LAURA HILLENBRAND is the author of the number-one bestseller *Seabiscuit*, which won the William Hill Sports Book of the Year and was a finalist for the National Book Critics Circle Award. The film it inspired was nominated for seven Academy Awards, including Best Picture. Hillenbrand's *New Yorker* article, 'A Sudden Illness', won the 2004 National Magazine Award, and she is a two-time winner of the Eclipse Award. She and actor Gary Sinise are the co-founders of Operation International Children, a charity that provides school supplies to children through American troops. She lives in Washington, D.C.

From the reviews of *Unbroken*:

'*Unbroken* is the unputdownable account of a remarkable life . . . This is tremendous stuff'

NICHOLAS SHAKESPEARE, *Daily Telegraph*

'*Unbroken* is a book with pages that almost turn themselves. It is a thrilling ride, vivid, swift, and easy to read'

BEN MACINTYRE, *The Times*

'If [Zamperini] didn't exist, you could scarcely credit his tale were true. It's so colourful it reads like fiction, and so agonising and uplifting it must surely be the most powerful story of prison endurance since *Papillon*. Hillenbrand is the perfect biographer for Zamperini . . . There is so much persuasive detail you'd think she'd been there herself. This book has become a massive bestseller, and rightly so. It is an instant classic' JAMES DELINGPOLE, *Mail on Sunday*

'Hillenbrand's storytelling is gripping . . . From a young Zamperini causing havoc in his California hometown, to the sight of an 81-year-old "Zamp" riding a skateboard, Hillenbrand's breathless narrative never lets up, sweeping the reader along in her subject's slipstream'

GEORGE PENDLE, *Financial Times*

'[Zamperini's] is surely one of the most extraordinary war stories of all . . . one of the most spectacular odysseys of this or any war . . . [Hillenbrand] is intelligent and restrained, and wise enough to let the story unfold for itself . . . *Unbroken* is gripping in an almost cinematic way . . . A startling narrative and an inspirational book' DAVID MARGOLICK, *Scotsman*

'This book's 500 pages literally have everything . . . Displaying the same qualities of meticulous research and identification with her subject that brought *Seabiscuit* alive, I'm sure that Laura Hillenbrand is already fighting off the major studios with a stick' NIGEL JONES, *Sunday Telegraph*

'Outstanding. An epic of individual heroism and fortitude in the second world war . . . Anyone who enjoyed *Seabiscuit* will know that [Hillenbrand] has a fine line in compelling narrative. *Unbroken* is no different: meticulously researched and powerful. With it Hillenbrand marches second world war literature right back into the spotlight'

KEVIN RUSHBY, *Guardian*

'An amazing tale of bravery and endurance, and Hillenbrand delivers it superbly . . . *Unbroken* is an extraordinarily compelling read, a match for any thriller . . . a remarkable book' DAVID SEXTON, *Evening Standard*

'Riveting . . . Zamperini's story keeps you turning the page with almost indecent haste'   *Metro*

'An astonishing tale of fortitude in the face of scarcely believable adversity . . . It is, at heart, a moralistic tale of good triumphing over unspeakable evil . . . In the hands of Hillenbrand, Zamperini's tale of tragedy, trauma and ultimately a form of triumph is a riveting read'

IAN BIRRELL, *Spectator*

'Edge-of-the-seat tale . . . Hillenbrand is a gifted writer'
The Economist

'An inspiring book that has kept me glued throughout'
Literary Review

By the same author

Seabiscuit

LAURA HILLENBRAND

Unbroken

An Extraordinary True Story of
Courage and Survival

FOURTH ESTATE • *London*

Fourth Estate
An imprint of HarperCollins*Publishers*
77–85 Fulham Palace Road
Hammersmith
London W6 8JB

This Fourth Estate paperback edition published 2012
6

First published in Great Britain by Fourth Estate in 2011

Originally published in the United States by Random House in 2010

Copyright © Laura Hillenbrand 2010

Laura Hillenbrand asserts the moral right to be identified as the author of this work

A catalogue record for this book is available from the British Library

ISBN 978-0-00-737803-6

Printed and bound in Great Britain by Clays Ltd, St Ives plc

MIX
Paper from
responsible sources
FSC
www.fsc.org
FSC® C007454

Find out more about HarperCollins and the environment at
www.harpercollins.co.uk/green

For the wounded and the lost

What stays with you latest and deepest? of curious panics,
Of hard-fought engagements or sieges tremendous what
*   deepest remains?*
                                    —Walt Whitman, "The Wound-Dresser"

CONTENTS

PART V

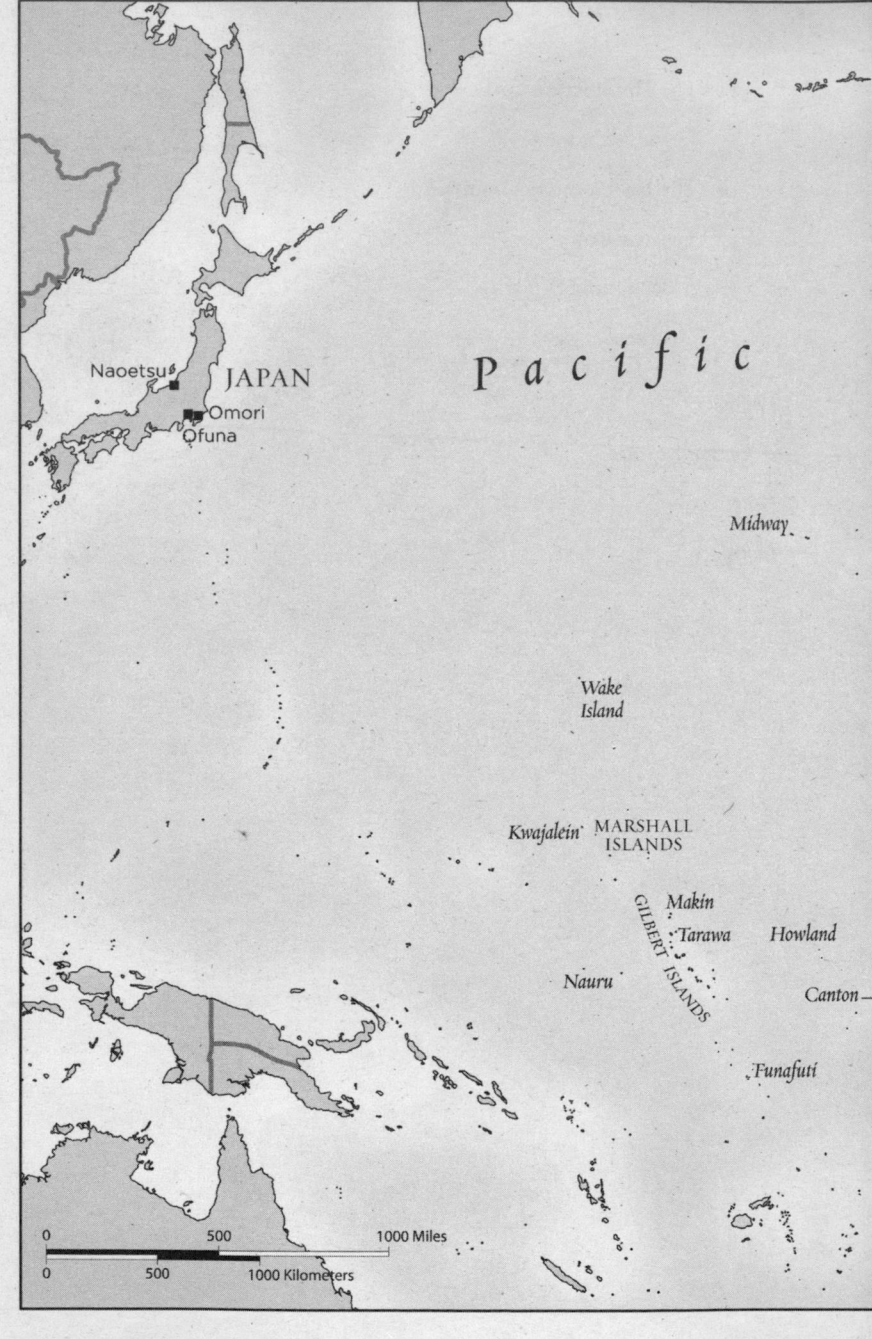

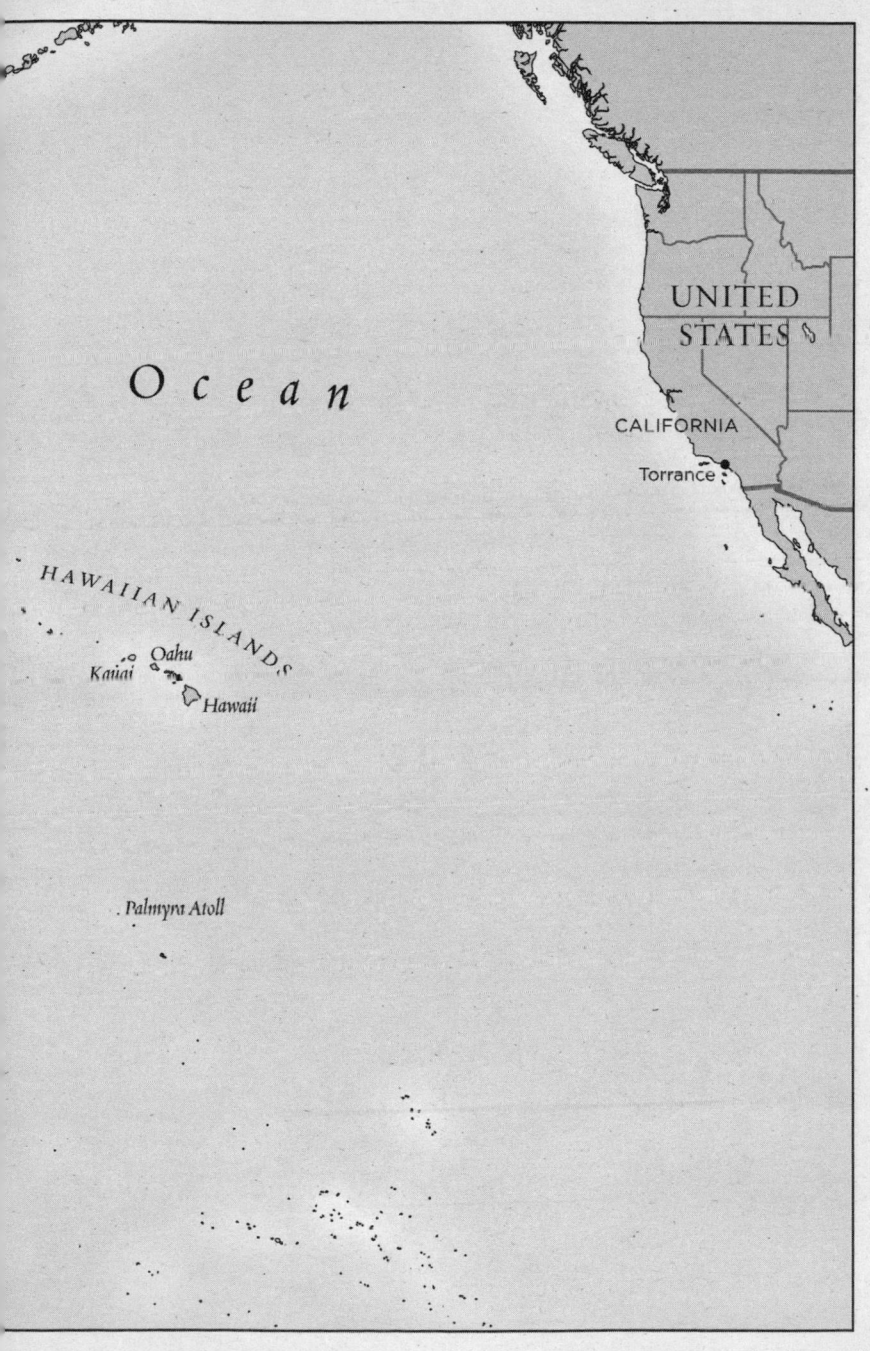

Ocean

UNITED
STATES

CALIFORNIA

Torrance

HAWAIIAN ISLANDS

Kauai   Oahu
        Hawaii

Palmyra Atoll

PREFACE

ALL HE COULD SEE, IN EVERY DIRECTION, WAS WATER.
It was June 23, 1943. Somewhere on the endless expanse of the Pacific Ocean, Army Air Forces bombardier and Olympic runner Louie Zamperini lay across a small raft, drifting westward. Slumped alongside him was a sergeant, one of his plane's gunners. On a separate raft, tethered to the first, lay another crewman, a gash zigzagging across his forehead. Their bodies, burned by the sun and stained yellow from the raft dye, had winnowed down to skeletons. Sharks glided in lazy loops around them, dragging their backs along the rafts, waiting.

The men had been adrift for twenty-seven days. Borne by an equatorial current, they had floated at least one thousand miles, deep into Japanese-controlled waters. The rafts were beginning to deteriorate into jelly, and gave off a sour, burning odor. The men's bodies were pocked with salt sores, and their lips were so swollen that they pressed into their nostrils and chins. They spent their days with their eyes fixed on the sky, singing "White Christmas," muttering about food. No one was even looking for them anymore. They were alone on sixty-four million square miles of ocean.

A month earlier, twenty-six-year-old Zamperini had been one of the greatest runners in the world, expected by many to be the first to break the four-minute mile, one of the most celebrated barriers in sport. Now his Olympian's body had wasted to less than one hundred pounds and his famous legs could no longer lift him. Almost everyone outside of his family had given him up for dead.

On that morning of the twenty-seventh day, the men heard a distant, deep strumming. Every airman knew that sound: pistons. Their eyes caught a glint in the sky—a plane, high overhead. Zamperini fired two flares and shook powdered dye into the water, enveloping the rafts in a circle of vivid orange. The plane kept going, slowly disappearing. The men sagged. Then the sound returned, and the plane came back into view. The crew had seen them.

With arms shrunken to little more than bone and yellowed skin, the castaways waved and shouted, their voices thin from thirst. The plane dropped low and swept alongside the rafts. Zamperini saw the profiles of the crewmen, dark against bright blueness.

There was a terrific roaring sound. The water, and the rafts themselves, seemed to boil. It was machine gun fire. This was not an American rescue plane. It was a Japanese bomber.

The men pitched themselves into the water and hung together under the rafts, cringing as bullets punched through the rubber and sliced effervescent lines in the water around their faces. The firing blazed on, then sputtered out as the bomber overshot them. The men dragged themselves back onto the one raft that was still mostly inflated. The bomber banked sideways, circling toward them again. As it leveled off, Zamperini could see the muzzles of the machine guns, aimed directly at them.

Zamperini looked toward his crewmates. They were too weak to go back in the water. As they lay down on the floor of the raft, hands over their heads, Zamperini splashed overboard alone.

Somewhere beneath him, the sharks were done waiting. They bent their bodies in the water and swam toward the man under the raft.

PART

I

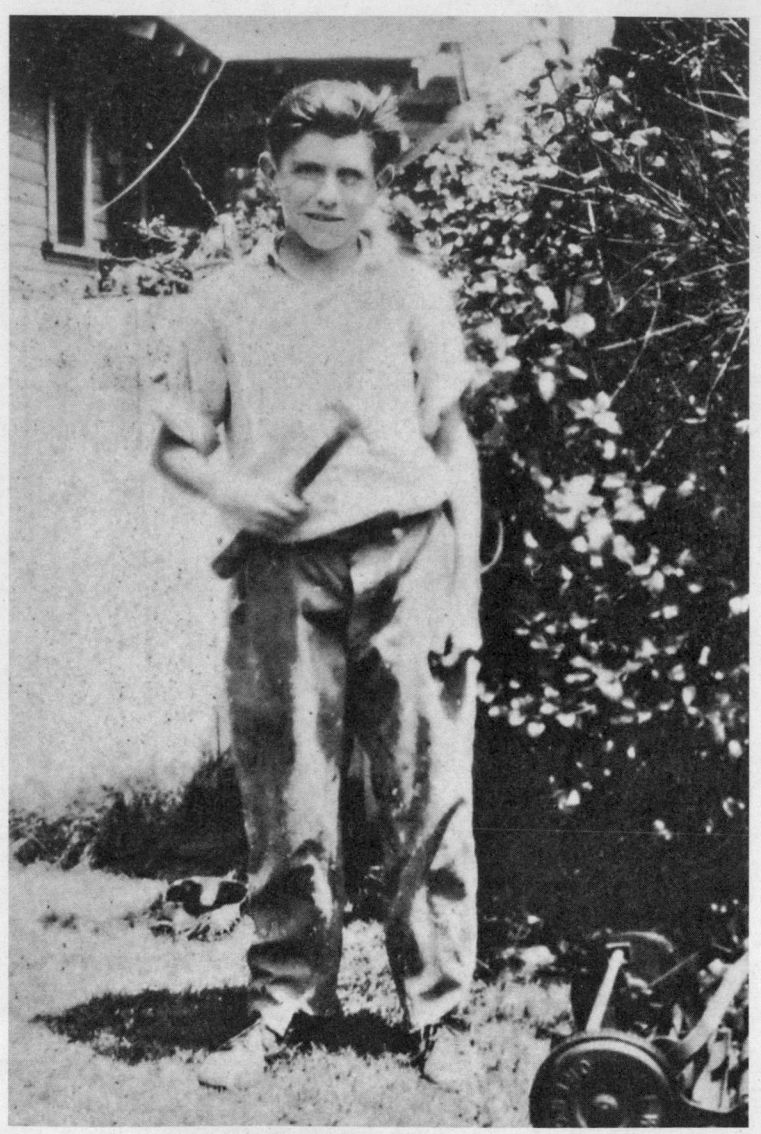

Courtesy of Louis Zamperini. Photo of original image by John Brodkin.

One

The One-Boy Insurgency

I N THE PREDAWN DARKNESS OF AUGUST 26, 1929, IN THE back bedroom of a small house in Torrance, California, a twelve-year-old boy sat up in bed, listening. There was a sound coming from outside, growing ever louder. It was a huge, heavy rush, suggesting immensity, a great parting of air. It was coming from directly above the house. The boy swung his legs off his bed, raced down the stairs, slapped open the back door, and loped onto the grass. The yard was otherworldly, smothered in unnatural darkness, shivering with sound. The boy stood on the lawn beside his older brother, head thrown back, spellbound.

The sky had disappeared. An object that he could see only in silhouette, reaching across a massive arc of space, was suspended low in the air over the house. It was longer than two and a half football fields and as tall as a city. It was putting out the stars.

What he saw was the German dirigible *Graf Zeppelin*. At nearly 800 feet long and 110 feet high, it was the largest flying machine ever crafted. More luxurious than the finest airplane, gliding effortlessly over huge distances, built on a scale that left spectators gasping, it was, in the summer of '29, the wonder of the world.

The airship was three days from completing a sensational feat of aeronautics, circumnavigation of the globe. The journey had begun on August 7, when the *Zeppelin* had slipped its tethers in Lakehurst, New Jersey, lifted up with a long, slow sigh, and headed for Manhattan. On Fifth Avenue that summer, demolition was soon to begin on the Waldorf-Astoria Hotel, clearing the way for a skyscraper of unprecedented proportions, the Empire State Building. At Yankee Stadium, in the Bronx, players were debuting numbered uniforms: Lou Gehrig wore No. 4; Babe Ruth, about to hit his five hundredth home run, wore No. 3. On Wall Street, stock prices were racing toward an all-time high.

After a slow glide around the Statue of Liberty, the *Zeppelin* banked north, then turned out over the Atlantic. In time, land came below again: France, Switzerland, Germany. The ship passed over Nuremberg, where fringe politician Adolf Hitler, whose Nazi Party had been trounced in the 1928 elections, had just delivered a speech touting selective infanticide. Then it flew east of Frankfurt, where a Jewish woman named Edith Frank was caring for her newborn, a girl named Anne. Sailing northeast, the *Zeppelin* crossed over Russia. Siberian villagers, so isolated that they'd never even seen a train, fell to their knees at the sight of it.

On August 19, as some four million Japanese waved handkerchiefs and shouted "*Banzai!*" the *Zeppelin* circled Tokyo and sank onto a landing field. Four days later, as the German and Japanese anthems played, the ship rose into the grasp of a typhoon that whisked it over the Pacific at breathtaking speed, toward America. Passengers gazing from the windows saw only the ship's shadow, following it along the clouds "like a huge shark swimming alongside." When the clouds parted, the passengers glimpsed giant creatures, turning in the sea, that looked like monsters.

On August 25, the *Zeppelin* reached San Francisco. After being cheered down the California coast, it slid through sunset, into darkness and silence, and across midnight. As slow as the drifting wind, it passed over Torrance, where its only audience was a scattering of drowsy souls, among them the boy in his pajamas behind the house on Gramercy Avenue.

Standing under the airship, his feet bare in the grass, he was transfixed. It was, he would say, "fearfully beautiful." He could feel the rumble of the craft's engines tilling the air but couldn't make out the silver skin, the sweeping ribs, the finned tail. He could see only the blackness of the space it inhabited. It was not a great presence but a great absence, a geometric ocean of darkness that seemed to swallow heaven itself.

——

The boy's name was Louis Silvie Zamperini. The son of Italian immigrants, he had come into the world in Olean, New York, on January 26, 1917, eleven and a half pounds of baby under black hair as coarse as barbed wire. His father, Anthony, had been living on his own since age fourteen, first as a coal miner and boxer, then as a construction worker. His mother, Louise, was a petite, playful beauty, sixteen at marriage and eighteen when Louie was born. In their apartment, where only Italian was spoken, Louise and Anthony called their boy Toots.

From the moment he could walk, Louie couldn't bear to be corralled. His siblings would recall him careening about, hurdling flora, fauna, and furniture. The instant Louise thumped him into a chair and told him to be still, he vanished. If she didn't have her squirming boy clutched in her hands, she usually had no idea where he was.

In 1919, when two-year-old Louie was down with pneumonia, he climbed out his bedroom window, descended one story, and went on a naked tear down the street with a policeman chasing him and a crowd watching in amazement. Soon after, on a pediatrician's advice, Louise and Anthony decided to move their children to the warmer climes of California. Sometime after their train pulled out of Grand Central Station, Louie bolted, ran the length of the train, and leapt from the caboose. Standing with his frantic mother as the train rolled backward in search of the lost boy, Louie's older brother, Pete, spotted Louie strolling up the track in perfect serenity. Swept up in his mother's arms, Louie smiled. "I knew you'd come back," he said in Italian.

In California, Anthony landed a job as a railway electrician and bought a half-acre field on the edge of Torrance, population 1,800. He and Louise hammered up a one-room shack with no running water, an outhouse behind, and a roof that leaked so badly that they had to keep buckets on the beds. With only hook latches for locks, Louise took to sitting by the front door on an apple box with a rolling pin in her hand, ready to brain any prowlers who might threaten her children.

There, and at the Gramercy Avenue house where they settled a year later, Louise kept prowlers out, but couldn't keep Louie in hand. Contesting a footrace across a busy highway, he just missed getting broadsided by a jalopy. At five, he started smoking, picking up discarded cigarette butts while walking to kindergarten. He began drinking one night when he was eight; he hid under the dinner table, snatched glasses of wine, drank them all dry, staggered outside, and fell into a rosebush.

On one day, Louise discovered that Louie had impaled his leg on a bamboo beam; on another, she had to ask a neighbor to sew Louie's severed toe back on. When Louie came home drenched in oil after scaling an oil rig, diving into a sump well, and nearly drowning, it took a gallon of turpentine and a lot of scrubbing before Anthony recognized his son again.

Thrilled by the crashing of boundaries, Louie was untamable. As he grew into his uncommonly clever mind, mere feats of daring were no longer satisfying. In Torrance, a one-boy insurgency was born.

———

If it was edible, Louie stole it. He skulked down alleys, a roll of lock-picking wire in his pocket. Housewives who stepped from their kitchens would return to find that their suppers had disappeared. Residents looking out their back windows might catch a glimpse of a long-legged boy dashing down the alley, a whole cake balanced on his hands. When a local family left Louie off their dinner-party guest list, he broke into their house, bribed their Great Dane with a bone, and cleaned out their icebox. At another party, he absconded with an entire keg of beer. When he discovered that the cooling tables at Meinzer's Bakery stood within an arm's length of the back door, he began picking the lock, snatching pies, eating until he was full, and reserving the rest as ammunition for ambushes. When rival thieves took up the racket, he suspended the stealing until the culprits were caught and the bakery owners dropped their guard. Then he ordered his friends to rob Meinzer's again.

It is a testament to the content of Louie's childhood that his stories about it usually ended with ". . . and then I ran like *mad*." He was often chased by people he had robbed, and at least two people threatened to shoot him. To minimize the evidence found on him when the police habitually came his way, he set up loot-stashing sites around town, including a three-seater cave that he dug in a nearby forest. Under the Torrance High bleachers, Pete once found a stolen wine jug that Louie had hidden there. It was teeming with inebriated ants.

In the lobby of the Torrance theater, Louie stopped up the pay telephone's coin slots with toilet paper. He returned regularly to feed wire behind the coins stacked up inside, hook the paper, and fill his palms with change. A metal dealer never guessed that the grinning Italian kid who often came by to sell him armfuls of copper scrap had stolen the same scrap from his lot the night before. Discovering, while scuffling with an enemy at a circus, that adults would give quarters to fighting kids to pacify them, Louie declared a truce with the enemy and they cruised around staging brawls before strangers.

To get even with a railcar conductor who wouldn't stop for him, Louie greased the rails. When a teacher made him stand in a corner for spitballing, he deflated her car tires with toothpicks. After setting a legitimate Boy Scout state record in friction-fire ignition, he broke his record by soaking his tinder in gasoline and mixing it with match heads, causing a small explosion. He stole a neighbor's coffee percolator tube, set up a sniper's nest in a tree, crammed pepper-tree berries into his mouth, spat them through the tube, and sent the neighborhood girls running.

His magnum opus became legend. Late one night, Louie climbed the steeple of a Baptist church, rigged the bell with piano wire, strung the wire into a nearby tree, and roused the police, the fire department, and all of Torrance with apparently spontaneous pealing. The more credulous townsfolk called it a sign from God.

Only one thing scared him. When Louie was in late boyhood, a pilot landed a plane near Torrance and took Louie up for a flight. One might have expected such an intrepid child to be ecstatic, but the speed and altitude frightened him. From that day on, he wanted nothing to do with airplanes.

In a childhood of artful dodging, Louie made more than just mischief. He shaped who he would be in manhood. Confident that he was clever, resourceful, and bold enough to escape any predicament, he was almost incapable of discouragement. When history carried him into war, this resilient optimism would define him.

———

Louie was twenty months younger than his brother, who was everything he was not. Pete Zamperini was handsome, popular, impeccably groomed, polite to elders and avuncular to juniors, silky smooth with girls, and blessed with such sound judgment that even when he was a child, his parents consulted him on difficult decisions. He ushered his mother into her seat at dinner, turned in at seven, and tucked his alarm clock under his pillow so as not to wake Louie, with whom he shared a bed. He rose at two-thirty to run a three-hour paper route, and deposited all his earnings in the bank, which would swallow every penny when the Depression hit. He had a lovely singing voice and a gallant habit of carrying pins in his pant cuffs, in case his dance partner's dress strap failed. He once saved a girl from drowning. Pete radiated a gentle but impressive authority that led everyone he met, even adults, to be swayed by his opinion. Even Louie, who made a religion out of heeding no one, did as Pete said.

Louie idolized Pete, who watched over him and their younger sisters, Sylvia and Virginia, with paternal protectiveness. But Louie was eclipsed, and he never heard the end of it. Sylvia would recall her mother tearfully telling Louie how she wished he could be more like Pete. What made it more galling was that Pete's reputation was part myth. Though Pete earned grades little better than Louie's failing ones, his principal assumed that he was a straight-A student. On the night of Torrance's church bell miracle, a well-directed flashlight would have revealed Pete's legs dangling from the tree alongside Louie's. And Louie wasn't always the only Zamperini boy who could be seen sprinting down the alley with food that had lately belonged to the neighbors. But it never occurred to anyone to suspect Pete of anything. "Pete never got caught," said Sylvia. "Louie always got caught."

Nothing about Louie fit with other kids. He was a puny boy, and in his first years in Torrance, his lungs were still compromised enough from the pneumonia that in picnic footraces, every girl in town could dust him. His features, which would later settle into pleasant collaboration, were growing at different rates, giving him a curious face that seemed designed by committee. His ears leaned sidelong off his head like holstered pistols, and above them waved a calamity of black hair that mortified him. He attacked it with his aunt Margie's hot iron, hobbled it in a silk stocking every night, and slathered it with so much olive oil that flies trailed him to school. It did no good.

And then there was his ethnicity. In Torrance in the early 1920s, Italians were held in such disdain that when the Zamperinis arrived, the neighbors petitioned the city council to keep them out. Louie, who knew only a smattering of English until he was in grade school, couldn't hide his pedigree. He survived kindergarten by keeping mum, but in first grade, when he blurted out *"Brutte bastarde!"* at another kid, his teachers caught on. They compounded his misery by holding him back a grade.

He was a marked boy. Bullies, drawn by his oddity and hoping to goad him into uttering Italian curses, pelted him with rocks, taunted him, punched him, and kicked him. He tried buying their mercy with his lunch, but they pummeled him anyway, leaving him bloody. He could have ended the beatings by running away or succumbing to tears, but he refused to do either. "You could beat him to death," said Sylvia, "and he wouldn't say 'ouch' or cry." He just put his hands in front of his face and took it.

———

As Louie neared his teens, he took a hard turn. Aloof and bristling, he lurked around the edges of Torrance, his only friendships forged loosely with rough boys who followed his lead. He became so germophobic that he wouldn't tolerate anyone coming near his food. Though he could be a sweet boy, he was often short-tempered and obstreperous. He feigned toughness, but was secretly tormented. Kids passing into parties would see him lingering outside, unable to work up the courage to walk in.

Frustrated at his inability to defend himself, he made a study of it. His father taught him how to work a punching bag and made him a barbell from two lead-filled coffee cans welded to a pipe. The next time a bully came at Louie, he ducked left and swung his right fist straight into the boy's mouth. The bully shrieked, his tooth broken, and fled. The feeling of lightness that Louie experienced on his walk home was one he would never forget.

Over time, Louie's temper grew wilder, his fuse shorter, his skills sharper. He socked a girl. He pushed a teacher. He pelted a policeman with rotten tomatoes. Kids who crossed him wound up with fat lips, and bullies learned to give him a wide berth. He once came upon Pete in their front yard, in a standoff with another boy. Both boys had their fists in front of their chins, each waiting for the other to swing. "Louie can't stand it," remembered Pete. "He's standing there, 'Hit him, Pete! Hit him, Pete!' I'm waiting there, and all of a sudden Louie turns around and smacks this guy right in the gut. And then he *runs*!"

Anthony Zamperini was at his wits' end. The police always seemed to be on the front porch, trying to talk sense into Louie. There were neighbors to be apologized to and damages to be compensated for with money that Anthony couldn't spare. Adoring his son but exasperated by his behavior, Anthony delivered frequent, forceful spankings. Once, after he'd caught Louie wiggling through a window in the middle of the night, he delivered a kick to the rear so forceful that it lifted Louie off the floor. Louie absorbed the punishment in tearless silence, then committed the same crimes again, just to show he could.

Louie's mother, Louise, took a different tack. Louie was a copy of herself, right down to the vivid blue eyes. When pushed, she shoved; sold a bad cut of meat, she'd march down to the butcher, frying pan in hand. Loving mischief, she spread icing over a cardboard box and presented it as a birthday cake to a neighbor, who promptly got the knife stuck. When Pete told her he'd drink his castor oil if she gave him a box of candy, she agreed, watched him drink it, then handed him an empty candy box. "You only asked for the box, honey," she said with a smile. "That's all I got." And she understood Louie's restiveness. One Halloween, she dressed as a boy and raced around town trick-or-treating with Louie and Pete. A gang of kids, thinking she was one of the local toughs, tackled her and tried to steal her pants. Little Louise Zamperini, mother of four, was deep in the melee when the cops picked her up for brawling.

Knowing that punishing Louie would only provoke his defiance, Louise took a surreptitious route toward reforming him. In search of an informant, she worked over Louie's schoolmates with homemade pie and turned up a soft boy named Hugh, whose sweet tooth was Louie's undoing. Louise suddenly knew everything Louie was up to, and her children wondered if she had developed psychic powers. Sure that Sylvia was snitching, Louie refused to sit at the supper table with her, eating his meals in spiteful solitude off the open oven door. He once became so enraged with her that he chased her around the block. Outrunning Louie for the only time in her life, Sylvia cut down the alley and dove into her father's work shed. Louie flushed her out by feeding his three-foot-long pet snake into the crawl space. She then locked herself in the family car and didn't come out for an entire afternoon. "It was a matter of life and death," she said some seventy-five years later.

For all her efforts, Louise couldn't change Louie. He ran away and wandered around San Diego for days, sleeping under a highway overpass. He tried to ride a steer in a pasture, got tossed onto the ragged edge of a fallen tree, and limped home with his gashed knee bound in a handkerchief. Twenty-seven stitches didn't tame him. He hit one kid so hard that he broke his nose. He upended another boy and stuffed paper towels in his mouth. Parents forbade their kids from going near him. A farmer, furious over Louie's robberies, loaded his shotgun with rock salt and blasted him in the tail. Louie beat one kid so badly, leaving him unconscious in a ditch, that he was afraid he'd killed him. When Louise saw the blood on Louie's fists, she burst into tears.

———

As Louie prepared to start Torrance High, he was looking less like an impish kid and more like a dangerous young man. High school would be the end of his education. There was no money for college; Anthony's paycheck ran out before the week's end, forcing Louise to improvise meals out of eggplant, milk, stale bread, wild mushrooms, and rabbits that Louie and Pete shot in the fields. With flunking grades and no skills, Louie had no chance for a scholarship. It was unlikely that he could land a job. The Depression had come, and the unemployment rate was nearing 25 percent. Louie had no real ambitions. If asked what he wanted to be, his answer would have been "cowboy."

In the 1930s, America was infatuated with the pseudoscience of eugenics and its promise of strengthening the human race by culling the "unfit" from the genetic pool. Along with the "feebleminded," insane, and criminal, those so classified included women who had sex out of wedlock (considered a mental illness), orphans, the disabled, the poor, the homeless, epileptics, masturbators, the blind and the deaf, alcoholics, and girls whose genitals exceeded certain measurements. Some eugenicists advocated euthanasia, and in mental hospitals, this was quietly carried out on scores of people through "lethal neglect" or outright murder. At one Illinois mental hospital, new patients were dosed with milk from cows infected with tuberculosis, in the belief that only the undesirable would perish. As many as four in ten of these patients died. A more popular tool of eugenics was forced sterilization, employed on a raft of lost souls who, through misbehavior or misfortune, fell into the hands of state governments. By 1930, when Louie was entering his teens, California was enraptured with eugenics, and would ultimately sterilize some twenty thousand people.

When Louie was in his early teens, an event in Torrance brought reality home. A kid from Louie's neighborhood was deemed feebleminded, institutionalized, and barely saved from sterilization through a frantic legal effort by his parents, funded by their Torrance neighbors. Tutored by Louie's siblings, the boy earned straight A's. Louie was never more than an inch from juvenile hall or jail, and as a serial troublemaker, a failing student, and a suspect Italian, he was just the sort of rogue that eugenicists wanted to cull. Suddenly understanding what he was risking, he felt deeply shaken.

The person that Louie had become was not, he knew, his authentic self. He made hesitant efforts to connect to others. He scrubbed the kitchen floor to surprise his mother, but she assumed that Pete had done it. While his father was out of town, Louie overhauled the engine on the family's Marmon Roosevelt Straight-8 sedan. He baked biscuits and gave them away; when his mother, tired of the mess, booted him from her kitchen, he resumed baking in a neighbor's house. He doled out nearly everything he stole. He was "bighearted," said Pete. "Louie would give away anything, whether it was his or not."

Each attempt he made to right himself ended wrong. He holed up alone, reading Zane Grey novels and wishing himself into them, a man and his horse on the frontier, broken off from the world. He haunted the theater for western movies, losing track of the plots while he stared at the scenery. On some nights, he'd drag his bedding into the yard to sleep alone. On others, he'd lie awake in bed, beneath pinups of movie cowboy Tom Mix and his wonder horse, Tony, feeling snared on something from which he couldn't kick free.

In the back bedroom he could hear trains passing. Lying beside his sleeping brother, he'd listen to the broad, low sound: faint, then rising, faint again, then a high, beckoning whistle, then gone. The sound of it brought goose bumps. Lost in longing, Louie imagined himself on a train, rolling into country he couldn't see, growing smaller and more distant until he disappeared.

Two

Run Like Mad

THE REHABILITATION OF LOUIE ZAMPERINI BEGAN IN 1931, with a key. Fourteen-year-old Louie was in a locksmith shop when he heard someone say that if you put any key in any lock, it has a one-in-fifty chance of fitting. Inspired, Louie began collecting keys and trying locks. He had no luck until he tried his house key on the back door of the Torrance High gym. When basketball season began, there was an inexplicable discrepancy between the number of ten-cent tickets sold and the considerably larger number of kids in the bleachers. In late 1931, someone caught on, and Louie was hauled to the principal's office for the umpteenth time. In California, winter-born students entered new grades in January, so Louie was about to start ninth grade. The principal punished him by making him ineligible for athletic and social activities. Louie, who never joined anything, was indifferent.

When Pete learned what had happened, he headed straight to the principal's office. Though his mother didn't yet speak much English, he towed her along to give his presentation weight. He told the principal that Louie craved attention but had never won it in the form of praise, so he sought it in the form of punishment. If Louie were recognized for doing something right, Pete argued, he'd turn his life around. He asked the principal to allow Louie to join a sport. When the principal balked, Pete asked him if he could live with allowing Louie to fail. It was a cheeky thing for a sixteen-year-old to say to his principal, but Pete was the one kid in Torrance who could get away with such a remark, and make it persuasive. Louie was made eligible for athletics for 1932.

Pete had big plans for Louie. A senior in 1931–32, he would graduate with ten varsity letters, including three in basketball and three in baseball. But it was track, in which he earned four varsity letters, tied the school half-mile record, and set its mile record of 5:06, that was his true forte. Looking at Louie, whose getaway speed was his saving grace, Pete thought he saw the same incipient talent.

As it turned out, it wasn't Pete who got Louie onto a track for the first time. It was Louie's weakness for girls. In February, the ninth-grade girls began assembling a team for an interclass track meet, and in a class with only four boys, Louie was the only male who looked like he could run. The girls worked their charms, and Louie found himself standing on the track, barefoot, for a 660-yard race. When everyone ran, he followed, churning along with jimmying elbows and dropping far behind. As he labored home last, he heard tittering. Gasping and humiliated, he ran straight off the track and hid under the bleachers. The coach muttered something about how that kid belonged anywhere but in a footrace. "He's my brother," Pete replied.

From that day on, Pete was all over Louie, forcing him to train, then dragging him to the track to run in a second meet. Urged on by kids in the stands, Louie put in just enough effort to beat one boy and finish third. He hated running, but the applause was intoxicating, and the prospect of more was just enough incentive to keep him marginally compliant. Pete herded him out to train every day and rode his bicycle behind him, whacking him with a stick. Louie dragged his feet, belly-ached, and quit at the first sign of fatigue. Pete made him get up and keep going. Louie started winning. At the season's end, he became the first Torrance kid to make the All City Finals. He finished fifth.

Pete had been right about Louie's talent. But to Louie, training felt like one more constraint. At night he listened to the whistles of passing trains, and one day in the summer of '32, he couldn't bear it any longer.

It began over a chore that Louie's father asked him to do. Louie resisted, a spat ensued, and Louie threw some clothes into a bag and stormed toward the front door. His parents ordered him to stay; Louie was beyond persuasion. As he walked out, his mother rushed to the kitchen and emerged with a sandwich wrapped in waxed paper. Louie stuffed it in his bag and left. He was partway down the front walk when he heard his name called. When he turned, there was his father, grim-faced, holding two dollars in his outstretched hand. It was a lot of money for a man whose paycheck didn't bridge the week. Louie took it and walked away.

He rounded up a friend, and together they hitchhiked to Los Angeles, broke into a car, and slept on the seats. The next day they jumped a train, climbed onto the roof, and rode north.

The trip was a nightmare. The boys got locked in a boxcar so hot that they were soon frantic to escape. Louie found a discarded strip of metal, climbed on his friend's shoulders, pried a vent open, squirmed out, and helped his friend out, badly cutting himself in the process. Then they were discovered by the railroad detective, who forced them to jump from the moving train at gunpoint. After several days of walking, getting chased out of orchards and grocery stores where they tried to steal food, they wound up sitting on the ground in a railyard, filthy, bruised, sunburned, and wet, sharing a stolen can of beans. A train rattled past. Louie looked up. "I saw . . . beautiful white tablecloths and crystal on the tables, and food, people laughing and enjoying themselves and eating," he said later. "And [I was] sitting here shivering, eating a miserable can of beans." He remembered the money in his father's hand, the fear in his mother's eyes as she offered him a sandwich. He stood up and headed home.

When Louie walked into his house, Louise threw her arms around him, inspected him for injuries, led him to the kitchen, and gave him a cookie. Anthony came home, saw Louie, and sank into a chair, his face soft with relief. After dinner, Louie went upstairs, dropped into bed, and whispered his surrender to Pete.

———

In the summer of 1932, Louie did almost nothing but run. On the invitation of a friend, he went to stay at a cabin on the Cahuilla Indian Reservation, in southern California's high desert. Each morning, he rose with the sun, picked up his rifle, and jogged into the sagebrush. He ran up and down hills, over the desert, through gullies. He chased bands of horses, darting into the swirling herds and trying in vain to snatch a fistful of mane and swing aboard. He swam in a sulfur spring, watched over by Cahuilla women scrubbing clothes on the rocks, and stretched out to dry himself in the sun. On his run back to the cabin each afternoon, he shot a rabbit for supper. Each evening, he climbed atop the cabin and lay back, reading Zane Grey novels. When the sun sank and the words faded, he gazed over the landscape, moved by its beauty, watching it slip from gray to purple before darkness blended land and sky. In the morning he rose to run again. He didn't run from something or to something, not for anyone or in spite of anyone; he ran because it was what his body wished to do. The restiveness, the self-consciousness, and the need to oppose disappeared. All he felt was peace.

He came home with a mania for running. All of the effort that he'd once put into thieving he threw into track. On Pete's instruction, he ran his entire paper route for the *Torrance Herald,* to and from school, and to the beach and back. He rarely stayed on the sidewalk, veering onto neighbors' lawns to hurdle bushes. He gave up drinking and smoking. To expand his lung capacity, he ran to the public pool at Redondo Beach, dove to the bottom, grabbed the drain plug, and just floated there, hanging on a little longer each time. Eventually, he could stay underwater for three minutes and forty-five seconds. People kept jumping in to save him.

Louie also found a role model. In the 1930s, track was hugely popular, and its elite performers were household names. Among them was a Kansas University miler named Glenn Cunningham. As a small child, Cunningham had been in a schoolhouse explosion that killed his brother and left Glenn with severe burns on his legs and torso. It was a month and a half before he could sit up, and more time still before he could stand. Unable to straighten his legs, he learned to push himself about by leaning on a chair, his legs floundering. He graduated to the tail of the family mule, and eventually, hanging off the tail of an obliging horse named Paint, he began to run, a gait that initially caused him excruciating pain. Within a few years, he was racing, setting mile records and obliterating his opponents by the length of a homestretch. By 1932, the modest, mild-tempered Cunningham, whose legs and back were covered in a twisting mesh of scars, was becoming a national sensation, soon to be acclaimed as the greatest miler in American history. Louie had his hero.

In the fall of 1932, Pete began his studies at Compton, a tuition-free junior college, where he became a star runner. Nearly every afternoon, he commuted home to coach Louie, running alongside him, subduing the jimmying elbows and teaching him strategy. Louie had a rare bio-mechanical advantage, hips that rolled as he ran; when one leg reached forward, the corresponding hip swung forward with it, giving Louie an exceptionally efficient, seven-foot stride. After watching him from the Torrance High fence, cheerleader Toots Bowersox needed only one word to describe him: "*Smoooooth.*" Pete thought that the sprints in which Louie had been running were too short. He'd be a miler, just like Glenn Cunningham.

In January 1933, Louie began tenth grade. As he lost his aloof, thorny manner, he was welcomed by the fashionable crowd. They invited him to weenie bakes in front of Kellow's Hamburg Stand, where Louie would join ukulele sing-alongs and touch football games played with a knotted towel, contests that inevitably ended with a cheerleader being wedged into a trash can. Capitalizing on his sudden popularity, Louie ran for class president and won, borrowing the speech that Pete had used to win his class presidency at Compton. Best of all, girls suddenly found him dreamy. While walking alone on his sixteenth birthday, Louie was ambushed by a giggling gaggle of cheerleaders. One girl sat on Louie while the rest gave him sixteen whacks on the rear, plus one to grow on.

When the school track season began in February, Louie set out to see what training had done for him. His transformation was stunning. Competing in black silk shorts that his mother had sewn from the fabric of a skirt, he won an 880-yard race, breaking the school record, co-held by Pete, by more than two seconds. A week later, he ran a field of milers off their feet, stopping the watches in 5:03, three seconds faster than Pete's record. At another meet, he clocked a mile in 4:58. Three weeks later, he set a state record of 4:50.6. By early April, he was down to 4:46; by late April, 4:42. "Boy! oh boy! oh boy!" read a local paper. "Can that guy fly? Yes, this means that Zamperini guy!"

Almost every week, Louie ran the mile, streaking through the season unbeaten and untested. When he ran out of high school kids to whip, he took on Pete and thirteen other college runners in a two-mile race at Compton. Though he was only sixteen and had never even trained at the distance, he won by fifty yards. Next he tried the two-mile in UCLA's Southern California Cross Country meet. Running so effortlessly that he couldn't feel his feet touching the ground, he took the lead and kept pulling away. At the halfway point, he was an eighth of a mile ahead, and observers began speculating on when the boy in the black shorts was going to collapse. Louie didn't collapse. After he flew past the finish, rewriting the course record, he looked back up the long straightaway. Not one of the other runners was even in view. Louie had won by more than a quarter of a mile.

He felt as if he would faint, but it wasn't from the exertion. It was from the realization of what he was.

Louie wins the 1933 UCLA Cross Country two-mile race by more than a quarter of a mile. Pete is running up from behind to greet him. *Courtesy of Louis Zamperini*

Three

The Torrance Tornado

IT HAPPENED EVERY SATURDAY. LOUIE WOULD GO TO THE track, limber up, lie on his stomach on the infield grass, visualizing his coming race, then walk to the line, await the pop of the gun, and spring away. Pete would dash back and forth in the infield, clicking his stopwatch, yelling encouragement and instructions. When Pete gave the signal, Louie would stretch out his long legs and his opponents would scatter and drop away, in the words of a reporter, "sadly disheartened and disillusioned." Louie would glide over the line, Pete would be there to tackle him, and the kids in the bleachers would cheer and stomp. Then there would be autograph-seeking girls coming in waves, a ride home, kisses from Mother, and snapshots on the front lawn, trophy in hand. Louie won so many wristwatches, the traditional laurel of track, that he began handing them out all over town. Periodically, a new golden boy would be touted as the one who would take him down, only to be run off his feet. One victim, wrote a reporter, had been hailed as "the boy who doesn't know how fast he can run. He found out Saturday."

Louie's supreme high school moment came in the 1934 Southern California Track and Field Championship. Running in what was celebrated as the best field of high school milers in history, Louie routed

Louie and Pete. *Bettmann/Corbis*

them all and smoked the mile in 4:21.3, shattering the national high
school record, set during World War I, by more than two seconds.* His
main rival so exhausted himself chasing Louie that he had to be carried
from the track. As Louie trotted into Pete's arms, he felt a tug of regret.
He felt too fresh. Had he run his second lap faster, he said, he might
have clocked 4:18. A reporter predicted that Louie's record would stand
for twenty years. It stood for nineteen.

Once his hometown's resident archvillain, Louie was now a super-
star, and Torrance forgave him everything. When he trained, people
lined the track fence, calling out, "Come on, Iron Man!" The sports

---

* Louie's time was called a "world interscholastic" record, but this was a mis-
nomer. There were no official world high school records. Later sources would list
the time as 4:21.2, but all sources from 1934 list it as 4:21.3. Because different
organizations had different standards for record verification, there is some confusion about whose record Louie broke, but according to newspapers at the time,
the previous recordholder was Ed Shields, who ran 4:23.6 in 1916. In 1925,
Chesley Unruh was timed in 4:20.5, but this wasn't officially verified. Cunningham was also credited with the record, but his time, 4:24.7 run in 1930, was far
slower than those of Unruh and Shields. Louie's mark stood until Bob Seaman
broke it in 1953.

pages of the Los Angeles *Times* and *Examiner* were striped with stories on the prodigy, whom the *Times* called the "Torrance Tempest" and practically everyone else called the "Torrance Tornado." By one report, stories on Louie were such an important source of revenue to the *Torrance Herald* that the newspaper insured his legs for $50,000. Torrancers carpooled to his races and crammed the grandstands. Embarrassed by the fuss, Louie asked his parents not to watch him race. Louise came anyway, sneaking to the track to peer through the fence, but the races made her so nervous that she had to hide her eyes.

Not long ago, Louie's aspirations had ended at whose kitchen he might burgle. Now he latched onto a wildly audacious goal: the 1936 Olympics, in Berlin. The Games had no mile race, so milers ran the 1,500 meters, about 120 yards short of a mile. It was a seasoned man's game; most top milers of the era peaked in their mid-twenties or later. As of 1934, the Olympic 1,500-meter favorite was Glenn Cunningham, who'd set the world record in the mile, 4:06.8, just weeks after Louie set the national high school record. Cunningham had been racing since the fourth grade, and at the 1936 Games, he would be just short of twenty-seven. He wouldn't run his fastest mile until he was twenty-eight. As of 1936, Louie would have only five years' experience, and would be only nineteen.

But Louie was already the fastest high school miler in American history, and he was improving so rapidly that he had lopped forty-two seconds off his time in two years. His record mile, run when he was seventeen, was three and a half seconds faster than Cunningham's fastest high school mile, run when he was twenty.* Even conservative track pundits were beginning to think that Louie might be the one to shatter precedent, and after Louie won every race in his senior season, their confidence was strengthened. Louie believed he could do it, and so did Pete. Louie wanted to run in Berlin more than he had ever wanted anything.

In December 1935, Louie graduated from high school; a few weeks later, he rang in 1936 with his thoughts full of Berlin. The Olympic trials track finals would be held in New York in July, and the Olympic committee would base its selection of competitors on a series of qualifying races. Louie had seven months to run himself onto the team. In

---

* Apparently because of his burns, Cunningham didn't start high school until he was eighteen.

the meantime, he also had to figure out what to do about the numerous college scholarships being offered to him. Pete had won a scholarship to the University of Southern California, where he had become one of the nation's top ten college milers. He urged Louie to accept USC's offer but delay entry until the fall, so he could train full-time. So Louie moved into Pete's frat house and, with Pete coaching him, trained obsessively. All day, every day, he lived and breathed the 1,500 meters and Berlin.

In the spring, he began to realize that he wasn't going to make it. Though he was getting faster by the day, he couldn't force his body to improve quickly enough to catch his older rivals by summer. He was simply too young. He was heartbroken.

———

In May, Louie was leafing through a newspaper when he saw a story on the Compton Open, a prestigious track meet to be held at the Los Angeles Coliseum on May 22. The headliner in the 5,000 meters—three miles and 188 yards—was Norman Bright, a twenty-six-year-old schoolteacher. Bright had set the American two-mile record in 1935 and was America's second-fastest 5,000-meter man, behind the legendary Don Lash, Indiana University's twenty-three-year-old record-smashing machine. America would send three 5,000-meter men to Berlin, and Lash and Bright were considered locks. Pete urged Louie to enter the Compton Open and try his legs at a longer distance. "If you stay with Norman Bright," he told Louie, "you make the Olympic team."

The idea was a stretch. The mile was four laps of the track; the 5,000 was more than twelve, what Louie would describe as a "fifteen-minute torture chamber," well over three times his optimal distance. He had only twice raced beyond a mile, and the 5,000, like the mile, was dominated by much older men. He had only two weeks to train for Compton and, with the Olympic trials in July, two months to become America's youngest elite 5,000-meter man. But he had nothing to lose. He trained so hard that he rubbed the skin right off one of his toes, leaving his sock bloody.

The race, contested before ten thousand fans, was a barn burner. Louie and Bright took off together, leaving the field far behind. Each time one took the lead, the other would gun past him again and the crowd would roar. They turned into the homestretch for the last time dead together, Bright inside, Louie outside. Ahead, a runner named

John Casey was on the verge of being lapped. Officials waved at Casey, who tried to yield, but Bright and Louie came to him before he could get out of the way. Bright squeezed through on the inside, but Louie had to shift right to go around Casey. Confused, Casey veered farther right, carrying Louie out. Louie sped up to go around him, but Casey sped up also, carrying Louie most of the way toward the grandstand. Finally, Louie took a half step to cut inside, lost his balance, and dropped one hand to the ground. Bright now had an advantage that looked, to Pete's eye, to be several yards. Louie took off after him, gaining rapidly. With the crowd on its feet and screaming, Louie caught Bright at the tape. He was a beat too late: Bright won by a glimmer. He and Louie had clipped out the fastest 5,000 run in America in 1936. Louie's Olympic dream was on again.

On June 13, Louie made quick work of another Olympic 5,000 qualifier, but the toe injured in training opened up again. He was too lame to train for his final qualifying race, and it cost him. Bright beat Louie by four yards, but Louie wasn't disgraced, clocking the third-fastest 5,000 run in America since 1931. He was invited to the final of the Olympic trials.

On the night of July 3, 1936, the residents of Torrance gathered to see Louie off to New York. They presented him with a wallet bulging with traveling money, a train ticket, new clothes, a shaving kit, and a suitcase emblazoned with the words TORRANCE TORNADO. Fearing that the suitcase made him look brash, Louie carried it out of view and covered the nickname with adhesive tape, then boarded his train. According to his diary, he spent the journey introducing himself to every pretty girl he saw, including a total of five between Chicago and Ohio.

When the train doors slid open in New York, Louie felt as if he were walking into an inferno. It was the hottest summer on record in America, and New York was one of the hardest-hit cities. In 1936, air-conditioning was a rarity, found only in a few theaters and department stores, so escape was nearly impossible. That week, which included the hottest three-day period in the nation's history, the heat would kill three thousand Americans. In Manhattan, where it would reach 106 degrees, forty people would die.

Louie and Norman Bright split the cost of a room at the Lincoln Hotel. Like all of the athletes, in spite of the heat, they had to train. Sweating profusely day and night, training in the sun, unable to sleep in stifling hotel rooms and YMCAs, lacking any appetite, virtually every athlete lost a huge amount of weight. By one estimate, no athlete dropped less than ten pounds. One was so desperate for relief that he moved into an air-conditioned theater, buying tickets to movies and sleeping through every showing. Louie was as miserable as everyone else. Chronically dehydrated, he drank as much as he could; after an 880-meter run in 106-degree heat, he downed eight orangeades and a quart of beer. Each night, taking advantage of the cooler air, he walked six miles. His weight fell precipitously.

The prerace newspaper coverage riled him. Don Lash was considered unbeatable, having just taken the NCAA 5,000-meter title for the third time, set a world record at two miles and an American record at 10,000 meters, and repeatedly thumped Bright, once by 150 yards. Bright was pegged for second, a series of other athletes for third through fifth. Louie wasn't mentioned. Like everyone else, Louie was daunted by Lash, but the first three runners would go to Berlin, and he believed he could be among them. "If I have any strength left from the heat," he wrote to Pete, "I'll beat Bright and give Lash the scare of his life."

On the night before the race, Louie lay sleepless in his sweltering hotel room. He was thinking about all the people who would be disappointed if he failed.

The next morning, Louie and Bright left the hotel together. The trials were to be held at a new stadium on Randall's Island, in the confluence of the East and Harlem rivers. It was a hair short of 90 in the city, but when they got off the ferry, they found the stadium much hotter, probably far over 100 degrees. All over the track, athletes were keeling over and being carted off to hospitals. Louie sat waiting for his race, baking under a scalding sun that, he said, "made a wreck of me."

At last, they were told to line up. The gun cracked, the men rushed forward, and the race was on. Lash bounded to the lead, with Bright in close pursuit. Louie dropped back, and the field settled in for the grind.

On the other side of the continent, a throng of Torrancers crouched around the radio in the Zamperinis' house. They were in agonies. The start time for Louie's race had passed, but the NBC radio announcer was lingering on the swimming trials. Pete was so frustrated that he considered putting his foot through the radio. At last, the announcer listed the positions of the 5,000-meter runners, but didn't mention

Louie. Unable to bear the tension, Louise fled to the kitchen, out of earshot.

The runners pushed through laps seven, eight, nine. Lash and Bright led the field. Louie hovered in the middle of the pack, waiting to make his move. The heat was suffocating. One runner dropped, and the others had no choice but to hurdle him. Then another went down, and they jumped him, too. Louie could feel his feet cooking; the spikes on his shoes were conducting heat up from the track. Norman Bright's feet were burning particularly badly. In terrible pain, he took a staggering step off the track, twisted his ankle, then lurched back on. The stumble seemed to finish him. He lost touch with Lash. When Louie and the rest of the pack came up to him, he had no resistance to offer. Still he ran on.

As the runners entered the final lap, Lash gave himself a breather, dropping just behind his Indiana teammate, Tom Deckard. Well behind him, Louie was ready to move. Angling into the backstretch, he accelerated. Lash's back drew closer, and then it was just a yard or two ahead. Looking at the bobbing head of the mighty Don Lash, Louie felt intimidated. For several strides, he hesitated. Then he saw the last curve ahead, and the sight slapped him awake. He opened up as fast as he could go.

Banking around the turn, Louie drew alongside Lash just as Lash shifted right to pass Deckard. Louie was carried three-wide, losing precious ground. Leaving Deckard behind, Louie and Lash ran side by side into the homestretch. With one hundred yards to go, Louie held a slight lead. Lash, fighting furiously, stuck with him. Neither man had any more speed to give. Louie could see that he was maybe a hand's width ahead, and he wouldn't let it go.

With heads thrown back, legs pumping out of sync, Louie and Lash drove for the tape. With just a few yards remaining, Lash began inching up, drawing even. The two runners, legs rubbery with exhaustion, flung themselves past the judges in a finish so close, Louie later said, "you couldn't put a hair between us."

The announcer's voice echoed across the living room in Torrance. Zamperini, he said, had won.

Standing in the kitchen, Louise heard the crowd in the next room suddenly shout. Outside, car horns honked, the front door swung open, and neighbors gushed into the house. As a crush of hysterical

Louie and Lash at the finish line at the 1936 Olympic trials.
Courtesy of Louis Zamperini

Torrancers celebrated around her, Louise wept happy tears. Anthony popped the cork on a bottle of wine and began filling glasses and singing out toasts, smiling, said one reveler, like a "jackass eating cactus." A moment later, Louie's voice came over the airwaves, calling a greeting to Torrance.

But the announcer was mistaken. The judges ruled that it was Lash, not Zamperini, who had won. Deckard had hung on for third. The announcer soon corrected himself, but it hardly dimmed the celebration in Torrance. The hometown boy had made the Olympic team.

A few minutes after the race, Louie stood under a cold shower. He could feel the sting of the burns on his feet, following the patterns of his cleats. After drying off, he weighed himself. He had sweated off three pounds. He looked in a mirror and saw a ghostly image looking back at him.

Across the room, Norman Bright was slumped on a bench with one ankle propped over the other knee, staring at his foot. It, like the other one, was burned so badly that the skin had detached from the sole. He had finished fifth, two places short of the Olympic team.*

By the day's end, Louie had received some 125 telegrams. TORRANCE HAS GONE NUTS, read one. VILLAGE HAS GONE SCREWEY, read another. There was even one from the Torrance Police Department, which must have been relieved that someone else was chasing Louie.

That night, Louie pored over the evening papers, which showed photos of the finish of his race. In some, he seemed to be tied with Lash; in others, he seemed to be in front. On the track, he'd felt sure that he had won. The first three would go to the Olympics, but Louie felt cheated nonetheless.

As Louie studied the papers, the judges were reviewing photographs and a film of the 5,000. Later, Louie sent home a telegram with the news: JUDGES CALLED IT A TIE. LEAVE NOON WEDNESDAY FOR BERLIN. WILL RUN HARDER IN BERLIN.

When Sylvia returned from work the next day, the house was packed with well-wishers and newsmen. Louie's twelve-year-old sister, Virginia, clutched one of Louie's trophies and told reporters of her plans to be the next great Zamperini runner. Anthony headed off to the Kiwanis club, where he and Louie's Boy Scout master would drink toasts to Louie until four in the morning. Pete walked around town to back slaps and congratulations. "Am I ever happy," he wrote to Louie. "I have to go around with my shirt open so that I have enough room for my chest."

Louie Zamperini was on his way to Germany to compete in the Olympics in an event that he had only contested four times. He was the youngest distance runner to ever make the team.

---

* Bright wouldn't have another shot at the Olympics, but he would run for the rest of his life, setting masters records in his old age. Eventually he went blind, but he kept right on running, holding the end of a rope while a guide held the other. "The only problem was that most guides couldn't run as fast as my brother, even when he was in his late seventies," wrote his sister Georgie Bright Kunkel. "In his eighties his grandnephews would walk with him around his care center as he timed the walk on his stopwatch."

Four

Plundering Germany

THE LUXURY STEAMER *MANHATTAN*, BEARING THE 1936 U.S. Olympic team to Germany, was barely past the Statue of Liberty before Louie began stealing things. In his defense, he wasn't the one who started it. Mindful of being a teenaged upstart in the company of such seasoned track deities as Jesse Owens and Glenn Cunningham, Louie curbed his coltish impulses and began growing a mustache. But he soon noticed that practically everyone on board was "souvenir collecting," pocketing towels, ashtrays, and anything else they could easily lift. "They had nothing on me," he said later. "I [was] Phi Beta Kappa in taking things." The mustache was abandoned. As the voyage went on, Louie and the other lightfingers quietly denuded the *Manhattan*.

Everyone was fighting for training space. Gymnasts set up their apparatuses, but with the ship swaying, they kept getting bucked off. Basketball players did passing drills on deck, but the wind kept jettisoning the balls into the Atlantic. Fencers lurched all over the ship. The water athletes discovered that the salt water in the ship's tiny pool sloshed back and forth vehemently, two feet deep one moment, seven feet the next, creating waves so large, one water polo man took up bodysurfing. Every large roll heaved most of the water, and everyone in it, onto the deck, so the coaches had to tie the swimmers to the wall. The situ-

ation was hardly better for runners. Louie found that the only way to
train was to circle the first-class deck, weaving among deck chairs, reclining movie stars, and other athletes. In high seas, the runners were
buffeted about, all staggering in one direction, then in the other. Louie

Courtesy of Louis Zamperini

had to move so slowly that he couldn't lose the marathon walker creeping along beside him.

For a Depression-era teenager accustomed to breakfasting on stale
bread and milk, and who had eaten in a restaurant only twice in his
life,* the *Manhattan* was paradise. Upon rising, the athletes sipped
cocoa and grazed from plates of pastries. At nine, there was steak and
eggs in the dining room. A coffee break, lunch, tea, and dinner followed, nose to tail. Between meals, a ring for the porter would bring
anything the heart desired, and late at night, the athletes raided the galley. Inching around the first-class deck, Louie found a little window in

---

* Louie would later recall eating at a restaurant only once, when a family friend
 bought him a sandwich at a lunch counter, but according to his Olympic diary,
 after his 5,000-meter trial, a fan treated him to dinner in a Manhattan skyscraper. The meal cost $7, a staggering sum to Louie, who had been paying be-
 tween 65 cents and $1.35 for his dinners, carefully recording the prices in his
 diary.

which pints of beer kept magically appearing. He made them magically disappear. When seasickness thinned the ranks of the diners, extra desserts were laid out, and Louie, who had sturdy sea legs, let nothing go to waste. His consumption became legendary. Recalling how the ship had to make an unscheduled stop to restock the pantries, runner James LuValle joked, "Of course, most of this was due to Lou Zamperini." Louie made a habit of sitting next to the mountainous shot putter Jack Torrance, who had an inexplicably tiny appetite. When Torrance couldn't finish his entrée, Louie dropped onto the plate like a vulture.

On the evening of July 17, Louie returned from dinner so impressed with his eating that he immortalized it on the back of a letter:

> 1 pint of pineapple juice
> 2 bowls of beef broth
> 2 sardine salads
> 5 rolls
> 2 tall glasses of milk
> 4 small sweet pickles
> 2 plates of chicken
> 2 helpings of sweet potatoes
> 4 pieces of butter
> 3 helpings of ice cream with wafers
> 3 chunks of angel food cake with white frosting
> 1½ pounds of cherries
> 1 apple
> 1 orange
> 1 glass of ice water

"Biggest meal I ever ate in my life," he wrote, "and I can't believe it myself, but I was there . . . Where it all went, I don't know."

He'd soon find out. Shortly before the athletes came ashore at Hamburg, a doctor noted that quite a few were expanding. One javelin competitor had gained eight pounds in five days. Several wrestlers, boxers, and weightlifters had eaten themselves out of their weight classes, and some were unable to compete. Don Lash had gained ten pounds. Louie outdid them all, regaining all the weight that he'd lost in New York, and then some. When he got off the *Manhattan,* he weighed twelve pounds more than when he'd gotten on nine days earlier.

On July 24, the athletes shuffled from the ship to a train, stopped over in Frankfurt for a welcoming dinner, and reboarded the train toting quite a few of their hosts' priceless wine glasses. The Germans chased down the train, searched the baggage, repatriated the glasses, and sent the Americans on to Berlin. There, the train was swamped by teenagers holding scissors and chanting, *"Wo ist Jesse? Wo ist Jesse?"* When Owens stepped out, the throng swarmed him and began snipping off bits of his clothing. Owens leapt back onto the train.

The athletes were driven to the Olympic Village, a masterpiece of design crafted by Wolfgang Fürstner, a Wehrmacht captain. Nestled in an undulating patchwork of beech forests, lakes, and clearings were 140 cottages, a shopping mall, a barbershop, a post office, a dentist's office, a sauna, a hospital, training facilities, and dining halls. A new technology called television was on exhibit in the village office. There were wooded trails, over which bounded a multitude of imported animals. The Japanese athletes were especially taken with the deer and began feeding them treats in such volume that the Germans discreetly moved the deer out. One British wag wondered aloud where the storks were. The next day, two hundred storks appeared.

Louie was housed in a cottage with several other athletes, including Owens. The great sprinter kept a fatherly eye on him; Louie repaid him by swiping his DO NOT DISTURB sign, leaving poor Owens besieged by autograph seekers. Louie swam in the lakes, ate appalling quantities of food, and socialized. The hit of the village was the Japanese contingent, whose tradition of prodigious gift giving made them the collective Santa Claus of the Games.

On the first of August, Louie and the other Olympians were driven through Berlin for the opening ceremonies. Every vista suggested coiled might. Nazi banners had been papered over everything. As much as a third of the male population was in uniform, as were many children. Military units drilled openly, and though powered aircraft were forbidden under the Versailles Treaty, the strength of the burgeoning Luftwaffe was on conspicuous display over an airfield, where gliders swooped over impressed tourists and Hitler Youth. The buses had machine gun mounts on the roofs and undercarriages that could be converted into tank-style tracks. The city was pristine. Even the wagon horses left no mark, their droppings instantly scooped up by uniformed street sweepers. Berlin's Gypsies and Jewish students had vanished—

the Gypsies had been dumped in camps, the Jews confined to the University of Berlin campus—leaving only smiling "Aryans." The only visible wisp of discord was the broken glass in the windows of Jewish businesses.

The buses drove to the Olympic stadium. Entering in a parade of nations and standing at attention, the athletes were treated to a thunderous show that culminated in the release of twenty thousand doves. As the birds circled in panicked confusion, cannons began firing, prompting the birds to relieve themselves over the athletes. With each report, the birds let fly. Louie stayed at attention, shaking with laughter.

Louie had progressed enough in four 5,000-meter races to compete with Lash, but he knew that he had no chance of winning an Olympic medal. It wasn't just that he was out of shape from the long idleness on the ship, and almost pudgy from gorging on board and in the village. Few nations had dominated an Olympic event as Finland had the 5,000, winning gold in 1912, '24, '28, and '32. Lauri Lehtinen, who had won gold in '32, was back for another go, along with his brilliant teammates Gunnar Höckert and Ilmari Salminen. When Louie watched them train, noted a reporter, his eyes bulged. Louie was too young and too green to beat the Finns, and he knew it. His day would come, he believed, in the 1,500 four years later.

In the last days before his preliminary heat, Louie went to the stadium and watched Owens crush the field in the 100 meters and Cunningham break the world record for the 1,500 but still lose to New Zealander Jack Lovelock. The atmosphere was surreal. Each time Hitler entered, the crowd jumped up with the Nazi salute. With each foreign athlete's victory, an abbreviated version of his or her national anthem was played. When a German athlete won, the stadium rang with every stanza of "Deutschland über Alles" and the spectators shouted "*Sieg heil!*" endlessly, arms outstretched. According to the swimmer Iris Cummings, the slavish nationalism was a joke to the Americans, but not to the Germans. The Gestapo paced the stadium, eyeing the fans. A German woman sitting with Cummings refused to salute. She shrank between Iris and her mother, whispering, "*Don't let them see me! Don't let them see me!*"

On August 4, three 5,000-meter qualifying heats were run. Louie drew the third, deepest heat, facing Lehtinen. The top five in each heat would make the final. In the first, Lash ran third. In the second, Tom Deckard, the other American, failed to qualify. Louie slogged through heat three, feeling fat and leaden-legged. He barely caught fifth place at the line. He was, he wrote in his diary, "tired as hell." He had three days to prepare for the final.

While he was waiting, an envelope arrived from Pete. Inside were two playing cards, an ace and a joker. On the joker Pete had written, "Which are you going to be, the joker, which is another word for horse's ass, or the *TOPS*: Ace of spades. The best in the bunch. The highest in the deck. Take your choice!" On the ace he had written, "Let's see you storm through as the best in the deck. If the joker does not appeal to you, throw it away and keep this for good luck. Pete."

On August 7, Louie lay facedown in the infield of the Olympic stadium, readying himself for the 5,000-meter final. One hundred thousand spectators ringed the track. Louie was terrified. He pressed his face to the grass, inhaling deeply, trying to settle his quivering nerves. When the time came, he rose, walked to the starting line, bowed forward, and waited. His paper number, 751, flapped against his chest.

At the sound of the gun, Louie's body, electric with nervous energy, wanted to bolt, but Louie made a conscious effort to relax, knowing how far he had to go. As the runners surged forward, he kept his stride short, letting the pacesetters untangle. Lash emerged with the lead, a troika of Finns just behind him. Louie floated left and settled into the second tier of runners.

The laps wound by. Lash kept leading, the Finns on his heels. Louie pushed along in the second group. He began breathing in a sickening odor. He looked around and realized that it was coming from a runner ahead of him, his hair a slick of reeking pomade. Feeling a swell of nausea, Louie slowed and slid out a bit, and the stench dissipated. Lash and the Finns were slipping out of reach, and Louie wanted to go with them, but his body felt sodden. As the clumps of men stretched and thinned into a long, broken thread, Louie sank through the field, to twelfth. Only three stragglers trailed him.

Ahead, the Finns scuffed and sidled into Lash, roughing him up. Lash held his ground. But on the eighth lap, Salminen cocked his elbow and rammed it into Lash's chest. Lash folded abruptly, in evident pain. The Finns bounded away. They entered the eleventh lap in a tight knot, looking to sweep the medals. Then, for an instant, they strayed too close to each other. Salminen's leg clipped that of Höckert. As Höckert stumbled, Salminen fell heavily to the track. He rose, dazed, and resumed running. His race, like Lash's, was lost.

Louie saw none of it. He passed the deflated Lash, but it meant little to him. He was tired. The Finns were small and distant, much too far away to catch. He found himself thinking of Pete, and of something that he had said as they had sat on their bed years earlier: A lifetime of glory is worth a moment of pain. Louie thought: *Let go.*

Nearing the finish line for the penultimate time, Louie fixed his eyes on the gleaming head of the pomaded competitor, who was many runners ahead. He began a dramatic acceleration. Around the turn and down the backstretch, Louie kicked, his legs reaching and pushing, his cleats biting the track, his speed dazzling. One by one, runners came up ahead and faded away behind. "All I had," Louie would say, "I gave it."

As Louie flew around the last bend, Höckert had already won, with Lehtinen behind him. Louie wasn't watching them. He was chasing the glossy head, still distant. He heard a gathering roar and realized that the crowd had caught sight of his rally and was shouting him on. Even Hitler, who had been contorting himself in concert with the athletes, was watching him. Louie ran on, Pete's words beating in his head, his whole body burning. The shining hair was far away, then nearer. Then it was so close that Louie again smelled the pomade. With the last of his strength, Louie threw himself over the line. He had made up fifty yards in the last lap and beaten his personal best time by more than eight seconds. His final time, 14:46.8, was by far the fastest 5,000 run by any American in 1936, almost twelve seconds faster than Lash's best for the year. He had just missed seventh place.

As Louie bent, gasping, over his spent legs, he marveled at the kick that he had forced from his body. It had felt very, very fast. Two coaches hurried up, gaping at their stopwatches, on which they had clocked his final lap. Both watches showed precisely the same time.

In distance running in the 1930s, it was exceptionally rare for a man to run a last lap in one minute. This rule held even in the comparatively short hop of a mile: In the three fastest miles ever run, the winner's final lap had been clocked at 61.2, 58.9, and 59.1 seconds, respectively. No lap in those three historic performances had been faster than 58.9. In the 5,000, well over three miles, turning a final lap in less than 70 seconds was a monumental feat. In his record-breaking 1932 Olympic 5,000, Lehtinen had spun his final lap in 69.2 seconds.

Louie had run his last lap in 56 seconds.

After cleaning himself up, Louie climbed into the stands. Nearby, Adolf Hitler sat in his box, among his entourage. Someone pointed out a cadaverous man near Hitler and told Louie that it was Joseph Goebbels, Hitler's minister of propaganda. Louie had never heard of him. Pulling out his camera, he carried it to Goebbels and asked him if he'd snap a picture of the führer. Goebbels asked him his name and event, then took the camera, moved away, snapped a photo, spoke with Hitler, returned, and told Louie that the führer wanted to see him.

Louie was led into the führer's section. Hitler bent from his box, smiled, and offered his hand. Louie, standing below, had to reach far up. Their fingers barely touched. Hitler said something in German. An interpreter translated.

"Ah, you're the boy with the fast finish."

Happy with his performance, Louie was itching to raise hell. He had hoped to pal around with Glenn Cunningham, but his hero proved too mature for him. Instead, he found a suitably irresponsible companion, donned his Olympic dress uniform, and descended on Berlin. The two prowled bars, wooed girls, chirped, *"Heil Hitler!"* at everyone in uniform, and stole anything Germanish that they could pry loose. In an automat, they discovered German beer. The serving size was a liter, which took Louie a good while to finish. Buzzing, they went walking, then circled back for another liter, which went down easier than the first.

Trolling around Berlin, they stopped across the street from the Reich Chancellery. A car pulled up and out stepped Hitler, who walked inside. Studying the building, Louie spotted a small Nazi flag near the doors. It would make a swell souvenir, and it looked easy to reach. The banner didn't yet carry much symbolic meaning for him, or many other Americans, in the summer of '36. Louie just had a hankering to steal in his head and two persuasive liters of German brew in his belly.

Two guards paced the apron before the Chancellery. Watching them walk, Louie noted that on each pass, there was a point at which both had their backs to the flag. As the soldiers turned, Louie ran to the flag and immediately realized that it was much higher than he had thought. He began jumping in the air, trying to catch the edge of it. He became so absorbed in his task that he forgot about the guards, who ran toward him, shouting. Taking one last lunge for the flag, Louie snagged the edge and fell to the pavement, tearing the banner down with him, then scrambled to his feet and ran like mad.

He heard a *crack!* Behind him, a guard was running at him, his gun pointed at the sky, yelling, *"Halten Sie!"* That much Louie understood. He stopped. The guard grabbed his shoulder, spun him around, saw his Olympic uniform, and hesitated. He asked Louie his name. The one thing that Louie knew about Nazis was that they were anti-Semitic, so when he gave his name, he delivered it in an exaggeratedly Italian fashion, rolling the *r*, he would say, "for about two minutes."

The guards conferred, went inside, and came out with someone who looked more important than they. The new German asked him why he had stolen the flag. Louie, laying it on thick, replied that he wanted a souvenir of the happy time he had had in beautiful Germany. The Germans gave him the flag and let him go.

When the press got wind of Louie's adventure, reporters took creative liberties. Louie had "stormed Hitler's palace" to steal the flag in a hail of gunfire that had "whistled around his head." Plunging "eighteen feet," he had raced away, pursued by "two columns" of armed guards, who had tackled and beat him. Just as a German rifle butt had been about to crush Louie's head, the German army's commander in chief had halted the attack, and Louie had talked the general into sparing his life. In one version, Hitler himself had allowed him to keep the flag. In another, Louie had concealed the flag so cleverly that it was never discovered. He had done it all, went the story, to win the heart of a girl.

On August 11, Louie packed his belongings, the flag, and an array of other stolen Teutonica and left his room in the Olympic Village. The Games were winding down, and the track athletes were leaving early to compete in meets in England and Scotland. A few days later, fireworks brought the Games to a booming close. Hitler's show had gone without a hitch. The world was full of praise.

The American basketball player Frank Lubin lingered in Berlin for a few days. His German hosts had invited him out to dinner, so they cruised the streets in search of a restaurant. A pretty place caught

Lubin's eye, but when he suggested it, his hosts balked: a Star of David hung in the window. To be seen there, they said, "might prove harmful to us." The group found a gentile restaurant, then visited a public swimming pool. As they walked in, Lubin saw a sign reading JUDEN VERBOTEN. The sign hadn't been there during the Games. All over Berlin, such signs were reappearing, and the Nazis' virulently anti-Semitic *Der Stürmer*, nowhere to be seen during the Games, was back on newsstands. Lubin had won a gold medal in Berlin, but when he left, he felt only relief. Something terrible was coming.

The Olympic Village wasn't empty for long. The cottages became military barracks. With the Olympics over and his usefulness for propaganda expended, the village's designer, Captain Fürstner, learned that he was to be cashiered from the Wehrmacht because he was a Jew. He killed himself. Less than twenty miles away, in the town of Oranienburg, the first prisoners were being hauled into the Sachsenhausen concentration camp.

On the evening of September 2, when Louie arrived in Torrance, he was plunked onto a throne on the flatbed of a truck and paraded to the depot, where four thousand people, whipped up by a band, sirens, and factory whistles, cheered. Louie shook hands and grinned for pictures. "I didn't only start too slow," he said, "I ran too slow."

As he settled back into home, Louie thought of what lay ahead. Running the 1936 Olympic 5,000 at nineteen on four races' experience had been a shot at the moon. Running the 1940 Olympic 1,500 at twenty-three after years of training would be another matter. The same thought was circling in Pete's mind. Louie could win gold in 1940, and both brothers knew it.

A few weeks before, officials had announced which city would host the 1940 Games. Louie shaped his dreams around Tokyo, Japan.

Five

Into War

AT THE UNIVERSITY OF SOUTHERN CALIFORNIA, LOUIE found himself on a campus infested with world-class track athletes. He spent mornings in class and afternoons training with his best friend, Payton Jordan. A sensationally fast sprinter, Jordan had seen nothing but Jesse Owens's back at the 1936 Olympic trials and, like Louie, was aiming for gold in Tokyo. In the evenings, Louie, Jordan, and their teammates wedged into Louie's '31 Ford and drove to Torrance for Louise Zamperini's spaghetti, considering themselves so close to family that Sylvia once found a high jumper asleep on her bed. In his spare time, Louie crashed society weddings, worked as a movie extra, and harassed his housemates with practical jokes, replacing their deviled ham with cat food and milk with milk of magnesia. He pursued coeds by all means necessary, once landing a date with a beauty by hurling himself into the side of her car, then pretending to have been struck.

Between classes, Louie, Jordan, and their friends congregated near the administration building, sitting at the foot of the statue of Tommy Trojan, the symbol of USC. On some days, they were joined by a neatly dressed Japanese émigré who lingered on the edges of the group. His name was Kunichi James Sasaki. Known as Jimmie, he had come to

America in his late teens and settled in Palo Alto, where he had endured
the social misery of attending elementary school as an adult. Among
Louie's friends, no one would remember what Sasaki studied at USC,
but they all recalled his quiet, anodyne presence; saying almost nothing, he smiled without interruption.

Sasaki was an ardent track fan, and he sought Louie's acquaintance.
Louie was especially impressed with Sasaki's scholarliness; prior to

Training for the Olympics, 1940. *Bettmann/Corbis*

coming to USC, Jimmie said, he had earned degrees at Harvard, Princeton, and Yale. Bonding over shared interests in sports and music, the
two became good friends.

Louie and Jimmie had something else in common. Sometime over
the course of the friendship, Louie learned that his friend was making
daily trips to Torrance. He asked Jimmie if he lived there, and Jimmie
said no. He explained that he was concerned about the poverty of his
Japanese homeland and was going to Torrance to give lectures to locals
of Japanese ancestry, encouraging them to send money and foil from
cigarette packs and gum wrappers to Japan to help the poor. Louie ad-

mired his friend for his efforts, but found it odd that he would travel to Torrance every day, given how few Japanese lived there.

Jimmie Sasaki wasn't what he seemed. He had never attended Harvard, Yale, or Princeton. His friends thought him about thirty; he was in fact nearly forty. He had a wife and two daughters, though neither Louie nor his friends knew that they existed. Though he spent a lot of time on campus and led everyone to believe that he was a student, he was not. He had graduated from USC some ten years earlier, with a B.A. in political science. Neither Louie nor anyone else knew that Jimmie's attempts to pass as a student were apparently an elaborate ruse.

On USC's track team, Louie was a juggernaut. Focused on winning in Tokyo in 1940, he smashed record after record at multiple distances and routinely buried his competition by giant margins, once winning a race by one hundred yards. By the spring of 1938, he'd whittled his mile time down to 4:13.7, some seven seconds off the world record, which now stood at 4:06.4. His coach predicted that Louie would take that record down. The only runner who could beat him, the coach said, was Seabiscuit.

One afternoon in 1938, Glenn Cunningham stood in the Los Angeles Coliseum locker room, talking with reporters after winning a race. "There's the next mile champion," he said, leveling his eyes across the room. "When he concentrates on this distance, he'll be unbeatable." The reporters turned to see who Cunningham was looking at. It was Louie, blushing to the roots of his hair.

In the 1930s, track experts were beginning to toss around the idea of a four-minute mile. Most observers, including Cunningham, had long believed that it couldn't be done. In 1935, when Cunningham's record of 4:06.7 reigned, science weighed in. Studying data on human structural limits compiled by Finnish mathematicians, famed track coach Brutus Hamilton penned an article for *Amateur Athlete* magazine stating that a four-minute mile was impossible. The fastest a human could run a mile, he wrote, was 4:01.6.

Pete disagreed. Since the Olympics, he'd been certain that Louie had a four-minute mile in him. Louie had always shaken this off, but in the spring of '38, he reconsidered. His coach had forbidden him to run hills on the mistaken but common belief that it would damage his heart, but Louie didn't buy the warnings. Every night that May, he climbed the coliseum fence, dropped into the stadium, and ran the stairs until his legs went numb. By June, his body was humming, capable of speed and stamina beyond anything he'd ever known. He began to think that Pete was right, and he wasn't alone. Running pundits, including Olympic champion sprinter Charlie Paddock, published articles stating that Louie could be the first four-minute man. Cunningham, too, had changed his mind. He thought that four minutes might be within Louie's reach. Zamperini, Cunningham told a reporter, was more likely to crack four minutes than he was.

In June 1938, Louie arrived at the NCAA Championships in Minneapolis, gunning for four minutes. Spilling over with eagerness, he babbled to other athletes about his new training regimen, his race strategy, and how fast he might go. Word spread that Louie was primed for a superlative performance. On the night before the race, a coach from Notre Dame knocked on Louie's hotel room door, a grave expression on his face. He told Louie that some of his rival coaches were ordering their runners to sharpen their spikes and slash him. Louie dismissed the warning, certain that no one would do such a thing deliberately.

He was wrong. Halfway through the race, just as Louie was about to move for the lead, several runners shouldered around him, boxing him in. Louie tried repeatedly to break loose, but he couldn't get around the other men. Suddenly, the man beside him swerved in and stomped on his foot, impaling Louie's toe with his spike. A moment later, the man ahead began kicking backward, cutting both of Louie's shins. A third man elbowed Louie's chest so hard that he cracked Louie's rib. The crowd gasped.

Bleeding and in pain, Louie was trapped. For a lap and a half, he ran in the cluster of men, unable to get free, restraining his stride to avoid running into the man ahead. At last, as he neared the final turn, he saw a tiny gap open before him. He burst through, blew past the race leader, and, with his shoe torn open, shins streaming blood, and chest aching, won easily.

He slowed to a halt, bitter and frustrated. When his coach asked him how fast he thought he had gone, Louie replied that he couldn't have beaten 4:20.

The race time was posted on the board. From the stands came a sudden *Woooo!* Louie had run the mile in 4:08.3. It was the fastest NCAA mile in history and the fifth-fastest outdoor mile ever run. Louie had missed the world record by 1.9 seconds. His time would stand as the NCAA record for fifteen years.

Weeks later, Japan withdrew as host of the 1940 Olympics, and the Games were transferred to Finland. Adjusting his aspirations from Tokyo to Helsinki, Louie rolled on. He won every race he contested in the 1939 school season. In the early months of 1940, in a series of eastern indoor miles against the best runners in America, he was magnificent, taking two seconds and two close fourths, twice

With a cracked rib and puncture wounds to both legs and one foot, Louie celebrates his record-setting NCAA Championship victory. *Courtesy of Louis Zamperini*

beating Cunningham, and getting progressively faster. In February at the Boston Garden, he ran a 4:08.2, six-tenths of a second short of the fastest indoor mile ever run.* At Madison Square Garden two weeks later, he scorched a 4:07.9, caught just before the tape by the great Chuck Fenske, whose time equaled the indoor world record. With the Olympics months away, Louie was peaking at the ideal moment.

---

* Because indoor tracks are shorter than outdoor ones, forcing runners to make more turns to cover the same distance, indoor records are generally slower. In 1940, the outdoor mile world record was one second faster than the indoor record.

As Louie blazed through college, far away, history was turning. In Europe, Hitler was laying plans to conquer the continent. In Asia, Japan's leaders had designs of equal magnitude. Poor in natural resources, its trade crippled by high tariffs and low demand, Japan was struggling to support a growing population. Eyeing their nation's resource-rich neighbors, Japan's leaders saw the prospect of economic independence, and something more. Central to the Japanese identity was the belief that it was Japan's divinely mandated right to rule its fellow Asians, whom it saw as inherently inferior. "There are superior and inferior races in the world," said the Japanese politician Nakajima Chikuhei in 1940, "and it is the sacred duty of the leading race to lead and enlighten the inferior ones." The Japanese, he continued, are "the sole superior race of the world." Moved by necessity and destiny, Japan's leaders planned to "plant the blood of the Yamato [Japanese] race" on their neighboring nations' soil. They were going to subjugate all of the Far East.

Japan's military-dominated government had long been preparing for its quest. Over decades, it had crafted a muscular, technologically sophisticated army and navy, and through a military-run school system that relentlessly and violently drilled children on the nation's imperial destiny, it had shaped its people for war. Finally, through intense indoctrination, beatings, and desensitization, its army cultivated and celebrated extreme brutality in its soldiers. "Imbuing violence with holy meaning," wrote the historian Iris Chang, "the Japanese imperial army made violence a cultural imperative every bit as powerful as that which propelled Europeans during the Crusades and the Spanish Inquisition." Chang cited a 1933 speech by a Japanese general: "Every single bullet must be charged with the Imperial Way, and the end of every bayonet must have National Virtue burnt into it." In 1931, Japan tested the waters, invading the Chinese province of Manchuria and setting up a fiercely oppressive puppet state. This was only the beginning.

In the late 1930s, both Germany and Japan were ready to move. It was Japan that struck first, in 1937, sending its armies smashing into the rest of China. Two years later, Hitler invaded Poland. America, long isolationist, found itself pulled into both conflicts: In Europe, its allies lay in Hitler's path; in the Pacific, its longtime ally China was being ravaged by the Japanese, and its territories of Hawaii, Wake, Guam, and Midway, as well as its commonwealth of the Philippines, were threatened. The world was falling into catastrophe.

On a dark day in April 1940, Louie returned to his bungalow to find the USC campus buzzing. Hitler had unleashed his blitzkrieg across Europe, his Soviet allies had followed, and the continent had exploded into total war. Finland, which was set to host the summer Games, was reeling. Helsinki's Olympic stadium was partially collapsed, toppled by Soviet bombs. Gunnar Höckert, who had beaten Louie and won gold for Finland in the 5,000 in Berlin, was dead, killed defending his homeland.* The Olympics had been canceled.

———

Louie was unmoored. He became ill, first with food poisoning, then with pleurisy. His speed abandoned him, and he lost race after race. When USC's spring semester ended, he collected his class ring and left campus. He was a few credits short of a degree, but he had all of 1941 to make them up. He took a job as a welder at the Lockheed Air Corporation and mourned his lost Olympics.

As Louie worked through the summer of '40, America slid toward war. In Europe, Hitler had driven the British and their allies into the sea at Dunkirk. In the Pacific, Japan was tearing through China and moving into Indochina. In an effort to stop Japan, President Franklin Roosevelt imposed ever-increasing embargoes on matériel, such as scrap metal and aviation fuel. In the coming months, he would declare an oil embargo, freeze Japanese assets in America, and finally declare a total trade embargo. Japan pushed on.

Lockheed was on a war footing, punching out aircraft for the Army Air Corps and the Royal Air Force. From the hangar where he worked, Louie could see P-38 fighters cruising overhead. Ever since his trip in the air as a boy, he'd been uneasy about planes, but watching the P-38s, he felt a pull. He was still feeling it in September when Congress enacted a draft bill. Those who enlisted prior to being drafted could choose their service branch. In early 1941, Louie joined the Army Air Corps.†

———

* Höckert's teammate Lauri Lehtinen, the 1932 5,000-meter Olympic champion, gave his gold medal to another Finnish soldier in Höckert's honor.
† Many other great runners also enlisted. When Norman Bright tried to sign up, he was rejected because of his alarmingly slow pulse, a consequence of his extreme fitness. He solved the problem by running three miles, straight into another enlistment office. Cunningham tried to join the navy, but recruiters, seeing his grotesquely scarred legs, assumed that he was too crippled to serve. When someone came in and mentioned his name, they realized who he was and signed him in.

Sent to the Hancock College of Aeronautics in Santa Maria, California, Louie learned that flying a plane was nothing like watching it from the ground. He was jittery and dogged by airsickness. He washed out of the air corps, signed papers that he didn't bother to read, and got a job as a movie extra. He was working on the set of *They Died with*

Louie in training.
Courtesy of Louis Zamperini

Their Boots On, starring Errol Flynn and Olivia de Havilland, when a letter arrived. He'd been drafted.

The induction date fell before the Flynn film would wrap, and Louie stood to earn a bonus if he stayed through the shoot. Just before his army physical, he ate a fistful of candy bars; thanks to the consequent soaring blood sugar, he failed the physical. Ordered to return a few days later to retake the test, he went back to the set and earned his bonus. Then, on September 29, he joined the army.

When he finished basic training, he had an unhappy surprise. Because he hadn't read his air corps washout papers, he had no idea that he'd agreed to rejoin the corps for future service. In November 1941, he arrived at Ellington Field, in Houston, Texas. The military was going to make him a bombardier.

That fall, while Louie was on his way to becoming an airman, an urgent letter landed on the desk of J. Edgar Hoover, director of the FBI.

It had come from a brigadier general at the War Department, Military Intelligence Division. The letter said that a credible informant had warned military officials that a California man, believed to be working for an innocuous local Japanese organization, had in fact been an employee of the Japanese navy, on assignment to raise money for Japan's war effort. Japanese naval superiors had recently transferred the man to Washington, D.C., the informant said, to continue acting under their orders. According to the informant, the man was known as "Mr. Sasaki." It was Louie's friend Jimmie.

Though the surviving records of the informant's report contain no details of Sasaki's alleged activities, according to notes made later by a captain of the Torrance police, Sasaki had been making visits to a field adjacent to a power station, just off of Torrance Boulevard. There, he had erected a powerful radio transmitter, which he had used to send information to the Japanese government. If the allegation was true, it would explain Sasaki's mysterious trips to Torrance. Louie's good friend may have been a spy.

Sasaki had indeed moved to Washington, D.C., in the employ of the Japanese navy. He worked in the Japanese embassy and lived in an apartment building popular among congressmen. He made himself well known among the Washington elite, mixing with legislators at building cocktail parties, playing golf at the Army Navy Country Club, socializing with police officers and State Department officials, and volunteering to serve as chauffeur after parties. Just whose side he was on is unclear; at a cocktail party, he gave a congressman sensitive information on Japanese aircraft manufacturing.

The letter to the FBI set off alarm bells. Hoover, concerned enough to plan on informing the secretary of state, ordered an immediate investigation of Sasaki.

———

Not long after sunrise on a Sunday in December, a pilot guided a small plane over the Pacific. Below him, the dark sea gave way to a strand of white: waves slapping the northern tip of Oahu Island. The plane flew into a brilliant Hawaiian morning.

Oahu was beginning to stir. At Hickam Field, soldiers were washing a car. On Hula Lane, a family was dressing for Mass. At the officers' club at Wheeler Field, men were leaving a poker game. In a barracks, two men were in the midst of a pillow fight. At Ewa Mooring Mast Field, a technical sergeant was peering through the lens of a camera at his three-year-old son. Hardly anyone had made it to the mess halls yet. Quite a few were still sleeping in their bunks in the warships, gently swaying in the harbor. Aboard the USS *Arizona*, an officer was about to suit up to play in the United States Fleet championship baseball game. On deck, men were assembling to raise flags as a band played the national anthem, a Sunday morning tradition.

Far above them, the pilot counted eight battleships, the Pacific Fleet's full complement. There was a faint sheet of fog settled low to the ground.

The pilot's name was Mitsuo Fuchida. He rolled back the canopy on his plane and sent a flare skidding green across the sky, then ordered his radioman to tap out a battle cry. Behind Fuchida, 180 Japanese planes peeled away and dove for Oahu.* On the deck of the *Arizona,* the men looked up.

In the barracks, one of the men in the pillow fight suddenly fell to the floor. He was dead, a three-inch hole blown through his neck. His friend ran to a window and saw a building heave upward and crumble down. A dive-bomber had crashed straight into it. There were red circles on its wings.

———

Pete Zamperini was at a friend's house that morning, playing a few hands of high-low-jack before heading out for a round of golf. Behind him, the sizzle of waffles on a griddle competed with the chirp of a radio. An urgent voice interrupted the broadcast. The players put down their cards.

In Texas, Louie was in a theater, on a weekend pass. The theater was thick with servicemen, taking breaks from the endless drilling that was the life of the peacetime soldier. Midway through the showing, the screen went blank, light flooded the theater, and a man hurried onto the stage. *Is there a fire?* Louie wondered.

All servicemen must return to their bases immediately, the man said. Japan has attacked Pearl Harbor.

Louie would long remember sitting there with his eyes wide, his mind floundering. America was at war. He grabbed his hat and ran from the building.

* One hundred and eighty-three planes were launched in this first of two waves, but two were lost on takeoff.

B-24 LIBERATOR

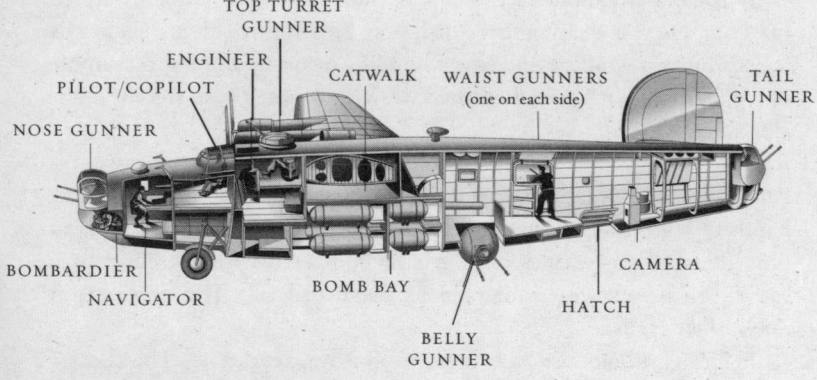

TOP TURRET
GUNNER

ENGINEER

PILOT/COPILOT

CATWALK

WAIST GUNNERS
(one on each side)

TAIL
GUNNER

NOSE GUNNER

BOMBARDIER

NAVIGATOR

BOMB BAY

BELLY
GUNNER

HATCH

CAMERA

PART

II

Six

The Flying Coffin

A S JAPANESE PLANES DOVE OVER OAHU, MORE THAN TWO thousand miles to the west, a few marines were sitting in a mess tent on Wake Atoll, having breakfast. Extremely small, lacking its own water supply, Wake would have been a useless atoll but for one enormous attribute: It lay far out in the Pacific, making it a strategically ideal spot for an air base. And so it was home to one runway and about five hundred bored American servicemen, mostly marines. Aside from the occasional refueling stopovers of Pan American World Airways planes, nothing interesting ever happened there. But that December morning, just as the marines were starting on their pancakes, an air-raid siren began wailing. By noon, the sky was streaked with Japanese bombers, buildings were exploding, and a few startled men on less than three square miles of coral found themselves on the front in the Second World War.

All over the Pacific that morning, the story was the same. In less than two hours over Pearl Harbor, Japan badly wounded the American navy and killed more than 2,400 people. Almost simultaneously, it attacked Thailand, Shanghai, Malaya, the Philippines, Guam, Midway, and Wake. In one day of breathtaking violence, a new Japanese onslaught had begun.

In America, invasion was expected at any moment. Less than an hour after the Japanese bombed Hawaii, mines were being laid in San Francisco Bay. In Washington, Civil Defense Minister Fiorello La Guardia looped around the city in a police car, sirens blaring, shouting the word *"Calm!"* into a loudspeaker. At the White House, Eleanor Roosevelt dashed off a letter to her daughter, Anna, urging her to get her children off the West Coast. A butler overheard the president speculating on what he'd do if Japanese forces advanced as far as Chicago. Meanwhile, just up Massachusetts Avenue, smoke billowed from the grounds of the Japanese embassy, where Jimmie Sasaki worked. Staffers were burning documents in the embassy yard. On the sidewalk, a crowd watched in silence.

On the night of December 7–8, there were four air-raid alerts in San Francisco. At Sheppard Field air corps school, in Texas, spooked officers ran through the barracks at four A.M., screaming that Japanese planes were coming and ordering the cadets to sprint outside and throw themselves on the ground. In coming days, trenches were dug along the California coast, and schools in Oakland were closed. From New Jersey to Alaska, reservoirs, bridges, tunnels, factories, and waterfronts were put under guard. In Kearney, Nebraska, citizens were instructed on disabling incendiary bombs with garden hoses. Blackout curtains were hung in windows across America, from solitary farmhouses to the White House. Shocking rumors circulated: Kansas City was about to be attacked. San Francisco was being bombed. The Japanese had captured the Panama Canal.

Japan galloped over the globe. On December 10, it invaded the Philippines and seized Guam. The next day, it invaded Burma; a few days later, British Borneo. Hong Kong fell on Christmas; North Borneo, Rabaul, Manila, and the U.S. base in the Philippines fell in January. The British were driven from Malaya and into surrender in Singapore in seventy days.

There was one snag: Wake, surely expected to be an easy conquest, wouldn't give in. For three days, the Japanese bombed and strafed the atoll. On December 11, a vast force, including eleven destroyers and light cruisers, launched an invasion attempt. The little group of defenders shoved them back, sinking two destroyers and damaging nine other ships, shooting down two bombers, and forcing the Japanese to abort, their first loss of the war. It wasn't until December 23 that the

Japanese finally seized Wake and captured the men on it. To the Americans' 52 military deaths, an estimated 1,153 Japanese had been killed.

For several days, the captives were held on the airfield, shivering by night, sweltering by day, singing Christmas carols to cheer themselves. They were initially slated for execution, but after a Japanese officer's intervention, most were crowded into the holds of ships and sent to Japan and occupied China as some of the first Americans to become POWs under the Japanese. Unbeknownst to America, ninety-eight captives were kept on Wake. The Japanese were going to enslave them.

Though Louie had been miserable over having to rejoin the air corps, it wasn't so bad after all. Training at Texas's Ellington Field, then Midland Army Flying School, he earned superb test scores. The flying was usually straight and level, so airsickness wasn't a problem. Best of all, women found the flyboy uniform irresistible. While Louie was out walking one afternoon, a convertible fringed in blondes pulled up, and he was scooped into the car and sped off to a party. When it happened a second time, he sensed a positive trend.

Louie was trained in the use of two bombsights. For dive-bombing, he had a $1 handheld sight consisting of an aluminum plate with a peg and a dangling weight. For flat runs, he had the Norden bombsight, an extremely sophisticated analog computer that, at $8,000, cost more than twice the price of the average American home. On a bombing run with the Norden sight, Louie would visually locate the target, make calculations, and feed information on air speed, altitude, wind, and other factors into the device. The bombsight would then take over flying the plane, follow a precise path to the target, calculate the drop angle, and release the bombs at the optimal moment. Once the bombs were gone, Louie would yell "Bombs away!" and the pilot would take control again. Norden bombsights were so secret that they were stored in guarded vaults and moved under armed escort, and the men were forbidden to photograph or write about them. If his plane was going down, Louie was under orders to fire his Colt .45 into the bombsight to prevent it from falling into enemy hands, then see about saving himself.

In August 1942, Louie, graduated from Midland, was commissioned a second lieutenant. He jumped into a friend's Cadillac and drove to California to say good-bye to his family before heading into his final round of training, then war. Pete, now a navy chief petty officer stationed in San Diego, came home to see Louie off.

On the afternoon of August 19, the Zamperinis gathered on the front steps for a last photograph. Louie and Pete, dashing in their dress uniforms, stood on the bottom step with their mother between them, tiny beside her sons. Louise was on the verge of tears. The August sun was sharp on her face, and she and Louie squinted hard and looked slightly away from the camera, as if all before them was lost in the glare.

A last family photograph as Louie leaves to go to war. Rear, left to right: Sylvia's future husband, Harvey Flammer; Virginia, Sylvia, and Anthony Zamperini. Front: Pete, Louise, and Louie.
Courtesy of Louis Zamperini

Louie and his father rode together to the train station. The platform was crowded with uniformed young men and crying parents, clinging to one another, saying good-bye. When Louie embraced his father, he could feel him shaking.

As his train pulled away, Louie looked out the window. His father stood with his hand in the air, a wavering smile on his face. Louie wondered if he'd ever see him again.

The train carried him to a perpetual dust storm known as Ephrata, Washington, where there was an air base in the middle of a dry lakebed. The lakebed was on a mission to bury the base, the men, and all of their planes, and it was succeeding. The air was so clouded with blowing dirt that men waded through drifts a foot and a half deep. Clothes left out of duffel bags were instantly filthy, and all of the meals, which the crews ate outside while sitting on the ground, were infused with sand. The ground crews, which had to replace twenty-four dirt-clogged aircraft engines in twenty-one days, resorted to spraying oil on the taxiways to keep the dust down. Getting the lakebed off the men was problematic; the hot water ran out long before the men did, and because the PX didn't sell shaving soap, practically everyone had a brambly, dust-catching beard.

Not long after his arrival, Louie was standing at the base, sweating and despairing over the landscape, when a squarish second lieutenant walked up and introduced himself. He was Russell Allen Phillips, and he would be Louie's pilot.

Born in Greencastle, Indiana, in 1916, Phillips had just turned twenty-six. He had grown up in a profoundly religious home in La Porte, Indiana, where his father had been a Methodist pastor. As a boy, he'd been so quiet that adults must have thought him timid, but he had a secret bold stripe. He snuck around his neighborhood with bags full of flour, launching guerrilla attacks on windshields of passing cars, and one Memorial Day weekend, he wedged himself into a car trunk to sneak into the infield of the Indy 500. He had gone to Purdue University, where he'd earned a degree in forestry and conservation. In ROTC, his captain had called him "the most unfit, lousy-looking soldier" he'd ever seen. Ignoring the captain's assessment, Phillips had enlisted in the air corps, where he'd proven to be a born airman. At home, they called him Allen; in the air corps, they called him Phillips.

The first thing people tended to notice about Phillips was that they hadn't noticed him earlier. He was so recessive that he could be in a room for a long time before anyone realized that he was there. He was smallish, short-legged. Some of the men called him Sandblaster because, said one pilot, "his fanny was so close to the ground." For unknown

Russell Allen Phillips.
Courtesy of Karen Loomis

reasons, he wore one pant leg markedly shorter than the other. He had a tidy, pleasant, boyish face that tended to blend with the scenery. This probably contributed to his invisibility, but what really did it was his silence. Phillips was an amiable man and was, judging by his letters, highly articulate, but he preferred not to speak. You could park him in a crowd of chattering partygoers and he'd emerge at evening's end having never said a word. People had long conversations with him, only to realize later that he hadn't spoken.

If he had a boiling point, he never reached it. He rolled along with every inexplicable order from his superiors, every foolish act of his inferiors, and every abrasive personality that military life could throw at an officer. He dealt with every manner of adversity with calm, adaptive acceptance. In a crisis, Louie would learn, Phillips's veins ran icewater.

Phillips had one consuming passion. When he had entered college, his father had taken a new pastorship in Terre Haute. There, Phillips's sister had introduced him to a girl from the church choir, a college student named Cecile Perry, known as Cecy. She had blond hair, a curvy figure, a buoyant disposition, a quick mind, and a family cat named Chopper. She was studying to be a teacher. At a prom in Terre Haute, Allen kissed Cecy. He was a goner, and so was she.

On a Saturday night in November 1941, when he left for the air corps, Phillips spent five last minutes with Cecy at the Indianapolis train station. When the fighting was over, he promised, he'd make her his bride. He kept her photo on his footlocker and wrote her love letters several times a week. When she turned twenty-one, he sent her his pay and asked her to find an engagement ring. Allen's ring was soon on Cecy's finger.

In June 1942, just after her graduation, Cecy traveled to Phoenix to see Allen get his wings. Crazy in love, the two talked about running off to get hitched right then, but reconsidered, deciding to marry at his next training venue and live together there until he was deployed. That venue was Ephrata, and when Phillips saw it, he kicked himself. "I've wished 100 times that we had gotten married when we were at Phoenix," he wrote to her, "but I wouldn't ask you now to come out here + live in a dump like Ephrata." Again, they postponed their wedding. In the fall, Allen's training would be finished. Then, they hoped, they'd have one more chance to see each other before he went to war.

In Ephrata, Louie and Phillips fell in together. Phillips floated along contentedly in Louie's chatty bonhomie; Louie liked Phillips's quiet

Phil's crew. Left to right: Phillips, temporary copilot Gross, Zamperini, Mitchell, Douglas, Pillsbury, and Glassman. Moznette, Lambert, and Brooks are not pictured. *Courtesy of Louis Zamperini*

steadiness, and thought him the kindest person he'd ever met. They never had a single argument and were almost never apart. Phillips called Louie "Zamp"; Louie called Phillips "Phil."

The rest of Phil's bomber crew assembled. Serving as engineer and top turret gunner would be twenty-two-year-old Stanley Pillsbury, who'd been running his family's Maine farm before joining up. The other engineer was Virginia native Clarence Douglas, who would operate one of the two side-directed waist guns, behind the wings. The navigator and nose gunner would be Robert Mitchell, a professor's son from Illinois. Tiny Frank Glassman, with his tightly curled hair, was a dead ringer for Harpo Marx. He would be their radioman and, later, their belly gunner. Because Frank hailed from Chicago, the men called him Gangster. Ray Lambert of Maryland would man the tail gun. The crew's girl magnet was Harry Brooks, a good-looking, ebullient radioman and waist gunner from Michigan. The copilot would be George Moznette, Jr. Because copilots were rotated from plane to plane as they qualified to be pilots, Moznette wouldn't stay with the crew, but he became fast friends with Phil and Louie.

Moznette, Mitchell, Phil, and Louie were officers; the others were enlisted. All were bachelors, but Harry Brooks, like Phil, had a steady girl back home. Her name was Jeannette, and before the war, she and Harry had set their wedding date for May 8, 1943.

The men were issued heavy sheepskin jackets and wool clothing, assembled, and photographed. They would make up crew No. 8 in the
nine-crew 372nd Bomb Squadron of the 307th Bomb Group, Seventh
Air Force. All they needed was a plane.

Louie was hoping to be assigned to a B-17 Flying Fortress. It was
the kind of plane that men wanted to be seen in: handsome, masculine,
nimble, fiercely armed, reliable, long-winded, and practically inde-
structible. The plane that no one wanted was a new bomber, Consolidated Aircraft's B-24 Liberator. On paper, it was generally comparable
to the B-17, but for one major advantage. Thanks to auxiliary fuel
tanks and slender, ultraefficient Davis wings, it could fly literally all
day, a decisive asset in the sprawling World War II theaters.

Flat-faced, rectangular, and brooding, the B-24 had looks only a
myopic mother could love. Crewmen gave it a host of nicknames,
among them "the Flying Brick," "the Flying Boxcar," and "the Consti-
pated Lumberer," a play on Consolidated Liberator. The cockpit was
oppressively cramped, forcing pilot and copilot to live cheek by jowl
for missions as long as sixteen hours. Craning over the mountainous
control panel, the pilot had a panoramic view of his plane's snout and
not much else. Navigating the nine-inch-wide bomb bay catwalk could
be difficult, especially in turbulence; one slip and you'd tumble into the
bay, which was fitted with fragile aluminum doors that would tear
away with the weight of a falling man.

Taxiing was an adventure. The B-24's wheels had no steering, so the
pilot had to cajole the bomber along by feeding power to one side's engines, then the other, and working back and forth on the left and right
brakes, one of which was usually much more sensitive than the other.
This made the taxiways a pageant of lurching planes, all of which,
sooner or later, ended up veering into places nowhere near where their
pilots intended them to go, and from which they often had to be extri-
cated with shovels.

A pilot once wrote that the first time he got into a B-24 cockpit, "it
was like sitting on the front porch and flying the house." The sentiment
was common. The Liberator was one of the heaviest planes in the
world; the D model then in production weighed 71,200 pounds loaded.
Flying it was like wrestling a bear, leaving pilots weary and sore. Because pilots usually manned the yoke with their left hands while their
right hands worked the other controls, B-24 pilots were instantly recog-

nizable when shirtless, because the muscles on their left arms dwarfed those on their right arms. The plane was so clumsy that it was difficult to fly in the tight formations that were critical to fending off attack. A squiggle of turbulence, or a crewman walking inside the fuselage, would tip the plane off its axis.

The B-24 was plagued with mechanical difficulties. If one of the four engines quit, staying airborne was challenging; the failure of two engines was often an emergency. Shortly after the plane was introduced, there were several incidents in which B-24 tails dropped off in midair. And though the war was young, the plane was winning a reputation for being delicate, especially in the skinny wings, which could snap off if struck in combat. Some of the men at Ephrata thought of the B-24 as a death trap.

After a long wait, the 372nd squadron's planes flew into Ephrata. Phil's crew walked out and squinted at the horizon. Even from a distance, there was no mistaking the silhouettes. As the men grumbled, Louie heard one voice pipe up.

"It's the Flying Coffin."

———

They were assigned to a B-24D that looked like all the others. For the next three months—in Ephrata in August and September and Sioux City in October—they practically lived in it. They flew in formation, fired at targets pulled by tow planes, simulated combat runs, and dive-bombed. One day they buzzed so low over Iowa that the propellers kicked up a storm of sand, skinning the paint off the plane's belly and scouring the legs of Pillsbury, who was sitting by the open hatch in the tail, trying to photograph their dummy bombs as they fell into target nets. Throughout it all, Louie perched in the glass-windowed "greenhouse" in the plane's nose, bombing targets. The COs soon learned of the squadron's prowess; angry farmers came calling after the 372nd's hundred-pound bombs flattened an outhouse and one unfortunate cow.

Phil's crew had their first scare at Ephrata. On a training flight, they had radio trouble and got lost, flew around in a blind confusion for hours, and ended up landing at nearly midnight in Spokane, half a state away from their slated destination. They'd been missing for three and a half hours, and the entire West Coast air corps had been hunting for them. When Phil stepped off the plane, he got one chewing out from a colonel. When he flew back to Ephrata, he got another, in stereo, from a colonel and major. "I grew a little older that night, sweet, believe me," he wrote to Cecy.

The panic had been justified, for accidents were common and deadly. Before Louie had begun his bombardier training, he had received a letter from a friend who was an air corps cadet.

> I guess you read about the cadet and instructor who was killed here last week. The poor devils never had a chance. They stalled their ship while turning from base leg onto landing approach. The ship made a one-turn spin and then really hit the ground . . . When they hit it tore their bodies to peaces. The safety belt cut the instructor half in-two. All over the wrecked part of the airplane it look like somebody took and threw about three pans of tomatoes and crakers all over it (blood and flesh) They were mangled to bits, couldn't even identify them looking at them.

It was the kind of story that was filling the letters of would-be airmen all over the country. Pilot and navigator error, mechanical failure, and bad luck were killing trainees at a stunning rate. In the Army Air Forces, or AAF,* there were 52,651 stateside aircraft accidents over the course of the war, killing 14,903 personnel. Though some of these personnel were probably on coastal patrol and other duties, it can be presumed that the vast majority were trainees, killed without ever seeing a combat theater. In the three months in which Phil's men trained as a crew, 3,041 AAF planes—more than 33 per day—met with accidents stateside, killing nine men per day. In subsequent months, death tallies exceeding 500 were common. In August 1943, 590 airmen would die stateside, 19 per day.

Louie, Phil, and their crew saw the dying firsthand. In July, Phil's close friend had been killed in a B-24, just after Phil had had dinner with him. On another day, Phil's crew spent part of a rainy morning sitting in a briefing room with another crew as they awaited flights. Both crews went to their planes, but at the last minute, Phil's crew was ordered back. The other crew took off, flew two miles, and crashed, killing the pilot and navigator. In October in Sioux City, another bomber from their group plowed onto a field, killing two. When he

---

* In June 1941, the air corps became a subordinate arm of the Army Air Forces. It remained in existence as a combat branch of the army until 1947.

learned that the press was reporting on the crash without giving the crewmen's names, Phil ran out of a meeting to get word to his family that he hadn't been on the plane.

The air corps did its best to teach men how to survive a crash. Men were drilled in preparing their planes for impact and equipping them-selves for postcrash survival. Each man was assigned to a crash station, which in Louie's case was by the waist window behind the right wing. They were also schooled in bailout simulations, jumping from parked planes. Some rolled off the catwalk and dropped through the open bomb bay doors; others leapt from the waist windows, wondering how, if jumping from an airborne plane, they'd avoid being cut in two by the twin rudders just behind the windows. They were also taught how to ditch, or make a controlled landing on water. Phil studied duti-fully, but he found the idea of landing a giant bomber on water "kind of silly." The training films surely deepened his doubts; in every film, the ditching B-24 broke apart.

Training was a crucible, and it transformed Phil's crew. They would not all live through what lay ahead, but the survivors would speak of their good fortune in serving among such skilled men. They worked to-gether with seamless efficiency, and judging by their training scores, in the grim business of bombs and bullets, there was no better crew in the squadron. Among surviving crewmen and men from other crews, the warmest praise would be reserved for Phil. B-24s were built for tall pi-lots, and though Phil needed a cushion to get his feet to the pedals and his eyes over the control panel, by all accounts he was superb at his job. Phil, Louie told a reporter, was "a damn swell pilot."

The B-24 assigned to Phil's crew had its own personality. It had a valve that oozed fuel into the bomb bay, prompting Pillsbury to de-velop a nervous habit of pacing the fuselage, sniffing the air. It had a curmudgeonly fuel transfer valve that Pillsbury and Douglas had to fi-nesse into place, lest it stick wide open, slow an engine, or trigger a deafening backfire. The fuel gauges were reliable only until the tanks neared empty, at which point they sometimes reported that the plane was magically gaining fuel. One engine, for reasons known only to the plane, was thirstier than the others, so the gauges had to be watched constantly.

In time, the men's misgivings about the Liberator fell away. In hun-dreds of hours of intense training, their plane never failed them. For all its ugliness and quirks, it was a noble thing, rugged and inexhaustible.

The ground crewmen felt the same, nursing Phil's plane with affection and fretting while it flew. When it returned, they received it with relief, scolding the crew for any scratches. Airmen talked of "flying boxcars," but Phil and Louie dismissed them. Louie described it as "our home."

On the ground, the crew drank together, swam in the local lakes, and cruised around Ephrata and Sioux City. In the latter, Louie discovered that the enlisted ground crewmen, who had preceded them into town, had convinced the local women that their insignia indicated that they were officers. As Louie set off to right this wrong, Phil pulled night duty at the operations office. Sometime one night, he drifted into a troubled dream. In it, he came home from the war only to find that Cecy had given him up.

―――

On a Saturday afternoon in mid-October of 1942, the men of the 372nd were told to pack their bags. Their training was being cut short, and they were to be sent to California's Hamilton Field, then rushed overseas. Phil was crestfallen; Cecy was about to come see him. He would miss her by three days. On October 20, the squadron flew out of Iowa.

At Hamilton Field, an artist was working his way down the planes, painting each one's name and accompanying illustration. Naming bombers was a grand tradition. Many B-24 crews dreamed up delightfully clever names, among them *E Pluribus Aluminum, Axis Grinder, The Bad Penny,* and *Bombs Nip On.* Quite a few of the rest were shamelessly bawdy, painted with scantily clad and unclad women. One featured a sailor chasing a naked girl around the fuselage. Its name was *Willie Maker.* Louie had a snapshot taken of himself grinning under one of the more ribald examples.

Phil's plane needed a name, and no one could think of one. After the war, the survivors would have different memories of who named the plane, but in a letter penned that fall, Phil would write that it was co-pilot George Moznette who suggested *Super Man.* Everyone liked it, and the name was painted on the plane's nose, along with the super-hero himself, a bomb in one hand and a machine gun in the other. Louie didn't think much of the painting—in photographs, the gun looks like a shovel—but Phil loved it. Most crews referred to their planes as "she." Phil insisted that his plane was all man.

The men were slated for combat, but they hadn't been told where they would serve. Judging by the heavy winter gear, Louie thought that they were bound for Alaska's Aleutian Islands, which had been invaded by the Japanese months before. He was happily wrong: they were going to Hawaii. On the evening of October 24, Louie called home for a last good-bye. He just missed Pete, who came for a visit only a few minutes after his brother hung up.

Sometime after speaking to Louie, Louise pulled out a set of note cards on which she kept lists of Christmas card recipients. After Louie's last visit home, she'd taken out one of the cards and, on it, jotted down the date and a few words about Louie's departure. This day, she noted Louie's phone call. These were the first two entries in what would become Louise's war diary.

Phil at the helm of *Super Man*.
Courtesy of Louis Zamperini

Before he left Hamilton Field, Louie dropped a little package in the mail, addressed to his mother. When Louise opened it, she found inside a pair of airman's wings. Every morning, through all that lay ahead for her, Louise would pin the wings to her dress. Every night, before she went to bed, she'd take them off her dress and pin them to her nightgown.

On November 2, 1942, Phil's crew climbed aboard *Super Man* and readied to go to war. They were heading into a desperate fight. North to south, Japan's new empire stretched five thousand miles, from the snowbound Aleutians to Java, hundreds of miles south of the equator. West to east, the empire sprawled over more than six thousand miles, from the border of India to the Gilbert and Marshall islands in the central Pacific. In the Pacific, virtually everything above Australia and west of the international date line had been taken by Japan. Only a few eastward islands had been spared, among them the Hawaiian Islands, Midway, Canton, Funafuti, and a tiny paradise called Palmyra. It was from these outposts that the men of the AAF were trying to win the Pacific, as the saying went, "one damned island after another."

That day, *Super Man* banked over the Pacific for the first time. The crew was bound for Oahu's Hickam Field, where the war had begun for America eleven months before, and where it would soon begin for them. The rim of California slid away, and then there was nothing but ocean. From this day forward, until victory or defeat, transfer, discharge, capture, or death took them from it, the vast Pacific would be beneath and around them. Its bottom was already littered with downed warplanes and the ghosts of lost airmen. Every day of this long and ferocious war, more would join them.

Seven

"This Is It, Boys"

OAHU WAS STILL RINGING FROM THE JAPANESE ATTACK. The enemy had left so many holes in the roads that the authorities hadn't been able to fill them all yet, leaving the local drivers swerving around craters. There were still a few gouges in the roof of the Hickam Field barracks, making for soggy airmen when it rained. The island was on constant alert for air raids or invasion, and was so heavily camouflaged, a ground crewman wrote in his diary, that "one sees only about ⅓ of what is actually there." Each night, the island disappeared; every window was fitted with lightproof curtains, every car with covered headlights, and blackout patrols enforced rules so strict that a man wasn't even permitted to strike a match. Servicemen were under orders to carry gas masks in hip holsters at all times. To reach their beloved waves, local surfers had to worm their way under the barbed wire that ran the length of Waikiki Beach.

The 372nd squadron was sent to Kahuku, a beachside base at the foot of a blade of mountains on the north shore. Louie and Phil, who would soon be promoted to first lieutenant, were assigned to a barracks with Mitchell, Moznette, twelve other young officers, and hordes of mosquitoes. "You kill one," Phil wrote, "and ten more come to the funeral." Outside, the building was picturesque; inside, Phil wrote, it looked "like a dozen dirty Missouri pigs have been wallowing on it." The nonstop revelry didn't help matters. After one four A.M. knockdown, drag-out water fight involving all sixteen officers, Phil woke up with floor burns on his elbows and knees. On another night, as Louie and Phil wrestled over a beer, they crashed into the flimsy partition separating their room from the next. The partition keeled over, and Phil and Louie kept staggering forward, toppling two more partitions before they stopped. When Colonel William Matheny, the 307th Bomb Group commander, saw the wreckage, he grumbled something about how Zamperini must have been involved.

There was one perk to life in the barracks. The bathroom was plastered in girlie pinups, a Sistine Chapel of pornography. Phil gaped at it, marveling at the distillation of frustrated flyboy libido that had inspired it. Here in the pornographic palace, he was a long way from his minister father's house in Indiana.

Everyone was eager to take a crack at the enemy, but there was no combat to be had. In its place were endless lectures, endless training, and, when Moznette was transferred to another crew, the breaking in of a series of temporary copilots. Eventually, Long Beach, California,

Louie, ready for the chill of high altitude.
Courtesy of Louis Zamperini

native Charleton Hugh Cuppernell joined the crew as Moznette's replacement. A smart, jovial ex–football player and prelaw student, built like a side of beef, Cuppernell got along with everyone, dispensing wisecracks through teeth clenched around a gnawed-up cigar.

When they first went up over Hawaii, the men were surprised to learn that their arctic gear hadn't been issued in error. At ten thousand feet, even in the tropics, it could be sharply cold, and occasionally the bombardier's greenhouse windows froze. Only the flight deck up front was heated, so the men in the rear tramped around in fleece jackets, fur-lined boots, and, sometimes, electrically heated suits. The ground crewmen used the bombers as flying iceboxes, hiding soda bottles in them and retrieving them, ice-cold, after missions.

Training mostly over Kauai, the men discovered their talent. Though they had a few mishaps—Phil once taxied *Super Man* straight into a telephone pole—in aerial gunning, they nailed targets at a rate more than three times the squadron average. Louie's bombing scores were outstanding. In one dive-bombing exercise, he hit the target dead center seven of nine times. The biggest chore of training was coping with the nitpicking, rank-pulling, much-loathed lieutenant who oversaw their flights. Once, when one of *Super Man*'s engines quit during a routine flight, Phil turned the plane back and landed at Kahuku, only to be accosted by the furious lieutenant in a speeding jeep, ordering them back up. When Louie offered to fly on three engines so long as the lieutenant joined them, the lieutenant abruptly changed his mind.

When the men weren't training, they were on sea search, spending ten hours a day patrolling a wedge of ocean, looking for the enemy. It was intensely dull work. Louie killed time by sleeping on Mitchell's navigator table and taking flying lessons from Phil. On some flights, he sprawled behind the cockpit, reading Ellery Queen novels and taxing the nerves of Douglas, who eventually got so annoyed at having to step over Louie's long legs that he attacked him with a fire extinguisher. Once, the gunners got so bored that they fired at a pod of whales. Phil yelled at them to knock it off, and the whales swam on, unharmed. The bullets, it turned out, carried lethal speed for only a few feet after entering the water. One day, this would be very useful knowledge.

One morning on sea search, Phil's crew passed over an American submarine sitting placidly on the surface, crewmen ambling over the deck. Louie flashed the identification code three times, but the sub crew ignored him. Louie and Phil decided to "scare the hell out of them." As

Louie rolled open the bomb bay doors, Phil sent the plane screaming down over the submarine. "The retreat from the deck was so hasty, it looked like they were sucked into the sub," Louie wrote in his diary. "I gave the skipper an F for identification, but an A+ for a quick dive."

The tedium of sea search made practical joking irresistible. When a loudmouth ground officer griped about the higher pay allotted to airmen, the crew invited him to fly the plane himself. During the flight, they sat him in the copilot's seat while Louie hid under the navigator's

Copilot Charleton Hugh Cuppernell.
Courtesy of Louis Zamperini

table, next to the chains that linked the plane's yokes to the control surfaces. When the officer took the yoke, Louie began tugging the chains, making the plane swoop up and down. The officer panicked, Louie smothered his laughter, and Phil kept a perfect poker face. The officer never again complained about airmen's pay.

Louie's two proudest moments as a prankster both involved chewing gum. After Cuppernell and Phil swiped Louie's beer, Louie retaliated by sneaking out to *Super Man* and jamming gum into the cockpit "piss pipe"—the urine relief tube. During that day's flight, the call of nature was followed by an inexplicably brimming piss pipe, turbulence, and at least one wet airman. Louie hid in Honolulu for two days to escape retribution. On another day, to get even with Cuppernell and Phil for regularly stealing his chewing gum, Louie replaced his ordinary gum with a laxative variety. Just before a long day of sea search, Cuppernell and Phil each stole three pieces, triple the standard dose. As *Super Man* flew over the Pacific that morning, Louie watched with delight as pilot and copilot, in great distress, made alternating dashes to the back of the plane, yelling for someone to get a toilet bag ready. On his last run, Cuppernell discovered that all the bags had been used. With nowhere else to go, he dropped his pants and hung his rear end out the waist window while four crewmen clung to him to prevent him from falling out. When the ground crew saw the results all over *Super Man*'s tail, they were furious. "It was like an abstract painting," Louie said later.

Phil's remedy for boredom was hotdogging. After each day of sea search, he and another pilot synchronized their returns to Oahu. The one in front would buzz the island with wheels up, seeing how low he could get without skinning the plane's underside, then goad the other into going lower. Phil hummed *Super Man* so close to the ground that he could look straight into the first-floor windows of buildings. It was, he said in his strolling cadence, "kind of daring."

———

For each day in the air, the crew got a day off. They played poker, divvied up Cecy's care packages, and went to the movies. Louie ran laps around the runway, keeping his body in Olympic condition. On the beach at Kahuku, he and Phil inflated their mattress covers, made a go at the waves, and nearly drowned themselves. Tooling around the island in borrowed cars, they came upon several airfields, but when they drew closer, they realized that all of the planes and equipment were fake, made of plywood, an elaborate ruse designed to fool Japanese reconnaissance planes. And in Honolulu, they found their Everest. It was the House of P. Y. Chong steakhouse, where for $2.50 they could get a steak nearly as fat as a man's arm and as broad as his head. Louie never saw a Chong diner finish his meal.

For the officer half of the crew, paradise was Honolulu's North Shore officers' club, where there were tennis courts, pretty girls with ten-thirty curfews, and boilermakers. When the crew got the best gunnery scores in the squadron, Louie rewarded the enlisted men by pinning his insignia to their uniforms and sneaking them into the club. Just after Louie got up to dance with a girl, Colonel Matheny sat down in

Waiting to fly.
Courtesy of Louis Zamperini

his place and began talking to the terrified Clarence Douglas, who was pretending to be a second lieutenant. When Louie finally got free and ran to Douglas's rescue, the unsuspecting colonel stood up and told him what a damn fine man Douglas was.

One day on the club's dance floor, Louie spotted the lieutenant who had ordered them to fly on three engines. He scrounged up a bag of flour, recruited a girl, and began dancing in circles near the lieutenant, dropping a pinch of flour down the officer's collar each time he swung past. After an hour of this, the whole club was watching. Finally, Louie snagged a glass of water, danced up behind his victim, dumped the water down his shirt, and took off. The lieutenant spun around, his back running with dough. Unable to find the culprit, he stormed out, and Louie was the toast of the club. "We had one more girl for us," he said.

November became December, and the crew still hadn't seen any Japanese. There was hard fighting down on Guadalcanal, and the men felt excluded, frustrated, and intensely curious about combat. Every time a B-17 was brought up from the fighting, Louie and his friends went to the airfield to gawk at it. At first, all the planes looked the same. Then an airman showed them a lone bullet hole. "My golly!" Louie said later. "Our hair stood on end."

Three days before Christmas, the crew's hour finally came. They and twenty-five other crews were told to pack three days' worth of clothes and report to their planes. Walking out to *Super Man*, Louie found the bomb bay fitted with two auxiliary fuel tanks and six five-hundred-pound bombs. Judging by the auxiliary tanks, Louie wrote in his diary, their destination was likely "a long hop somewhere." Instead of the Norden bombsight, Louie was given the handheld sight, which probably meant that they'd be dive-bombing. The crew was handed a packet of orders and told not to open them until airborne.

Five minutes after *Super Man* lifted off, the crewmen tore open the orders and learned that they were to make a heading for Midway. When they landed there eight hours later, they were greeted with a case of Budweiser and very big news: The Japanese had built a base on Wake Atoll. In the biggest raid yet staged in the Pacific war, the AAF was going to burn the base down.

The next afternoon, the crew was called to the briefing room, which was actually the base theater, strung with limp Christmas tinsel and streamers. They were going to hit Wake that night, with dive-bombing. The mission would take sixteen hours, nonstop, the longest combat flight the war had yet seen. This would push the B-24s as far as they could go. Even with auxiliary fuel tanks, they would be cutting it extremely close.

Before the flight, Louie walked to the airfield. The ground crewmen were preparing the planes, stripping out every ounce of excess weight and rolling black paint on the bellies and wings to make them harder to see against a night sky. Coming to *Super Man,* Louie climbed into the bomb bay, where the bombs sat ready. In honor of his college buddy Payton Jordan, who had just married his high school sweetheart, Louie scrawled *Marge and Payton Jordan* on a bomb.

At 4:00 P.M. on December 23, 1942, twenty-six B-24s, laden with some 73,000 gallons of fuel and 75,000 pounds of bombs, rose up from Midway. *Super Man* slipped toward the rear of the procession. All afternoon and into the evening, the planes flew toward Wake. The sun set, and the bombers pressed on under the timid glow of moon and stars.

At eleven P.M., when his plane was about 150 miles from Wake, Phil switched off the outside lights. Clouds closed in. The bombers were supposed to approach the atoll in formation, but with clouds around and the lights off, the pilots couldn't find their flightmates. They couldn't risk breaking radio silence, so each plane went on alone. The pilots craned into the dark, swerving away from the faint shadows of others, trying to avoid collisions. Wake was very close now, but they couldn't see it. Sitting in the top turret of *Super Man,* Stanley Pillsbury wondered if he'd make it back alive. In the greenhouse below, Louie felt a buzzing inside himself, the same sensation that he had felt before races. Ahead, Wake slept.

At exactly midnight, Colonel Matheny, piloting the lead plane, *Dumbo the Avenger,* broke radio silence.

"This is it, boys."

Matheny dropped *Dumbo's* nose and sent the bomber plunging out of the clouds. There beneath him was Wake, three slender islands joining hands around a lagoon. As his copilot called out speed and altitude figures, Matheny pushed his plane toward a string of buildings on Peacock Point, the atoll's southern tip. On either side of Matheny's plane, B-24s followed him down. When he reached his bombing altitude, Matheny hauled the plane's nose up and yelled to the bombardier.

"When are you going to turn loose those incendiaries?"

"Gone, sir!"

At that instant, the buildings on Peacock Point exploded. It was forty-five seconds past midnight.

Matheny tipped his bomber and looked down. Peacock Point, struck by *Dumbo*'s bombs and those of its flanking planes, was engulfed in fire. Matheny knew he'd been lucky; the Japanese had been caught sleeping, and no one had yet manned the antiaircraft guns. As Matheny turned back toward Midway, wave after wave of B-24s dove at Wake. The Japanese ran for their guns.

Up in *Super Man*, well behind and above Matheny's plane, Louie saw broad, quick throbs of light in the clouds. He hit the bomb bay door control valve, and the doors rumbled open. He set his bomb rack on the "select" position, flipped on his bomb switches, and fixed the settings. Phil's orders were to dive to 4,000 feet before dropping the bombs, but when he reached that altitude, he was still lost in clouds. Louie's target was the airstrip, but he couldn't see it. Phil pushed the plane still lower, moving at terrific speed. Suddenly, at 2,500 feet, *Super Man* speared through the clouds and Wake stretched out, sudden and brilliant, beneath it.

Pillsbury would never shake the memory of what he saw. "It looked like a star storm," he remembered. The islands, sealed in blackness a moment before, were a blaze of garish light. Several large infernos, spewing black smoke, were consuming the atoll's oil tanks. Everywhere, bombs were striking targets, sending up mushrooms of fire. Searchlights swung about, their beams reflecting off the clouds and back onto the ground, illuminating scores of Japanese, wearing only *fundoshi* undergarments, sprinting around in confusion. What neither Pillsbury nor any of the other airmen knew was that among the men under their bombers that night were the ninety-eight Americans who had been captured and enslaved.

Waist and tail gunners in the bombers fired downward, and one by one, the searchlights blew to pieces. To Pillsbury, "every gun in the world" seemed to be firing skyward. Antiaircraft guns lobbed shells over the planes, where they erupted, sending shrapnel showering down. Tracers from the firing above and below streaked the air in yellow, red, and green. As Pillsbury watched the clamor of colors, he thought of Christmas. Then he remembered: They had crossed the international date line and passed midnight. It *was* Christmas.

Phil wrestled *Super Man* out of its dive. As the plane leveled off, Louie spotted the taillight of a Zero rolling down the north-south runway. He began synchronizing on the light, hoping to hit the Zero before it took off. Below, very close, something exploded, and *Super Man* rocked. A shell burst by the left wing, another by the tail. Louie could see tracers cutting neat lines in the sky to the right. He loosed a bomb over the south end of the runway, counted two seconds, then dropped his five other bombs over a set of bunkers and parked planes beside the runway.

Relieved of three thousand pounds of bombs, *Super Man* bobbed upward. Louie yelled "Bombs away!" and Phil rolled the plane roughly to the left, through streams of antiaircraft fire. Louie looked down. His group of five bombs landed in splashes of fire on the bunkers and planes. He'd been a beat too late to hit the Zero. His bomb fell just behind it, lighting up the runway. Phil turned *Super Man* back for Midway. Wake was a sea of fire and running men.

The crew was jumpy, coursing with adrenaline. There were several Zeros in the air, but in the darkness, no one knew where they were. Somewhere in the galaxy of planes, a Zero fired on a bomber, which fired back. The Zero disappeared. Pillsbury looked to the side and saw yellow dashes of tracer fire, heading directly toward them. A B-24 gunner had mistaken them for an enemy plane and was firing on them. Phil saw it just as Pillsbury did, and swung the plane away. The firing stopped.

The bomb bay doors were stuck open. The motors strained, but couldn't budge them. Louie climbed back and looked. When Phil had wrenched the plane out of its dive, the enormous g-forces had nudged the auxiliary fuel tanks out of place, just enough to block the doors. Nothing could be done. With the bomb bay yawning open and dragging against the air, the plane was burning much more fuel than usual. Given that this mission was stretching the plane's range to the limit, it was sobering news.

The men could do nothing but wait and hope. They passed around pineapple juice and roast beef sandwiches. Louie was drained, both from the combat and the incessant quivering of the plane. He stared out, sleepy, watching the stars through breaks in the clouds.

Seventy-five miles away from Wake, one of the men looked back. He could still see the island burning.

As day broke over the Pacific, Brigadier General Howard K. Ramey stood by the Midway airstrip, looking at the clouds and waiting for his bombers. His face was furrowed. A brow of fog hung two hundred feet over the ocean, spilling rain. In some places, visibility was down to a few yards. Finding tiny, flat Midway would be difficult, and there was the question of whether the bombers' fuel would last long enough to bring them home.

One plane appeared, then another and another. One by one, they landed, all critically low on fuel, one with a dead engine. *Super Man* wasn't in sight.

Out in the fog, Phil must have looked at his fuel gauge and known that he was in real trouble. With his bomb bay open and wind howling through the fuselage, he had dragged away most of his fuel and was running on empty. He didn't know if he'd be able to find Midway, and he didn't have enough fuel to make a second pass. At last, at around eight A.M., he saw Midway dimly through the mist. A moment later, one of *Super Man*'s engines sputtered and died.

Phil knew that the other engines would quit almost immediately. He nursed the plane along, spotting the runway and aiming for it. The engines kept turning. Phil dropped *Super Man* and touched down. Just after the plane turned off the runway, a second engine died. As it reached its bunker, the other two engines quit. Had the route been only slightly longer, *Super Man* would have hit the ocean.

General Ramey ran to each bomber, calling out congratulations. The tired *Super Man* crewmen dropped out of the plane and into a mob of marines, who'd spent a year waiting to deliver retribution to the Japanese for what they'd done to their brothers at Wake. The marines passed out shots of liquor and feted the airmen.

The mission had been a smashing success. Every plane had returned safely. Only one bomb had missed its target, plopping into the water twenty feet offshore. The Japanese base had been gravely damaged— by one estimate, half of its personnel had been killed—and America had demonstrated the reach and power of its B-24s. And though the men didn't know it, the American captives had all survived.

Phil's crew spent the day sitting in the rain, watching several albatrosses make comically inept attempts at landing on the flooded runway. Early the next morning, *Super Man* carried them back to Kahuku. Louie spent New Year's Eve at a party with Moznette and his bombardier, James Carringer, Jr., and didn't drag himself back to the pornographic palace until four-thirty. He pulled himself together a few hours later, when Admiral Chester Nimitz presented the Wake pilots with Distinguished Flying Crosses and their crewmen with Air Medals.

News of the raid broke, and the men were lauded as heroes. The press played up their Christmas gift to the Allies. STEEL FILLS JAP SOX, read one headline. In Tokyo, radio broadcasters had a different take. They reported that the Americans, upon encountering Japanese defenses, had "fled in terror." In the *Honolulu Advertiser*, Louie found a cartoon depicting his role in bombing Wake. He clipped it out and tucked it in his wallet.

With the dawn of 1943 and the success at Wake, the men felt cocky. It had all been so easy. One admiral predicted that Japan might be finished within the year, and Phil overheard men talking about going home.

"Methinks," he wrote to his mother, "it's a little premature."

Eight

"Only the Laundry Knew
How Scared I Was"

I T WAS EARLY MORNING ON JANUARY 8, 1943. THE SUN HADN'T yet risen. George Moznette and James Carringer, who had spent New Year's Eve with Louie, joined their crew at the beachside airstrip at Barking Sands on Kauai, preparing to lead a three-plane training run over Pearl Harbor. The pilot was Major Jonathan Coxwell, one of Phil's closest friends.

As he taxied out for his flight, Coxwell tried to reach the control tower, but the tower's radio was down. He powered his plane down the runway, lifted off, and flew over the beach and into the darkness. The two other planes took off after Coxwell. Later that morning, they returned. Coxwell's plane did not. No one had seen it since takeoff.

During a briefing at eight, Louie was told that Coxwell's plane was missing. Phil's crew was slated for practice bombing off Barking Sands that morning, so they went early and walked the beach, looking for some sign of their friends. Someone found a $400 paycheck that had washed ashore. It was made out to Moznette.

The *Super Man* crew was fifteen thousand feet up when the lost B-24 was found, lying on the ocean floor not far offshore. All ten crewmen were dead.

Coxwell had barely made it past takeoff. He had cleared the runway, turned, and slammed into the water. Several crewmen had survived the crash and tried to swim to land, but sharks had found them. The men were, Louie wrote in his diary, "literally ripped to pieces." Five, including Moznette, had lived in the pornographic palace with Louie and Phil. Carringer had just been promoted to first lieutenant,

The B-24 *Stevenovich II* just after being struck by flak. The plane spun several times, then exploded. The radar operator, First Lieutenant Edward Walsh, Jr., was thrown from the plane and managed to open his parachute. He survived. The other crewmen were presumed dead.

but had died before anyone could tell him. They were buried in the cemetery in Honolulu, joining the men killed at Pearl Harbor.

Louie was shaken. He'd been in Hawaii for only two months, yet already several dozen men from his bomb group, including more than a quarter of the men in his barracks, had been killed.

The first loss had come on the flight from San Francisco, when a B-24 had simply vanished. This fate was sadly common; between 1943 and 1945, four hundred AAF crews were lost en route to their theaters. Next, a plane had caught fire and crashed at Kahuku, killing four men. Another plane had hit a mountain. A bomber had been forced down after losing all four engines, killing two. In one bomber, a green engineer transferring fuel across the wings had caused gasoline to pool on the floor of the bomb bay. When the bomb bay doors had scraped open, igniting a spark, the plane had exploded. Three men had survived, including a passenger whose hand had happened to be resting on a parachute when the blast flung him from the plane. After the Wake raid, a plane sent to photograph the damage had been hit by antiaircraft fire. The crew had sent out a last message—"Can't make it"—and was never heard from again. Then had come Coxwell's crash.

These losses, only one due to enemy action, were hardly anomalous. In World War II, 35,933 AAF planes were lost in combat and accidents. The surprise of the attrition rate is that only a fraction of the ill-fated planes were lost in combat. In 1943 in the Pacific Ocean Areas theater in which Phil's crew served, for every plane lost in combat, some six planes were lost in accidents. Over time, combat took a greater toll, but combat losses never overtook noncombat losses.

As planes went, so went men. In the air corps, 35,946 personnel died in nonbattle situations, the vast majority of them in accidental crashes.* Even in combat, airmen appear to have been more likely to die from accidents than combat itself. A report issued by the AAF surgeon general suggests that in the Fifteenth Air Force, between November 1, 1943, and May 25, 1945, 70 percent of men listed as killed in action died in operational aircraft accidents, not as a result of enemy action.

In many cases, the problem was the planes. In part because they were new technology, and in part because they were used so heavily, planes were prone to breakdowns. In January 1943 alone, Louie recorded in his diary ten serious mechanical problems in *Super Man* and other planes in which he flew, including two in-flight engine failures, a gas leak, oil-pressure problems, and landing gear that locked—fortunately, in the

---

* The military didn't break down nonbattle deaths by cause, but statistics strongly indicate that accidental crashes accounted for most deaths. First, the nonbattle death figure excludes those who died while interned, captured, or MIA. Disease, too, can be excluded as a major cause of death: given that in the entire army, including infantry fighting in malarial jungles, 15,779 personnel died of disease, disease deaths in the air corps had to be a small percentage of nonbattle deaths. Finally, given that some 15,000 airmen died in accidental crashes stateside, it seems highly likely that the huge number of accidental crashes in the war would have produced similarly high numbers of deaths.

Flak.

down position. Once, *Super Man*'s brakes failed on landing. By the time Phil got the plane stopped, the bomber was three feet short of the runway's end. Just beyond it lay the ocean.

The weather also took a toll. Storms reduced visibility to zero, a major problem for pilots searching for tiny islands or threading through the mountains that flanked some Hawaiian runways. B-24s were hard to manage even in smooth skies; in some tropical tempests, not even the combined strength of pilot and copilot could keep the plane in hand. Twice in one week, *Super Man* flew into storms that buffeted the plane so violently that Phil lost control. Once, the plane was flung around the sky for ten minutes, leaving the temporary copilot so paralyzed with fear that Phil had to call Louie to take his place.

One day after sea search, as Phil was detouring around a squall, Cuppernell asked him if he'd dare fly into it. "I can fly this thing anywhere," Phil said, turning the plane into the storm. *Super Man* was instantly swallowed, and Phil could see nothing. Rain drummed on the plane, wind pivoted it sideways, and it began porpoising, leaving the crewmen clinging to anything bolted down. They had only been at one thousand feet when they'd flown into the storm. Now the plane was pitching so erratically that they couldn't read their altitude, and with no visibility, they didn't know where the ocean was. Each time the plane plunged, the men braced for a crash. Oahu had been in sight before they entered the storm, but now they had no idea where it was. Phil gripped the yoke, sweat streaming down his face. Pillsbury strapped on his parachute.

Riding the bucking plane at his radio table, Harry Brooks picked up a signal from a Hawaiian radio station. The plane was equipped with a radio compass that enabled Harry to determine the direction from which the signal was coming. Phil strong-armed the plane around and headed toward it. They broke out of the storm, found the airfield, and landed. Phil was exhausted, his shirt wringing wet.

The runways were another headache. Many islands were so short that engineers had to plow coral onto one end to create enough length for a runway. Even with the amendments, there often wasn't enough space. After long missions, groups of planes occasionally came back so low on fuel that none of them could wait for the others to land, so they'd land simultaneously, with the lead pilot delaying his touchdown until he was far enough down the runway for the planes behind him to land at the same time. So many planes shot off the end of Funafuti's runway and into the ocean that the ground crews kept a bulldozer equipped with a towing cable parked by the water.

For loaded B-24s, which needed well over four thousand feet for takeoff, the cropped island runways, often abutted by towering palm trees, were a challenge. "The takeoff proved exciting," wrote Staff Sergeant Frank Rosynek of one overloaded departure. "Six of us had to stand on the narrow beam between the bomb bay doors with our arms spread out on each side over the tops of the twin auxiliary fuel tanks. The smell of the high-octane aviation fuel was almost intoxicating. The plane lumbered down the runway for an eternity and we could see the hard packed coral through the cracks where the bomb bay doors came up against the beam we were standing on, one foot in front of the other. There was a SWOOSH and pieces of palm fronds suddenly appeared jammed in the cracks, on both sides! . . . Only the laundry knew how scared I was."

And then there was human error. Pilots flew or drove their planes into each other. In B-24s notorious for fuel leaks, airmen lit cigarettes and blew up their planes. On one flight, when *Super Man*'s No. 3 engine died, Pillsbury found the temporary copilot, oblivious, sitting with his boot resting against the engine's ignition switch, pushing it into the "off" position. Louie was once asked to join a crew whose bombardier had gotten sick. Louie, too, was feeling ill, so the crew found another man. During the flight, the tower warned the pilot that he was heading toward a mountain. The pilot replied that he saw it, then flew right into it. The strangest incident occurred when a bomber made a sharp pull-up on a training run. A man inside, trying to avoid falling, inadvertently grabbed the life raft–release handle. The raft sprang from the roof and wrapped around the plane's horizontal stabilizer. Barely able to control the plane, the pilot ordered his men to bail out. He and his copilot somehow landed safely, and everyone survived.

Finally, there was the formidable difficulty of navigation. Making extraordinarily complex spherical trigonometry calculations based on figures taken from a crowd of instruments, navigators groped over thousands of miles of featureless ocean toward targets or destination islands that were blacked out at night, often only yards wide, and flat to the horizon. Even with all the instruments, the procedures could be comically primitive. "Each time I made a sextant calibration," wrote navigator John Weller, "I would open the escape hatch on the flight deck and stand on my navigation desk and the radio operator's desk while [the radioman] held on to my legs so I would not be sucked out of the plane." At night, navigators sometimes resorted to following the stars, guiding their crews over the Pacific by means not so different from those used by ancient Polynesian mariners. In a storm or clouds, even that was impossible.

Given that a plane had to be only a tick off course to miss an island, it's amazing that any crews found their destinations. Many didn't. Martin Cohn, an ordnance officer on Oahu, was once in a radar shack as a lost plane, unequipped with radar, tried to find the island. "We just sat there and watched the plane pass the island, and it never came back," he said. "I could see it on the radar. It makes you feel terrible. Life was cheap in war."

The risks of flying were compounded exponentially in combat. From the sky came Japanese fighters, chief among them the swift, agile Zero, which dominated the sky in the first half of the war. Zero pilots pummeled bombers with machine gun fire and massively destructive 20mm cannon shells, which rammed gaping holes in their targets. When these failed, some Zero pilots rammed their planes into bombers, kamikaze-style; one B-24 returned to base with half of a Zero hanging from his wing. From the ground came antiaircraft fire, including flak, which burst into razor-sharp metal shards that sliced planes open. To survive

AA fire and enemy aircraft, bomber pilots needed to change their altitude and direction constantly. But on approach, the Norden bombsight, not the pilot, flew the plane, so evasive action was impossible. B-24s were in the control of the bombsight for three to five minutes on approach; Japanese range finders needed less than sixty seconds to pinpoint bomber altitude. The math favored the Japanese.

In combat, bombers even posed risks to one another. To fend off fighter attack and hit narrow target islands, planes had to bunch very close together. In the chaos, planes collided, fired on each other, and worse. In one incident, three B-24s on a mission to mine a harbor flew in tight formation through a narrow canyon at fifty feet, under intense ground fire. As they dropped over the harbor, the right wingtip of a plane piloted by Lieutenant Robert Strong struck the greenhouse window on the plane to his right, piloted by a Lieutenant Robinson. The collision rotated Strong's bomber onto its left side and under Robinson's plane just as Robinson's bombardier dropped a thousand-pound mine. The mine crashed into Strong's plane, and though it didn't detonate, it tore an eighteen-square-foot hole in the fuselage and lodged itself just behind the waist gunners. Strong's B-24 was nearly cut in two, and the mine's parachute deployed, dragging the plane down. Crewmen cut the parachute free and shoved at the mine, but it wouldn't budge, so they dismantled their guns and used the barrels to crowbar the mine out. As Strong tried to get the nearly bisected plane home, the tail flapped in the wind, and a huge crack crept up the fuselage. Impossibly, Strong flew his Liberator eight hundred miles and landed. When Jesse Stay, a pilot in Louie's squadron, went to see the bomber, he was nearly able to pull its tail off with one hand.

The risks of combat created grim statistics. In World War II, 52,173 AAF men were killed in combat. According to Stay, who would become a squadron commander, airmen trying to fulfill the forty combat missions that made up a Pacific bomber crewman's tour of duty had a 50 percent chance of being killed.*

Along with safe return, injury, and death, airmen faced another possible fate. During the war, thousands of airmen vanished, some during combat missions, some on routine flights. Many had been swallowed by the ocean. Some were alive but lost on the sea or islands. And some

---

* When Louie and Phil were deployed, a tour was thirty missions. The number was later adjusted upward.

had been captured. Unable to find them, the military declared them missing. If they weren't found within thirteen months, they were declared dead.

Most of the time, stricken Pacific bombers came down on water, either by ditching or by crashing. Crewmen who crashed were very unlikely to survive, but ditching offered better odds, depending on the bomber. The B-17 and its soon-to-be-introduced cousin, the gigantic B-29, had wide, low wings that, with the fuselage, formed a relatively flat surface that could surf onto water. Their sturdy bomb bay doors sat flush to the fuselage and tended to hold in a ditching, enabling the plane to float. The first ditched B-29 not only survived, it floated onto an Indian beach, completely intact, the following day. The B-24 was another story. Its wings were narrow and mounted high on the fuselage, and its delicate bomb bay doors protruded slightly from the bottom of the plane. In most B-24 ditchings, the bomb bay doors would catch on the water and tear off and the plane would blow apart. Less than a quarter of ditched B-17s broke up, but a survey of B-24 ditchings found that nearly two-thirds broke up and a quarter of the crewmen died.

For B-24 survivors, quick escape was crucial. Without sealed fuselages, Liberators sank instantly; one airman recalled watching his ditched B-24 sink so quickly that he could still see its lights when it was far below the surface. Every airman was given a "Mae West" life vest,* but because some men stole the vests' carbon dioxide cartridges for use in carbonating drinks, some vests didn't inflate. Life rafts were deployed manually: from inside the plane, crewmen could pull a release handle just before ditching or crashing; from outside a floating plane, they could climb on the wings and turn raft-release levers. Once deployed, rafts inflated automatically.

Survivors had to get to rafts immediately. Airmen would later speak of sharks arriving almost the moment that their planes struck the water. In 1943, navy lieutenant Art Reading, Louie's USC track teammate, was knocked unconscious as he ditched his two-man plane. As the plane sank, Reading's navigator, Everett Almond, pulled Reading out, inflated their Mae Wests, and lashed himself to Reading. As Reading woke, Almond began towing him toward the nearest island, twenty

---

* It was called a Mae West because it gave the wearer a bountiful bust. In the 1970s, service personnel updated the name, calling them Dolly Partons.

miles away. Sharks soon began circling. One swept in, bit down on Almond's leg, and dove, dragging both men deep underwater. Then something gave way and the men rose to the surface in a pool of blood. Almond's leg had apparently been torn off. He gave his Mae West to Reading, then sank away. For the next eighteen hours, Reading floated alone, kicking at the sharks and hacking at them with his binoculars. By the time a search boat found him, his legs were slashed and his jaw broken by the fin of a shark, but thanks to Almond, he was alive. Almond, who had died at twenty-one, was nominated for a posthumous medal for bravery.*

Everyone had heard stories like Reading's, and everyone had looked from their planes to see sharks roaming below. The fear of sharks was so powerful that most men, faced with the choice of riding a crippled plane to a ditching or bailing out, chose to take their chances in a ditching, even in the B-24. At least that would leave them near the rafts.

The military was dedicated to finding crash and ditching survivors, but in the sprawling Pacific theater, the odds of rescue were extremely daunting. Many doomed planes sent no distress call, and often, no one knew a plane was down until it missed its estimated time of arrival, which could be as long as sixteen hours after the crash. If the absence went unnoticed until night, an air search couldn't be commenced until morning. In the meantime, raft-bound men struggled with injuries and exposure and drifted far from their crash site.

For rescuers, figuring out where to look was tremendously difficult. To keep radio silence, many crews didn't communicate any position during flights, so all searchers had to go on was the course the plane would have followed had everything gone right. But downed planes had often been flying over huge distances, and may have veered hundreds of miles off course. Once a plane was down, currents and wind could carry a raft dozens of miles a day. Because of this, search areas often extended over thousands of square miles. The longer rafts floated, the farther they drifted, and the worse the odds of rescue became.

The most heartbreaking fact was that, if searchers were lucky enough to fly near a raft, chances were good that they wouldn't see it. Rafts for small planes were the size of small bathtubs; those for large

---

* Two published accounts of this incident mistakenly identify Reading as the one who was eaten by the shark. Newspaper reports in which Reading was interviewed confirm that it was Almond.

planes were the length of a reclining man. Though search planes generally flew at just one thousand feet, even from that height, a raft could easily be mistaken for a whitecap or a glint of light. On days with low clouds, nothing could be seen at all. Many planes used for rescue searches had high stall speeds, so they had to be flown so fast that crewmen barely had a moment to scan each area before it was gone behind them.

In mid-1944, in response to the dismal results of Pacific rescue searches, the AAF implemented a vastly enhanced rescue system. Life rafts were stocked with radios and better provisions, boats were set out along the paths flown by military planes, and searches were handled by designated rescue squadrons equipped with float planes. These advances improved the odds of rescue, but even after their advent, most downed men were never found. According to reports made by the Far East Air Force air surgeon, fewer than 30 percent of men whose planes went missing between July 1944 and February 1945 were rescued. Even when the plane's location was known, only 46 percent of men were saved. In some months, the picture was far worse. In January 1945, only 21 of 167 downed XXI Bomber Command airmen were rescued—just 13 percent.

As bleak as these odds were late in the war, men who went down before mid-1944 faced far worse. Flying before the rescue system was modernized, they faced a situation in which searches were disorganized, life rafts poorly equipped, and procedures ineffective. Everyone on Phil's crew knew that should they go down, their chances of rescue were very low.

The improbability of rescue, coupled with the soaring rate of accidental crashes, created a terrible equation. Search planes appear to have been more likely to go down themselves than find the men they were looking for. In one time frame, in the Eastern Air Command, half of the Catalina flying boats attempting rescues crashed while trying to land on the ocean. It seems likely that for every man rescued, several would-be rescuers died, especially in the first years of the war.

With every day that passed without rescue, the prospects for raft-bound men worsened dramatically. Raft provisions lasted a few days at most. Hunger, thirst, and exposure to blistering sun by day and chill by night depleted survivors with frightening rapidity. Some men died in days. Others went insane. In September 1942, a B-17 crashed in the Pacific, stranding nine men on a raft. Within a few days, one had died and the rest had gone mad. Two heard music and baying dogs. One was convinced that a navy plane was pushing the raft from behind. Two scuffled over an imaginary case of beer. Another shouted curses at a sky that he believed was full of bombers. Seeing a delusory boat, he pitched himself overboard and drowned. On day six, when a plane flew by, the remaining men had to confer to be sure that it was real. When they were rescued on day seven, they were too weak to wave their arms.

There were fates even worse than this. In February 1942, a wooden raft was found drifting near Christmas Island, in the Indian Ocean. Upon it was the body of a man, lying in a makeshift coffin that appeared to have been built on the raft. The man's boilersuit had been in the sun for so long that its blue fabric had been bleached white. A shoe that didn't belong to the man lay beside him. No one ever determined who he was, or where he had come from.

Of all of the horrors facing downed men, the one outcome that they feared most was capture by the Japanese. The roots of the men's fear lay in an event that occurred in 1937, in the early months of Japan's invasion of China. The Japanese military surrounded the city of Nanking, stranding more than half a million civilians and 90,000 Chinese soldiers. The soldiers surrendered and, assured of their safety, submitted to being bound. Japanese officers then issued a written order: ALL PRISONERS OF WAR ARE TO BE EXECUTED.

What followed was a six-week frenzy of killing that defies articulation. Masses of POWs were beheaded, machine-gunned, bayoneted, and burned alive. The Japanese turned on civilians, engaging in killing contests, raping tens of thousands of people, mutilating and crucifying them, and provoking dogs to maul them. Japanese soldiers took pictures of themselves posing alongside hacked-up bodies, severed heads, and women strapped down for rape. The Japanese press ran tallies of the killing contests as if they were baseball scores, praising the heroism of the contestants. Historians estimate that the Japanese military murdered between 200,000 and 430,000 Chinese, including the 90,000 POWs, in what became known as the Rape of Nanking.

Every American airman knew about Nanking, and since then, Japan had only reinforced the precedent. Among the men of Louie's squadron, there was a rumor circulating about the atoll of Kwajalein, in the Marshall Islands, a Japanese territory. On Kwajalein, the rumor said, POWs were murdered. The men called it "Execution Island." It is testament to the reputation of the Japanese that of all the men in one fatally damaged B-24 falling over Japanese forces, only one chose to bail out. The rest were so afraid of capture that they chose to die in the crash.

———

For airmen, the risks were impossible to shrug off. The dead weren't numbers on a page. They were their roommates, their drinking buddies, the crew that had been flying off their wing ten seconds ago. Men didn't go one by one. A quarter of a barracks was lost at once. There were rarely funerals, for there were rarely bodies. Men were just gone, and that was the end of it.

Airmen avoided the subject of death, but privately, many were tormented by fear. One man in Louie's squadron had chronic, stress-induced nosebleeds. Another had to be relieved because he froze with terror in the air. Pilot Joe Deasy recalled a distraught airman who came to him with a question: If a crewman went mad during a mission, would the crew shoot him? The man was so jittery that he accidentally fired his sidearm into the ground as he spoke.

Some men were certain that they'd be killed; others lived in denial. For Louie and Phil, there was no avoiding the truth. After only two months and one combat mission, five of their friends were already dead, and they had survived several near misses themselves. Their room and icebox, inherited from friends whose bodies were now in the Pacific, were constant reminders.

Before Louie had left the States, he'd been issued an olive-drab Bible. He tried reading it to cope with his anxiety, but it made no sense to him, and he abandoned it. Instead, he soothed himself by listening to classical music on his phonograph. He often left Phil sprawled on his bed, penning letters to Cecy on an upturned box, as he headed out to run off his worries on the mile-long course that he had measured in the sand around the runway. He also tried to prepare for every contingency. He went to the machine shop, cut a thick metal slab, lugged it to *Super Man,* and plunked it down in the greenhouse in hopes that it would protect him from ground fire. He took classes on island survival and wound care, and found a course in which an elderly Hawaiian offered tips on fending off sharks. (Open eyes wide and bare teeth, make football-style stiff-arm, bop shark in nose.)

And like everyone else, Louie and Phil drank. After a few beers, Louie said, it was possible to briefly forget dead friends. Men were given a ration of four beers a week, but everyone scoured the landscape for alternatives. Alcohol was to Louie what acorns are to squirrels; he consumed what he wanted when he found it and hid the rest. In training, he had stashed his hooch in a shaving cream bottle. Once deployed, he graduated to mayonnaise jars and ketchup bottles. He stowed a bottle of a local rotgut called Five Island Gin—nicknamed Five Ulcer Gin—in radioman Harry Brooks's gas mask holster. When an MP tapped Brooks's hip to check for the mask, the bottle broke and left Brooks with a soggy leg. It was probably for the best. Louie noticed that when he drank the stuff, his chest hair spontaneously fell out. He later discovered that Five Island Gin was often used as paint thinner. After that, he stuck to beer.

Phil, like all airmen, had to cope with the possibility of dying, but he had an additional burden. As a pilot, he was keenly conscious that if he made a mistake, eight other men could die. He began carrying two talismans. One was a bracelet Cecy had given him. Believing that it kept him from harm, he wouldn't go up without it. The other was a silver dollar that jingled endlessly in his pocket. On the day that he finally ran away with Cecy, he said, he'd use it to tip the bellboy. "When I do get home," he wrote to her, "I'm going to hide with you where no one will find us."

In the early days of 1943, as men died one after another, every man dealt with the losses in a different way. Somewhere along the way, a ritual sprang up. If a man didn't return, the others would open his footlocker, take out his liquor, and have a drink in his honor. In a war without funerals, it was the best they could do.

Nine

Five Hundred and Ninety-four Holes

IN FEBRUARY 1943, DURING A BRIEF VISIT TO THE EQUATO-rial island of Canton, the *Super Man* crew had its first encounter with exploding sharks. Canton was a seething purgatory in the shape of a pork chop, consisting mostly of coral and scrubby plants huddled close to the ground, as if cringing from the heat. There was only one tree on the entire island. The surrounding waters were tumbling with sharks, which got trapped in the lagoon at low tide. Bored out of their wits, the local servicemen would tie garbage to long sticks and dangle them over the lagoon. When the sharks snapped at the bait, the men would lob hand grenades into their mouths and watch them blow up.

The *Super Man* crew had been sent to Canton for two missions over Japanese-occupied Makin and Tarawa, in the Gilbert Islands. On the first mission, the lead plane made a wrong turn, and the men found themselves over Howland, the island that Amelia Earhart had been aiming for when she had vanished six years earlier. They noticed gouges in the Howland runway, the calling cards of the Japanese. Once they got sorted out and found Makin, Louie couldn't see his target through the clouds. They made three circles with no luck, so their colonel ordered them to drop the bombs anywhere and get going. Through a gap in the clouds, Louie spotted a row of outhouses and, with giggling glee, walloped them with three thousand pounds of de-molition bombs. To a cheer from the crew, the outhouses blew sky-high.

Two days later, the men flew back to the Gilberts to photograph the islands, bringing a six-man camera crew. They buzzed several islands under fire, snapping photos. With *Super Man*'s nose bloodied from an antiaircraft round, they turned back for Canton. Three hundred miles from home, engineer Douglas made a discovery. *Super Man*'s eccentric fuel gauges, which had been jiggling around, had settled very low. Doug-las announced that at their current rate, they wouldn't make Canton.

Phil slowed the propellers as far as he dared and "leaned" the fuel mixture so that the least possible fuel was used. The crew shoved out almost everything that wasn't bolted down, and all fifteen men crowded into the front of the plane, in the belief that it would improve air speed. Knowing that their chances of making Canton were slim, they considered Howland, but then recalled the pitted runway. They discussed ditching near Howland, but that raised the issue of sharks. In the end, they agreed to try for Canton.

Wedged together in the front of the plane, all the men could do was wait. The sun set. Louie stared into the dark below and thought about what it would feel like to crash. The fuel gauges inched lower, and everyone waited to hear the engines sputtering out. At last, with the fuel gauges at absolute bottom, Phil spotted a searchlight craning around the sky and runway lights dotting the dark below. Realizing that he was way too high, Phil dropped the plane so sharply that Pills-bury bobbed into the air and hung there a moment, weightless, before slapping down.

As *Super Man* touched down on Canton, its tail settled lower than it had been in the air, causing the last drops of fuel to shift back. A mo-ment later, one engine quit.

Two weeks later, the men saw what would have awaited them had they gone down at sea. A B-25 flying off Oahu radioed that it was low on fuel, then went silent. *Super Man* was scrambled to hunt for it. After an hour and a half of searching, Louie spotted a curl of gray smoke. Two Catalina flying boats were heading toward it. *Super Man* fol-lowed.

When they arrived at the crash site, the men were astonished by what they saw. Two life rafts, holding the entire five-man B-25 crew, floated amid plane debris. Around them, the ocean was churning with hundreds of sharks, some of which looked twenty feet long. Knifing agitated circles in the water, the creatures seemed on the verge of overturning the rafts.

The Catalinas reached the men before the sharks could, and the B-25 men treated their rescuers to drinks that night. But the *Super Man* crew now understood the feelings of the grenade throwers on Canton. On a later flight, when they saw several sharks harassing six whales, they dove low over the water and shot at the sharks. Later, they felt guilty. On future flights, when they saw sharks, they let them be.

Nauru was a little afterthought of land, eight square miles of sand sitting alone in the Pacific, about twenty-five hundred miles southwest of Hawaii. It was the kind of place that the world might have left alone, were it not for the fifty thousand tons of high-grade phosphate that lay under the feet of the grass-skirted natives. A central ingredient in fertilizer and munitions, the phosphate had been discovered in 1900, and since then the island had been home to a community of European businessmen and Chinese workers who mined the land. When the war began, Nauru became a priceless prize.

Japan seized Nauru in August 1942, imprisoning the Europeans who had not fled and forcing the natives and the Chinese to mine phosphate and build a runway. They enforced their authority with the sword, beheading people for infractions as trivial as the theft of a pumpkin. When the runway was complete, Japan had a rich source of phosphate and an ideal base for air strikes.

On April 17, upon returning from a run, Louie was called to a briefing. America was going after Nauru in a big way, sending *Super Man* and twenty-two other B-24s to hit the phosphate works. No one in the squadron saw a bed that night. They left just before midnight, refueled on Canton, and flew to Funafuti, the tiny atoll from which they would launch their attack. They found it jostling with journalists brought in by the military to cover the raid.

At a briefing, the crews were told to approach Nauru at eight thousand feet. The altitude gave Louie and the others pause. That week, they had made practice runs from eight to ten thousand feet, and the potential for antiaircraft fire to butcher them at that altitude had alarmed the whole crew. "We only hope," Louie had written in his diary two days earlier, "we don't bomb that low in actual combat." Pillsbury couldn't stop thinking about something else that the briefing officer had said. There would be ten to twelve Zeros waiting for them. He'd seen a distant Zero at Wake, but had never been engaged by one. The idea of a single Zero was daunting. The prospect of twelve scared him to death.

Before dawn the next day, the men walked together to *Super Man*. With them was a lieutenant named Donald Nelson. He wasn't on the crew, but asked if he could tag along so he could see combat. At five A.M., *Super Man* was airborne.

––––

Doglegging to the west to hide their point of origin, the planes took six and a half hours to reach Nauru. No one spoke. *Super Man* led the mass of bombers, flying with a plane on each wing. The sun rose, and the planes flew into a clear morning. The Japanese would see them coming.

At about twenty past eleven, navigator Mitchell broke the silence: They'd be over the island in fifteen minutes. In the greenhouse, Louie could just make out an apostrophe of land, flat to the horizon. Below, there was a black shadow in the water. It was an American submarine, ready to pick up survivors if bombers were shot down. *Super Man* passed over it and slid over Nauru. Louie shivered.

It was eerily silent. The first nine planes, *Super Man* out front, crossed the island unopposed. The air was very still, and the plane glided along without a ripple. Phil relinquished control to the Norden bombsight. *Super Man*'s first target, a knot of planes and structures beside a runway, came into view. Louie lined up on the gleaming backs of the planes.

And then, shattering. The sky became a fury of color, sound, and motion. Flak hissed up, trailing streamers of smoke over the planes, then burst into black puffs, sparkling with shrapnel. Metal flew everywhere, streaking up from below and raining down from above. With the bombsight in control, Phil could do nothing.

Something struck the bomber on *Super Man*'s left wing, piloted by Lieutenant John Jacobs. The plane sank as if drowning. At almost the same moment, the plane to *Super Man*'s right was hit. Just a few feet away, Pillsbury watched the bomber falter, drop, and disappear under *Super Man*'s wing. Pillsbury could see the men inside, and his mind briefly registered that all of them were about to die. *Super Man* was alone.

Louie kept his focus below, trying to aim for the parked planes. As he worked, there was a tremendous *bang!* and a terrific shudder. Much of *Super Man*'s right rudder, a chunk the size of a dinner table, blew off. Louie lost the target. As he tried to find it again, a shell bit a wide hole in the bomb bay, and the plane rocked again.

At last, Louie had his aim, and the first bombs dropped, spun down, and struck their targets. Then *Super Man* passed over a set of red-roofed barracks and an antiaircraft battery, Louie's second and third targets. Louie lined up and watched the bombs crunch into the buildings and battery. He had one bomb left for a target of opportunity. North of the airfield, he saw a shack and took aim. The bomb fell clear, and Louie yelled "Bombs away!" and turned the valve to close the bomb bay doors. In the cockpit, the bomb-release light flicked on, and Phil took control of the plane. As he did, behind and below the plane, there was a pulse of white light and an orb of fire. Louie had made a lucky guess and a perfect drop. The shack was a fuel depot, and he had struck it dead center. In the top turret, Pillsbury pivoted backward and watched a vast cloud of smoke billow upward.

The air battle over Nauru.

There was no time for celebration: Zeros were suddenly all around. Louie counted nine of them, slashing around the bombers, machine guns blazing. The boldness and skill of the Japanese pilots astounded the bomber crews. The Zeros flew at the bombers head-on, cannons firing, slicing between planes that were just feet apart. They passed so close that Louie could see the faces of the pilots. Firing furiously, the bomber gunners tried to take out the Zeros. The shooting was all point-blank, and bullets were flying everywhere. One bomber sustained seventeen hits from friendly planes, or possibly from its own waist guns.

Stricken bombers began slipping behind, and the Zeros pounced. One bomber was hounded by four Zeros and a biplane. Its gunners shot down one Zero before their pilot found a cloud to hide in, scattering his pursuers. Below, Lieutenant Jacobs, Phil's lost wingman, was still airborne, his plane laboring along on three engines and no right rudder in a circle of Zeros. His gunners sent one Zero down. Thor Hamrin, pilot of the B-24 *Jab in the Ass,* saw Jacobs struggling. Circling back and speeding down, he opened up on the Zeros with all of his guns. The Zeros backed off, and Jacobs flew on with Hamrin on his wing.

The first bombers, pursued by Zeros, headed out to sea. With its fighters gone and many of its guns destroyed, the Japanese base was left exposed. The trailing B-24s swept in, crossing through rivers of smoke to rain bombs on the phosphate plant. In the last plane over the island, a reporter raised his binoculars. He saw "a volcano-like mass of smoke and fire," a burning Japanese bomber, a few bursts of antiaircraft fire, and not a single moving person.

———

Phil and Cuppernell pushed *Super Man* full-throttle for home. The plane was gravely wounded, trying to fly up and over onto its back. It wanted to stall and wouldn't turn, and the pilots needed all their strength to hold it level. Three Zeros orbited it, spewing streams of bullets and cannon shells. The gunners, engulfed in scalding-hot spent cartridges, fired back: Mitchell in the nose, Pillsbury in the top turret, Glassman in the belly, Lambert in the tail, and Brooks and Douglas standing exposed at the broad, open waist windows. Louie, still in the greenhouse, saw rounds ripping through the Zeros' fuselages and wings, but the planes were relentless. Bullets streaked through *Super Man* from every direction. In every part of the plane, the sea and sky were visible through gashes in the bomber's skin. Every moment, the holes multiplied.

Just as Louie turned to leave the greenhouse, he saw a Zero dive straight for *Super Man*'s nose. Mitchell and the Zero pilot fired simultaneously. Louie and Mitchell felt bullets cutting the air around them, one passing near Mitchell's arm, the other just missing Louie's face. One round sizzled past and struck the turret's power line, and the turret went dead. At the same instant, Louie saw the Zero pilot jerk. Mitchell had hit him. For a moment, the Zero continued to speed directly at the nose of *Super Man*. Then the weight of the stricken pilot on the yoke forced the Zero down, ducking under the bomber. The fighter powered down and splashed into the ocean just short of the beach.

Louie rotated the dead turret by hand and Mitchell climbed out. The gunners kept firing, and *Super Man* trembled on. There were still two Zeros circling it.

In the top turret, facing backward, Stanley Pillsbury had fearsome weapons, twin .50-caliber machine guns. Each gun could fire eight hundred rounds per minute, the bullets traveling about three thousand feet per second. Pillsbury's guns could kill a man from four miles away, and they could take out a Zero if given the chance. But the Zeros were staying below, where Pillsbury couldn't hit them. He could feel their rounds thumping into *Super Man*'s belly, but all he could see were his plane's wings. Fixated on the nearest Zero, Pillsbury thought, *If he'd just come up, I can knock him down.*

He waited. The plane groaned and shook, the gunners fired, the Zeros pounded them from below, and still Pillsbury waited. Then Louie saw a Zero swoop up on the right. Pillsbury never saw it. The first he knew of it was an earsplitting *ka-bang! ka-bang! ka-bang!*, a sensation of everything tipping and blowing apart, and excruciating pain.

The Zero had sprayed the entire right side of *Super Man* with cannon shells. The first rounds hit near the tail, spinning the plane hard on its side. Shrapnel tore into the hip and left leg of tail gunner Ray Lambert, who hung on sideways as *Super Man* rolled. The plane's twist saved him; a cannon round struck exactly where his head had been an instant earlier, hitting so close to him that his goggles shattered. Ahead, shrapnel dropped Brooks and Douglas at the waist guns. In the belly turret, two hunks of shrapnel penetrated the back of Glassman, who was so adrenalized that he felt nothing. Another round hit the passenger, Nelson. Finally, a shell blew out the wall of the top turret, disintegrating on impact and shooting metal into Pillsbury's leg from foot to knee. Half of the crew, and all of the working gunners, had been hit. *Super Man* reeled crazily on its side, and for a moment it felt about to spiral out of control. Phil and Cuppernell wrenched it level.

Clinging to his gun as the shrapnel struck his leg and the plane's spin nearly flung him from his seat, Pillsbury shouted the only word that came to mind.

"*Ow!*"

Louie heard someone scream. When the plane was righted, Phil yelled to him to find out how bad the damage was. Louie climbed from the nose turret. The first thing he saw was Harry Brooks, in the bomb bay, lying on the catwalk. The bomb bay doors were wide open, and Brooks was dangling partway off the catwalk, one hand gripping the catwalk and one leg swinging in the air, with nothing but air and ocean below him. His eyes bulged, and his upper body was wet with blood. He lifted one arm toward Louie, a plaintive expression on his face.

Louie grabbed Brooks by the wrists and pulled him into a seated position. Brooks slumped forward, and Louie could see holes dotting the back of his jacket. There was blood in his hair.

Louie dragged Brooks to the flight deck and pulled him into a corner. Brooks passed out. Louie found a cushion and slid it under him, then returned to the bomb bay. He remembered having turned the valve to close the doors, and couldn't understand why they were open. Then he saw: There was a slash in the wall, and purple fluid was splattered everywhere. The hydraulic lines, which controlled the doors, had been severed. With these lines broken, Phil would have no hydraulic control of the landing gear or the flaps, which they would need to slow the plane on landing. And without hydraulics, they had no brakes.

Louie cranked the bomb bay doors shut by hand. He looked to the rear and saw Douglas, Lambert, and Nelson lying together, bloody. Douglas and Lambert were pawing along the floor, trying to reach their guns. Nelson didn't move. He'd taken a shot to the stomach.

Louie shouted to the cockpit for help. Phil yelled back that he was losing control of the plane and needed Cuppernell. Louie said that this

was a dire emergency. Phil braced himself at the controls, and Cuppernell got up, saw the men in back, and broke into a run. He found morphine, sulfa, oxygen masks, and bandages and dropped down next to
each man in turn.

Louie knelt beside Brooks, who was still unconscious. Feeling
through the gunner's hair, he found two holes in the back of his skull.
There were four large wounds in his back. Louie strapped an oxygen
mask to Brooks's face and bandaged his head. As he worked, he thought
about the state of the plane. The waist, nose, and tail gunners were out,
the plane was shot to hell, Phil was alone in the cockpit, barely keeping the plane up, and the Zeros were still out there. *One more pass,* he
thought, *will put us down.*

Louie was bending over Brooks when he felt a tickle on his shoulder, something dripping. He looked up and saw Pillsbury in the top turret. Blood was streaming from his leg. Louie rushed to him.

Pillsbury was still in his seat, facing sideways, gripping the gun and
sweeping his eyes around the sky. He looked absolutely livid. His leg
dangled below him, his pant leg hanging in shreds and his boot blasted.
Next to him was a jagged hole, the shape of Texas and almost as large
as a beach ball, clawed out of the side of the plane. The turret was shot
with holes, and the floor was jingling with flakes of metal and turret
motor.

Top turret gunner Stanley Pillsbury, shown at the waist gun.
Courtesy of Louis Zamperini

Louie began doctoring Pillsbury's wounds. Pillsbury, swinging his head back and forth, ignored him. He knew that the Zero would come back to finish the kill, and he had to find it. The urgency of the moment drove the pain into a distant place.

Suddenly, there was a whoosh of dark, close, upward motion, a gray shining body, a red circle. Pillsbury shouted something unintelligible, and Louie let go of his foot just as Pillsbury banged the high-speed rotator on his turret. The turret grunted to life, whirling Pillsbury around ninety degrees.

The Zero reached the top of its arc, leveled off, and sped directly toward *Super Man*. Pillsbury was terrified. In an instant, the end would come with the most minute of gestures—the flick of the Zero pilot's finger on his cannon trigger—and *Super Man* would carry ten men into the Pacific. Pillsbury could see the pilot who would end his life, the tropical sun illuminating his face, a white scarf coiled about his neck. Pillsbury thought: *I have to kill this man.*

Pillsbury sucked in a sharp breath and fired. He watched the tracers skim away from his gun's muzzle and punch through the cockpit of the Zero. The windshield blew apart and the pilot pitched forward.

The fatal blow never came to *Super Man*. The Zero pilot, surely seeing the top turret smashed and the waist windows vacant, had probably assumed that the gunners were all dead. He had waited too long.

The Zero folded onto itself like a wounded bird. Pillsbury felt sure that the pilot was dead before his plane struck the ocean.

The last Zero came up from below, then faltered and fell. Clarence Douglas, standing at the waist gun with his thigh, chest, and shoulder torn open, brought it down.

In the ocean behind them, the men on the submarine watched the planes tussle over the water. One by one, the Zeros dropped, and the bombers flew on. The submarine crew would later report that not one Zero made it back to Nauru. It is believed that thanks to this raid and others, the Japanese never retrieved a single shipment of phosphate from the island.

The pain that had been far away during the gunfight surged over Pillsbury. Louie pushed the release on the turret chair, and the gunner slid into his arms. Louie eased him to the floor next to Brooks. Grasping Pillsbury's boot, he began easing it off as gently as he could. Pillsbury

hollered for all he was worth. The boot slid off. Pillsbury's left big toe
was gone; it was still in the boot. The toe next to it hung by a string of
skin, and portions of his other toes were missing. So much shrapnel
was embedded in his lower leg that it bristled like a pincushion. Louie
thought that there would be no way to save the foot. He bandaged
Pillsbury, gave him a shot of morphine, fed him a sulfa pill, then hurried away to see if they could save the plane.

Super Man was dying. Phil couldn't turn it from side to side with
the normal controls, and the plane was pulling upward so hard, trying
to flip, that Phil couldn't hold it with his arms. He put both feet on the
yoke and pushed as hard as he could. The nose kept rearing up so high
that the plane was on the verge of stalling. It was porpoising, up and
down.

The men who could walk rushed through the plane, assessing its
condition. The peril of their situation was abundantly clear. The right
rudder was completely shot, a large portion of it missing and its cables
severed. The cables for the elevators, which controlled the plane's
pitch, were badly damaged. So were the cables for the trim, which gave
the pilot fine control of the plane's attitude—its orientation in the air—
and thus greatly reduced the effort needed to handle the plane. Fuel
was trickling onto the floor under the top turret. No one knew the condition of the landing gear, but with the entire plane perforated, it was
likely that the tires had been struck. The bomb bay was sloshing with
hydraulic fluid.

Phil did what he could. Slowing the engines on one side created a
power differential that forced the plane to turn. Pushing the plane to
higher speed eased the porpoising and reduced the risk of stalling. If
Phil kept his feet on the yoke and pushed hard, he could stop the plane
from flipping. Someone shut off the fuel feed near Pillsbury, and the
leaking stopped. Louie took a bomb-arming wire and spliced the severed rudder and elevator cables together. It didn't result in immediate
improvement, but if the left rudder cables failed, it might help.

Funafuti was five hours away. If *Super Man* could carry them that
far, they would have to land without hydraulic control of the landing
gear, flaps, or brakes. They could lower the gear and extend the flaps
with hand pumps, but there was no manual alternative to hydraulic
brakes. Without bombs or much fuel aboard, the plane weighed some
forty thousand pounds. A B-24 without brakes, especially one coming

in "hot"—over the standard of 90 to 110 miles per hour landing speed—could eat up 10,000 feet before it stopped. Funafuti's runway was 6,660 feet long. At its end were rocks and sea.

Hours passed. *Super Man* shook and struggled. Louie and Cuppernell moved among the injured men. Pillsbury lay on the floor, watching his leg bleed. Mitchell hunched over his navigation table, and Phil wrestled with the plane. Douglas limped about, looking deeply traumatized, his shoulder and arm, said Pillsbury, "all torn to pieces." Brooks lay next to Pillsbury, blood pooling in his throat, making him gurgle as he breathed. Pillsbury couldn't bear the sound. Once or twice, when Louie knelt before him, Brooks opened his eyes and whispered something. Louie put his ear near Brooks's lips, but couldn't understand him. Brooks drifted off again. Everyone knew he was almost surely dying. No one spoke of it.

It was likely, they all knew, that they'd crash on landing, if not before. Whatever thoughts each man had, he kept them to himself.

——

Daylight was fading when the palms of Funafuti brushed over the horizon. Phil began dropping the plane toward the runway. They were going much too fast. Someone went to the hand crank on the catwalk and opened the bomb bay doors, and the plane, dragging on the air, began to slow. Douglas went to the pump for the landing gear, just under the top turret. He needed two hands to work it—one to push the valve and one to work the pump—but he was in too much pain to hold up either of his arms for more than a few seconds. Pillsbury couldn't stand, but by stretching as far as he could, he reached the selector valve. Together, they got the gear down while Louie peered out the side window, looking for a yellow tab that would signify that the gear was locked. The tab appeared. Mitchell and Louie pumped the flaps down.

Louie scrounged up parachute cord and went to each injured man, looping cord around him as a belt, then wrapping the rope around stationary parts of the plane. Nelson, with his belly wound, couldn't have a rope wrapped around his torso, so Louie fed the line around his arm and under his armpit. Fearing that they'd end up on fire, he didn't knot the cords. Instead, he wound the ends around the hands of the injured men, so they could free themselves easily.

The question of how to stop the bomber remained. Louie had an idea. What if they were to tie two parachutes to the rear of the plane, pitch them out of the waist windows at touchdown, and pull the rip cords? No one had ever tried to stop a bomber in this manner. It was a long shot, but it was all they had. Louie and Douglas placed one parachute in each waist window and tied them to a gun mount. Douglas went to his seat, leaving Louie standing between the waist windows, a rip cord in each hand.

Super Man sank toward Funafuti. Below, the journalists and the other bomber crews stood, watching the crippled plane come in. Super Man dropped lower and lower. Just before it touched down, Pillsbury looked at the airspeed gauge. It read 110 miles per hour. For a plane without brakes, it was too fast.

For a moment, the landing was perfect. The wheels kissed the runway so softly that Louie stayed on his feet. Then came a violent gouging sensation. What they had feared had happened: The left tire was flat. The plane caught hard, veered left, and careened toward two parked bombers. Cuppernell, surely more out of habit than hope, stomped on the right brake. There was just enough hydraulic fluid left to save them. Super Man spun in a circle and lurched to a stop just clear of the other bombers. Louie was still in the back, gripping the parachute cords. He had not had to use them.*

Douglas popped open the top hatch, dragged himself onto the roof, raised his injured arm over his head, and crossed it with his other arm, the signal that there were wounded men inside. Louie jumped down from the bomb bay and gave the same signal. There was a stampede across the airfield, and in seconds the plane was swarming with marines. Louie stood back and ran his eyes over the body of his ruined plane. Later, ground crewmen would count the holes in Super Man, marking each one with chalk to be sure that they didn't count any twice. There were 594 holes. All of the Nauru bombers had made it back, every one of them shot up, but none so badly as this.

Brooks was laid on a stretcher, placed on a jeep, and driven to a rudimentary, one-room infirmary. He was bleeding inside his skull.

* Eight months later, Charlie Pratte became the first pilot to stop a B-24 with parachutes. His bomber, Belle of Texas, had been shot up over the Marshall Islands and had no brakes, leaving Pratte to attempt a landing on a runway far too short for bombers. To make matters worse, Pratte had eaten bad eggs and was vomiting as he flew. Touching down at a scorching 140 miles per hour, Pratte ordered his men to deploy three parachutes. With the parachutes open behind it, the plane shot off the end of the runway and onto the beach before stopping just short of the ocean. Pratte and his crew were given special commendations.

They carried Pillsbury to a barracks to await treatment. He was lying there about an hour later when the doctor came in and asked him if he knew Harry Brooks. Pillsbury said yes.

"He didn't make it," the doctor said.

————

Technical Sergeant Harold Brooks died one week before his twenty-third birthday. It took more than a week for word to reach his widowed mother, Edna, at 511½ Western Avenue in Clarksville, Michigan. Across town on Harley Road, the news reached his fiancée, Jeannette Burtscher. She learned that he was gone nine days before the wedding date that they had set before he left for the war.

Harry Brooks.

Ten

The Stinking Six

AS EVENING FELL OVER FUNAFUTI, THE GROUND CREWS nursed the damaged bombers. When the holes were patched and mechanical problems repaired, the planes were fueled up and loaded with six five-hundred-pound bombs each, ready for a strike on Tarawa the next day. *Super Man*, still standing where it had spun to a halt, its entire length honeycombed, wouldn't join them. It would probably never fly again.

Worn out from the mission and hours spent helping at the infirmary, Louie walked to a grove of coconut trees where there were tents that served as barracks. He found his tent and flopped down on a cot, near Phil. The journalists were in a tent next to theirs. At the infirmary, Stanley Pillsbury lay with his bleeding leg hanging off his cot. Nearby, the other wounded *Super Man* crewmen tried to sleep. Blackout descended, and a hush fell.

At about three in the morning, Louie woke to a forlorn droning, rising and falling. It was a small plane, crossing back and forth overhead. Thinking that it was a crew lost in the clouds, Louie lay there listening, hoping they'd find home. Eventually, the sound faded away.

Before Louie could fall back asleep, he heard the growl of heavy aircraft engines. Then, from the north end of the atoll, came a *BOOM!* A siren began sounding, and there was distant gunfire. Then a marine ran past the airmen's tents, screaming, "Air raid! Air raid!" The droning overhead hadn't been a lost American crew. It had probably been a scout plane, leading Japanese bombers. Funafuti was under attack.

The airmen and journalists, Louie and Phil among them, jammed their feet into their boots, bolted from the tents, and stopped, some shouting, others spinning in panic. They couldn't see any bomb shelters. From down the atoll, the explosions were coming in rapid succession, each one louder and closer. The ground shook.

"I looked around and said, 'Holy hell! Where are we going to go?' " remembered pilot Joe Deasy. The best shelter he could find was a shallow pit dug around a coconut sapling, and he plowed into it, along with most of the men near him. Herman Scearce, Deasy's radioman, leapt into a trench next to an ordnance truck, joining five of his crewmates. Pilot Jesse Stay jumped into another hole nearby. Three men crawled under the ordnance truck; another flung himself into a garbage pit. One man ran right off the end of the atoll, splashing into the ocean even though he didn't know how to swim. Some men, finding nowhere to go, dropped to their knees to claw foxholes in the sand with their helmets. As he dug in the dark with the bombs coming, one man noisily cursed the sonofabitch generals who had left the atoll without shelters.

Dozens of natives crowded into a large missionary church that stood in a clearing. Realizing that the white church would stand out brilliantly on the dark atoll, a marine named Fonnie Black Ladd ran in and yelled at the natives to get out. When they wouldn't move, he drew his sidearm. They scattered.

In the infirmary, Stanley Pillsbury lay in startled confusion. One moment he'd been sleeping, and the next, the atoll was rocking with explosions, a siren was howling, and people were sprinting by, dragging patients onto stretchers and rushing them out. Then the room was empty, and Pillsbury was alone. He had apparently been forgotten. He sat up, frantic. He couldn't stand.

Louie and Phil ran through the coconut grove, searching for anything that might serve as shelter. The bombs were overtaking them, making a sound that one man likened to the footfalls of a giant: *Boom . . . boom . . . BOOM . . . BOOM!* At last, Louie and Phil spotted a native hut built on flood stilts. They dove under it, landing in a heap of more than two dozen men. The bombs were now so close that the men could hear them spinning in the air; Deasy remembered the sound as a *whirr*, Scearce as a piercing whistle.

An instant later, everything was scalding whiteness and splintering noise. The ground heaved, and the air whooshed around, carrying an acrid smell. Trees blew apart. A bomb struck the tent in which Louie and Phil had been sleeping a minute before. Another burst beside a pile of men in a ditch, and something speared into the back of the man on top. He said, "This feels like it, boys," and passed out. A bomb hit the ordnance truck, sending it into the air in thousands of pieces. The remains of the truck and the men under it skimmed past Jesse Stay's head. A nose gunner heard a singing sound as the parts of the truck flew by him. It was apparently this truck that landed on one of the tents, where two airmen were still on their cots. Another bomb tumbled into Scearce's trench, plopping right on top of a tail gunner. It didn't go off, but sat there hissing. The gunner shouted, "Jesus!" It took them a moment to realize that what they'd thought was a bomb was actually a fire extinguisher. Yards away, Louie and Phil huddled. The hut shook, but still stood.

The bombs moved down the atoll. Each report sounded farther away, and then the explosions stopped. A few men climbed from their shelters to help the wounded and douse fires. Louie and the others stayed where they were, knowing that the bombers would be back. Matches were struck and cigarettes were pinched in trembling fingers. If we're hit, one man grumbled, there'll be nothing left of us but gravy. Far away, the bombers turned. The booming began again.

Someone running by the infirmary saw Pillsbury, hurried in, threw him on a stretcher, and dragged him into a tiny cement building where the other wounded had been taken. The building was so crowded that men had been laid on shelves. It was pitch-dark, and doctors were shuffling around, peering at their patients by flashlight. Pillsbury lay panting in the darkness, listening to the bombs coming, feeling claustrophobic, his mind flashing with images of bombs entombing them. With men stacked everywhere and no one speaking, he thought of a morgue. His leg hurt. He began groaning, and the doctor felt his way to him and gave him morphine. The booming was louder, louder, and then it was over them again, tremendous crashing. The ceiling shuddered, and cement dust sifted down.

Outside, it was hell on earth. Men moaned and screamed, one calling for his mother. A pilot thought the voices sounded "like animals crying." Men's eardrums burst. A man died of a heart attack. Another man's arm was severed. Others sobbed, prayed, and lost control of their bowels. "I wasn't only scared, I was terrified," one airman would write to his parents. "I thought I was scared in the air, but I wasn't. [It was] the first time in my life I saw how close death could come." Phil felt the same; never, even during the fight over Nauru, had he known such terror. Louie crouched beside him. As he had run through the co-conut grove, he had moved only on instinct and roaring adrenaline, feeling no emotion. Now, as explosions went off around him, fear seized him.

Staff Sergeant Frank Rosynek huddled in a coral trench, wearing nothing but a helmet, untied shoes, and boxer shorts. The tonnage coming down, he later wrote, "seemed like a railroad carload. The bombs sounded like someone pushing a piano down a long ramp be-fore they hit and exploded. Big palm trees were shattered and splin-tered all around us; the ground would rise up in the air when a bomb exploded and there was this terrific flash of super bright light that it made. The concussion blew pieces of coral into our hole and we blindly groped for them and tossed them out as quick as we could find them. At intervals between a bomb falling it sounded like church: voices from nearby slit trenches all chanting the Lord's prayer together—over and over again. Louder when the bombs hit closer. I thought I even heard some guys crying. You were afraid to look up because you felt your face might be seen from above."

Two more soldiers were killed on the third pass. On the fourth pass, the Japanese hit the jackpot. Two bombs bull's-eyed the gassed-up, loaded B-24s parked by the runway. The first went up in a huge explo-sion, sending bomber parts showering all over the island. Another burst into flames. The fires set off machine gun bullets, which whizzed in all directions, their tracers drawing ribbons in the air. Then the five-hundred-pound bombs on the planes started going off.

Finally, the atoll fell silent. A few of the men, shaking, stood up. As they walked among the wreckage, another B-24 blew up, the explosion accelerated by its 2,300 gallons of fuel, 3,000 pounds of bombs, and cache of .50-caliber ammunition. A copilot wrote that it sounded "like the whole island was blowing up." With that, it was over.

When dawn broke, men began creeping from their hiding places. The man who had run into the ocean waded ashore, having clung to a rock for three hours as the tide rose. With the morning light, the man who had cursed his generals as he had dug his foxhole discovered that those generals had been digging right next to him. Louie and Phil crawled out from beneath the hut. Phil was unscathed; Louie had only a cut on his arm. They joined a procession of exhausted, stunned men.

Funafuti, the morning after. *Courtesy of Louis Zamperini*

Funafuti was wrecked. A bomb had struck the church roof, sending the building down onto itself, but thanks to Corporal Ladd, there had been no one inside. There was a crater where Louie and Phil's tent had been. Another tent lay collapsed, a bomb standing on its nose in the middle of it. Someone tied the bomb to a truck, dragged it to the beach, and turned sharply, sending the bomb skidding into the ocean. Rosynek walked up the runway and found six Japanese bombs lying in a neat row. The bombs were armed by spinning as they fell, but whoever had dropped them had come in too low, not leaving the bombs enough drop space to arm themselves. The men dragged them into the ocean too.

Where the struck B-24s had been, there were deep holes ringed by decapitated coconut trees. One crater, Louie noted in his diary, was thirty-five feet deep and sixty feet across. Bits of bomber were sprinkled everywhere. Landing gear and seats that had seen the sunset from one side of Funafuti greeted the sunrise from the other. All that was left of one bomber was a tail, two wingtips, and two propellers, connected by a black smudge. There was a 1,200-horsepower Pratt and Whitney engine sitting by itself on the runway; the plane that it belonged to was nowhere to be found. Louie came upon a reporter staring into a crater, in tears. Louie walked to him, bracing to see a dead body. Instead, he saw a typewriter, flattened.

The wounded and dead were everywhere. Two mechanics who'd been caught in the open were bruised all over from the concussive force of the explosions. They were so traumatized that they couldn't talk, and were using their hands to communicate. Men stood in a solemn circle around a couple of seats and twisted metal, all that was left of the ordnance truck. The three men who had sought shelter under it were beyond recognition. A radioman was found dead, a bomb shard in his head. Louie came upon the body of a native, dressed in a loincloth, lying on his back. Half of his head was missing.

A radio operator would say that there had been about fourteen Japanese bombers, but thinking that there had been two sets of three, someone dubbed them "the Stinking Six." Everyone expected them to return. Phil and Louie joined a group of men digging foxholes with shovels and helmets. When they had a moment, they walked to the beach and sat together for an hour, trying to collect their thoughts.

Sometime that day, Louie went to the infirmary to help out. Pillsbury was back in his cot. His leg was burning terribly, and he lay with it dangling in the air, dripping blood into a puddle on the floor. Cuppernell sat with him, thanking him for shooting down that Zero.

The doctor was concerned that Pillsbury's foot wouldn't stop bleeding. Surgery was necessary, but there was no anesthetic, so Pillsbury was just going to have to do without. With Pillsbury gripping the bed with both hands and Louie lying over his legs, the doctor used pliers to tear tissue from Pillsbury's foot, then pulled a long strip of hanging skin over his bone stump and sewed it up.

Super Man sat by the airstrip, listing left on its peg-legged landing gear, the shredded tire hanging partway off. The air raid had missed the plane, but it didn't look like it. Its 594 holes were spread over every part of it: swarms of bullet holes, slashes from shrapnel, four cannon-fire gashes at least as large as a man's head, the gaping punch hole beside Pillsbury's turret, and the hole in the rudder, as big as a doorway. The plane looked as if it had flown through barbed wire, its paint scoured off the leading edge of the engines and sides. Journalists and airmen circled it, amazed that it had stayed airborne for five hours with so much damage. Phil was hailed as a miracle worker, and everyone had cause to reassess the supposedly fainthearted B-24. A photographer climbed inside the plane and snapped a picture. Taken in daylight in the dark of the plane's interior, the image showed shafts of light streaming through the holes, a shower of stars against a black sky.

Louie, looking as battered as his plane, walked to *Super Man*. He leaned his head into one of the cannon holes and saw the severed right rudder cables, still spliced together as he had left them. He ran his fingers along the tears in *Super Man*'s skin. The plane had saved him and all but one of his crew. He would think of it as a dear friend.

Louie at *Super Man* on the day after Nauru. *Courtesy of Louis Zamperini*

Louie boarded another plane and began his journey back to Hawaii with Phil, Cuppernell, Mitchell, and the bandaged Glassman. Pillsbury, Lambert, and Douglas were too badly wounded to rejoin the crew. In a few days, they'd be sent to Samoa, where a doctor would take one look at Pillsbury's leg and announce that it had been "hamburgered." Lambert would be hospitalized for five months.* When a general presented him with a Purple Heart, Lambert apparently couldn't sit up, so the general pinned the medal to his sheet. Douglas's war was done. Brooks was lying in a grave in Funafuti's Marine Corps cemetery.

The crew was broken up forever. They would never see *Super Man* again.

An oppressive weight settled on Louie as he flew away from Funafuti. He and the remains of the crew stopped at Canton, then flew on to Palmyra Atoll, where Louie took a hot shower and watched *They Died with Their Boots On* at the base theater. It was the movie he'd been working on as an extra when the war had begun, a lifetime ago.

Back on Hawaii, he sank into a cold torpor. He was irritable and withdrawn. Phil, too, was off-kilter, drinking a few too many, seeming not himself. With a gutted crew and no plane, the men weren't called for assignments, so they killed time in Honolulu. When a drunken hothead tried to pick a fight, Phil stared back indifferently, but Louie obliged. The two stomped outside to have it out, and the hothead backed out. Later, drinking beer with friends, Louie couldn't bring himself to be sociable. He holed up in his room, listening to music. His only other solace was running, slogging through the sand around the Kahuku runway, thinking of the 1944 Olympics, trying to forget Harry Brooks's plaintive face.

On May 24, Louie, Phil, and the other *Super Man* veterans were transferred to the 42nd squadron of the 11th Bomb Group. The 42nd would be stationed on the eastern edge of Oahu, on the gorgeous beach at Kualoa. Six new men were brought in to replace the lost *Super Man* crewmen. Flying with unfamiliar men worried Louie and Phil. "Don't like the idea a bit," Louie once wrote in his diary. "Every time they mix up a crew, they have a crack up." Among the *Super Man* veterans, the only thing that seemed noteworthy about the new men was that their tail gunner, a sergeant from Cleveland named Francis McNamara, had such an affinity for sweets that he ate practically nothing but dessert. The men called him "Mac."

For the moment, they had no plane. Liberators destined for the

---

* Lambert eventually returned to duty with another crew and amassed an astounding record, completing at least ninety-five missions.

11th Bomb Group were being flown in from other combat areas, and the first five, peppered with bullet holes, had just arrived. One of them, *Green Hornet*, looked haggard, its sides splattered with something black, the paint worn off the engines. Even with an empty bomb bay and all four engines going, it was only just able to stay airborne. It tended to fly with its tail dragging below its nose, something the airmen called "mushing," a reference to the mushy feel of the controls of a faltering plane. Engineers went over the bomber, but found no explanation. All of the airmen were wary of *Green Hornet*. The bomber was relegated to errands, and the ground crewmen began prying parts off it for use on other planes. Louie went up in it for a short hop, came away referring to it as "the craziest plane," and hoped he'd never have to fly in it again.

On May 26, Louie packed up his belongings and caught a ride to his new Kualoa digs, a private cottage thirty feet from the ocean. Louie, Phil, Mitchell, and Cuppernell would have the place all to themselves. That afternoon, Louie stayed in, transforming the garage into his private room. Phil went to a squadron meeting, where he met a rookie pilot, George "Smitty" Smith, by coincidence a close friend of Cecy's. After the meeting, Phil lingered late with Smitty, talking about Cecy. At the cottage, Louie turned in. The next day, he, Phil, and Cuppernell were going to go to Honolulu to take another crack at P. Y. Chong's steaks.

Across the island at Hickam Field, nine crewmen and one passenger climbed aboard a B-24. The crew, piloted by a Tennessean named Clarence Corpening, had just come from San Francisco and was on its way to Canton, then Australia. As men on the ground watched, the plane lifted off, banked south, and flew out of sight.

Eleven

"Nobody's Going to Live Through This"

ON THURSDAY, MAY 27, 1943, LOUIE ROSE AT FIVE A.M. Everyone else in the cottage was asleep. He tiptoed out and hiked up the hill behind the cottage to rouse himself, then walked back, pulled on his workout clothes, and started for the runway. On his way, he found a sergeant and asked him to pace him in a jeep. The sergeant agreed, and Louie jogged off with the jeep beside him. He turned a mile in 4:12, a dazzling time given that he was running in sand. He was in the best shape of his life.

He walked back to the cottage, cleaned himself up, and dressed, donning a pair of tropical-weight khaki pants, a T-shirt, and a muslin top shirt that he'd bought in Honolulu. After breakfast and some time spent fixing up his new room, he wrote a letter to Payton Jordan, tucked the letter into his shirt pocket, climbed into a borrowed car with Phil and Cuppernell, and headed for Honolulu.

At the base gate, they were flagged down by the despised lieutenant who had ordered them to fly *Super Man* on three engines. The lieutenant was on urgent business. Clarence Corpening's B-24, which had left for Canton the day before, had never landed. The lieutenant, who was under the impression that the plane was a B-25 instead of a much larger B-24, was looking for volunteers to hunt for it. Phil told him that they had no plane. The lieutenant said they could take *Green Hornet*. When Phil said that the plane wasn't airworthy, the lieutenant replied that it had passed inspection. Both Louie and Phil knew that though the word "volunteer" was used, this was an order. Phil volunteered. The lieutenant woke pilot Joe Deasy and talked him into volunteering as well. Deasy and his crew would take the B-24 *Daisy Mae*.

Phil, Louie, and Cuppernell turned back to round up their crew. Stopping at the cottage, Louie grabbed a pair of binoculars that he had bought at the Olympics. He flipped open his diary and jotted down a few words on what he was about to do. "There was only one ship, 'The Green Hornet,' a 'musher,' " he wrote. "We were very reluctant, but Phillips finally gave in for rescue mission."

Just before he left, Louie scribbled a note and left it on his foot-locker, in which he kept his liquor-filled condiment jars. *If we're not back in a week,* it read, *help yourself to the booze.*

———

The lieutenant met the crews at *Green Hornet*. He unrolled a map. He believed that Corpening had gone down two hundred miles north of Palmyra. His reason for believing this is unclear; the official report of the downing states that the plane wasn't seen or heard from after take-off, so it could have been anywhere. Whatever his reason, he told Phil to follow a heading of 208 and search to a point parallel to Palmyra. He gave Deasy roughly the same instruction but directed him to a slightly different area. Both crews were told to search all day, land at Palmyra, then resume searching the next day, if necessary.

As they prepared for takeoff, everyone on Phil's crew worried about *Green Hornet*. Louie tried to reassure himself that without bombs or ammunition aboard, the plane should have enough power to stay air-borne. Phil was concerned that he'd never been in this plane and didn't know its quirks. He knew that it had been cannibalized, and he hoped that critical parts weren't missing. The crew reviewed crash procedures and made a special inspection to be sure that the survival equipment was aboard. There was a provisions box in the plane, and retrieving this was the tail gunner's responsibility. There was also an extra raft, stored in a yellow bag on the flight deck. This raft was Louie's respon-sibility, and he checked to be sure it was there. He put on his Mae West, as did some other crewmen. Phil left his off, perhaps because it was dif-ficult to fly with it on.

At the last moment, an enlisted man ran to the plane and asked if he

Green Hornet. Courtesy of Louis Zamperini

could hitch a ride to Palmyra. There were no objections, and the man found a seat in the back. With the addition of the enlisted man, there were eleven on board.

As Phil and Cuppernell turned the plane up the taxiway, Louie remembered his letter to Payton Jordan. He fished it from his pocket, leaned from the waist window, and tossed it to a ground crewman, who said he'd mail it for him.

———

Daisy Mae lifted off at almost the same time as *Green Hornet,* and the planes flew side by side. On *Green Hornet,* other than the four *Super Man* veterans, the crewmen were strangers and had little to say to one another. Louie passed the time on the flight deck, chatting with Phil and Cuppernell.

Green Hornet, true to form, flew with its tail well below its nose, and couldn't keep up with *Daisy Mae.* After about two hundred miles, Phil radioed to Deasy to go on without him. The crews lost sight of each other.

Sometime around two P.M., *Green Hornet* reached the search area,

about 225 miles north of Palmyra. Clouds pressed around the plane, and no one could see the water. Phil dropped the plane under the clouds, leveling off at eight hundred feet. Louie took out his binoculars, descended to the greenhouse, and began scanning. Phil's voice soon crackled over the interphone, asking him to come up and pass the binoculars around. Louie did as told, then remained on the flight deck, just behind Phil and Cuppernell.

While they searched the ocean, Cuppernell asked Phil if he could switch seats with him, taking over the first pilot's duties. This was a common practice, enabling copilots to gain experience to qualify as first pilots. Phil assented. The enormous Cuppernell squeezed around Phil and into the left seat as Phil moved to the right. Cuppernell began steering the plane.

A few minutes later, someone noticed that the engines on one side were burning more fuel than those on the other, making one side progressively lighter. They began transferring fuel across the wings to even out the load.

Suddenly, there was a shudder. Louie looked at the tachometer and saw that the RPMs on engine No. 1—on the far left—were falling. He looked out the window. The engine was shaking violently. Then it stopped. The bomber tipped left and began dropping rapidly toward the ocean.

Phil and Cuppernell had only seconds to save the plane. They began working rapidly, but Louie had the sense that they were disoriented by their seat swap. To minimize drag from the dead No. 1 engine, they needed to "feather" it—turn the dead propeller blades parallel to the wind and stop the propeller's rotation. Normally, this was Cuppernell's job, but now he was in the pilot's seat. As he worked, Cuppernell shouted to the new engineer to come to the cockpit to feather the engine. It is unknown if he or anyone else specified which engine needed feathering. It was a critical piece of information; because a dead engine's propeller continues turning in the wind, it can look just like a running engine.

On the control panel, there were four feathering buttons, one for each engine, covered by a plastic shield. Leaning between Cuppernell and Phil, the engineer flipped the shield and banged down on a button. The moment he did it, *Green Hornet* heaved and lurched left. The engineer had hit the No. 2 button, not the No. 1 button. Both leftward engines were now dead, and No. 1 still wasn't feathered.

Phil pushed the two working engines full on, trying to keep the plane aloft long enough to restart the good left engine. The racing right engines, pulling against the dragging, liftless side, rolled the plane halfway onto its left side, sending it into a spiral. The engine wouldn't start. The plane kept dropping.

Green Hornet was doomed. The best Phil could do was to try to level it out to ditch. He grunted three words into the interphone:

"Prepare to crash."

Louie ran from the flight deck, yelling for everyone to get to crash stations. As the plane whirled, he dug out the extra life raft, then clambered toward his crash position by the right waist window. He saw Mac, the new tail gunner, clutching the survival provisions box. Other men were frantically pulling on Mae Wests. Louie was distantly aware that Mitchell hadn't emerged from the nose. It was Mitchell's duty to calculate the plane's position, relay this to the radioman so he could send a distress signal, and strap the sextant and celestial navigation kit to his body. But with the plane gyrating down nose first and the escape passage narrow, perhaps the navigator couldn't pull himself out.

As the men behind the cockpit fled toward the comparative safety of the waist and rear of the plane, one man, almost certainly the engineer who had hit the wrong feathering button, apparently stayed in front. Because life rafts didn't deploy automatically in a crash, it was the engineer's duty to stand behind the cockpit to pull the overhead raft-release handle. To ensure that the rafts would be near enough to the plane for survivors to swim to them, he would have to wait until just before the crash to pull the handle. This meant that he would have little or no chance to get to a crash position, and thus, little chance of survival.

Phil and Cuppernell fought the plane. *Green Hornet* rolled onto its left side, moving faster and faster as the right engines thundered at full power. There was no time to radio a distress call. Phil looked for a swell over which to orient the plane for ditching, but it was no use. He couldn't haul the plane level, and even if he'd been able to, he was going much too fast. They were going to crash, very hard. Phil felt strangely devoid of fear. He watched the water rotating up at him and thought: *There's nothing more I can do.*

Louie sat down on the floor by the bulkhead, facing forward. There were five men near him. Everyone looked stunned; no one said anything. Louie looked out the right waist window. All he saw was the cloudy sky, turning around and around. He felt intensely alive. He recalled the bulkhead in front of him and thought of how his skull would strike it. Sensing the ocean coming up at the plane, he took a last glance at the twisting sky, then pulled the life raft in front of him and pushed his head into his chest.

One terrible, tumbling second passed, then another. An instant before the plane struck the water, Louie's mind throbbed with a single, final thought: *Nobody's going to live through this.*

For Louie, there were only jagged, soundless sensations: his body catapulted forward, the plane breaking open, something wrapping itself around him, the cold slap of water, and then its weight over him. *Green Hornet*, its nose and left wing hitting first at high speed, stabbed into the ocean and blew apart.

As the plane disintegrated around him, Louie felt himself being pulled deep underwater. Then, abruptly, the downward motion stopped and Louie was flung upward. The force of the plane's plunge had spent itself, and the fuselage, momentarily buoyed by the air trapped inside, leapt to the surface. Louie opened his mouth and gasped. The air hissed from the plane, and the water rushed up over Louie again. The plane slipped under and sank toward the ocean floor as if yanked downward.

Louie tried to orient himself. The tail was no longer behind him, the wings no longer ahead. The men who'd been around him were gone. The impact had rammed him into the waist gun mount and wedged him under it, facedown, with the raft below him. The gun mount pressed against his neck, and countless strands of something were coiled around his body, binding him to the gun mount and the raft. He felt them and thought: *Spaghetti*. It was a snarl of wires, *Green Hornet*'s nervous system. When the tail had broken off, the wires had snapped and whipped around him. He thrashed against them but couldn't get free. He felt frantic to breathe, but couldn't.

In the remains of the cockpit, Phil was fighting to get out. When the plane hit, he was thrown forward, his head striking something. A wave of water punched through the cockpit, and the plane carried him under.

From the darkness, he knew that he was far below the surface, sinking deeper by the second. He apparently saw Cuppernell push his big body out of the plane. Phil found what he thought was the cockpit window frame, its glass missing. He put his foot on something hard and pushed himself through the opening and out of the cockpit. He swam toward the surface, the light coming up around him.

He emerged in a puzzle of debris. His head was gushing blood and his ankle and one finger were broken. He found a floating hunk of wreckage, perhaps four feet square, and clung to it. It began to sink. There were two life rafts far away. No one was in them. Cuppernell was nowhere to be seen.

Far below, Louie was still ensnared in the plane, writhing in the wires. He looked up and saw a body, drifting passively. The plane coursed down, and the world fled away above. Louie felt his ears pop, and vaguely recollected that at the swimming pool at Redondo Beach, his ears would pop at twenty feet. Darkness enfolded him, and the water pressure bore in with greater and greater intensity. He struggled uselessly. He thought: *Hopeless*.

He felt a sudden, excruciating bolt of pain in his forehead. There was an oncoming stupor, a fading, as he tore at the wires and clenched his throat against the need to breathe. He had the soft realization that this was the last of everything. He passed out.

He woke in total darkness. He thought: *This is death*. Then he felt the water still on him, the heavy dropping weight of the plane around him. Inexplicably, the wires were gone, as was the raft. He was floating inside the fuselage, which was bearing him toward the ocean floor, some seventeen hundred feet down. He could see nothing. His Mae West was uninflated, but its buoyancy was pulling him into the ceiling of the plane. The air was gone from his lungs, and he was now gulping reflexively, swallowing salt water. He tasted blood, gasoline, and oil. He was drowning.

Louie flung out his arms, trying to find a way out. His right hand struck something, and his USC ring snagged on it. His hand was caught. He reached toward it with his left hand and felt a long, smooth length of metal. The sensation oriented him: He was at the open right waist window. He swam into the window, put his feet on the frame, and pushed off, wrenching his right hand free and cutting his finger. His back struck the top of the window, and the skin under his shirt scraped off. He kicked clear. The plane sank away.

Louie fumbled for the cords on his Mae West, hoping that no one had poached the carbon dioxide canisters. Luck was with him: The chambers ballooned. He was suddenly light, the vest pulling him urgently upward in a stream of debris.

He burst into dazzling daylight. He gasped in a breath and immediately vomited up the salt water and fuel he had swallowed. He had survived.

PART
III

Twelve

Downed

THE OCEAN WAS A JUMBLE OF BOMBER REMAINS. THE LIFE-blood of the plane—oil, hydraulic fluid, and some one thousand gallons of fuel—slopped about on the surface. Curling among the bits of plane were threads of blood.

Louie heard a voice. He turned toward it and saw Phil, a few dozen feet away, clinging to what looked like a fuel tank. With him was the tail gunner, Mac. Neither man had a Mae West on. Blood spouted in rhythmic arcs from Phil's head and washed in sheets down his face. His eyes lolled about in dazed bewilderment. Phil looked at the head bobbing across the debris field and registered that it was Louie. None of the other men had surfaced.

Louie saw one of the life rafts bobbing on the water. It was possible that the raft had been thrown loose by the disintegrating plane, but it was much more likely that the engineer, in the last act of his life, had yanked the raft-release handle just before the crash. The raft had inflated itself and was drifting away rapidly.

Louie knew that he had to get Phil's bleeding stopped, but if he went to him, the raft would be lost and all of them would perish. He swam for the raft. His clothing and shoes weighed him down, and the current and wind carried the raft away faster than he could swim. As it slipped farther and farther from reach, Louie gave up. He looked back at Phil and Mac, sharing the recognition that their chance was lost. Then he saw a long cord trailing off the raft, snaking not two feet from his face. He snatched the cord, reeled the raft to him, and climbed aboard. A second raft was sliding away. Louie pulled out his raft's oars, rowed as hard as he could, and just managed to catch the cord and pull the raft to him. He fed the cords through grommets in the rafts and tied them together.

He rowed to Phil and Mac. Realizing that the jagged hunk that he was clinging to might perforate the rafts, Phil pushed it away. Louie pulled Phil aboard, and Mac climbed up under his own power. Both men, like Louie, were filmy with fuel and oil. With all three of them in one raft, it was cramped; the raft was only about six feet long and a little more than two feet wide.

There were two gashes on the left side of Phil's forehead, by the hairline. Blood was spurting from the wounds and, mixed with seawater, sloshing in the bottom of the raft. Remembering what he had learned in Boy Scouts and his Honolulu first aid course, Louie ran his fingers down Phil's throat until he felt a pulse, the carotid artery. He showed Mac the spot and told him to press down. He pulled off his muslin top shirt and T-shirt and pulled Phil's shirts off as well. He asked Mac to do the same. Setting aside the top shirts, Louie dipped Phil's T-shirt in the water, folded it into a compress, and pressed it to the wounds. He took the other T-shirts and tied them tightly around Phil's head, then slid Phil into the second raft.

Phil's mind was woozy. He knew that he'd crashed, that someone had pulled him from the water, that he was in a raft, and that Louie was with him. He felt frightened, though not panicked. As the pilot, he was officially in command, but he grasped his situation well enough to know that he was in no condition to make decisions. He could see that Louie had a nasty cut on his finger, near his USC ring, but was otherwise unhurt and lucid. He asked Louie to take command, and Louie agreed.

"I'm glad it was you, Zamp," Phil said softly. Then he fell quiet.

From somewhere nearby, there was a small sound, a moan trailing off into a gargle, a mouth trying to form a word, a throat filling with water—then silence. Louie grabbed an oar and circled around as rapidly as he could, searching for the drowning man. Maybe it was Cuppernell, who hadn't been seen since he was deep underwater. They would never know. Whoever had made the sound had slipped under. He didn't come up again.

———

With Phil relatively stable, Louie turned his attention to the rafts. Made of two layers of canvas coated in rubber and divided into two air pockets bisected by a bulkhead, each was in good condition. The critical question regarded provisions. The provisions box, which Mac had been holding as the plane went down, was gone, either ripped from his hands during the crash or lost in his escape from the wreckage. In their pockets, the men had only wallets and a few coins. Their watches were still on their wrists, but the hands had stopped when the plane had hit the water. Probably for the first time since Phil had arrived in Oahu, Cecy's lucky bracelet wasn't on his wrist, and the silver dollar he'd been keeping for his reunion with her wasn't in his pocket. Maybe in the hurry to dress for the flight, he had forgotten them, or maybe they'd been lost in the crash.

Pockets in the rafts contained some survival provisions. Whatever was in them was all that they'd have. Louie untied the pocket flaps and looked inside. He found several thick chocolate bars—probably the Hershey Company's military-issue Ration D bars—divided into segments and packaged in wax-dipped containers to resist gas attack. Designed to be unpalatably bitter so soldiers would eat them only in dire circumstances, they were formulated to be highly caloric and melt-resistant. The package instructions said that each man was to be given two segments a day, one in the morning, one in the evening, to be held on the tongue and allowed to dissolve over thirty minutes.

With the chocolate, Louie found several half-pint tins of water, a brass mirror, a flare gun, sea dye, a set of fishhooks, a spool of fishing line, and two air pumps in canvas cases. There was also a set of pliers with a screwdriver built into the handle. Louie pondered it for a long while, trying to come up with a reason why someone would need a screwdriver or pliers on a raft. Each raft also had a patch kit, to be used if the raft leaked. That was all there was.

The provisions were grossly inadequate. One year later, each B-24 raft would be equipped with a sun tarpaulin for shade, blue on one side, yellow on the other. For camouflage in enemy waters, the tarpaulin could be spread blue side up; for signaling, the yellow side could be waved. Each standard 1944 raft would also be equipped with a bailing bucket, a mast and sail, a sea anchor, sun ointment, a first aid kit, puncture plugs, a flashlight, fishing tackle, a jackknife, scissors, a whistle, a compass, and religious pamphlets. None of these items, not even a knife, was in *Green Hornet*'s rafts. The rafts also had no "Gibson Girl," a radio transmitter that could send signals over some two hundred miles. Newer planes had been carrying them for nearly a year, and in two months, all planes would be equipped, but *Green Hornet* hadn't been furnished with one. And they had no navigation instruments. It had been Mitchell's job to strap them to his body, but if he had done so, the instruments had gone to the bottom with him.

Most worrisome was the water situation. A few half-pints wouldn't last them long. The men were surrounded by water, but they couldn't drink it. The salt content in seawater is so high that it is considered a poison. When a person drinks seawater, the kidneys must generate urine to flush the salt away, but to do so, they need more water than is contained in the seawater itself, so the body pulls water from its cells. Bereft of water, the cells begin to fail. Paradoxically, a drink of seawater causes potentially fatal dehydration.

Adrift near the equator with little water and no shelter, Phil, Louie, and Mac would soon be in dire trouble. The rafts hadn't been equipped with water desalinizing or distilling materials, nor did they have containers in which to catch rain. Five months earlier, General Hap Arnold had ordered that all life rafts be equipped with the Delano Sunstill, a device that could generate small amounts of drinking water indefinitely. Delivery had been delayed.

From the moment that he had come out of the water, Mac hadn't said a word. He had somehow escaped the crash without injury. He had done everything that Louie had asked of him, but his face had never lost its glazed, startled expression.

Louie was bent over the raft when Mac suddenly began wailing, "We're going to die!" Louie reassured him that the squadron would come for them, that they were likely to be found that night, at the latest the next day. Mac continued to shout. Louie, exasperated, threatened to report Mac when they returned. It had no effect. At his wits' end, Louie whacked Mac across the cheek with the back of his hand. Mac thumped back and fell silent.

Louie came up with ground rules. Each man would eat one square of chocolate in the morning, one in the evening. Louie allotted one water tin per man, with each man allowed two or three sips a day. Eating and drinking at this rate, they could stretch their supplies for a few days.

With inventory taken and rules established, there was nothing to do but wait. Louie made a deliberate effort to avoid thinking about the men who had died, and had to push away the memory of the gurgling voice in the water. Considering the crash, he was amazed that three men had survived. All three had been on the plane's right side; the fact that the plane had struck on its left had probably saved them. What mystified Louie was his escape from the wreckage. If he had passed out from the pressure, and the plane had continued to sink and the pressure to build, why had he woken again? And how had he been loosed from the wires while unconscious?

The men watched the sky. Louie kept his hand on Phil's head, stanching the bleeding. The last trace of *Green Hornet*, the shimmer of gas, hydraulic fluid, and oil that had wreathed the rafts since the crash, faded away. In its place, rising from below, came dark blue shapes, gliding in lithe arcs. A neat, sharp form, flat and shining, cut the surface and began tracing circles around the rafts. Another one joined it. The sharks had found them. Fluttering close to their sides were pilot fish, striped black and white.

The sharks, which Louie thought were of the mako and reef species, were so close that the men would only have to extend their hands to touch them. The smallest were about six feet long; some were double that size, twice the length of the rafts. They bent around the rafts, testing the fabric, dragging their fins along them, but not trying to get at the men on top. They seemed to be waiting for the men to come to them.

The sun sank, and it became sharply cold. The men used their hands to bail a few inches of water into each raft. Once their bodies warmed the water, they felt less chilled. Though exhausted, they fought the urge to sleep, afraid that a ship or submarine would pass and they'd miss it. Phil's lower body, under the water, was warm enough, but his upper body was so cold that he shook.

It was absolutely dark and absolutely silent, save for the chattering of Phil's teeth. The ocean was a flat calm. A rough, rasping tremor ran through the men. The sharks were rubbing their backs along the raft bottoms.

Louie's arm was still draped over the side of his raft, his hand resting on Phil's forehead. Under Louie's hand, Phil drifted to sleep, attended by the sensation of sharks scraping down the length of his back. In the next raft, Louie, too, fell asleep.

Mac was alone in his wakefulness, his mind spinning with fear. Grasping at an addled resolution, he began to stir.

Thirteen

Missing at Sea

DAISY MAE TOUCHED DOWN ON PALMYRA LATE THAT AF-
ternoon. The crew had searched for Corpening's plane all day
but had seen no trace of it. Deasy had dinner, then went to the base theater. He was watching the film when someone told him to report to the
base commander immediately. When he got there, he was told that
Green Hornet had never come in. "Holy smoke!" he said. He knew
that there were two possibilities. One was that Phillips's crew had
turned back to Hawaii; the other was that they were, as Deasy phrased
it, "in the drink." Someone went to check with Hawaii. Knowing that
if *Green Hornet* was indeed down, they'd still have to wait until morning to search, Deasy went to bed.

At around midnight, a sailor woke Deasy's radioman, Herman
Scearce, and told him that Phil's plane was missing. The navy wanted
to check Scearce's radio log to see when the last contact with the plane
was. Scearce asked the sailor to wake Deasy, and he, Deasy, and navy
officials reviewed the log at the base office. It yielded little information.

At four-thirty A.M., *Green Hornet* was declared missing. Two planes
were now down—Corpening's and Phillips's—taking twenty-one men
with them.

The navy assumed command of the rescue effort. Once the sun was up, *Daisy Mae* would be sent out, along with at least two navy flying boats and at least one other AAF plane. Because *Daisy Mae* and *Green Hornet* had flown side by side early in the journey, the searchers knew that *Green Hornet* had not crashed during the first two hundred miles of the trip. It had apparently gone down somewhere between the point at which *Daisy Mae* had left it and Palmyra, a stretch of eight hundred miles. The trick was figuring out the direction in which any survivors would be drifting. The ocean around Palmyra was a whorl of currents, lying at the meeting point of the westward-carrying north equatorial current and the eastward-carrying equatorial countercurrent. A few miles of difference in latitude could mean a 180-degree difference in current direction, and no one knew where the plane had hit. The search area would have to be enormous.

Each crew was given search coordinates. From Palmyra, *Daisy Mae* would fly north. From Oahu, several planes would fly south. Not long after sunup, the planes took off. Everyone knew that the odds of finding the crew were very long, but, said Scearce, "we kept hoping, hoping, hoping . . ."

———

Louie woke with the sun. Mac was beside him, lying back. Phil lay in his raft, his mind still fumbling. Louie sat up and ran his eyes over the sky and ocean in search of rescuers. Only the sharks stirred.

Louie decided to divvy up breakfast, a single square of chocolate. He untied the raft pocket and looked in. All of the chocolate was gone. He looked around the rafts. No chocolate, no wrappers. His gaze paused on Mac. The sergeant looked back at him with wide, guilty eyes.

The realization that Mac had eaten all of the chocolate rolled hard over Louie. In the brief time that Louie had known Mac, the tail gunner had struck him as a decent, friendly guy, although a bit of a reveler, confident to the point of flippancy. The crash had undone him. Louie knew that they couldn't survive for long without food, but he quelled the thought. A rescue search was surely under way. They'd be on Palmyra later today, maybe tomorrow, and the loss of the chocolate wouldn't matter. Curbing his irritation, Louie told Mac that he was disappointed in him. Understanding that Mac had acted in panic, he reassured him that they'd soon be rescued. Mac said nothing.

The chill of the night gave way to a sweltering day. Louie watched the sky. Phil, weak from blood loss, slept. Mac, a shade short of being a redhead, burned in the sun. He remained in a dreamy, distant place. All three men were hungry, but they could do nothing about it. The fishhooks and line were useless. There was no bait.

As the men lay in silence, a purring sound began drifting gently between their thoughts. Then all three realized that they were hearing a plane. Searching the sky, they saw a B-25, high up and well to the east. Flying much too high to be a search plane, it was probably on its way to Palmyra.

Louie lunged for the raft pocket, retrieved the flare gun, and loaded a flare cartridge. He couldn't stand in the soft-bottomed raft, so he tipped up onto his knees and raised the gun. He squeezed the trigger, the gun bucked in his hand, and the flare, roaring red, streaked up. As it shot overhead, Louie dug out a dye pack and shook it hurriedly into the water, and a pool of vivid greenish yellow bloomed over the ocean.

With the flare arcing over them, Louie, Phil, and Mac watched the bomber, willing the men aboard to see them. Slowly, the flare sputtered out. The bomber kept going, and then it was gone. The circle of color around the rafts faded away.

The sighting left the castaways with one important piece of information. They had known that they were drifting, but without points of reference, they hadn't known in which direction, or how fast. Since planes on the north-south passage from Hawaii followed a flight lane that ran close to *Green Hornet*'s crash site, the appearance of a B-25 far to the east almost certainly meant that the rafts were drifting west, away from the view of friendly planes. Their chances of rescue were already dimming.

That evening, the search planes turned back for their bases. No one had seen anything. They would be back in the air at first light.

Over the rafts, the daylight died. The men took sips of water, bailed seawater around themselves, and lay down. The sharks came to the rafts again to rub their backs on the undersides.

Phil slept for most of the next day. Louie sipped water and thought about food. Mac continued to hunker down, speaking little. For another day, rescue did not come.

It was sometime early the next morning, May 30, when Louie, Mac, and Phil heard a broad, deep rumble of B-24 engines, the sound of home. Then there it was, low and right overhead, a blunt-faced whale of a plane, heading southeast, plowing through the clouds, disappearing and reappearing. It was a search plane. It was so near the rafts that Louie thought he recognized the insignia of their squadron, the 42nd, on the plane's tail.

Louie grabbed the flare gun, loaded it, and fired. The flare shot straight at the bomber; for a moment, the men thought that it would hit the plane. But the flare missed, passing alongside the plane, making a fountain of red that looked huge from the raft. Louie reloaded and fired again. The plane turned sharply right. Louie fired two more flares, past the tail.

The plane was *Daisy Mae*. Its crewmen were straining their eyes at the ocean, passing a pair of binoculars between them. Searching was difficult that day, with loaves of clouds closing and parting, offering the men only brief glimpses of the sea. Everyone felt a particular urgency; the missing men were their squadron mates and friends. "If we ever looked for something on a mission," remembered Scearce, "that day we were looking."

The flares spent themselves, and *Daisy Mae* flew on. No one aboard saw anything. The plane's pivot had only been a routine turn. Louie, Phil, and Mac watched *Daisy Mae*'s twin tails grow smaller in the distance, then disappear.

For a moment, Louie felt furious with the airmen who had passed so close to them, yet had not seen them. But his anger soon cooled. From his days searching for missing planes, he knew how hard it was to see a raft, especially among clouds. For all he knew, he too had overlooked raft-bound men below him.

But what had probably been their best chance of rescue had been lost. With every hour, they were drifting farther west, away from the flight lanes. If they weren't found, the only way they could survive would be to get to land. To their west, they knew, there wasn't a single island for some two thousand miles.* If by some miracle they floated that far and were still alive, they might reach the Marshall Islands. If they veered a little south, they might reach the Gilberts. If they were lucky enough to drift to those islands, rather than passing by and out again into the open Pacific, they'd have another problem. Both sets of

---

* There was one spot directly west, about halfway to the Marshall Islands, where the ocean floor was just five feet below the surface. It was almost an island, but not quite.

islands belonged to the Japanese. Watching *Daisy Mae* fly away, Louie had a sinking feeling.

As the castaways watched their would-be rescuers disappear over the horizon, not far away, George "Smitty" Smith, who had sat up the night before the crash talking to Phil about Cecy, was piloting his B-24 over the ocean, searching for any sign of the lost men. About fifty miles short of Barbers Point, a base on the leeward side of Oahu, his crew spotted something. Spiraling in for a closer look, Smitty saw a muddle of yellow rectangular boxes, jostling on the surface. Large fish were circling them.

The boxes had not come from *Green Hornet*. They were too close to Oahu to have traveled that far, especially as the currents wouldn't have carried them in that direction. But Corpening's plane had probably gone down somewhere along the north-south flight lane, the lane over which Smitty was searching. The boxes may well have been the last remains of Corpening's plane, and the men aboard it.

The boxes weren't the only sighting that Smitty had that day. In the same region where *Green Hornet* had crashed, he spotted a shock yellow object bobbing in the water. He swung his bomber down toward it. It appeared to be a provisions box, like the ones carried on B-24s, but he wasn't sure. Smitty flew loops around the box for fifteen minutes. There was nothing anywhere near it: no debris, no rafts, no men. Smitty probably believed that he was looking at a piece of Phil's plane, and if he did, he was probably right. He flew back to Oahu, thinking of his friend Cecy and all the pain she would feel when she learned that her fiancé was missing.

On Oahu, the men of the 42nd squadron were losing hope. "Cuppernell, Phillips, Zamperini (the Olympic miler), and Mitchell, lost, on their way to Palmyra," a ground crewman wrote in his diary. "I find it hard to get used to such a thing. Just the other day I drove them all to Kahuku and around—kidded around with them but now they're probably dead! The other pilots act as though nothing has happened and speak of sending the other fellow's clothes home as though it were an everyday occurrence. That's the way it has to be played because that's the way it is—it's an everyday occurrence!"

The castaways' bodies were declining. Other than Mac's feast on the chocolate bars, none of them had eaten since their early morning breakfast before their last flight. They were intensely thirsty and hungry. After the B-24 sighting, they spent another frigid night, then a long fourth day. There were no planes, no ships, no submarines. Each man drank the last drops of his water.

Sometime on the fifth day, Mac snapped. After having said almost nothing for days, he suddenly began screaming that they were going to die. Wild-eyed and raving, he couldn't stop shouting. Louie slapped him across the face. Mac abruptly went silent and lay down, appearing strangely contented. Maybe he was comforted by Louie's assertion of control, protected thereby from the awful possibilities that his imagination hung before him.

Mac had good reason to lose faith. Their water was gone. After the B-24 had passed over, no more planes had come, and the current was carrying them far from the paths trafficked by friendly aircraft. If the search for them hadn't been called off, the men knew, it soon would be.

That night, before he tried to sleep, Louie prayed. He had prayed only once before in his life, in childhood, when his mother was sick and he had been filled with a rushing fear that he would lose her. That night on the raft, in words composed in his head, never passing his lips, he pleaded for help.

As the lost men drifted farther and farther out of reach, their last letters reached their families and friends, who did not yet know that they were missing. It was apparently military policy to wait for initial searches to be conducted before informing loved ones.

On the day after the crash, Phil's final letter to his father arrived in Virginia. Reverend Phillips—who called his son by his middle name, Allen—had joined the army and was now Chaplain Phillips at Camp Pickett. The last news of Allen had reached him weeks earlier, in newspaper stories about *Super Man*'s saga over Nauru. Chaplain Phillips had carried clippings about the raid to the offices of a local newspaper, which had run a story on Allen's heroism. As proud as he was, Chaplain Phillips was also frightened. "I sure hope that is the closest call he ever has," he wrote to his daughter.

It was probably this fear that had led Chaplain Phillips to write to Allen to ask about the fate of the raft-bound men his crew had found, encircled by sharks, that spring. In his last letter to his father, Allen was reassuring: The men were all safe. As for himself, Allen wrote, "I'm still in the same place I have been . . . I'll write again soon. So long for now. —Al."

On the weekend after the crash, Pete, Virginia, and Louise Zamperini made an impromptu visit to the home of Cuppernell's parents, who lived in Long Beach. It was a merry meeting, and they all talked of their boys. After the visit, Pete wrote to Louie, asking him to tell Cuppernell that his parents were doing great. Before sealing the envelope, he tucked in a photo of himself, smiling. On the back, he had scribbled an inscription: "Don't let 'em clip your wings."

In Saranap, California, Payton Jordan opened the letter that Louie had tossed out the window of *Green Hornet* as the plane taxied for its last takeoff. "Dear Payton and Marge," it read. "I am still alive and kickin around, why I don't know."

That little turkey'd better take care of himself, Jordan thought.

Phil's last letter to Cecy reached her in Princeton, Indiana, where she was finishing her first year as a high school teacher. In his letter, Phil had written of the moon over Hawaii and how it reminded him of the last time he was with her. "I never will forget that time I spent there with you. There are a lot of things which I'll never forget while I was with you, sweet—I'm waiting for the day when we can begin doing things together again as we used to do." He had closed this letter as he had so many others: "I love you, I love you, I love you."

No more messages would come from the lost men. Pete's letter to Louie made its way to the postmaster in San Francisco, where the 11th Bomb Group's mail was sorted. Someone wrote *Missing at sea* on the outside and dropped it back in the mail to Pete.

———

A week had passed since *Green Hornet* had vanished. Intensive searching had yielded nothing. Every man on Phil's crew was officially declared missing, and in Washington, the process of informing family members was set in motion. The men from *Daisy Mae* were told to return the plane from Palmyra to Oahu. The search had been abandoned. The crew was dejected—they wanted to go on looking. As they flew back to Oahu, they talked of the lost men.

At Kualoa, a second lieutenant named Jack Krey walked into the cottage to perform the grim duty of cataloging the men's things and sending them to their families. Louie's room was mostly as it had been when Louie had walked out that Thursday morning: clothes, a footlocker, a diary that ended with a few words about a rescue mission, a pinup of actress Esther Williams on the wall. The note that Louie had left on the locker was gone, as was the liquor. Among Louie's things, Krey found photographs that Louie had taken inside his plane. In some of them, Louie had forgotten to aim the camera away from the Norden bombsight, so Krey had to confiscate those. The rest of Louie's belongings were packed into his footlocker and readied to be sent to Torrance.

———

On the evening of Friday, June 4, 1943, Phil's mother, Kelsey, was in Princeton, Indiana. In the absence of her husband and son, she had sold the family house in Terre Haute and moved to Princeton to be closer to her daughter, Martha, and future daughter-in-law, Cecy, with whom she had become dear friends. That evening, when Kelsey was visiting Martha, someone brought her a telegram:

> I REGRET TO INFORM YOU THAT THE COMMANDING GENERAL
> PACIFIC AREA REPORTS YOUR SON—FIRST LIEUTENANT RUSSELL A
> PHILLIPS—MISSING SINCE MAY TWENTY-SEVEN. IF FURTHER
> DETAILS OR OTHER INFORMATION OF HIS STATUS ARE RECIEVED
> YOU WILL BE PROMPTLY NOTIFIED

The telegram reached the Zamperinis that same evening. Louise called Sylvia, who had recently married a firefighter, Harvey Flammer, and now lived in a nearby suburb with her husband. Upon hearing that her brother was missing, Sylvia became hysterical, sobbing so loudly that her neighbor ran to her. When the neighbor asked her what was wrong, Sylvia was crying too hard to speak. Eventually she pulled herself together enough to call Harvey at the fire station. She was frantic and confused and didn't know what to do. Harvey told her to go to her mother. Sylvia put the phone down and ran straight out the door.

Sylvia sobbed for the entire forty-five-minute drive. Weeks before, just after the Nauru raid, she had picked up her morning paper and seen, on the front page, a photograph of Louie, looking haunted, staring through a gaping hole in the side of *Super Man*. The image had horrified her. Now, as she absorbed the news that Louie was missing, she couldn't stop seeing that image. When she pulled up at her parents' house, she had to compose herself before she walked in.

Her father was calm but quiet; her mother was consumed in anguish. Sylvia, who, like the rest of the family, assumed that Louie had gone down in the ocean, told her mother not to worry. "With all those islands," Sylvia said, "he's teaching someone hula." Pete arrived from San Diego. "If he has a toothbrush and a pocket knife and he hits land," he told his mother, "he'll make it."

Perhaps that day, or perhaps later, Louise found the tiny snapshot that had been taken on the afternoon Louie had left, when he had stood beside her on her front steps, his arm around her waist. On the back of the photograph, Louise wrote, *Louis Reported missing   May 27, 1943.*

The news of Louie's disappearance headlined California newspapers and led radio broadcasts on June 5. The *Los Angeles Evening Herald and Express* ran a feature on the "Life of Zamp," which looked an awful lot like an obituary. Payton Jordan, now a navy officer, was driving to his base when he heard the news on the radio. Jordan gasped. He drove into the base feeling numb, and for a while did nothing at all. Then he started speaking to his fellow officers. Jordan's job was to train cadets in survival techniques, and he and the others considered the possibilities that might face Louie. All of the officers agreed that if Louie had the right training, he might survive.

Pete called Jordan, and they talked about Louie. As Pete spoke of his hope that Louie would be found, Jordan could hear his voice wavering. Jordan thought about calling Louie's parents, but he couldn't bring himself to do it. He had no idea what to say. That evening, he drove home and told his wife, Marge, who had known Louie well at USC. They moved through their routines in a quiet fog, then went to bed and lay awake, in silence.

In Torrance, Anthony Zamperini remained stoic. Louise cried and prayed. From the stress, open sores broke out all over her hands. Sylvia thought her hands looked like raw hamburger.

Somewhere in those jagged days, a fierce conviction came over Louise. She was absolutely certain that her son was alive.

On Samoa, Stanley Pillsbury and Clarence Douglas were still in the hospital, trying to recover from the wounds incurred over Nauru. Douglas's shoulder was far from healed, and to Pillsbury, he seemed emotionally gutted. Pillsbury was in considerable pain. The doctors had been unable to remove all of the shrapnel from his leg, and he could feel every shard, burning. He wasn't close to being able to walk. In his dreams, planes dove at him, endlessly.

Pillsbury was in his bed when Douglas came in, his face radiating shock.

"The crew went down," he said.

Pillsbury could barely speak. His first emotion was overwhelming guilt. "If I had only been there," he said later, "I could have saved it."

Douglas and Pillsbury said little more to each other. They parted, each man swimming in grief. Douglas would soon be granted transfer back to the States. Pillsbury would linger on his cot in Samoa, hoping that he would one day walk again.*

On Oahu, Louie's friends gathered in a barracks. In the corner of one of the rooms, they hung a small flag in memory of Zamp. It would hang there as Louie, Phil, and Mac drifted west and the Allies, the 11th Bomb Group's 42nd squadron among them, carried the war across the Pacific and into the throat of Japan.

---

* As soon as he could walk, Pillsbury was assigned to a new crew to replace a dead waist gunner. Superstitious about adding a new man, the crew received him coldly. On a mission, a Zero tried to ram the plane, and one of its rounds exploded inside the fuselage. The engineer found Pillsbury on the floor with a hunk of metal embedded just above his eye, the white of which was clouding with blood. The plane made a hasty landing, and Pillsbury was bandaged up and sent back to his gun. Somehow, Pillsbury survived the war, a fistful of medals and a permanent limp testifying to all he'd endured. "It was awful, awful, awful," he said through tears sixty years later. ". . . If you dig into it, it comes back to you. That's the way war is."

Fourteen

Thirst

PHIL FELT AS IF HE WERE ON FIRE. THE EQUATORIAL SUN LAY upon the men, scalding their skin. Their upper lips burned and cracked, ballooning so dramatically that they obstructed their nostrils, while their lower lips bulged against their chins. Their bodies were slashed with open cracks that formed under the corrosive onslaught of sun, salt, wind, and fuel residue. Whitecaps slapped into the fissures, a sensation that Louie compared to having alcohol poured onto a wound. Sunlight glared off the ocean, sending barbs of white light into the men's pupils and leaving their heads pounding. The men's feet were cratered with quarter-sized salt sores. The rafts baked along with their occupants, emitting a bitter smell.

The water cans were empty. Desperately thirsty and overheated, the men could do no more than use their hands to bail seawater over themselves. The coolness of the ocean beckoned and couldn't be answered, for the sharks circled. One shark, six or eight feet long, stalked the rafts without rest, day and night. The men became especially wary of him, and when he ventured too close, one of them would jab him with an oar.

On the third day without water, a smudge appeared on the horizon. It grew, darkened, billowed over the rafts, and lidded the sun. Down came the rain. The men threw back their heads, spilled their bodies back, spread their arms, and opened their mouths. The rain fell on their chests, lips, faces, tongues. It soothed their skin, washed the salt and sweat and fuel from their pores, slid down their throats, fed their bodies. It was a sensory explosion.

They knew it wouldn't last. They had to find a way to save the water. The narrow water tins, opened to the downpour, caught virtually nothing. Louie, keeping his head tipped up and his mouth open, felt around the raft for something better. He dug into the raft pockets and pulled out one of the air pumps. It was sheathed in a canvas case about fourteen inches long, stitched down one side. He tore the seam open, spread the fabric to form a triangular bowl, and watched happily as the rain pooled on the fabric.

He had collected some two pints of water when a whitecap cracked into the raft, crested over, and slopped into the canvas, spoiling the water. Not only had the most productive part of the storm been wasted, but the canvas had to be rinsed in the rain before Louie could resume capturing water. Even when that was done, there was no way to avoid the next whitecap, because Louie couldn't see them coming.

Louie tried a new technique. Instead of allowing large pools of water to gather, he began continuously sucking the captured water into his mouth, then spitting it in the cans. Once the cans were full, he kept harvesting the rain, giving one man a drink every thirty seconds or so. They tore open the second pump case to form another rain catcher. When the sun emerged, they found that the canvas cases also made excellent hats. They began rotations with them, two men in, one man out.

The men were ravenous. It was now clear that Mac's binge on the chocolate, which had seemed only moderately worrisome at the time, was a catastrophe. Louie resented Mac, and Mac seemed to know it. Though Mac never spoke of it, Louie sensed that he was consumed with guilt over what he had done.

As hunger bleated inside them, the men experienced a classic symptom of starvation, the inability to direct their thoughts away from food. They stared into the ocean, undulating with edible creatures; but without bait, they couldn't catch even a minnow. Occasionally, a bird passed, always out of reach. The men studied their shoes and wondered if they could eat the leather. They decided that they couldn't.

Days passed. Each evening, the roasting heat gave way to cold.

Sleep was elusive. Phil, alone in his raft and lacking the heat of another man to warm the water around him, suffered particularly badly. He shook through each night, too cold to sleep. In the daytime, exhaustion, heat, and the lolling of the raft made all of them drowsy. They slept through much of each day and spent the rest lying back, saving their precious, evaporating energy.

It occurred to Phil that from the point of view of the birds, their still forms, obscured by canvas hoods, must have looked like lifeless debris. He was right. One day, nine or ten days into their odyssey, Louie felt something alight on his hood, and saw its shadow fall before him. It was an albatross. With Louie's head hidden, the bird hadn't recognized that he was landing on a man.

Slowly, slowly, Louie raised his hand toward the bird, his motion so gradual that it was little more noticeable than the turning of a minute hand on a clock. The bird rested calmly. In time, Louie's hand was beside the bird, his fingers open. All at once, Louie snapped his hand shut, clamping down on the bird's legs. The bird pecked frantically, slashing his knuckles. Louie grabbed its head and broke its neck.

Louie used the pliers to tear the bird open. A gust of fetid odor rose from the body, and all three men recoiled. Louie handed a bit of meat to Phil and Mac and took one for himself. The stench hung before them, spurring waves of nausea. Gagging, they couldn't get the meat into their mouths. Eventually, they gave up.

Though they couldn't eat the bird, they finally had bait. Louie took out the fishing gear, tied a small hook to a line, baited it, and fed it into the water. In a moment, a shark cruised by, bit down on the hook, and severed the line, taking the bait, the hook, and a foot or two of line with him. Louie tried with another hook, and again, a shark took it. A third try produced the same result. Finally, the sharks let a hook hang unmolested. Louie felt a tug and pulled up the line. On its end hung a slender pilot fish, about ten inches long. As Louie pulled it apart, everyone felt apprehensive. None of them had eaten raw fish before. They each put a bit of meat into their mouths. It was flavorless. They ate it down to the bones.

It was the first food to cross their lips in more than a week. Between three men, a small fish didn't go far, but the protein gave them a push of energy. Louie had demonstrated that if they were persistent and resourceful, they could catch food, and both he and Phil felt inspired. Only Mac remained unchanged.

Phil felt uneasy about the albatross. Like many schoolboys of his era, he had read Samuel Taylor Coleridge's "Rime of the Ancient Mariner." In the poem, a sailor kills a friendly albatross that, it is said, had made the winds blow. In consequence, the sailor and his crew are stranded in infernal, windless waters, tormented by thirst and monstrous creatures. The crewmen all die, and the sailor is left in a hellish limbo, the albatross hung about his neck, his eyes closed against the accusing stares of his dead crewmen.

Louie wasn't superstitious, but he'd grown fond of albatrosses on that Christmas he'd spent watching them crash-land on Midway. He felt sorry for the bird. Phil reminded Louie that killing an albatross was said to bring bad luck. After a plane crash, Louie replied, what more bad luck could they have?

———

Several more days passed. Louie caught nothing, and his hook supply dwindled. No more birds landed on the raft. Periodically, rain replenished the water tins, but only partway.

The men floated in a sensory vacuum. When the weather was calm, the ocean was silent. There was nothing to touch but water, skin, hair, and canvas. Other than the charred smell of the raft, there were no odors. There was nothing to look at but sky and sea. At some point, Louie stuck his finger in his ear and felt wax there. He smelled his finger, and by virtue of being new, the scent of the wax was curiously refreshing. He developed a habit of twisting his finger in his ear and sniffing it. Phil began doing it too.

When Louie slept, he dreamed of being on land, trying to sleep, but there was never a place to rest safely—only rocks, sucking mud, beds of cactus. He would be on perilous cliffs or unstable boulders, and the ground would heave and shift under his weight. Phil was having the same dreams.

As time passed, Phil began thinking about an article, written by the World War I ace pilot Eddie Rickenbacker, that he had read in _Life_ magazine that winter. The previous October, a B-17 carrying Rickenbacker and a crew over the Pacific had become lost and run out of fuel. The pilot had ditched the plane, and it had floated long enough for the men to get into rafts. The men had drifted for weeks, surviving on stores in the rafts, rainwater, fish, and bird meat. One man had died, and the rest had hallucinated, babbling at invisible companions, singing bizarre songs, arguing about where to pull over the imaginary car in which they were riding. One lieutenant had been visited by a specter who had tried to lure him to the bottom of the ocean. Finally, the rafts had split up, and one had reached an island. Natives had radioed to Funafuti, and the other men had been rescued.

It seemed that Rickenbacker's crew had stretched the capacity for human survival as far as it would go. Rickenbacker had written that he had drifted for twenty-one days (he had actually drifted for twenty-four), and Phil, Louie, and Mac believed that this was a survival record. In fact, the record for inflated raft survival appears to have been set in 1942, when three navy plane crash victims survived for thirty-four days on the Pacific before reaching an island, where they were sheltered by natives.*

At first, Phil gave no thought to counting days, but when time stretched on, he began paying attention to how long they'd been out there. He had no trouble counting days without confusion; because they were on the raft for only part of the day they crashed, Phil and Louie counted the following day as day 1. With each new day, Phil told himself that surely they'd be picked up before reaching Rickenbacker's mark. When he considered what they'd do if they passed that mark, he had no answer.

Rickenbacker's story, familiar to Louie also, was important for another reason. Exposure, dehydration, stress, and hunger had quickly driven many of Rickenbacker's party insane, a common fate for raft-bound men. Louie was more concerned about sanity than he was about sustenance. He kept thinking of a college physiology class he had taken, in which the instructor had taught them to think of the mind as a muscle that would atrophy if left idle. Louie was determined that no matter what happened to their bodies, their minds would stay under their control.

Within a few days of the crash, Louie began peppering the other two with questions on every conceivable subject. Phil took up the challenge, and soon he and Louie turned the raft into a nonstop quiz show. They shared their histories, from first memories onward, recounted in minute detail. Louie told of his days at USC; Phil spoke of Indiana. They recalled the best dates they'd ever had. They told and retold sto-

---

* In 1942, Poon Lim survived for 133 days alone on a raft after his ship was sunk by a German submarine. Lim's feat was a record, but his vessel was a large, wood-and-metal "Carley float boat" raft, equipped with ten gallons of water, a fair amount of food, an electric torch, and other supplies.

ries of practical jokes that they'd played on each other. Every answer was followed by a question. Phil sang church hymns; Louie taught the other two the lyrics to "White Christmas." They sang it over the ocean, a holiday song in June, heard only by circling sharks.

Every conversation meandered back to food. Louie had often boasted to Phil about his mother's cooking, and at some point, Phil asked Louie to describe how she made a meal. Louie began describing a dish, and all three men found it satisfying, so Louie kept going, telling them about each dish in the greatest possible detail. Soon, Louise's kitchen floated there with them: Sauces simmered, spices were pinched and scattered, butter melted on tongues.

So began a thrice-daily ritual on the raft, with pumpkin pie and spaghetti being the favorite subjects. The men came to know Louise's recipes so well that if Louie skipped a step or forgot an ingredient, Phil, and sometimes Mac, would quickly correct him and make him start over. When the imaginary meal was prepared, the men would devour every crumb, describing each mouthful. They conjured up the scene in such vivid detail that somehow their stomachs were fooled by it, if only briefly.

Once the food was eaten and the past exhausted, they moved to the future. Louie laid plans to buy the Torrance train depot and turn it into a restaurant. Phil fantasized about getting back to Indiana, maybe to teach school. He couldn't wait to see the Indy 500 again. The race had been suspended because of the war, but Phil revived it in his mind, spreading a blanket on the infield grass, heaping it with food, and watching the cars blur past. And he thought about Cecy. It hadn't occurred to him to tuck her picture in his wallet before he left the cottage, but in his mind, she never left him.

For Louie and Phil, the conversations were healing, pulling them out of their suffering and setting the future before them as a concrete thing. As they imagined themselves back in the world again, they willed a happy ending onto their ordeal and made it their expectation. With these talks, they created something to live for.

In all of these bull sessions, not once did they broach the subject of the crash. Louie wanted to talk about it, but something about Phil stopped him. There were times when Phil seemed lost in troubled thoughts, and Louie guessed that he was reliving the crash, and perhaps holding himself responsible for the deaths of his men. Louie wanted to reassure Phil that he'd done nothing wrong, but he decided that raising the issue would deepen Phil's preoccupation. So he said nothing.

———

As Louie and Phil grilled each other, Mac usually sat in silence. Sometimes he'd ask Louie to describe a recipe, and occasionally he would interject, but getting him to fully participate was rough going. He shared few memories, and though the other two encouraged him, he couldn't imagine a future. To him, it seemed, the world was too far gone.

Given the dismal record of raft-bound men, Mac's despair was reasonable. What is remarkable is that the two men who shared Mac's plight didn't share his hopelessness. Though Phil was constantly wondering how long this would go on, it had not yet occurred to him that he might die. The same was true for Louie. Though they both knew that they were in an extremely serious situation, both had the ability to warn fear away from their thoughts, focusing instead on how to survive and reassuring themselves that things would work out.

It remains a mystery why these three young men, veterans of the same training and the same crash, differed so radically in their perceptions of their plight. Maybe the difference was biological; some men may be wired for optimism, others for doubt. As a toddler, Louie had leapt from a train and watched it bear his family away, yet had remained cheerfully unconcerned about his safety, suggesting that he may have been a born optimist. Perhaps the men's histories had given them opposing convictions about their capacity to overcome adversity. Phil and Louie had survived Funafuti and performed uncommonly well over Nauru, and each trusted the other. "If there was one thing left, he'd a given it to me," Phil once said of Louie. Mac had never seen combat, didn't know these officers, and was largely an unknown quantity to himself. All he knew about his ability to cope with this crisis was that on the first night, he had panicked and eaten the only food they had. As time passed and starvation loomed, this act took on greater and greater importance, and it may have fed Mac's sense of futility.

For Phil, there was another source of strength, one of which even Louie was unaware. According to his family, in his quiet, private way, Phil was a deeply religious man, carrying a faith instilled in him by his parents. "I had told Al several times before to always do his best as he knew how to do it," Phil's father once wrote, "and when things get beyond his skill and ability to ask the Lord to step in and help out." Phil never spoke of his faith, but as he sang hymns over the ocean, conjuring up a protective God, perhaps rescue felt closer, despair more distant.

From earliest childhood, Louie had regarded every limitation placed on him as a challenge to his wits, his resourcefulness, and his determination to rebel. The result had been a mutinous youth. As maddening as his exploits had been for his parents and his town, Louie's success in carrying them off had given him the conviction that he could think his way around any boundary. Now, as he was cast into extremity, despair and death became the focus of his defiance. The same attributes that had made him the boy terror of Torrance were keeping him alive in the greatest struggle of his life.

Though all three men faced the same hardship, their differing perceptions of it appeared to be shaping their fates. Louie and Phil's hope displaced their fear and inspired them to work toward their survival, and each success renewed their physical and emotional vigor. Mac's resignation seemed to paralyze him, and the less he participated in their efforts to survive, the more he slipped. Though he did the least, as the days passed, it was he who faded the most. Louie and Phil's optimism, and Mac's hopelessness, were becoming self-fulfilling.

———

Two weeks had passed. The men's skin was burned, swollen, and cracked. Mysterious white lines striped their fingernails and toenails, and salt sores were marching up their legs, buttocks, and backs. The rafts were decomposing in the sun and salt water, bleeding vivid yellow dye onto the men's clothing and skin and making everything sticky.

The men's bodies slowly winnowed. Each day, Louie noticed incremental differences in his weight, and the weight of his raftmates, from the day before: the pants looser, the faces narrower. As they passed the fortnight mark, they began to look grotesque. Their flesh had evaporated. Their cheeks, now bearded, had sunken into concavity. Their bodies were digesting themselves.

They were reaching a stage of their ordeal that for other castaways had been a gruesome turning point. In 1820, after the whaling ship *Essex* was sunk by an enraged whale, the lifeboat-bound survivors, on the brink of death, resorted to cannibalism. Some sixty years later, after nineteen days adrift, starving survivors of the sunken yacht *Mignonette* killed and ate a teenaged crewman. Stories of cannibalism among castaways were so common that the British gave a name to the practice of choosing a victim, dubbing it the "custom of the sea." To well-fed men on land, the idea of cannibalism has always inspired revulsion. To many sailors who have stood on the threshold of death, lost in the agony and mind-altering effects of starvation, it has seemed a reasonable, even inescapable solution.

For Louie, the idea of consuming a human being was revolting and unthinkable. To eat a human being, even if the person had died naturally, would be abhorrent for him. All three men held the same conviction. Cannibalism wouldn't be considered, then or ever.

The two-week mark was a different kind of turning point for Louie. He began to pray aloud. He had no idea how to speak to God, so he recited snippets of prayers that he'd heard in movies. Phil bowed his head as Louie spoke, offering "Amen" at the end. Mac only listened.

The rafts slid on the current, their tethers snaking behind them. It seemed that they were still drifting west, but without any points of reference, the men weren't sure. At least they were going somewhere.

————

The second albatross fluttered onto Louie's head sometime around the fourteenth day. Again Louie slowly raised his hand, snatched it, and killed it. The men sat there looking at it, remembering the stench of the first albatross. When Louie opened it up, they were happily surprised to find that it didn't smell that bad. Still, no one wanted to eat it. Louie portioned the meat and insisted that everyone eat. All three men forced the meat down. Because Mac seemed to need food the most, they gave him all of the blood.

In the bird's stomach they found several small fish, which they decided to use as bait, and with them, Louie caught one more fish. He saved some of the bird meat for bait and set the bones out to dry in hopes that they might be useful as fishhooks.

————

Time spun out endlessly. Louie caught a few fish, once parlaying a tiny one, thrown into the raft by a whitecap, into bait that yielded a comparatively fat pilot fish. Rains came intermittently, leaving the men sucking up every drop that fell into their rain catchers. Louie and Phil took turns leading prayers each night. Mac remained in his own world.

The men grew thinner. Phil was gradually regaining his strength after his initial state of concussed exhaustion; Mac's body grew weaker, following his broken spirit. Then the rains stopped and the water tins dried up. They reached day twenty-one. They caught a fish and had a little celebration for passing what they thought was Rickenbacker's mark.

For some time, Louie had noticed a stomach-turning reek wafting to and fro over them. It was coming from Phil's head. The blood on his T-shirt bandage was rotting, and cakes of it were chipping off and falling into the raft. Phil couldn't smell it, but Louie couldn't bear it. Louie untied the T-shirt and gently unwrapped it. Beneath a thick cake of dried blood, the wounds had knit neatly. The bleeding didn't resume. The T-shirt could go.

A few days later, Louie saw something bizarre. The edge of the sea, flush to the horizon, was peeling upward. A vast black rim formed, rose up, and began speeding toward them with a tumbling motion. Louie shouted a warning and the other two men wheeled around toward it. They dropped down, getting their weight as low as possible so they wouldn't be flipped over. As the wave closed in, they braced themselves.

Just as the wave reached them, they realized it wasn't a wave at all. It was a giant school of dolphins, swimming with astonishing speed. The dolphins rushed at the rafts and were soon muscling all around them. Looking into the water, Phil saw small fish, thousands of them, seeming to fill the ocean. The dolphins were chasing them. The men thrust their arms into the water and tried to grab some, but the fish slipped through their fingers. If they had had a net, they could have whisked it through the water and filled the rafts. But with only their fingers, they couldn't snare even one.

Louie was out of bait. Other than the sharks, the only fish that ventured near the rafts were pilot fish, which hugged the sides of the sharks as they circled. They were within easy reach, only when Louie tried to grab them, they squirted away. The sharks had stolen every hook small enough to fit in the mouths of pilot fish, so Louie tried albatross bones, but the fish spat them out.

Looking at the fish line that he had left, he got an idea. He cut off small portions of line, tied them to the large fishhooks, and then tied three hooks to the fingers of one hand, one on his pinkie, one on his middle finger, one on his thumb, orienting them as if they were claws. He held his hand over the water's surface and waited.

A shark, attended by a pilot fish, swam by. Once its head had passed, Louie sank his hand into the water. When the unsuspecting pilot fish moved under his hand, he snapped his fingers shut around its back. The hooks dug in. Louie yanked the fish out of the water, jubilant.

Sometime that week, a small tern landed on the wall of the raft, right between the men. It was closest to Phil, and without speaking, the men indicated to each other that he'd catch it. Phil clapped down on the bird. It was tiny, and offered little meat, but not long after, another tern settled on the raft. This time, Mac caught it. Louie was so famished that he went at it with his teeth, ripping the feathers loose and spitting them out in whuffs. Almost immediately, he felt a crawling sensation on his chin. The tern had been covered in lice, which were now hopping over his face.

Something about the tickle of lice on his skin rattled Louie more than anything he had yet encountered. He began scratching and rubbing at his face, but he couldn't get at the lice, which had burrowed into his beard and were moving up his head and into his hair. He pitched his upper body into the water. Phil and Mac, realizing that Louie was going to get his head ripped off, grabbed the oars and bumped the sharks away while Louie splashed about, trying to drown the lice. After about half a dozen dunks, the tickle was gone.

As the days passed, the men caught three, perhaps four more birds. One bird kept dipping low over the raft, then soaring off again. Mac suddenly shot his hand up and snagged the bird by the leg in midair, then handed the squirming animal to Louie, who was amazed at Mac's alacrity. The men ate every morsel of the bird, and every other bird that they caught, leaving only feathers and bones.

————

For days, Louie lay over the side of the raft, fishhooks tied to his fingers, trying to catch another pilot fish. He caught none. The water ran out again, and the thirst was agonizing. Day after day passed with no rain. Twice, the men rowed toward distant squalls, but each time, the rain sputtered out just as they reached it, leaving them exhausted and demoralized. When the next squall inched along the horizon, none of them had the strength to chase it.

The intense thirst and overheating drove Phil to do something almost suicidal. He waited for the sharks to wander a short distance away, then pulled himself overboard. Louie and Mac knelt near him, jabbing at sharks with the oars as Phil hung on the raft, savoring the cool water and swishing big mouthfuls of it over his tongue before spitting them out. He only just had the strength to drag himself back in. Since Phil had gotten away with it, the other two thought it worth a try, and took their turns in the water. The men were able to keep the sharks away long enough for all three to have a dip.

On the sixth day without water, the men recognized that they weren't going to last much longer. Mac was failing especially quickly.

They bowed their heads together as Louie prayed. If God would quench their thirst, he vowed, he'd dedicate his life to him.

The next day, by divine intervention or the fickle humors of the tropics, the sky broke open and rain poured down. Twice more the water ran out, twice more they prayed, and twice more the rain came. The showers gave them just enough water to last a short while longer. If only a plane would come.

Fifteen

Sharks and Bullets

ON THE MORNING OF THE TWENTY-SEVENTH DAY, A PLANE came.

It began with a rumble of engines, and then a spot in the sky. It was a twin-engine bomber, moving west at a brisk clip. It was so far away that expending the flares and dye was questionable. The men conferred and voted. They decided to take a shot.

Louie fired one flare, reloaded, then fired a second, drawing vivid lines across the sky. He opened a dye container and spilled its contents into the ocean, then dug out the mirror and angled a square of light toward the bomber.

The men waited, hoping. The plane grew smaller, then faded away.

As the castaways slumped in the rafts, trying to accept another lost chance, over the western horizon there was a glimmer, tracing a wide curve, then banking toward the rafts. The bomber was coming back. Weeping with joy, Louie, Phil, and Mac tugged their shirts over their heads and snapped them back and forth in the air, calling out. The bomber leveled off, skimming over the water. Louie squinted at the cockpit. He made out two silhouettes, a pilot and copilot. He thought of Palmyra, food, solid ground underfoot.

And then, all at once, the ocean erupted. There was a deafening noise, and the rafts began hopping and shuddering under the castaways. The gunners were firing at them.

Louie, Phil, and Mac clawed for the raft walls and threw themselves overboard. They swam under the rafts and huddled there, watching bullets tear through the rafts and cut bright slits in the water around them. Then the firing stopped.

The men surfaced. The bomber had overshot them and was now to the east, moving away. Two sharks were nosing around. The men had to get out of the water immediately.

Clinging to the side of Louie and Mac's raft, Phil was completely done in. The leap into the water had taken everything that was left in him. He floundered, unable to pull himself over the raft wall. Louie swam up behind him and gave him a push, and Phil slopped up on board. Mac, too, needed Louie's help to climb over the wall. Louie then dragged himself up, and the three sat there, stunned but uninjured. They couldn't believe that the airmen, mistaking them for Japanese, would strafe unarmed castaways. Under them, the raft felt doughy. It was leaking air.

In the distance, the bomber swung around and began flying at the rafts again. Louie hoped that the crew had realized the mistake and was returning to help them. Flying about two hundred feet over the water, the bomber raced at them, following a path slightly parallel to the rafts, so that its side passed into view. All three men saw it at once. Behind the wing, painted over the waist, was a red circle. The bomber was Japanese.

Louie saw the gunners taking aim and knew he had to go back in the water. Phil and Mac didn't move. They were both exhausted. They knew that if they went overboard again, they wouldn't be strong enough to get back in, and the sharks would take them. If they stayed on the raft, it seemed impossible that the gunners could miss them.

As the bomber flew toward them, they lay down. Phil pulled his knees to his chest and covered his head in his hands. Mac balled himself up beside him. Louie took a last glance at them, then dropped into the water and swam back under the rafts.

The bullets showered the ocean in a glittering downpour. Looking up, Louie saw them popping through the canvas, shooting beams of intensely bright tropical sunlight through the raft's shadow. But after a few feet, the bullets spent their force and fluttered down, fizzing. Louie straightened his arms over his head and pushed against the bottom of one of the rafts, trying to get far enough down to be outside the bullets' lethal range. Above him, he could see the depressions formed by Mac and Phil's bodies. Neither man was moving.

As the bullets raked overhead, Louie struggled to stay under the rafts. The current clutched at him, rotating his body horizontally and dragging him away. He kicked against it, but it was no use. He was being sucked away, and he knew that if he lost touch with the rafts, he wouldn't be able to swim hard enough against the current to get back. As he was pulled loose, he saw the long cord that strayed off the end of one of the rafts. He grabbed it and tied it around his waist.

As he lay underwater, his legs tugged in front of him by the current, Louie looked down at his feet. His left sock was pulled up on his shin; his right had slipped halfway off. He watched it flap in the current. Then, in the murky blur beyond it, he saw the huge, gaping mouth of a shark emerge out of the darkness and rush straight at his legs.

Louie recoiled, pulling his legs toward his body. The current was too strong for him to get his legs beneath him, but he was able to swing them to the side, away from the shark's mouth. The shark kept coming, directly at Louie's head. Louie remembered the advice of the old man in Honolulu: Make a threatening expression, then stiff-arm the shark's snout. As the shark lunged for his head, Louie bared his teeth, widened his eyes, and rammed his palm into the tip of the shark's nose. The shark flinched, circled away, then swam back for a second pass. Louie waited until the shark was inches from him, then struck it in the nose again. Again, the shark peeled away.

Above, the bullets had stopped coming. As quickly as he could, Louie pulled himself along the cord until he reached the raft. He grabbed its wall and lifted himself clear of the shark.

Mac and Phil were lying together in the fetal position. They were absolutely still, and bullet holes dappled the raft around them. Louie shook Mac. Mac made a sound. Louie asked if he'd been hit. Mac said no. Louie spoke to Phil. Phil said he was okay.

The bomber circled back for another go. Phil and Mac played dead, and Louie tipped back into the ocean. As bullets knifed the water around him, the shark came at him, and again Louie bumped its snout and repelled it. Then a second shark charged at him. Louie hung there, gyrating in the water and flailing his arms and legs, as the sharks snapped at him and the bullets came down. The moment the bomber sped out of firing range, he clambered onto the raft again. Phil and Mac were still unhit.

Four more times the Japanese strafed them, sending Louie into the water to kick and punch at the sharks until the bomber had passed. Though he fought them to the point of exhaustion, he was not bitten. Every time he emerged from the water, he was certain that Phil and Mac would be dead. Impossibly, though there were bullet holes all the way around the men, even in the tiny spaces between them, not one bullet had hit either man.

The bomber crew made a last gesture of sadism. The plane circled back, and Louie ducked into the water again. The plane's bomb bay doors rolled open, and a depth charge tumbled out, splashing down some fifty feet from the rafts. The men braced themselves for an explosion, but none came. Either the charge was a dud or the bombardier had forgotten to arm it. *If the Japanese are this inept,* Phil thought, *America will win this war.*

Louie rolled back onto the raft and collapsed. When the bomber came back, he was too tired to go overboard. As the plane passed a final time, Louie, Mac, and Phil lay still. The gunners didn't fire. The bomber flew west and disappeared.

———

Phil's raft had been slashed in two. A bullet had struck the air pump and ricocheted straight across the base of the raft, slitting it from end to end. Everything that had been in the raft had been lost in the water. Because the ruined raft was made from rubberized canvas, it didn't sink, but it was obviously far beyond repair. Shrunken and formless, it lapped about on the ocean surface.

The men were sardined together on what remained of Mac and Louie's raft, which was far too small for all three of them. The canvas was speckled with tiny bullet holes. The raft had two air chambers, but both were punctured. Each time one of the men moved, air sighed out of the chambers and the canvas wrinkled a little more. The raft sat lower and lower in the water. The sharks whipped around it, surely excited by the bullets, the sight and smell of men in the water, and the sinking raft.

As the men sat together, exhausted and in shock, a shark lunged up over a wall of the raft, mouth open, trying to drag a man into the ocean. Someone grabbed an oar and hit the shark, and it slid off. Then another shark jumped on and, after it, another. The men gripped the oars and wheeled about, frantically swinging at the sharks. As they turned and swung and the sharks flopped up, air was forced out of the bullet holes, and the raft sank deeper. Soon, part of the raft was completely submerged.

If the men didn't get air into the raft immediately, the sharks would take them. One pump had been lost in the strafing; only the one from Mac and Louie's raft remained. The men hooked it up to one of the two valves and took turns pumping as hard as they could. Air flowed into the chamber and seeped out through the bullet holes, but the men found that if they pumped very quickly, just enough air passed through the raft to lift it up in the water and keep it mostly inflated. The sharks kept coming, and the men kept beating them away.

As Phil and Mac pumped and struck at the sharks, Louie groped for the provisions pocket and grabbed the patching kit, which contained sheets of patching material, a tube of glue, and sandpaper to roughen up the raft surface so the glue could adhere. The first problem declared itself immediately: The sandpaper wasn't waterproof. When Louie pulled it out, only the paper emerged; the sand that had been stuck to it had washed off. For the umpteenth time, Louie cursed whoever had stocked the raft. He had to devise something that could etch up the patch area so the glue would stick. He pondered the problem, then picked up the brass mirror that he had used to hail the bomber. Using the pliers, he cut three teeth into the edge of the mirror. Phil and Mac kept fighting the sharks off.

Louie began patching, starting with the holes on the top of the raft. He lifted the perforated area clear of the water, wiped the water from the surface, and held it away from the waves, letting it dry in the sun. Then, with each perforation, he used the mirror edge to cut an X across the hole. The material consisted of two layers of canvas with rubber between. After cutting the X, he peeled back the canvas to reveal the rubber layer, used the mirror to scratch up the rubber, squeezed glue onto it, and stuck the patch on. Then he waited for the sun to dry the glue. Sometimes, a whitecap would drench the patch before it dried, and he'd have to begin again.

As Louie worked, keeping his eyes on the patches, the sharks kept snapping at him. Growing wiser, they gave up flinging themselves haphazardly at the men and began stalking about, waiting for a moment when an oar was down or a back was turned before bulling their way aboard. Over and over again, they lunged at Louie from behind, where he couldn't see them. Mac and Phil smacked them away.

Hour after hour, the men worked, rotating the duties, clumsy with fatigue. The pumping was an enormous exertion for the diminished men. They found that instead of standing the pump up and pushing the handle downward, it was easier to press the pump handle to their chests and pull the base toward themselves. All three men were indispensable. Had there been only two, they couldn't have pumped, patched, and repelled the sharks. For the first time on the raft, Mac was truly helpful. He was barely strong enough to pull the pump handle a few times in a row, but with the oar he kept every shark away.

Night fell. In the darkness, patching was impossible, but the pumping couldn't be stopped. They pumped all night long, so drained that they lost the feeling in their arms.

In the morning the patching resumed. The rate of air loss gradually lessened, and they were able to rest for longer periods. Eventually, the air held enough for them to begin brief sleep rotations.

Once the top was patched, there was the problem of patching the bottom, which was underwater. All three men squeezed onto one side of the raft, balancing on one air tube. They opened up the valve and let the air out of the side they weren't sitting on, lifted it clear of the water, turned it over so the bottom faced skyward, wiped it off, and held it up to dry. Then Louie began patching. When that half of the bottom was patched, they reinflated it, crawled onto the repaired side, deflated the other side, and repeated the process. Again, whitecaps repeatedly washed over the raft and spoiled the patches, and everything had to be redone.

Finally, they could find no more holes to patch. Because bubbles kept coming up around the sides of the raft, they knew there were holes someplace where they couldn't reach. They had to live with them. The patches had slowed the air loss dramatically. Even when struck by whitecaps, the patches held. The men found that they could cut back on their pumping to one session every fifteen minutes or so during the day, and none at night. With the raft now reasonably inflated, the sharks stopped attacking.

Losing Phil's raft was a heavy blow. Not only had they lost all of the items stored on it, but now three men were wedged in a two-man raft, so close together that to move, each man had to ask the others to give him room. There was so little space that they had to take turns straightening their legs. At night, they had to sleep in a bony pile, feet to head.

But two good things came from the strafing. Looking at the dead raft, Louie thought of a use for it. Using the pliers, he pulled apart the layers of canvas on the ruined raft, creating a large, light sheet. At last, they had a canopy to block the sun in daytime and the cold at night.

The other benefit of the strafing was the information it gave the men. When they had a moment to collect themselves, Louie and Phil discussed the Japanese bomber. They thought that it must have come from the Marshall or Gilbert islands. If they were right in their belief that they were drifting directly west, then the Marshalls and Gilberts were roughly equidistant from them. They thought that the bomber had probably been on sea search, and if the Japanese followed the same sea search procedures as the Americans, it would have taken off at around seven A.M., a few hours before it had reached the rafts.

Estimating the bomber's cruising speed and range, they made rough calculations to arrive at how many hours the bomber could remain airborne after it left them, and thus how far they were from its base. They guessed that they were some 850 miles from the bomber's base. If this was correct, given that they had crashed about 2,000 miles east of the Marshalls and Gilberts, they had already traveled more than half the distance to those islands and were covering more than 40 miles per day. Phil thought over the numbers and was surprised. They had had no idea that they were so far west.

Extrapolating from these figures, they made educated guesses of when they'd reach the islands. Phil guessed the forty-sixth day; Louie guessed the forty-seventh. If their figures were right, they were going to have to last about twice as long as Rickenbacker. That meant surviving on the raft for almost three more weeks.

It was frightening to imagine what might await them on those islands. The strafing had confirmed what they'd heard about the Japanese. But it was good to feel oriented, to know that they were drifting toward land somewhere out there, on the far side of the earth's tilt. The bomber had given them something to ground their hope.

Mac didn't join in on the prognostication. He was slipping away.

Sixteen

Singing in the Clouds

LOUIE SAT AWAKE, LOOKING INTO THE SEA. PHIL WAS ASLEEP. Mac was virtually catatonic.

Two sharks, about eight feet long, were placidly circling the raft. Each time one slid past, Louie studied its skin. He had banged sharks on the nose many times but had never really felt the hide, which was said to feel like sandpaper. Curious, he dropped a hand into the water and laid it lightly on a passing shark, feeling its back and dorsal fin as it slid beneath him. It felt rough, just as everyone said. The shark swished on. The second shark passed, and Louie again let his hand follow its body. *Beautiful,* he thought.

Soon after, Louie noticed something odd. Both sharks were gone. Never in four weeks had the sharks left. Louie got up on his knees and leaned out over the water, looking as far down as he could, puzzled. No sharks.

He was kneeling there, perched over the edge of the raft, when one of the sharks that he had touched leapt from the water at terrific speed, mouth wide open, lunging straight at his head. Louie threw both hands in front of his face. The shark collided with him head-on, trying to get its mouth around his upper body. Louie, his hands on the animal's snout, shoved as hard as he could, and the shark splashed back into the water. A moment later, the second shark jumped up. Louie grabbed an oar and struck the shark in the nose, and it jerked back and slid away. Then the first shark lunged for him again. Louie was recoiling when he saw an oar swing past, sending the animal backward into the ocean. To Louie's surprise, it wasn't Phil who had saved him. It was Mac.

Louie had no time to thank him. One of the sharks jumped up again, followed by the other. Louie and Mac sat side by side, clubbing each shark as it lunged at them. Mac was a new man. A moment before, he had seemed almost comatose. Now he was infused with frantic energy.

For several minutes, the sharks took turns bellying onto the raft with gaping mouths, always launching themselves from the same spot. Finally, they gave up. Louie and Mac collapsed. Phil, who had been startled awake but had been unable to help because there were only two oars, stared at them in groggy confusion.

"What happened?" he said.

Louie looked at Mac with happy amazement and told him how grateful and proud of him he was. Mac, crumpled on the bottom of the raft, smiled back. He had pushed himself beyond his body's capacities, but the frightened, childlike expression had left his face. Mac had reclaimed himself.

Louie was furious at the sharks. He had thought that they had an understanding: The men would stay out of the sharks' turf—the water—and the sharks would stay off of theirs—the raft. That the sharks had taken shots at him when he had gone overboard, and when the raft had been mostly submerged after the strafing, had seemed fair enough. But their attempt to poach men from their reinflated raft struck Louie as dirty pool. He stewed all night, scowled hatefully at the sharks all day, and eventually made a decision. If the sharks were going to try to eat him, he was going to try to eat them.

He knelt by the raft wall and watched the sharks, searching for a beatable opponent. One that looked about five feet long passed. Louie thought he could take it. Louie and Phil made a plan.

They had a little bait on the raft, probably the remains of their last bird. Phil hung it on a fishhook and strung it into the water at one end of the raft. At the other end, Louie knelt, facing the water. Smelling the bait, the shark swam toward Phil, orienting itself so that its tail was under Louie. Louie leaned as far overboard as he could without losing his balance, plunged both hands into the water, and grabbed the tail. The shark took off. Louie, gripping the tail, flew out of the raft and crashed into the water, sending a large serving of the Pacific up his nose. The shark whipped its tail and flung Louie off. Louie bolted back onto the raft so quickly that he later had no memory of how he had done it.

Soaking and embarrassed, Louie rethought his plan. His first error had been one of appraisal: Sharks were stronger than they looked. His second had been to fail to brace himself properly. His third had been to allow the shark's tail to stay in the water, giving the animal something to push against. He settled in to wait for a smaller shark.

In time, a smaller one, perhaps four feet long, arrived. Louie knelt at the raft's side, tipping his weight backward and keeping his knees far apart to brace himself. Phil dangled a baited hook in the water.

The shark swam for the bait. Louie clapped his hands around the tail and heaved it out of the water. The shark thrashed, but could neither get free nor pull Louie into the water. Louie dragged the animal onto the raft. The shark twisted and snapped, and Phil grabbed a flare cartridge and jammed it into the shark's mouth. Pinning the shark down, Louie took the pliers and stabbed the screwdriver end of the handle through the animal's eye. The shark died instantly.

In his Honolulu survival course, Louie had been told that the liver was the only part of a shark that was edible. Getting at it was no mean feat. Even with a knife, sharkskin is about as easy to cut as a coat of mail; with only the edge of a mirror to cut with, the labor was draining. After much sawing, Louie managed to break the skin. The flesh underneath stank of ammonia. Louie cut the liver out, and it was sizable. They ate it eagerly, giving Mac a larger portion, and for the first time since breakfast on May 27, they were all full. The rest of the shark reeked, so they threw it overboard. Later, using the same technique, they caught a second shark and again ate the liver.

Among the sharks, word seemed to get around; no more small sharks came near. Large sharks, some as long as twelve feet, lumbered alongside the raft, but Louie thought better of taking them on. The men's stomachs were soon empty again.

Mac was in a sharp downward spiral. He rarely moved. All three men had lost a staggering amount of weight, but Mac had shriveled the most. His eyes, sunken in their sockets, stared out lifelessly.

It was nightfall somewhere around the thirtieth day. The men went through their usual routine, bailing water into the raft and entwining themselves for warmth. The sky was clear and starry, and the moon shone on the water. The men fell asleep.

Louie woke to a tremendous crash, stinging pain, and the sensation of weightlessness. His eyes snapped open and he realized that he, Mac, and Phil were airborne. They flopped down together onto the raft and twisted about in confusion. Something had struck the bottom of the raft with awesome power. The garden-variety sharks that made up their entourage weren't large enough to hit them with such force, and had never behaved in this way.

Looking over the side of the raft, they saw it. Swelling up from under the water came a leviathan: a vast white mouth, a broad back parting the surface, and a long dorsal fin, ghostly in the moonlight. The animal was some twenty feet long, more than three times the length of the raft. Louie recognized its features from his survival school training. It was a great white shark.

As the castaways watched in terrified silence, the shark swam the length of one side of the raft, then bent around to the other side, exploring it. Pausing on the surface, it swished its tail away, then slapped it into the raft, sending the raft skidding sideways and splashing a wave of water into the men. Louie, Mac, and Phil came up on their knees in the center of the raft and clung to one another. The shark began to swim around to the other side. Louie whispered, *"Don't make a noise!"* Again came the mighty swing, the shower of water, the jolt through the raft and the men.

Around and around the shark went, drenching the raft with each pass. It seemed to be playing with the raft. With every pass, the men cringed and waited to be capsized. Finally, the great back slid under, and the sea smoothed behind it. It did not surface again.

Louie, Phil, and Mac lay down again. The water around them was now cold, and none of them could sleep.

The next morning, Mac could no longer sit up. He lay on the floor of the raft, little more than a wrinkled mummy, his gaze fixed far away.

One last albatross landed. Louie caught it, wrenched its head off, and handed it to Phil. Phil turned it upside down over Mac and let the blood flow into his mouth. As Louie and Phil ate the meat, dipping it into the ocean to give it flavor, they fed bits to Mac, but it didn't revive him.

In subsequent days, Mac became a faint whisper of a man. His water tins ran dry. When Phil opened his tin and took a sip of the little he had left, Mac asked if he could drink from it. For Phil, thirst had been the cruelest trial, and he knew that the water left in his tin, essential to his own survival, couldn't save Mac. He gently told Mac that he didn't have enough left to share. Louie was sympathetic to Phil, but he couldn't bring himself to refuse Mac. He gave him a small sip of his own water.

That evening, Phil heard a small voice. It was Mac, asking Louie if he was going to die. Louie looked over at Mac, who was watching him. Louie thought it would be disrespectful to lie to Mac, who might have something that he needed to say or do before life left him. Louie told him that he thought he'd die that night. Mac had no reaction. Phil and Louie lay down, put their arms around Mac, and went to sleep.

Sometime that night, Louie was lifted from sleep by a breathy sound, a deep outrushing of air, slow and final. He knew what it was.

Francis McNamara on May 26, 1943, the day before the crash.
Courtesy of Louis Zamperini

Sergeant Francis McNamara had begun his last journey with a panicked act, consuming the rafts' precious food stores, and in doing so, he had placed himself and his raftmates in the deepest jeopardy. But in the last days of his life, in the struggle against the deflating raft and the jumping sharks, he had given all he had left. It wasn't enough to save him—it had probably hastened his death—but it may have made the difference between life and death for Phil and Louie. Had Mac not survived the crash, Louie and Phil might well have been dead by that thirty-third day In his dying days, Mac had redeemed himself.

In the morning, Phil wrapped Mac's body in something, probably part of the ruined raft. They knelt over the body and said aloud all of the good things they knew of Mac, laughing a little at his penchant for mess hall pie. Louie wanted to give him a religious eulogy but didn't know how, so he recited disjointed passages that he remembered from movies, ending with a few words about committing the body to the sea. And he prayed for himself and Phil, vowing that if God would save them, he would serve heaven forever.

When he was done, Louie lifted the shrouded body in his arms. It felt as if it weighed no more than forty pounds. Louie bent over the side of the raft and gently slid Mac into the water. Mac sank away. The sharks let him be.

The next night, Louie and Phil completed their thirty-fourth day on the raft. Though they didn't know it, they had passed what was almost certainly the record for survival adrift in an inflated raft. If anyone had survived longer, they hadn't lived to tell about it.

The raft bobbed westward. Petulant storms came over now and then, raining enough to keep the water supply steady. Because the water ration was now divided by two instead of three, each man had more to drink. Louie made a hook out of his lieutenant's pin and caught one fish before the pin broke.

Phil and Louie could see the bend of their thighbones under their skin, their knees bulging in the centers of birdlike legs, their bellies hollow, their ribs stark. Each man had grown a weedy beard. Their skin glowed yellow from the leached raft dye, and their bodies were patterned with salt sores. They held their sun-scorched eyes to the horizon, searching for land, but there was none. Their hunger dimmed, an ominous sign. They had reached the last stage of starvation.

One morning, they woke to a strange stillness. The rise and fall of the raft had ceased, and it sat virtually motionless. There was no wind. The ocean stretched out in all directions in glossy smoothness, regarding the sky and reflecting its image in crystalline perfection. Like the ancient mariner, Louie and Phil had found the doldrums, the eerie pause of wind and water that lingers around the equator. They were, as Coleridge wrote, "as idle as a painted ship upon a painted ocean."

It was an experience of transcendence. Phil watched the sky, whispering that it looked like a pearl. The water looked so solid that it seemed they could walk across it. When a fish broke the surface far away, the sound carried to the men with absolute clarity. They watched as pristine ringlets of water circled outward around the place where the fish had passed, then faded to stillness.

For a while they spoke, sharing their wonder. Then they fell into reverent silence. Their suffering was suspended. They weren't hungry or thirsty. They were unaware of the approach of death.

As he watched this beautiful, still world, Louie played with a thought that had come to him before. He had thought it as he had watched hunting seabirds, marveling at their ability to adjust their dives to compensate for the refraction of light in water. He had thought it as he had considered the pleasing geometry of the sharks, their gradation of color, their slide through the sea. He even recalled the thought coming to him in his youth, when he had lain on the roof of the cabin in the Cahuilla Indian Reservation, looking up from Zane Grey to watch night settling over the earth. Such beauty, he thought, was too perfect to have come about by mere chance. That day in the center of the Pacific was, to him, a gift crafted deliberately, compassionately, for him and Phil.

Joyful and grateful in the midst of slow dying, the two men bathed in that day until sunset brought it, and their time in the doldrums, to an end.

Given how badly the men's bodies were faring, it would seem likely that their minds, too, would begin to fail. But more than five weeks into their ordeal, both Louie and Phil were enjoying remarkable precision of mind, and were convinced that they were growing sharper every day. They continued quizzing each other, chasing each other's stories down to the smallest detail, teaching each other melodies and lyrics, and cooking imaginary meals.

Louie found that the raft offered an unlikely intellectual refuge. He had never recognized how noisy the civilized world was. Here, drifting in almost total silence, with no scents other than the singed odor of the raft, no flavors on his tongue, nothing moving but the slow procession of shark fins, every vista empty save water and sky, his time unvaried and unbroken, his mind was freed of an encumbrance that civilization had imposed on it. In his head, he could roam anywhere, and he found that his mind was quick and clear, his imagination unfettered and supple. He could stay with a thought for hours, turning it about.

He had always enjoyed excellent recall, but on the raft, his memory became infinitely more nimble, reaching back further, offering detail that had once escaped him. One day, trying to pinpoint his earliest memory, he saw a two-story building and, inside, a stairway broken into two parts of six steps each, with a landing in between. He was there in the image, a tiny child toddling along the stairs. As he crawled down the first set of steps and moved toward the edge of the landing, a tall yellow dog stepped in front of him to stop him from tumbling off. It was his parents' dog, Askim, whom they had had in Olean, when Louie was very little. Louie had never remembered him before.*

On the fortieth day, Louie was lying beside Phil under the canopy when he abruptly sat up. He could hear singing. He kept listening; it sounded like a choir. He nudged Phil and asked him if he heard anything. Phil said no. Louie slid the canopy off and squinted into the daylight. The ocean was a featureless flatness. He looked up.

Above him, floating in a bright cloud, he saw human figures, silhouetted against the sky. He counted twenty-one of them. They were singing the sweetest song he had ever heard.

Louie stared up, astonished, listening to the singing. What he was seeing and hearing was impossible, and yet he felt absolutely lucid. This was, he felt certain, no hallucination, no vision. He sat under the singers, listening to their voices, memorizing the melody, until they faded away.

Phil had heard and seen nothing. Whatever this had been, Louie concluded, it belonged to him alone.

---

* Askim was notorious for his kleptomania; the Zamperinis lived above a grocery, and the dog made regular shoplifting runs downstairs, snatching food and fleeing. His name was a clever joke: When people asked what the dog's name was, they were invariably confused by the reply, which sounded like "Ask him."

On the men drifted. Several days passed with no food and no rain. The raft was a gelatinous mess, its patches barely holding on, some spots bubbling outward, on the verge of popping. It wouldn't bear the men's weight much longer.

In the sky, Phil noticed something different. There were more birds. Then they began to hear planes. Sometimes they'd see a tiny speck in the sky, sometimes two or more together, making a distant buzz. They were always much too far away to be signaled, and both men knew that as far west as they had probably drifted, these planes were surely Japanese. As the days passed, more and more specks appeared, every day arriving earlier.

Louie had come to love sunrise and the warmth it brought, and each morning he'd lie with his eyes on the horizon, awaiting it. On the morning of July 12, the forty-sixth day, the day that Phil had picked for their arrival at land, no sunrise came. There was only a gradual, gloomy illumination of a brooding sky.

Phil and Louie looked up apprehensively. The wind caught them sharply. The sea began to arch its back under the raft, sending the men up to dizzying heights. Louie looked out over the churning water and thought how lovely it was. Phil was fond of roller-coastering over the big swells that came with storms, thrilled as he skidded down one and turned his face up to see the summit of the next, but this was ominous.

To the west, something appeared, so far away that it could be glimpsed only from the tops of the swells. It was a low, gray-green wiggle on the horizon. Phil and Louie would later disagree on who saw it first, but the moment the sea tossed them up, the horizon rolled westward, and their eyes grasped it, they knew what it was.

It was an island.

Seventeen

Typhoon

ALL DAY, UNDER A DARK, GYRATING SKY, LOUIE AND PHIL rode the swells, straining their eyes westward and feeling a weary thrill as the bump on the horizon peeked into view. Slowly, as the current carried them toward it, the island became more distinct. They could see a bright white line where waves dashed against something, maybe a beach, maybe a reef. In the afternoon, one island became two, and then a dozen or so, lined up like railcars. The castaways had expected that if they ever saw land, they'd be rapturous. Instead, they discussed it matter-of-factly. They were too weak for anything more, and there were pressing worries. Overhead, a huge storm was gathering.

In training, Louie and Phil had memorized the geography of the central Pacific. They knew that the islands ahead had to be part of the Gilberts or Marshalls, enemy territory. Between them, the two island groups had dozens of atolls and islands, so there was a good likelihood that there were places unoccupied by the Japanese. Louie and Phil decided to hang offshore until they found an island that looked uninhabited, or inhabited only by natives. They began rowing over the wind-chapped sea, turning parallel to the islands so they could wait until night to slip ashore.

The sky broke all at once. A sudden, slashing rain came down, and the islands vanished. The ocean began heaving and thrashing. The wind slapped the raft in one direction, then another, sending it spinning up swells, perhaps forty feet, then careening down into troughs as deep as canyons. Phil and Louie had drifted into what was almost certainly a typhoon.

Wave after wave slammed into the raft, tipping it sideways and peeling it upward, on the verge of overturning. To try to stop it from flipping, Louie and Phil bailed in water as ballast, positioned themselves on opposite sides to balance their weight, and lay on their backs to keep the center of gravity low. Knowing that if they were thrown loose, they'd never get back in, Louie reeled in the raft cord, looped it around the cushion sewn into the center of the raft, threaded it through a grommet, then wound it around his waist and Phil's waist, pulling it taut. They pushed their feet under the cushion, leaned back, and held on.

Night fell, and the storm pounded. The raft raced up and down hundreds of mountains of water. At times, in the darkness, they felt the strange lightness of flying as the raft was swept into the air off the tops of the waves. Louie felt more intensely afraid than he had felt as *Green Hornet* was falling. Across from him, Phil lay in grim silence. Both men thought of the nearness of the land they could no longer see. They feared that any second, they'd be flung into a reef.

Sometime in the night, the storm sagged and softened, then moved on.* The swells remained, but their tops became smooth. Louie and Phil freed themselves from the raft cord and awaited daylight.

In the dark, they could smell soil, greenness, rain washing over living things. It was the smell of land. It flirted with them all night, growing stronger. As dawn neared, they could hear the hiss of water scouring a reef. Exhausted, they decided to take turns napping, with one man on the lookout for land. Somewhere along the way, they both fell asleep.

They woke in a new universe. They had drifted into the embrace of two small islands. On one island, they saw huts, trees heavy with fruit, but no people. They had heard of the Japanese enslaving native popula-

---

* Several days later, a catastrophic typhoon, almost certainly the same storm, plowed into the coast of China, collapsing homes, uprooting telephone poles, and causing extensive flooding.

tions and moving them en masse off their home islands, and they thought that perhaps this had been the fate of this island's inhabitants. They pulled their shoes over their sore-pocked feet and began rowing for shore. From overhead came the whine of engines. They looked up and saw Zeros looping through combat maneuvers, far too high for their pilots to notice the raft below. They rowed on.

Louie had predicted that they'd find land on the forty-seventh day. Phil had chosen the day before. Because they had spotted land on the day Phil had chosen and were about to reach it on the day Louie had chosen, they decided that they had both been right.

They could see more islands now. Louie spotted a tiny island to their left and pointed it out to Phil, describing it as having one tree on it. Then a strange thing happened. The lone tree became two trees. After a moment's confusion, the men suddenly understood. It wasn't an island, and those weren't trees. It was a boat. It had been perpendicular to them, leaving only one mast visible, and then it had turned, bringing the rearward mast into view.

Louie and Phil ducked. They rowed as fast as they could, trying to get to shore before the sailors spotted them. They were too late. The boat made a sharp turn and sped toward them. The weakened men couldn't row fast enough to escape. They gave up and stopped.

The boat drew alongside the raft, and Louie and Phil looked up. Above them was a machine gun, mounted on the boat's bow. Along the deck stood a line of men, all Japanese. Each one held a weapon, pointed at the castaways.

One of the Japanese opened his shirt and pointed to his chest. He seemed to want the Americans to do the same. As Louie opened his shirt, he braced himself, expecting to be shot, but no shot came. The man had only wanted to see if they were armed.

One of the sailors threw a rope at the raft, and Louie caught it. Louie and Phil tried to climb onto the boat, but their legs were too weak. The sailors brought out a rope ladder, tied the castaways to it, and dragged them up, then pulled the raft aboard. On the deck, Louie and Phil attempted to rise, but their legs buckled. The Japanese were impatient for the men to move across the deck, so the Americans crawled on all fours. When they reached the mast, they were picked up and lashed to it. Their hands were bound behind their backs.

One of the sailors began speaking to them in Japanese. He seemed to be asking questions. Louie and Phil offered responses, trying to guess what the man wanted to know. A soldier waved a bayonet past Louie's face, trying to hack off his beard. Another man cracked a pistol across Phil's jaw, then moved to do the same to Louie. Louie tipped his head forward in hopes that the sailor would aim for the front of his face; when the sailor swung, Louie jerked his head back. The man missed, but Louie smacked his head against the mast.

The boat's captain approached and chastised the crewmen. The mood changed, and Louie's and Phil's hands were untied. Someone gave the castaways cigarettes, but the ends kept lighting their beards on fire. Someone else brought them cups of water and one biscuit each. Louie took a bite of the biscuit and held it in his mouth, caressing it, feeling the flavor. He ate slowly, savoring each crumb. It was his first food in eight days.

A second boat pulled alongside the first. Louie and Phil were helped onto it, and it began moving. As it sailed, a crewman came to the castaways and fed them more biscuits and some coconut. Then a young sailor approached, Japanese-English dictionary in hand, and asked questions. Phil and Louie gave brief accounts of their journey.

In time, the boat drew up to a large island. A sailor approached with two blindfolds and tied them around Louie's and Phil's heads. Men got on either side of them, grabbed their arms, and half-dragged, half-carried them off the boat. After a few minutes, Louie felt himself being laid down on something soft. His blindfold was taken off.

He was inside an infirmary, lying on a soft mattress on an iron bed. Phil was on a bed beside his. There was a small window nearby, and through it, he could see Japanese soldiers thrusting bayonets into dummies. An officer spoke to the Japanese surrounding the castaways, then spoke in English, apparently repeating his statement so Louie and Phil would understand him.

"These are American fliers," he said. "Treat them gently."

A doctor came in, smiled warmly, and examined Phil and Louie, speaking English. He smoothed ointment on their salt sores and burned lips, palpated their abdomens, took their temperatures and pulses, and pronounced them healthy. Louie and Phil were helped to their feet and led to a scale. They took turns standing on it, each with a man ready to catch him if his legs failed.

Phil had weighed about 150 pounds when he had stepped aboard *Green Hornet*. Louie's war diary, begun shortly after he arrived in

Hawaii, noted that he weighed 155 pounds. He believed that weight training had added another 5 pounds by the time of the crash. Now Phil weighed about 80 pounds. According to different accounts, five-foot, ten-inch Louie weighed 67 pounds, 79.5 pounds, or 87 pounds. Whatever the exact number, each man had lost about half of his body weight, or more.

On the doctor's orders, in came a bottle of Russian cognac and two glasses, which Louie and Phil quickly emptied. Then came a platter of eggs, ham, milk, fresh bread, fruit salad, and cigarettes. The castaways dug in. When they were done, they were helped into another room and seated before a group of Japanese officers, who gaped at the shrunken, canary yellow men. An officer, speaking English, asked how they had ended up there. Louie told the story as the Japanese listened in silent fascination, tracing the journey on a map.

Louie and Phil knew where their journey had begun, but did not yet know where it had ended. The officers told them. They were on an atoll in the Marshall Islands. They had drifted two thousand miles.

As Japanese servicemen crowded around, the raft was spread out and the bullet holes counted. There were forty-eight. The curious servicemen pressed toward the Americans, but the officers kept them back. An officer asked Louie where the bullet holes had come from. Louie replied that a Japanese plane had strafed them. The officer said that this was impossible, a violation of their military code of honor. Louie described the bomber and the attack. The officers looked at one another and said nothing.

Two beds were made up, and Louie and Phil were invited to get as much rest as they wished. Slipping between cool, clean sheets, their stomachs full, their sores soothed, they were deeply grateful to have been received with such compassion. Phil had a relieved thought: *They are our friends.*

Louie and Phil stayed in the infirmary for two days, attended by Japanese who cared for them with genuine concern for their comfort and health. On the third day, the deputy commanding officer came to them. He brought beef, chocolate, and coconuts—a gift from his commander—as well as news. A freighter was coming to transport them to another atoll. The name he gave sent a tremor through Louie: Kwajalein. It was the place known as Execution Island.

"After you leave here," Louie would long remember the officer saying, "we cannot guarantee your life."

The freighter arrived on July 15. Louie and Phil were taken into the hold and housed separately. The captain had bountiful portions of food sent to them. The prisoners ate all they could.

One of the cruelties of starvation is that a body dying of hunger often rejects the first food it is given. The food on the atoll had apparently agreed with the castaways, but not the food on the freighter. Louie spent much of that day hunched over the ship railing, vomiting into the sea, while a guard held him. Phil's meal left him almost as quickly, but by a different route; that evening, he had to be taken on at least six runs to the head.

As the freighter drew up to Kwajalein on July 16, the Japanese became harsh. On came the blindfolds, and Louie and Phil were taken onto what seemed to be a barge. When the barge stopped, they were picked up, heaved over men's shoulders, and carried. Louie felt himself bobbing through the air, then slapped down on a hard surface. Phil was dropped beside him. Louie said something to Phil, and immediately felt a boot kick into him as a voice shouted, "No!"

An engine started, and they were moving. They were on the flatbed of a truck. In a few minutes, the truck stopped, and Louie was tugged out and flung over a shoulder again. There was walking, two steps up, a darkening, the sense that Phil was no longer near him, and the disorienting feeling of being thrown backward. Louie's back struck a wall, and he fell to a floor. Someone yanked off his blindfold. A door slammed, a lock turned.

At first, Louie could barely see. His eyes darted about uncontrollably. His mind raced, flitting incoherently from thought to thought. After weeks of endless openness, he was disoriented by the compression of the space around him. Every nerve and muscle seemed in a panic.

Slowly, his thoughts quieted and his eyes settled. He was in a wooden cell, about the length of a man and not much wider than his shoulders. Over his head was a thatched roof, about seven feet up. The only window was a hole, about a foot square, in the door. The floor was strewn with gravel, dirt, and wiggling maggots, and the room hummed with flies and mosquitoes, already beginning to swarm onto him. There was a hole in the floor with a latrine bucket below it. The air hung hot and still, oppressive with the stench of human waste.

Louie looked up. In the dim light, he saw words carved into the wall: NINE MARINES MAROONED ON MAKIN ISLAND, AUGUST 18, 1942. Below that were names: Robert Allard, Dallas Cook, Richard Davis, Joseph Gifford, John Kerns, Alden Mattison, Richard Olbert, William Pallesen, and Donald Roberton.

In August 1942, after a botched American raid on a Japanese base at Makin in the Marshall Islands, nine marines had been mistakenly left behind. Captured by the Japanese, they had disappeared. Louie was almost certainly the first American to learn that they had been taken to Kwajalein. But other than Phil and Louie, there were no prisoners here now. Louie felt a wave of foreboding.

He called to Phil. Phil's voice answered, distant and small, somewhere to the left. He was down the hall in a squalid hole like Louie's. Each man asked the other if he was okay. Both knew that this was likely the last time they would talk, but if they wished to say good-bye, neither had the chance. There was shuffling in the corridor as a guard took up his station. Louie and Phil said nothing else.

Louie looked down at his body. Legs that had sprung through a 4:12 mile over bright sand on that last morning on Kualoa were now useless. The vibrant, generous body that he had trained with such vigilance had shrunken until only the bones remained, draped in yellow skin, crawling with parasites.

All I see, he thought, *is a dead body breathing.*

Louie dissolved into hard, racking weeping. He muffled his sobs so the guard wouldn't hear him.

PART
IV

Eighteen

A Dead Body Breathing

SOMETHING FLEW THROUGH THE WINDOW IN THE DOOR of Louie's cell and struck the floor, breaking into white bits. It was two pieces of hardtack, the dry biscuit that was the standard fare of sailors. A tiny cup of tea—so weak that it was little more than hot water, so small that it constituted a single swallow—was set on the sill. Phil received food also, but no water. He and Louie crawled about their cells, picking up slivers of biscuit and putting them into their mouths. A guard stood outside.

There was a rustle outside Louie's cell, and a face appeared. The man greeted Louie cheerfully, in English, by name. Louie stared up at him.

The man was a Kwajalein native, and he explained that the American castaways were the talk of the island. A sports fanatic, he had recognized Louie's name, which Louie had given to his captors. Prattling about track, football, and the Olympics, he paused only rarely to ask Louie questions. Once Louie got one or two words off, the native bounded back into his narrative.

After a few minutes, the native glanced at his watch and said he had to leave. Louie asked him what had happened to the marines whose names were carved into the wall. In the same chipper tone, the native

replied that the marines were dead. All of the POWs held on that island, he said, were executed.

As the native walked out, the guard looked challengingly at Louie,
lifted a flattened hand to his throat, and made a slashing gesture. He
pointed to the names on the wall, then to Louie.

That night, Louie rested his head next to the door, trying to get as
far as possible from the waste hole. He had only just settled there when
the door swung open and the guard grabbed him and spun him around,
pushing his head against the hole. Louie resisted, but the guard became
angry. Louie gave up and lay as the guard ordered. He could see that
the guard wanted him to lie in this position so he could see him through
the window in the door. Every few minutes, all night long, the guard
peered in, making sure that Louie didn't move.

———

The morning of the second day began. Phil and Louie lay in sweltering
silence, thinking that at any moment they'd be dragged out and beheaded. The guards stalked back and forth, snarling at the captives and
drawing the sides of their hands across their necks with sadistic smiles.

For Louie, the digestive miseries continued. His diarrhea became
explosive, and cramps doubled him over. He lay under a blanket of flies
and mosquitoes, keeping his buttocks over the waste hole for as long as
he could, until the guard snapped at him to move his face back to the
hole.

The day passed. Three times, a single wad of rice, a little bigger than
a golf ball, sailed through the door window and broke against the floor.
Once or twice, a swallow of tea in a cup was left on the sill, and Louie
sucked it down. Night came.

Another day came and went, then another. The heat was smother-
ing. Lice hopped over the captives' skin. Mosquitoes preyed on them in
swarms so thick that when Louie snapped his fingers into a fist, then
opened his hand, his entire palm was crimson. His diarrhea worsened,
becoming bloody. Each day, Louie cried out for a doctor. One day, a
doctor came. He leaned into the cell, looked at Louie, chuckled, and
walked away.

Curled up on the gravelly floor, both men felt as if their bones were
wearing through their skin. Louie begged for a blanket to sit on, but
was ignored. He passed the time trying to strengthen his legs, pulling
himself upright and standing for a minute or two while holding the
wall, then sinking down. He missed the raft.

Two sips of water a day weren't nearly enough to replace Louie's torrential fluid loss. His thirst became worse than anything he'd known on the raft. He crawled to the door and pleaded for water. The guard left, then returned with a cup. Louie, grateful, drew close to the door to take a drink. The guard threw scalding water in his face. Louie was so dehydrated that he couldn't help but keep begging. At least four more times, the response was the same, leaving Louie's face speckled with blisters. Louie knew that dehydration might kill him, and part of him hoped it would.

One day, as he lay in misery, Louie heard singing. The voices he had heard over the raft had come to him again. He looked around his cell, but the singers weren't there. Only their music was with him. He let it wash over him, finding in it a reason to hope. Eventually, the song faded away, but silently, in his mind, Louie sang it over and over to himself. He prayed intensely, ardently, hour after hour.

Down the hall, Phil languished. Rats were everywhere, climbing up his waste bucket and wallowing in his urine pail, waking him at night by skittering over his face. Periodically, he was prodded outside, halted before a pan of water, and ordered to wash his face and hands. Phil dropped his face into the pan and slurped up the water.

Louie often stared at the names of the marines, wondering who they were, if they'd had wives and children, how the end had come for them. He began to think of them as his friends. One day he pulled off his belt and bent the buckle upward. In tall, block letters, he carved his name into the wall beside theirs.

Louie couldn't speak to Phil, nor Phil to him, but occasionally one of them would cough or scuff the floor to let the other know that he was there. Once, the guards left the cells unattended, and for the first time, Phil and Louie were alone. Louie heard Phil's voice.

"What's going to happen?"

Louie had no answer. There was a beating of boots in the hall and the Americans fell silent.

The guards maintained a fixed state of fury at the captives, glaring at them wrathfully, making threatening gestures, shouting at them. Virtually every day, they flew into rages that usually ended in Phil and Louie being bombarded with stones and lit cigarettes, spat upon, and poked with sticks. Louie always knew that he was in for it when he heard a guard arriving in a stomping fit—a consequence, he hoped, of an American victory. The situation worsened when the guard had company; the guards used the captives to impress each other with their cruelty.

The pretext for many of the outbursts was miscommunication. The captives and their guards came from cultures with virtually no overlap in language or custom. Louie and Phil found it almost impossible to understand what was being asked of them. Sign language was of little help, because even the cultures' gestures were different. The guards, like nearly all citizens of their historically isolated nation, had probably never seen a foreigner before, and probably had no experience in communicating with a non-Japanese. When misunderstood, they often became so exasperated that they screamed at and beat the captives.

For self-preservation, Louie and Phil studied everything they heard, developing small Japanese vocabularies. *Kocchi koi* meant "come here." *Ohio* was a greeting, used by the occasional civil guard. Though Louie soon knew what it meant, his stock reply was "No, California." Phil learned that *mizu* meant water, but the knowledge got him nowhere; his cries for *mizu* were ignored.

When the guards weren't venting their fury at the captives, they entertained themselves by humiliating them. Every day, at gunpoint, Louie was forced to stand up and dance, staggering through the Charleston while his guards roared with laughter. The guards made Louie whistle and sing, pelted him with fistfuls of gravel, taunted him as he crawled around his cell to pick up bits of rice, and slid long sticks through the door window so they could stab and swat him, finding his helpless contortions hilarious. Down the hall, the guards did the same to Phil. Sometimes Louie could hear Phil's voice, tiny and thin, groaning. Once, driven to his breaking point by a guard jabbing him, Louie yanked the stick from the guard's hands. He knew he might get killed for it, but under this unceasing degradation, something was happening to him. His will to live, resilient through all of the trials on the raft, was beginning to fray.

The crash of *Green Hornet* had left Louie and Phil in the most desperate physical extremity, without food, water, or shelter. But on Kwajalein, the guards sought to deprive them of something that had sustained them even as all else had been lost: dignity. This self-respect and sense of self-worth, the innermost armament of the soul, lies at the heart of humanness; to be deprived of it is to be dehumanized, to be cleaved from, and cast below, mankind. Men subjected to dehumanizing treatment experience profound wretchedness and loneliness and find that hope is almost impossible to retain. Without dignity, identity is erased. In its absence, men are defined not by themselves, but by their captors and the circumstances in which they are forced to live. One American airman, shot down and relentlessly debased by his Japanese captors, described the state of mind that his captivity created: "I was literally becoming a lesser human being."

Few societies treasured dignity, and feared humiliation, as did the Japanese, for whom a loss of honor could merit suicide. This is likely one of the reasons why Japanese soldiers in World War II debased their prisoners with such zeal, seeking to take from them that which was most painful and destructive to lose. On Kwajalein, Louie and Phil learned a dark truth known to the doomed in Hitler's death camps, the slaves of the American South, and a hundred other generations of betrayed people. Dignity is as essential to human life as water, food, and oxygen. The stubborn retention of it, even in the face of extreme physical hardship, can hold a man's soul in his body long past the point at which the body should have surrendered it. The loss of it can carry a man off as surely as thirst, hunger, exposure, and asphyxiation, and with greater cruelty. In places like Kwajalein, degradation could be as lethal as a bullet.

Louie had been on Kwajalein for about a week when his cell door was thrown open and two guards pulled him out. He flushed with fear, thinking that he was being taken to the sword. As he was hustled toward what seemed to be an officers' quarters, he passed two girls with Asian features, walking with heads down, eyes averted, as they retreated from the building. Louie was pulled into a room and stopped before a table covered with a white tablecloth, on which was arranged a selection of foods. Around it sat Japanese officers in dress uniforms, smoking cigarettes. Louie wasn't here to be executed. He was here to be interrogated.

The officers took long draws on their cigarettes and sighed the smoke toward Louie. Periodically, one of them would open a bottle of cola, pour it into a cup, and drink it slowly, making a show of his enjoyment.

The ranking officer stared coolly at his captive. How do American soldiers satisfy their sexual appetites? he asked. Louie replied that they don't—they rely on willpower. The officer was amused. The Japanese military, he said, provides women for its soldiers, an allusion to the thousands of Chinese, Korean, Indonesian, and Filipino women whom the Japanese military had kidnapped and forced into sexual slavery. Louie thought of the girls outside.

The interrogators asked about Louie's plane. They knew, probably from Louie's conversation with the officers on the first atoll, that it was a B-24. What model was it? On Oahu, Louie had heard that during a battle, a B-24D had crashed on a reef and had been retrieved by the Japanese. *Green Hornet* had been a D model. Knowing that the Japanese already knew about this model, he decided not to lie, and told them that he had been in a D. They handed him a pencil and paper and asked him to draw the plane. When he was done, his interrogators held up a photograph of a D model. They had been testing him.

What did he know about the E-model B-24? Nothing, he told them. It was a lie; *Super Man,* while always officially a D model, had undergone upgrades that had effectively made it an E. Where was the radar system? The location of the radar had no bearing on how it worked, so Louie told the truth. How do you operate it? Louie knew the answer, but he replied that as a bombardier, he wouldn't know. The interrogators asked him to draw the radar system. Louie invented an imaginary system, making a drawing so elaborate that, it was later written, the system looked like "a ruptured octopus." The interrogators nodded.

They moved on to the Norden bombsight. How do you work it? You just twist two knobs, Louie said. The officers were annoyed. Louie was sent back to his cell.

Suspecting that he'd be brought back, Louie brainstormed, trying to anticipate questions. He thought about which things he could divulge and which things he couldn't. For the latter, he came up with lies and practiced until he could utter them smoothly. Because he'd been partially truthful in the first session, he was now in a better position to lie.

Phil was pulled in for interrogation. He, too, knew about the captured B-24D, so he spoke freely about the plane's components. The interrogators asked him to describe American war strategy. He replied that he thought they would attack the outlying captured territories, then work their way in until they defeated Japan. The interrogators responded with whoops of laughter. Phil sensed something forced. These men, he suspected, thought that Japan was going to lose.

Louie was sitting in his cell when a new guard appeared at the door. Louie looked up, saw a face he didn't recognize, and felt an upswell of dread, knowing that a new guard would likely assert his authority.

"You Christian?" the guard asked.

Louie, whose parents had tried to raise him Catholic, hadn't gone near church since one Sunday in his boyhood, when a priest had punished him for tardiness by grabbing him by the ear and dragging him out. But though Louie emerged with a sore ear, a little religion had stuck with him. He said yes. The guard smiled.

"Me Christian."

The guard gave his name, which Louie would later recall, with some uncertainty, as Kawamura. He began babbling in English so poor that all Louie could pick out was something about Canadian missionaries and conversion. The guard slipped two pieces of hard candy into Louie's hand, then moved down the hall and gave two pieces to Phil. A friendship was born.

Kawamura brought a pencil and paper and began making drawings to illustrate things he wished to talk about. Walking back and forth between the cells, he'd draw a picture of something—a car, a plane, an ice cream cone—and say and write its Japanese name. Louie and Phil would then write and say the English name. The prisoners understood almost nothing of what Kawamura said, but his goodwill needed no translation. Kawamura could do nothing to improve the physical conditions in which the captives lived, but his kindness was lifesaving.

When Kawamura was off guard duty, a new guard came. He launched himself at Louie, ramming a stick through the door window and into Louie's face, as if trying to put out his eyes. The next day, Kawamura saw Louie's bloody face and asked who had done it. Upon hearing the guard's name, Kawamura hardened, lifting his arm and flexing his biceps at Louie. When his shift was up, he sped away with an expression of furious determination.

For two days, Louie saw nothing of Kawamura or the vicious guard. Then Kawamura returned, opened Louie's cell door a crack, and proudly pointed out the guard who had beaten Louie. His forehead and mouth were heavily bandaged. He never guarded the cell again.

As Louie and Phil lay in their cells one day, they heard a commotion outside, the clamoring sounds of a mob. Then faces pressed into Louie's door window, shouting. Rocks started flying in. More men came, one after another, screaming, spitting on Louie, hitting him with rocks, hurling sticks like javelins. Down the hall, the men were doing the same to Phil. Louie balled himself up at the far end of the cell.

On and on the procession went. There were eighty, perhaps ninety men, and each one spent some thirty seconds attacking each captive. At last, the men left. Louie sat in pools of spit and jumbled rocks and sticks, bleeding.

When Kawamura saw what had happened, he was livid. He explained that the attackers were a submarine crew stopping over on the island. When Louie was taken to interrogation, he complained about the attack. The officers replied that this was what he ought to expect.

The interrogators wanted Louie to tell them the numbers of aircraft, ships, and personnel in Hawaii. Louie told them that the last time he'd seen Hawaii, it had been May. Now it was August. He couldn't be expected to have current information. He was sent back to his cell.

Some three weeks after his arrival on Kwajalein, Louie was again pulled from his cell. Outside for the first time since his arrival on the island, he saw Phil. Their eyes met. It looked like this might be the end.

They were taken to the interrogation building, but this time they were halted on the front porch, Phil on one end, Louie on the other. Two men in white medical coats joined them, along with four aides holding paperwork and stopwatches. Japanese began collecting below the porch to watch.

Louie and Phil were ordered to lie down. The doctors pulled out two long hypodermic syringes and filled each with a murky solution. Someone said it was the milk of green coconuts, though whether or not this was true remains unknown. The doctors said that what they were about to do would be good for the prisoners. If the solution worked as hoped—improving their condition, they were told—it would be given to Japanese troops.

The doctors turned the captives' hands palm-up and swabbed their arms with alcohol. The needles slid in, the plungers depressed, and the aides clicked the stopwatches. The doctors told the captives to describe their sensations.

For Louie, within a few seconds, the porch started gyrating. The doctor pushed more solution into his vein, and the spinning worsened. He felt as if pins were being jabbed all over his body. Then the blood rushed from his head, the same sensation that he used to feel when Phil lifted *Super Man* out of a dive. His skin burned, itched, and stung. The porch pitched and turned. Across the porch, Phil was experiencing the same symptoms. The doctors, speaking in sterile tones, continued to question them. Then everything blurred. Louie cried out that he was going to faint. The doctor withdrew the needle.

The captives were taken back to their cells. Within fifteen minutes, Louie's entire body was covered in a rash. He lay awake all night, itching and burning. Several days later, when the symptoms subsided, he and Phil were again taken to the porch and again injected, this time with more solution. Again they rolled through vertigo and burned with rashes. After another few days, they were subjected to a third experiment, and a few days later came a fourth. In the last infusion, a full pint of the fluid was pumped into their veins.

Both men survived, and as terrible as their experience had been, they were lucky. All over their captured territories, the Japanese were using at least ten thousand POWs and civilians, including infants, as test subjects for experiments in biological and chemical warfare. Thousands died.

Back in his cell, Louie felt a sharp headache coming on, and was soon dizzy and baking with fever. His bones ached. Phil was going through the same ordeal. The guards summoned a doctor. Louie picked out a familiar word: dengue. The prisoners had dengue fever, a potentially fatal mosquito-borne illness that was ravaging the tropics. The doctor offered no treatment.

Louie drifted into a febrile fog. Time slid by, and he felt little connection to his body. As he lay there, feet tramped outside, livid faces appeared again at the door, and Louie felt himself struck with rocks, stabbed with sticks, and slapped with wads of spit. A new crop of submariners had come.

Louie floated through it, too sick to resist. The faces streamed past, and the stones and sticks cracked off his burning bones. Time passed with merciful speed, and the abuse was soon over.

Louie was brought to interrogation again. The officers pushed a map of Hawaii in front of him and told him to mark where the air bases were.

Louie resisted for some time, but the interrogators leaned hard on him. At last, he broke. He dropped his head and, with an expression of ashamed resignation, told them everything—the exact location of the bases, the numbers of planes.

The Japanese broke into jubilant smiles. They opened up a bottle of cola and gave it to Louie, along with a biscuit and a pastry. As they celebrated, they had no idea that the "bases" that Louie had identified were the fake airfields he had seen when tooling around Hawaii with Phil. If the Japanese bombed there, the only planes they would hit would be made of plywood.

Louie and Phil's usefulness had been exhausted. At headquarters, the officers discussed what to do with the captives. The decision was probably easy; the same Japanese officers had been responsible for killing the marines whose names were written on Louie's cell wall. Louie and Phil would be executed.

On August 24, men gathered before Louie's cell, and once more he was dragged out. *Is this it?* he thought. He was tugged to the interrogation building. Expecting to learn that he was condemned to execution, he was told something else: A Japanese navy ship was coming to Kwajalein, and he was going to be put on it and taken to a POW camp in Yokohama, Japan. At the last minute, the officers had decided not to kill him. It would be a long time before Louie learned why.

Louie felt deep relief, believing that at a POW camp, he would be treated under the humane rules of international law, put in contact with the Red Cross, and allowed to contact his family. Phil, too, was told that he was going to Yokohama. He was amazed and hopeful.

On August 26, 1943, forty-two days after arriving at Execution Island, Louie and Phil were led from their cells, stripped naked, splashed with buckets of water, allowed to dress again, and taken toward the ship that would carry them to Japan.

As he walked from his cell for the last time, Louie looked back, searching for Kawamura. He couldn't find him.

Nineteen

Two Hundred Silent Men

LOUIE AND PHIL WERE SITTING IN A HOLDING ROOM ON the navy ship when the door slapped open and a crowd of agitated, sloppy-drunk Japanese sailors pushed in. One of them asked if Japan would win the war.

"No," said Phil.

A fist caught Phil in the face, then swung back and struck him again. Louie was asked who would win the war.

"America."

The sailors fell onto the captives, fists flying. Something connected with Louie's nose, and he felt a crunch. An officer ran in, peeled the crewmen off, and ordered them out. Louie's nose was bleeding. When he touched it, he felt a gash and a bone elbowing out sideways.

In choppy English, the officer told them that the crewmen had been rifling through the captives' wallets, which had been confiscated when they came on board. In Louie's wallet, they had found a folded, stained bit of newspaper. It was the cartoon that Louie had cut from the *Honolulu Advertiser* many months before, depicting his service in the raid on Wake. The officer said that about half of the ship's crew had been on Wake that night, and their ship, apparently anchored offshore, had been sunk.

The crewmen had regrets about attacking the captives. Later, the

This clipping was in Louie's wallet throughout his raft journey, and was stained purple by the wallet dye. Its discovery by the Japanese resulted in Louie and Phil being beaten.
Courtesy of Louis Zamperini

door opened again, and two of them lurched in, muttered apologies, draped their arms around Louie, and gave him *sake*.

Louie and Phil were separated again, and Louie was locked in an officer's cabin. Every few days, he had strange visits from a grinning sailor who would lean into the room, say, "Thump on the head for a biscuit?," rap his knuckles on Louie's head, hand him a biscuit, and amble away.

Between the sailor's visits, Louie had nothing to do but sit, pinching his fingers around his nose to set the bones. Bored, he rummaged through the cabin and found a bottle of *sake*. He began taking furtive sips of the rice wine, little enough that its absence might not be missed. When, during a submarine alert, he panicked and drank so much that no one could fail to notice it, he decided that he might as well finish it off. In the last days of the journey, the skinny American and the fat Japanese bottle had a grand time together.

After a three-week journey, including a stopover at Truk Atoll, the ship docked at Yokohama, on the eastern coast of Japan's central island,

Honshu. Louie was blindfolded and led out. Solid ground came under-foot. Through a gap in his blindfold, Louie's first glimpse of Japan was the word CHEVROLET, stamped on a hubcap. He was standing before a car.

He heard someone stomping off the ship, shouting. The men around Louie froze; the man approaching, he assumed, must be an officer. Louie felt the officer grabbing him and shoving him into the car's jump seat. As he struggled to get his legs in, the officer cracked him in the face with a flashlight. Louie felt his nose bones splay again. He thought of the *sake* and wondered if this man was its owner. He folded himself into the seat, alongside Phil.

The Chevy motored up through hilly country. After the better part of an hour, it stopped. Hands pulled Louie onto his feet and led him into an enclosed, humid space. The blindfold was untied. He was in a bathhouse, apparently in the promised POW camp. Phil was no longer with him. There was a tub before him, filled with water that carried the tart smell of disinfectant. Told to undress and get in, he stepped into the water, luxuriating in the warmth, scrubbing himself clean for the first time since he'd left Oahu.

When his bath was over, he was told to dress again. A man came with clippers and shaved his head and beard. Louie was escorted out, led down a hallway, and stopped at a door. The guard told him to go in and wait for orders.

Louie walked into the room. The lights were out, and he could only just make out the silhouette of a man in civilian clothing, facing away from him. Someone flipped on a light, the man turned, and Louie saw his face.

It was his college friend Jimmie Sasaki.

———

"We meet again," Sasaki said. Louie gaped at him in astonishment. He knew nothing of Sasaki's alleged spying, and was stunned to see his friend in the service of his enemy. Sasaki looked at him warmly. He'd been prepared to see Louie, but he was disturbed by how thin he was. He made a playful crack about how ugly Louie looked bald.

What followed was a strange and stilted conversation. Sasaki asked a few questions about Louie's odyssey, then began reminiscing about USC, meals at the student union, ten-cent movies on campus. Louie, uneasy, waited for questions on military matters, but they never came. The closest Sasaki got was to express confidence that Japan would win the war. He told Louie that he was a civilian employee of the Japanese navy, which had made him head interrogator of all POWs in Japan. He said he bore a rank equal to that of admiral.

Louie was taken outside. He was in a large compound with several one-story buildings surrounded by a high fence topped with barbed wire. There was something spooky about this place. Louie, like every man brought there, noticed it immediately. Gathered in drifts against the buildings were some two hundred whisper-thin captive Allied servicemen. Every one of them had his eyes fixed on the ground. They were as silent as snow.

Louie was led to a bench, some distance from the other captives. He saw Phil far away, sitting alone. A couple of captives sat on other benches across the compound, hiding their hands from the guards' view and gesturing to each other in Morse code—fists for dots and flat hands for dashes. Louie watched them until a captive approached. The man seemed to have permission to speak. He began to tell Louie about where he was.

This wasn't a POW camp. It was a secret interrogation center called Ofuna, where "high-value" captured men were housed in solitary confinement, starved, tormented, and tortured to divulge military secrets. Because Ofuna was kept secret from the outside world, the Japanese operated with an absolutely free hand. The men in Ofuna, said the Japanese, weren't POWs; they were "unarmed combatants" at war against Japan and, as such, didn't have the rights that international law accorded POWs. In fact, they had no rights at all. If captives "confessed their crimes against Japan," they'd be treated "as well as regulations permit." Over the course of the war, some one thousand Allied captives would be hauled into Ofuna, and many would be held there for years.

The man told Louie the rules. He was forbidden to speak to anyone but the guards, to put his hands in his pockets, or to make eye contact with other captives. His eyes were to be directed downward at all times. He had to learn to count in Japanese, because every morning there was *tenko,* a roll call and inspection in which men had to count off. To use the *benjo*—latrine—he had to ask in broken Japanese: "*Benjo kudasai,*" said while bowing. He wouldn't be given a cup, so if he was thirsty he'd have to beg the guard to escort him to the washstand. There were rules about every detail of life, from the folding of blankets to the buttoning of clothes, each reinforcing isolation and total obedience. The slightest violation would bring a beating.

The Japanese were abundantly clear about one thing. In this secret place, they could, and did, do anything they wanted to their captives, and no one would ever know. They stressed that they did not guarantee that captives would survive Ofuna. "They can kill you here," Louie was told. "No one knows you're alive."

After nightfall, Louie was taken into a barracks and led to a tiny cell. On the floor was a thin *tatami* (straw mat), which would be his bed, with three paper sheets. There was a small window, but it had no glass, so wind eddied through the room. The walls were flimsy, the floorboards gapped, the ceiling was tarpaper. It was mid-September, and with winter approaching, Louie would be living in a building that was, in one captive's words, barely a windbreak.

Louie curled up under the paper sheets. There were dozens of men in cells near him, but no one made a sound. Phil was in a cell far down the hall, and for the first time in months, Louie wasn't near him. In this warren of captive men, he was alone.

Each day began at six: a bell clanging, a shouting guard, captives running outside to *tenko*. Louie would fall into a line of haggard men. Guards stalked them, clubs or baseball bats in their hands and rifles with fixed bayonets over their shoulders, making menacing postures and yelling unintelligibly. The captives were hounded through a frenzied routine: counting off, bowing toward Emperor Hirohito, rushing to the washstand and *benjo*, then rushing back to the assembly area five minutes later. Then it was back to the barracks, where guards rifled through the men's things in search of contraband, misfolded blankets, misaligned buttons—anything to justify a beating.

Breakfast came from captives who handed out bowls of watery, fetid slop, which each man ate alone in his cell. Then men were paired off, given clots of wet rope, and forced to bend double, put the rope on the floor, and wash the 150-foot-long barracks aisle floor at a run, or sometimes waddling duck-style, while the guards trotted behind them, swatting them. Then it was back outside, where the guards made the men run circles or perform calisthenics, often until they collapsed. When the exercise was over, the men had to sit outside, regardless of the weather. The only breaks in the silence were the screams coming from the interrogation room.

Punctuating the passage of each day were beatings. Men were beaten for folding their arms, for sitting naked to help heal sores, for cleaning their teeth, for talking in their sleep. Most often, they were beaten for not understanding orders, which were almost always issued in Japanese. Dozens of men were lined up and clubbed in the knees for one man's alleged infraction. A favorite punishment was to force men to stand, sometimes for hours, in the "Ofuna crouch," a painful and strenuous position in which men stood with knees bent halfway and arms overhead. Those who fell over or dropped their arms were clubbed and kicked. Captives who tried to assist victims were attacked themselves, usually far more violently, so victims were on their own. Any attempt to protect oneself—ducking, shielding the face—provoked greater violence. "My job," remembered captive Glenn McConnell, "was to keep my nose on my face and keep from being disassembled." The beatings, he wrote, "were of such intensity that many of us wondered if we'd ever live to see the end of the war."

At night, in the cell again, Louie awaited dinner, eaten alone in the dark. Then he just sat there. He wasn't permitted to speak, whistle, sing, tap, read, or look out his window. There was another inspection outside, another haranguing, and then the uneasy pause of night, the pacing of the guards, before the dawn again brought shouting and running and the thud of clubs.

———

At Ofuna, as at the scores of POW camps scattered throughout Japan and its conquests, the men used for guard duty were the dregs of the Japanese military. Many had washed out of regular soldierly life, too incompetent to perform basic duties. Quite a few were deranged. According to captives, there were two characteristics common to nearly all Ofuna guards. One was marked stupidity. The other was murderous sadism.

In the Japanese military of that era, corporal punishment was routine practice. "Iron must be beaten while it's hot; soldiers must be beaten while they're fresh" was a saying among servicemen. "No strong soldiers," went another, "are made without beatings." For all Japanese soldiers, especially low-ranking ones, beating was inescapable, often a daily event. It is thus unsurprising that camp guards, occupying the lowest station in a military that applauded brutality, would vent their frustrations on the helpless men under their authority. Japanese historians call this phenomenon "transfer of oppression."

This tendency was powerfully reinforced by two opinions common in Japanese society in that era. One held that Japanese were racially and morally superior to non-Japanese, a "pure" people divinely destined to rule. Just as Allied soldiers, like the cultures they came from, often held virulently racist views of the Japanese, Japanese soldiers and civilians, intensely propagandized by their government, usually carried their own caustic prejudices about their enemies, seeing them as brutish, subhuman beasts or fearsome "Anglo-Saxon devils." This racism, and the hatred and fear it fomented, surely served as an accelerant for abuse of Allied prisoners.

In Japan's militaristic society, all citizens, from earliest childhood, were relentlessly indoctrinated with the lesson that to be captured in war was intolerably shameful. The 1941 Japanese Military Field Code made clear what was expected of those facing capture: "Have regard for your family first. Rather than live and bear the shame of imprisonment, the soldier must die and avoid leaving a dishonorable name." As a result, in many hopeless battles, virtually every Japanese soldier fought to the death. For every Allied soldier killed, four were captured; for every 120 Japanese soldiers killed, one was captured. In some losing battles, Japanese soldiers committed suicide en masse to avoid capture. The few who were captured sometimes gave false names, believing that their families would rather think that their son had died. The depth of the conviction was demonstrated at Australia's Cowra camp in 1944, when hundreds of Japanese POWs flung themselves at camp machine guns and set their living quarters afire in a mass suicide attempt that became known as "the night of a thousand suicides." The contempt and revulsion that most Japanese felt for those who surrendered or were captured extended to Allied servicemen. This thinking created an atmosphere in which to abuse, enslave, and even murder a captive or POW was considered acceptable, even desirable.

Some guards, intoxicated by absolute power and indoctrinated in racism and disgust for POWs, fell easily into sadism. But those less inclined toward their culture's prejudices may still have been vulnerable to the call to brutality. To be made responsible for imprisoning people is surely, to many guards, an unsettling experience, especially when they are tasked with depriving their prisoners of the most basic necessities. Perhaps some guards forced their prisoners to live in maximally dehumanizing conditions so that they could reassure themselves that they were merely giving loathsome beasts their due. Paradoxically, then, some of the worst abuses inflicted on captives and POWs may have arisen from the guards' discomfort with being abusive.

Writing of his childhood in slavery, Frederick Douglass told of being acquired by a man whose wife was a tenderhearted woman who had never owned a slave. "Her face was made of heavenly smiles and her voice of tranquil music," Douglass wrote. She lavished him with motherly love, even giving him reading lessons, unheard of in slave-holding society. But after being ordered by her husband to treat the boy like the slave he was, she transformed into a vicious "demon." She, like the Ofuna guards more than a century later, had succumbed to what Douglass called "the fatal poison of irresponsible power."

Of all of the warped, pitiless men who persecuted captives at Ofuna, Sueharu Kitamura stood above all others. In civilian life, by different accounts, he was either a *sake* salesman or a movie scenario writer. In Ofuna, he was the medical officer. Fascinated by suffering, he forced sick and injured captives to come to him for "treatment," then tortured and mutilated them while quizzing them on their pain, his mouth curved in a moist smile. Known as "the Butcher" and "the Quack," Kitamura was Ofuna's most eager instigator of beatings. He was a massive man, built like a bison, and he punched like a heavyweight. No official in Ofuna was more hated or feared.

Though under great pressure to conform to a culture of brutality, a few guards refused to participate in the violence. In one incident, a captive was clubbed so savagely that he was certain he was going to be killed. In the middle of the assault, the attacking guard was called away, and a guard known as Hirose* was ordered to finish the beating. Out of sight of other guards, Hirose told the captive to cry out as if he were being struck, then pounded his club harmlessly against the floor. The two acted out their parts until it seemed enough "beating" had been done. The captive believed that Hirose may have saved his life.

What Hirose did took nerve. Everywhere in Japan, demonstrating sympathy for captives or POWs was taboo. When a child living near the Zentsuji POW camp expressed compassion for the prisoners, her comments became a national scandal. Camp personnel caught trying to improve conditions for POWs, or even voicing sympathy for them, were sometimes beaten by their superiors. "The general opinion towards POWs at that time was very bad," wrote Yukichi Kano, a private at another camp who was beloved by POWs he tried to assist. "There was always some risk of to be misunderstood by other Japanese by making

* Probably Lieutenant Hiroetsu Narushima.

humane interpretation of our duty. To resist against the wrong hostile feeling, prejudice, and lack of knowledge was not very easy for the lower rank soldier like me."

At Ofuna, merciful guards paid the price. One officer, upon learning that another guard had shown leniency to captives, assaulted the guard with a sword. During his nightly walk from his kitchen job to his cell, one captive would regularly see a guard who refused to beat prisoners being singled out for gang attacks from his fellow guards.

At Ofuna, captives weren't just beaten, they were starved. The thrice-daily meals usually consisted of a bowl of broth with a bit of vegetable and a bowl or half bowl of rancid rice, sometimes mixed with barley. It contained virtually no protein and was grossly lacking in nutritive value and calories. It was camp policy to give diminished and/or spoiled rations to captives suspected of withholding information, and at times the entire camp's rations were cut to punish one captive's reticence. The food was infested with rat droppings, maggots, and so much sand and grit that Louie's teeth were soon pitted, chipped, and cracked. The men nicknamed the rations "all dumpo."

The extremely low caloric intake and befouled food, coupled with the exertion of the forced exercise, put the men's lives in great danger. "We were dying," wrote captive Jean Balch, "on about 500 calories a day." Scurvy was common. Foodborne parasites and pathogens made diarrhea almost ubiquitous. Most feared was beriberi, a potentially deadly disease caused by a lack of thiamine. There were two forms of beriberi, and they could occur concurrently. "Wet" beriberi affected the heart and the circulatory system, causing marked edema—swelling—of the extremities; if untreated, it was often fatal. "Dry" beriberi affected the nervous system, causing numbness, confusion, unsteady gait, and paralysis. When wet beriberi victims pressed on their swollen limbs, deep indentations would remain long after the pressure was removed, giving the men the unnerving impression that their bones were softening. In some cases, wet beriberi caused extreme swelling of the scrotum. Some men's testicles swelled to the size of bread loaves.

In Ofuna's theater of cruelty, survival was an open question, and deaths were common. For Louie, Phil, and the other captives, the only hope lay in the Allies rescuing them, but this prospect also carried tremendous danger.

In the fall of 1942, when the Americans attacked Japanese ships off Tarawa, in the Gilbert Islands, the Japanese beheaded twenty-two POWs held on the island. A similar horror played out on Japanese-held Ballale, in the Shortland Islands, where British POWs were being used as slaves to build an airfield. According to a Japanese officer, in the spring of 1943, when it appeared that the Americans were soon to land on Ballale, Japanese authorities issued a directive that in the event of an invasion, the POWs were to be killed. No landing occurred, but in response to an Allied bombing, the Japanese executed all of the POWs anyway, some seventy to one hundred men.

A few weeks after Louie arrived at Ofuna, an American carrier force began bombing and shelling Wake Atoll, where the Americans captured during the Japanese invasion were still being held as slaves. Mistakenly believing that an invasion was imminent, the Japanese commander had the prisoners blindfolded, bound, shot, and dumped in a hole. One man escaped. When he was caught three weeks later, the commander himself beheaded him. The only trace of the men was found years afterward. In the atoll lagoon, on a hunk of coral, one of the POWs had scraped a message:

98

US

P.W.

5-10-43

These murders were the first applications of what would come to be known as the "kill-all" rule. Japanese policy held that camp commanders could not, under any circumstances, allow Allied forces to recapture POWs. If Allied advances made this a possibility, POWs were to be executed. "If there is any fear that the POWs would be retaken due to the tide of battle turning against us," read a May 1944 order issued to every POW branch camp commander, "decisive measures must be taken without returning a single POW."

That August, the Japanese War Ministry would issue a clarification of this order, sending it to all POW camp commanders:

At such time as the situation becomes urgent and it be extremely important, the POWs will be concentrated and confined in their present location and under heavy guard the preparation for the final disposition will be made . . . Whether they are destroyed individually or in groups, or however it is done, with mass bombing, poisonous smoke, poisons, drowning, decapitation, or what, dispose of them as the situation dictates . . . In any case it is the aim not to allow the escape of a single one, to annihilate them all, and not to leave any traces.

As the Allies fought their way toward Japan, the captives in Ofuna and POWs everywhere else faced the very real threat that Allied successes would bring the kill-all policy to bear on them. While none of the captives knew of the incidents in which this order had already been followed, the guards at Ofuna enjoyed warning them about the policy. Like every other captive, Louie knew that most of the guards would be eager to carry it out.

Twenty

Farting for Hirohito

AT FIRST, THERE WAS ONLY SILENCE AND ISOLATION. AT night, all Louie could see were walls, stripes of ground through the gaps in the floorboards, and his own limbs, as slender as reeds. The guards would stomp down the aisles, occasionally dragging a man out to be beaten. There were men in cells around Louie, but no one spoke. Come daylight, Louie was suddenly among them, hustled outside and herded in crazy circles; with his eyes trained obediently on the ground and his mouth obediently closed, Louie was no less alone. The only break in the gloom came in the form of a smiling guard who liked to saunter down the barracks aisle, pause before each cell, raise one leg, and vent a surly fart at the captive within. He never quite succeeded in farting his way down the entire cell block.

In stolen glances, nods, and hushed words, Louie sorted out the constellations of Ofuna. His barracks was inhabited by new captives, mostly Americans, survivors of downed aircraft and sunken seacraft. Down the hall lived two emaciated American navy officers, the ranking Allied servicemen. First in rank was Commander Arthur Maher, who had survived the sinking of his ship, the *Houston,* in Indonesia's Sunda Strait. He had swum to Java and fled into the mountains, only to be hunted down. Second in rank was thirty-five-year-old Commander

John Fitzgerald, who had fallen into Japanese hands after he'd scuttled his burning submarine, the *Grenadier,* which had been bombed. The Japanese had attempted, in vain, to torture information out of Fitzgerald, clubbing him, jamming penknives under his fingernails, tearing his fingernails off, and applying the "water cure"—tipping him backward,

Louie's barracks at Ofuna. His cell window was
the third from the right. *Frank Tinker*

holding his mouth shut, and pouring water up his nose until he passed out. Both Maher and Fitzgerald spoke Japanese, and they served as the camp's only resident interpreters. All captives, regardless of nationality, deferred to them.

During forced exercise one day, Louie fell into step with William Harris, a twenty-five-year-old marine officer, the son of marine general Field Harris. Tall and dignified, with a face cut in hard lines, Harris had been captured in the surrender of Corregidor in May 1942. With another American,* he had escaped and embarked on an eight-and-a-half-hour swim across Manila Bay, kicking through a downpour in darkness as fish bit him. Dragging himself ashore on the Japanese-occupied Bataan Peninsula, he had begun a run for China, hiking through jungles and over mountains, navigating the coast in boats donated by sympathetic Filipinos, hitching rides on burros, and surviving in part by eating ants. He had joined a Filipino guerrilla band, but when he had heard of the American landing at Guadalcanal, the marine in him had called. Making a dash by boat toward Australia in

---

* Future Indiana governor Edgar Whitcomb.

William Harris.
Courtesy of Katherine H. Meares

hopes of rejoining his unit, he had gotten as far as the Indonesian island of Morotai before his journey ended. Civilians had turned him in to the Japanese, who had discovered that he was a general's son and sent him to Ofuna. Even here, he was itching to escape.

Each day, Louie and Harris hung together, laboring through forced exercise, bearing blows from the guards, and whispering. The curious thing about Harris was that while he was certainly a tall man—six foot two or three, according to his daughter—virtually everyone, including Louie, would remember him as a giant, by one account six foot eight, by another six-ten. Figuratively, though, Harris was indeed a giant. He was probably a genius. Impeccably educated, conversant in several languages, including Japanese, he had a perfect photographic memory. With a single glance, he could memorize a huge volume of information and retain it for years. In Ofuna, this attribute would be a blessing and a terrible curse.

Jimmie Sasaki made frequent visits to Ofuna, and he liked to call Louie to his office. Among ragged captives and guards in drab uniforms, Sasaki was a spectacle, dressing like a movie star and wearing his hair slicked back and parted down the middle, like Howard Hughes. The captives dubbed him "Handsome Harry." Louie expected interrogation, but it never came. Sasaki only wanted to reminisce about USC and boast of Japan's coming victory. He knew that Louie had lied in his interrogation on Kwajalein, but he didn't pursue the truth. Louie couldn't understand it. Every other captive was grilled, at least at first, but no effort was made to interrogate him. He suspected that Sasaki was using his influence to protect him.

Ofuna had one other notable resident. Gaga was a duck who bobbed around in a fire trough, paddling with a broken leg that a captive had fitted with a little splint. The duck trailed the captives around like a puppy, limping in and out of the kitchen, where the workers apparently fed him. Every morning at *tenko*, Gaga peg-legged to the parade ground and stood with the men, and one captive would later swear that when the men bowed toward the emperor, Gaga bowed in imitation. In so dark a place, this cheerful bird became especially beloved. For the captives, wrote Ofuna survivor "Pappy" Boyington, Gaga became a creature on which "to rest their tortured brains a moment while they [were] praying and worrying if anyone [would] ever free them."

Louie rarely crossed paths with Phil, who was housed far down the hall. The pilot seemed to be handling Ofuna well enough, but he remained shrunken and frail, a hollow distance in his eyes. During forced exercise, he wasn't strong enough to run, so he and a few others were separated and harangued through calisthenics.

Once, when Louie and Phil shuffled up next to each other on the parade ground, Phil finally spoke of the crash. Filled with anguish, he said that he felt responsible for the deaths of all of those men. Louie reassured him that the crash hadn't been his fault, but Phil was unswayed.

"I'll never fly again," he said.

In time, Louie discovered that both the forced silence of Ofuna and the bowing submission of its captives were illusions. Beneath the hush was a humming underground of defiance.

It began with sidelong whispers. The guards couldn't be everywhere, and as soon as an area was left unattended, the captives became absorbed in stealthy muttering. Men scribbled notes on slips of toilet paper and hid them for each other in the *benjo*. Once, when given permission to speak aloud so he could translate orders, Commander Maher advised another captive on stealing techniques, right in front of the oblivious guards. The boldest captives would walk up to the guards, look straight at them, and speak in English, using a querying tone. The confused guards thought they were being asked questions, when in fact the men were speaking to each other.

When words couldn't be used, Morse code could. At night, in the small intervals when the guards left the building, the whole barracks would start tapping. Outside, men would whisper in code, using "tit" for "dot" and "da" for "dash," words that could be spoken without moving the lips. Louie used his hands for code, obscuring them from the guards. Most of the discussions were trivial—Louie would be remembered for descriptions of his mother's cooking—but the content didn't matter. The triumph was in the subversion.

Louie soon learned a critical rule of conversation: Never use a guard's real name. Guards who discovered that they were being discussed often delivered savage beatings, so the men invented nicknames for them. The sluggish, quiet camp commander was called the Mummy. Guard nicknames included Turdbird, Flange Face, the Weasel, Liver Lip, Fatty, and Termite. A particularly repugnant guard was known as Shithead.

The defiance took on a life of its own. Men would smile and address the guards in friendly tones, cooing out insults filthy enough to curl a man's hair. One captive convinced a particularly dim-witted guard that a sundial would work at night if he used a match. A fragrant favorite involved saving up intestinal gas, explosively voluminous thanks to chronic dysentery, prior to *tenko*. When the men were ordered to bow toward the emperor, the captives would pitch forward in concert and let thunderclaps fly for Hirohito.

Louie had another, private act of rebellion. A fellow captive, a bookbinder in civilian life, gave him a tiny book that he'd made in camp with rice paste flattened into pages and sewn together. Louie either found or stole a pencil and began keeping a diary. In it, he recorded what had happened since his crash, then continued with life in the camp. On the book's central pages, in bold print, he wrote hometown contact information for other captives, making it seem to be an innocuous address book. He wrote his diary entries in faint script upside down in the back of the book, where they might be overlooked. He pried up a board on his cell floor and hid the diary underneath. With daily room inspections, discovery was likely, and would probably bring a clubbing. But this small declaration of self mattered a great deal to Louie. He knew that he might well die here. He wanted to leave a testament to what he had endured, and who he had been.

After food, what every man wanted most was war news. The Japanese sealed their camps from outside information and went to some lengths to convince their captives of Allied annihilation, first by trumpeting Japanese victories, and later, when victories stopped coming, by inventing stories of Allied losses and ridiculously implausible Japanese feats. Once, they announced that their military had shot Abraham Lincoln and torpedoed Washington, D.C. "They couldn't understand why we laughed," said a prisoner. Ofuna officials had no idea that the captives had found ways to follow the war in spite of them.

New captives were fonts of information, and no sooner had they arrived than their minds were picked clean, the news tapping its way down the cell blocks in minutes. Newspapers rarely appeared, but when one did, stealing it became a campwide obsession. Rations were sometimes delivered to camp wrapped in newspapers, and the two kitchen laborers, Al Mead and Ernest Duva, would quietly pocket them. The boldest men even managed to pinch papers from the interrogation room as they were being questioned. Once stolen, the papers made elaborate secret journeys, passed hand to hand until they reached the translators, Harris, Fitzgerald, and Maher. As translations were done, lookouts stood by, pretending to tie their shoes or adjust their belts. When guards neared, warnings were issued, and the papers vanished, soon to be put to their final use. In a camp with a lot of dysentery and little toilet paper, newspapers were priceless.

In a secret place inside his cell, Harris stored the tools of his clandestine translating trade. Sometime during his stay at Ofuna, he had scavenged or stolen bits of wire and string, strips of cardboard, scraps of paper, and a pencil. The cardboard had been cut from a Canadian Red Cross POW relief package; because the Red Cross didn't know of Ofuna's existence, the package had probably been brought from another camp by the Japanese, who routinely purloined the contents of such parcels for their own consumption. Cutting or tearing the paper into small pages, Harris had used the wire and string to bind them into two books, sewing on the cardboard as covers.

In one book, Harris had recorded the addresses of his fellow captives, including Louie. In the other, he had begun creating an elaborate Japanese-English dictionary. Inside, he had written sentences in Japanese and English—"I feel like eating melon," "Don't you intend to buy a piano"—followed by notes on proper phrasing, verbs, and tenses. Other pages were devoted to a comprehensive list of translations of military terms, words like "torpedo plane," "tank," "bomber," "antiaircraft gun," and "captive." In creating the dictionary, Harris may have had more in mind than translating stolen documents; if he ever escaped from Ofuna, the Japanese translations of words like "compass," "seacoast," and "ashore" might be critical to know. Along with the books, Harris kept a collection of hand-drawn war maps; he'd seen the original maps in stolen newspapers, memorized them, and re-created them. He stored all of these items, along with a newspaper clipping, in a small bag that he kept carefully hidden from the guards.

Thanks to the work of thieves and translators, most captives were well enough informed on the war's progress that they had wagers riding on when it would end. Knowing that the Allies were winning was immensely inspiring, enabling men to go on a little longer. Though the captives' resistance was dangerous, through such acts, dignity was preserved, and through dignity, life itself. Everyone knew what the consequences would be if anyone were caught stealing newspapers or hiding items as incriminating as Harris's maps and dictionary. At the time, it seemed worth the risk.

———

In the fall, the snow came, gliding through the gaps in the barracks walls. During the morning mopping, the water in the aisle froze. Nearly every captive fell ill. Louie, still wearing only the clothes he'd crashed in, developed an ominous cough. Shut outside all day, he and the others stood in large huddles, mixing slowly to give each man time in the middle, where it was warmest.

The rations dwindled. The central authorities were allotting scant food to Ofuna, but this wasn't the half of it. Unloading the ration trucks, captives saw beans, vegetables, and other nutritious fare, yet at mealtime, these items were almost never in their bowls. Camp officials, including the commander, were stealing them. The most flagrant thief was the cook, a ringlet-haired civilian known as Curley. Curley would stand in full view of the captives as he hoisted their food over the fence to civilians, or packed it onto his bicycle and pedaled off to sell it on the black market, where it would bring astronomical prices. Sometimes he'd call Louie over, give him a package of the captives' food, and order him to walk it over to the fence, where a woman would take it in exchange for barter payment. According to one captive, it was widely known that Curley had bought and furnished a house with his profits.

The stealing left Ofuna in a state of famine. "To give you an idea of how hungry we were," wrote Commander Fitzgerald, "it can best be explained by the fact that it took an awful lot of will power to take the last part of starch from my rice bowl in order to stick a snapshot of my wife to a piece of plywood." Commander Maher pleaded for more food. Officials punished his impertinence by slashing the prisoners' rations and intensifying their exercise.

In search of something to occupy their hungry mouths, the captives were seized by a mania for smoking. Small allotments of foul tobacco were handed out, and Louie, like almost all captives, resumed the habit. Men became fiercely addicted. The few who didn't smoke still received the tobacco ration; they were richer than kings. One of Louie's friends, an aging Norwegian sailor named Anton Minsaas, became so hooked that he began trading his food for smokes. Louie urged him to eat, but Minsaas couldn't be persuaded. He grew ever thinner.

Every man in camp was thin, many emaciated, but Louie and Phil were thinner than anyone else. The rations weren't nearly enough, and Louie was plagued by dysentery. He couldn't get warm, and he was racked by a cough. He teetered through the exercise sessions, trying to keep his legs from buckling. At night, he folded his paper blankets to create loft, but it barely helped; the unheated, drafty rooms were only a few degrees warmer than the frigid outside air. When camp officials staged a baseball game, Louie was sent to bat. He hit the ball, took one step, and collapsed. Sprawled on the ground, he heard laughing.

One day that fall, a Japanese newspaper editor came to camp. He had learned that a Louis Zamperini was being held there. In Japan, track was wildly popular, and international running stars were well known. The editor carried a file full of information on Louie, and showed it to the guards.

The guards were fascinated to learn that the sick, emaciated man in the first barracks had once been an Olympic runner. They quickly found a Japanese runner and brought him in for a match race against the American. Hauled out and forced to run, Louie was trounced, and the guards made tittering mockery of him. Louie was angry and shaken, and his growing weakness scared him. POWs were dying by the thousands in camps all over Japan and its captured territories, and winter was coming.

Louie went to Sasaki to ask for help. Since Sasaki was, by his own account, a bigwig, it seemed that it would be easy for him to intervene. But after talking about what "we" would do, Sasaki never followed through. The most he did for Louie was to give him an egg and a tangerine, which Louie shared with other captives. Louie began to believe that Sasaki wasn't his ally, and wasn't protecting him from interrogation. It now seemed that the Japanese simply weren't interested in what he knew. They had brought him to Ofuna to soften him up for something else, but he had no idea what it was.

Where Sasaki failed Louie, the kitchen workers, Mead and Duva, came through, at considerable risk to themselves. Each day as they walked the barracks hall to deliver rations, they balled up an extra portion of rice and sometimes a bit of fish, waited for a moment when the guards glanced away, and tossed it to Louie. Mead whispered his only request: Give half to Phil. Louie would hide half the rice, inch up to Phil on the parade ground, and slip it into his hand.

In October, Anton Minsaas, still trading his food for cigarettes, sank to the ground during an exercise session. The guards dropped on him, clubs flying. Not long after, beriberi set in, and Minsaas became too weak to walk, then could no longer speak. Camp officials brought in a doctor, who injected Minsaas with a green fluid. Minsaas died immediately. Of the green fluid, captive Johan Arthur Johansen wrote, "We . . . believed that it was an attempt to end his life."*

Louie sat in his cell, shivering and praying. A Norwegian sailor, Thorbjørn Christiansen, felt for him, and gave him a gift that may well have saved his life. Digging through his possessions, he pulled out a coat and passed it to Louie. Louie bundled up, hung on, and hoped he wouldn't end up like Minsaas.

———

As 1943 drew to its end, the men in Ofuna had a taste of liberation. The veteran captives, Louie included, were allowed to speak to one another when they were outside. When new captives arrived, they were whisked into solitary confinement and banned from speaking until they were done with the initial interrogation. Veterans began loitering outside the new men's windows, pretending to speak to each other when in fact they were grilling the neophytes.

In the early weeks of 1944, Louie got word that a new captive, just out of solitary, was looking for him. When he tracked the man down, he found a wavy-haired blond from Burbank, not far from Torrance. One of the man's legs was gone, his pant leg tied above the knee. He introduced himself as Fred Garrett, a B-24 pilot. He seemed amazed to see Louie. As Louie listened, Garrett told a remarkable story.

---

* They may have been right. Later, two other captives were given similar injections, and both died. The doctor's intent may have been compassionate; mercy killing was then an accepted practice in Japan.

Before Christmas, the Americans had gone after the Japanese bases in the Marshall Islands, sending waves of bombers. Flying on one such mission, Garrett was shot down over the ocean, incurring a compound ankle fracture. After floating for ten hours on a raft, he was picked up by a Japanese tugboat crew. They took him to an island, where Japanese soldiers took turns kicking his dangling ankle. Then Garrett was flown to another island and thrown into a cell block where nineteen other downed American airmen were being held. His ankle festered, maggots hatched in it, and Garrett began to run a high fever. He was told that he'd be given medical care only if he divulged military secrets. If not, he'd be killed. Garrett lied in interrogation, and the Japanese knew it.

Two days after Christmas, Garrett was tied down, given a spinal anesthetic, and forced to watch as a Japanese corpsman sawed at his leg, then snapped it off. Though the infection was limited to the ankle, the corpsman cut the entire leg off, because, he told Garrett, this would make it impossible for him to fly a plane again. Garrett, delirious, was dumped back in his cell. The next morning, he was thrown onto a truck and taken toward mainland Japan with two other captives. Their journey brought them to Ofuna. The seventeen Americans who were left behind were never seen again.

Garrett then told Louie why he had sought him out. As he had lain in fevered agony in his cell on the second island, he had looked up to see ten names scratched into the wall. He had asked about them and had been told that the first nine men had been executed. No one had told him what had happened to the tenth man. Garrett had spent much of his time mulling over that last name on the wall, perhaps thinking that if this man had survived, so might he. When he had arrived at Ofuna, he had asked if anyone had heard of that man, Louis Zamperini. Garrett and Zamperini, both Los Angeles–area natives, had been held in the same tiny Kwajalein cell almost five thousand miles from home.

Plodding around the parade ground that winter, Louie and Harris befriended Frank Tinker, a dive-bomber pilot and opera singer who had been brought from Kwajalein with Garrett. The three spent most of their outdoor time together, sitting on benches or tracing the edges of the compound, distracting one another from the tooth-chattering cold with mind exercises. Harris and Tinker were experiencing the sparkling mental clarity, prompted by starvation, that Louie had first known on the raft. Tinker became conversant in Norwegian in a single week, taking lessons from his cell neighbors. He saw Harris arguing with another captive about medieval history and the Magna Carta, and he once found the marine sitting with his hands parted as if holding a book, staring at them and mumbling to himself. When Tinker asked what he was doing, Harris said he was reading a text that he had studied at Annapolis many years earlier. Harris could see the book in front of him, as if its words were written across his outspread fingers.

With the help of Christiansen's coat, Duva and Mead's rice, and Harris, Tinker, and Garrett's friendship, Louie survived the winter. Buoyed by the extra calories, he strengthened his legs, lifting his knees up and down as he walked the compound. The guards began goading him into running around the compound alone.

When spring arrived, Ofuna officials brought in a Japanese civilian and ordered Louie to race him. Louie didn't want to do it, but he was told that if he refused, all captives would be punished. The race was about a mile and a half, in laps around the compound. Louie had no intention of winning, and lagged behind for most of it. But as he ran, he found that his body was so light that carrying it was surprisingly easy. All around the compound, the captives watched him, breathless. As the finish approached, they started cheering.

Louie looked ahead at the Japanese runner and realized that he had it within himself to pass the man. He knew what would happen if he won, but the cheering and the accumulation of so many months of humiliation brought something in him to a hard point. He lengthened his stride, seized the lead, and crossed the finish line. The captives whooped.

Louie didn't see the club coming at his skull. He just felt the world tip and go away. His eyes opened to the sight of the sky, ringed with the faces of captives. It had been worth it.

The guards thought they had taught him a lesson. Another runner, his girlfriend in tow, arrived. Louie was ready to beat him too, but before the race, the runner spoke to him kindly, in English, offering to give him a rice ball if he'd throw the race. It would mean a lot to him, he said, to win in front of his girlfriend. Louie lost, the girlfriend was impressed, and the runner delivered one rice ball, plus a second as interest. The payment, Louie said, "made me a professional."

In March, Phil was taken away. It seemed that he had at last gotten lucky; officials said that he was being sent to a POW camp called

Zentsuji. Every captive longed to be transferred to a POW camp, where, it was said, men were registered with the Red Cross and could write home and enjoy vastly better living conditions. Of all POW camps, Zentsuji was rumored to be the best. The interrogators had long dangled this "plush" camp before the captives as a reward for co-operation.

Phil and Louie had only a brief good-bye. They spoke of finding each other again someday, when the war was over. Phil was led through the gate and driven away.

The Zentsuji story was false. Phil was sent to Ashio, a camp north of Tokyo. The POWs of Ashio were handed over to a wire-and-cable firm, which herded them underground to mine copper in conditions that were almost unlivable. This work was usually, but not always, restricted to enlisted POWs. Whether or not Phil was forced into slavery is unknown.

There was, it seemed, one good thing about Ashio. Phil hadn't seen Cecy or his family in well over two years, and knew that they probably thought he was dead. At Ashio, he was told that he could write home. Given paper and pen, he wrote about his days on the life raft with Zamp, his capture, and his yearning for home. "The first night home will hear some interesting tales," he wrote. "Much love til we're together again. Al."

Sometime after Phil turned in his letter, someone found it in a garbage heap, burned. Though the edges were charred, the text was still visible. Phil took back his letter and tucked it away. If he got out of this war alive, he'd deliver it in person.

Twenty-one

Belief

BEHIND TORRANCE HIGH SCHOOL STOOD A HUDDLE OF trees. On many evenings in the months after her brother went missing, Sylvia Zamperini Flammer would drive to the school, turn her car under the trees, and park there, then sit in the quiet and the dimness, alone. As the car cooled over the pavement, tears would stream down Sylvia's cheeks. Sometimes she'd let herself sob, knowing that no one would hear her. After a few minutes, she'd dab away her tears, straighten herself, and start the car again.

On the drive home, she'd think of a lie to explain why her post office trip had again taken so long. She never let anyone know how frightened she was.

––––––

In Torrance, the June 4, 1943, telegram announcing Louie's disappearance was followed by excruciating silence. Many weeks passed, and the military's search yielded no trace of Louie, his crew, or his plane. In town, hope dissolved. When the Zamperinis went out, they saw resignation in their neighbors' faces.

Inside the white house on Gramercy Avenue, the mood was different. In the first days after the telegram arrived, Louise Zamperini had been seized with the conviction that her son was alive. Her husband

and children had felt the same. Days passed, then weeks; spring became summer; and no word came. But the family's conviction remained unshaken. To the family, Louie was among them still, spoken of in the present tense, as if he were just down the street, expected at any moment.

What the Zamperinis were experiencing wasn't denial, and it wasn't hope. It was belief. Louise, Anthony, Pete, and Virginia still sensed Louie's presence; they could still *feel* him. Their distress came not from grief but from the certainty that Louie was out there, in trouble, and they couldn't reach him.

On July 13, Louise felt a wave of urgency. She penned a letter to Major General Willis Hale, commander of the Seventh Air Force. In it, she begged Hale not to give up searching; Louie, she wrote, was alive. Unbeknownst to Louise, on that same day, Louie was captured.

Several weeks later, a reply came from Hale's office. The letter said that given the failure of the search to yield any clues, the military had been forced to accept that Louie and the rest of the men on the plane were gone. It was hoped, the letter said, that Louise would accept this also. Louise ripped up the letter.

Pete was still in San Diego, training navy recruits. The stress wore on him. Sometimes he drove to Torrance to visit his family, and when he arrived, everyone quietly worried about how thin he was. In September, his last letter to Louie, mailed hours before his family was notified of his crash, came back to him. Scribbled on the front were the words *Missing at sea*. On the back, there was a stamp: CASUALTY STATUS VERIFIED. The photograph of Pete was still sealed in the envelope.

That same month, Sylvia's husband, Harvey, left for the war. He wouldn't see his wife again for two years. Living alone, Sylvia was racked with anxiety for her brother and her husband, and she had no one to share it with. Like Pete, she was barely able to eat. Her body had become a slender, taut line. Yearning to connect with someone, she decided to move back in with her parents.

Sylvia held a yard sale to get rid of all of her possessions. She had a clothes washer and dryer, both rationed items that were almost impossible to buy new. One woman wanted to buy them, but Sylvia refused, in hopes that she could sell everything in one lot. The woman promptly bought the entire house's contents for $1,000, just to get the appliances. Sylvia took what little she had left and drove to Torrance.

She found her father just as he had been since the news had come:

chin up, smiling bravely, sometimes through tears. Virginia, living at home and building military ships at Western Pipe and Steel, was as distraught as Sylvia. Their mother was the biggest worry. At first Louise cried often. Then, as the months passed, she hardened down. The weeping rash on her hands, which had appeared almost the moment she'd learned of Louie's disappearance, raged. She couldn't wear gloves, and could no longer do anything with her hands. Sylvia and her father took over the cooking.

Sylvia quit her job in a dentist's office and took a new one as a dental assistant in an army hospital, hoping that the job might give her access to information about Louie. There, she heard talk of a plane shortage in the military, so she took a second job, moonlighting on the evening shift in the blueprint office of an aircraft factory. She was almost unbearably tense. One night, leaving work late, she came upon a group of workers sitting under a plane, gambling. She suddenly found herself shouting at them, saying that her brother was missing, America needed planes, and here they were goofing off. Sylvia was startled by her outburst, but she didn't regret it. It made her feel better.

On October 6, Louie's army trunk bumped onto his parents' doorstep, heavy and final. Louise couldn't bring herself to look inside. She had it dragged to the basement and covered with a blanket. It would sit there, unopened, for the rest of her life.

Everyone in the family was suffering, but the children wanted to insulate their mother. They never cried together, instead telling each other invented stories of Louie's adventures on a tropical island. Most of the time, Anthony simply couldn't talk about Louie. Sylvia spent a lot of time in church, praying for Louie and Harvey. Sometimes she and Virginia drove to San Diego to see Pete, and they'd all go out for a drink to cheer one another up. They never discussed the possibility that Louie was dead. When Sylvia walked through downtown Torrance with her family, she noticed oblique glances from passersby. Their expressions seemed to say that they pitied the Zamperinis for being unable to accept the truth.

Every evening, Sylvia wrote a letter to her husband. Every week or so, she wrote one to Louie. She made a point of writing as if everything were normal, sharing the trivial news of home. She had an address for Harvey; for Louie she had nothing, so she addressed his letters to the Red Cross. She'd tell her mother that she was mailing letters, get in the car, drive to the post office, and drop the letters in the box. Then she'd drive to Torrance High, park under the trees, and cry.

At night, when the lights were out and she was alone in her childhood bed, Sylvia often broke down again. When sleep came, it was fitful and haunted. Because she knew nothing of what had happened to her brother, her mind latched onto the image she had seen in the newspaper after Nauru: Louie peering through a hole in the side of *Super Man*. The image had fixed in her mind the idea of Louie being shot, and this was the point around which her nightmares circled: never a crash, never water, only bullets bloodying Louie as he sat in his plane. Sylvia was always trying to get to Louie, but she was never able. As bad as the nightmares were, in them, Louie was never killed. Even Sylvia's imagination didn't allow for her brother's death.

In December 1943, the family prepared to celebrate their first Christmas without Louie. The mailman knocked at the door each day to deliver a harvest of cards and letters, most of them offering sympathy. The holiday tree was strung with popcorn and cranberries, and beneath it sat a collection of gifts for Louie. The gifts would be tucked away in the belief that one day, Louie would come home to open them himself.

Louise bought a little Christmas card depicting a cherub in a red dress blowing a horn as she stood surrounded by lambs. Inside, she wrote a message.

Dear Louis. Where ever you are, I know you want us to think of you as well and safe. May God be with you, + guide you. Love from all. Mother Dad Pete Sylvia and Virginia. Christmas 25 43.

Two months later, after a campaign of saturation bombing, America seized Kwajalein. The island's dense jungle had been bombed away; in its place were massive craters, burned tree stumps, and churned earth. "The entire island looked as if it had been picked up twenty thousand feet and then dropped," said one serviceman. In what was left of an administrative building, someone found a stack of documents. Outside, a serviceman, climbing through the remains of a wooden structure, saw something in the wreckage and dug it out. It was a long splinter of wood. Etched along the slat, in capital letters, was the name LOUIS ZAMPERINI.

On Oahu, Joe Deasy was summoned to Hickam Field. When he arrived, he was handed translations of some of the Japanese documents that had been taken from Kwajalein. He began to read. Two American airmen, the documents said, had been fished from a life raft and brought to Kwajalein. Their names weren't given, but they were described as a pilot and a bombardier. They'd been in a plane crash—the date was apparently provided—and three men had survived, but one had died on the raft. The other two had drifted for forty-seven days. Included among the papers were interrogation reports and drawings of B-24s made by the captives. The report stated that the men had been beaten, then sent to Japan by boat.

The moment that Deasy read the report, he knew who the men were. Deasy had been long at war, and the experience had ground away his emotions, but this revelation broke through: Phillips and Zamperini had survived their crash. Deasy's elation was tailed by a sinking sense of guilt: In their painstaking search of the ocean, they had missed seeing the lost men, but the enemy had not.

"I was happy to have found them," Deasy recalled, "but the next thing is, where the hell are they?" If the report of their transport to Japan was correct, it still didn't mean they had gotten there alive, or that they had survived whatever lay in store for them there.

The military now knew with a fair amount of certainty that everyone who had gone up on *Green Hornet,* with the exception of Zamperini and Phillips, was dead. Apparently because of the sketchiness of the reports and the fact that Louie's and Phil's fates were still unknown, the families of the dead and the two still missing weren't notified.

Like the Zamperinis, the Phillips family had been largely in the dark since Allen had disappeared. Allen's father was at Camp Pickett in Virginia; his mother, Kelsey, rattled around in her empty house in Princeton, Indiana. After the telegram informing them that Allen was missing, they received a letter from an adjutant from the 42nd squadron, giving details on how Allen had disappeared. The adjutant wrote with a tone of finality, speaking of "your hour of grief," noting that Allen "will always be revered by the members of this organization" and offering to "extend myself to you to ease your sorrow." The next month, a package came to Allen's father at Camp Pickett. In it were two bronze oakleaf clusters, awarded to Allen for his valor in the missions of Makin, Tarawa, and Nauru. "Pending final determination of your son's status," the cover letter read, "the Oak Leaf Clusters are being sent to you for safe-keeping." Though the Phillipses didn't know it, the medals arrived the same week Allen was captured.

Chaplain Phillips wanted to send the oak-leaf clusters to his wife but feared losing them in the mail, so he kept them with him in Virginia. He took a picture of them, along with Allen's service ribbons, wings, insignia, and Air Medal, attached the picture to a maroon piece of felt he'd cut from a lady's hat, and glued the felt to a walnut plaque. When he got back to Indiana, he planned to attach the actual medals and ribbons to the felt and stand the plaque on the bookcase, under Allen's picture. "It certainly is swell," he wrote to his daughter.

In the absence of information, all the Phillipses could do was ponder what little they knew. They, like the Zamperinis, refused to conclude that their boy was dead. "I think I have thought of every conceivable angle to what Allen did and I have not dismissed any of them from my mind yet," Chaplain Phillips wrote to his daughter in August. "So many things could be true about it all that they build up for me a feeling of confidence that will not be shaken. Some day we are all going to have that reunion we are hoping and waiting for."

For Cecy Perry, the news that her fiancé was missing was followed by a letter from her old friend Smitty, one of the pilots who had searched

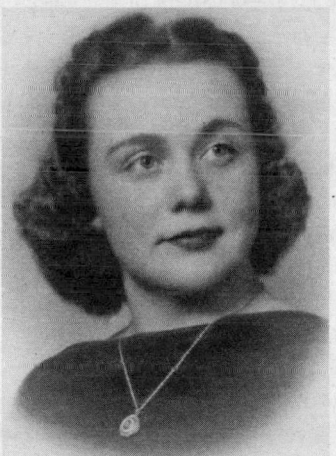

Phil's fiancée, Cecy Perry.
Courtesy of Karen Loomis

for *Green Hornet.* In his letter, Smitty told Cecy everything that was known about Allen's disappearance and how dedicated the searchers were to finding him. He didn't tell her that he had seen what had probably been the provisions box for the lost plane, floating by itself on the ocean. He wrote about having sat with Allen on the night before he disappeared, and how Allen had been thinking of her and hoping to get leave to see her.

After Smitty's letter, no news came. Cecy, desperate for information, felt isolated in Indiana. One of her friends was living in a suburb of Washington, D.C., and Cecy thought that in the capital, she could find out more about Allen. She gave up teaching, traveled east, and moved into her friend's apartment, which she decorated with pictures of Allen. She got a job with TWA, thinking that through the airline, she might learn something. She spent much of her time asking questions, but learned nothing.

Cecy was a sensible, educated woman, but in her anguish, she did something completely out of character. She went to a fortune-teller and asked about Allen.

The fortune-teller told her that Allen wasn't dead. He was injured but alive. He would be found, she said, before Christmas. Cecy latched onto those words and believed them.

———

By the spring of 1944, the mothers of the *Green Hornet* crewmen, as well as other family members, had begun to correspond. In dozens of letters that crisscrossed America, they shared their emotions and bolstered each other's hopes about "our boys." Kelsey would later say that she came to love all of them through those letters.

"This year sure has been an awful long year just waiting of some word from them," wrote Delia Robinson, the sister of *Green Hornet* gunner Otto Anderson, that June. "We just have to keep on hoping." The waiting had taken its toll on crewman Leslie Dean's mother, Mable—her failing health had sent her to Wichita for weeks of treatment—but she, like the others, had not given up. "We thought surely we would have heard something when the year was up," she wrote to Louise. "So it seems they are *not sure* the crew were killed, or they would have notified us long before this. So I feel that we can still have hope of them being alive somewhere."

Mable Dean wrote those words on June 27, 1944. On that very day, exactly thirteen months after *Green Hornet* had gone down, messages were typed up at the War Department and sent to the families of the plane's crewmen. When Louise Zamperini's message reached her door, she opened it and burst into tears. The military had officially declared Louie, and all the other crewmen, dead.

Kelsey Phillips was not persuaded. She either learned or guessed that the *La Porte Herald-Argus*, the newspaper of their former home-town, would publish the news. She contacted the paper and asked them not to print the death notice; her son, she told them, was not gone. The editors honored her request. Russell Allen Phillips had officially been declared dead, but no obituary appeared.

The feeling in the Zamperini home was the same as in the Phillipses'. When the initial shock from the death notice faded, all of the Zamperi-nis realized that it changed nothing. The notice had been generated as a bureaucratic matter of course, a designation made for all missing ser-vicemen after thirteen months had passed. Louie's official death date was listed as May 28, 1944, a year and a day after his plane had van-ished. The notice was just a piece of paper. "None of us believed it. None of us," Sylvia would say. "Never once. Not underneath, even."

Inside themselves, the Zamperinis still felt that persistent little echo of Louie, the sense that he was still in the world somewhere. Until it was gone, they would go on believing that he was alive.

During family dinners, Pete and his father began drawing up plans to hunt for Louie. When the war was over, they'd rent a boat and sail from island to island until they found him. They'd go on for as long as it took.

Twenty-two

Plots Afoot

T HE PLOT BEGAN WITH A QUESTION. IT WAS THE SUMMER of 1944, and Louie and Frank Tinker were walking together in the Ofuna compound. Louie could hear small planes coming and going from an airstrip somewhere in the distance, and the sound started him thinking. If we could get out of here, he asked Tinker, could you fly a Japanese plane?

"If it has wings," Tinker replied.

From that brief exchange, an idea took root. Louie, Tinker, and Harris were going to escape.

———

They'd been driven to this point by a long, desperate spring and summer. Every day, the men were slapped, kicked, beaten, humiliated, and driven through forced exercises. There were sudden explosions of violence that left captives spilled over the ground, hoping they wouldn't be killed. And that spring, the central authorities had cut rations to all prisoners dramatically. With only about half of the official ration ending up in the captives' bowls, the men were wasting away. When the Japanese weighed the captives, Bill Harris, over six feet tall, tipped the scale at 120 pounds. He had developed beriberi.

Louie was driven to ever more reckless efforts to find food. He stole an onion and secretly cooked it under a water heater, but divided between several men, it didn't amount to much. He stole a package of miso paste and, when the guards weren't looking, shoveled it into his mouth and swallowed it in one gulp, not knowing that miso paste is extremely concentrated, meant to be diluted in water. He was soon doubled over behind the barracks, heaving his guts out. He was so mad for food that he snuck from his cell late at night, broke into the kitchen, and crammed his mouth full of chestnuts that were to be served to the guards. When he looked up, Shithead was there, watching him. Louie backed away, then sprinted back to his cell. Shithead didn't beat him for it, but the guard's appearance was enough to scare Louie out of another go at the kitchen. The best he could do was volunteer to starch the guards' shirts. The starch was made from rice water pressed through cloth; after Louie pressed the rice, he spent the rest of his time picking flecks of it off the cloth and eating them.

Finally, opportunity knocked. Camp officials asked for a volunteer to work as barber for the guards, offering payment of one rice ball per job. The idea of working around the guards was intimidating, but Louie had to eat. When he came forward, he was given not just electric clippers but a straight razor. He'd never used one before, and he knew what the guards would do to him if they were nicked. He took the razor to his cell and practiced on himself until he could shave without drawing blood. When he walked out to do his first job, the guard balled up his fist at him, then made a demand that, to an American, seemed bizarre. He wanted his forehead shaved, a standard barbering practice in Japan. All of the guards expected Louie to do this. Louie managed not to cut anyone, and the rice balls kept him alive.

A notoriously cruel guard called the Weasel began coming to Louie for shaves, but every time, he left without paying. Louie knew what he would risk in evening the score, but he couldn't resist. While shaving the Weasel's forehead, he let the blade stray a little low. By the time he was done, all that was left of the Weasel's bushy eyebrows was a coquettish line. The Weasel stood, left without paying, and entered the guardhouse. A moment later, Louie heard a shout.

"Marlene Dietrich!"

Louie backed away, waiting for the Weasel to burst out. Several other guards went into the guardhouse, and Louie could hear laughing. The Weasel never punished Louie, but the next time he needed a shave, he went elsewhere.

For the captives, every day was lived with the knowledge that it could be their last. The nearer the Allies came to Japan, the larger loomed the threat of the kill-all order. The captives had only a vague idea of how the war was going, but the Japanese were clearly worried. In an interrogation session in late spring, an official told Fitzgerald that if Japan lost, the captives would be executed. "Hope for Japan's victory," he said. The quest for news of the war took on special urgency.

One morning, Louie was on the parade ground, under orders to sweep the compound. He saw the Mummy—the camp commander—sitting under a cherry tree, holding a newspaper. He was nodding off. Louie loitered near him, watching. The Mummy's head tipped, his fingers parted, and the paper fluttered to the ground. Louie swept his way over, reached out with the broom, and, as quietly as he could, forked the newspaper to himself. The text was in Japanese, but there was a war map on one page. Louie ran to the barracks, found Harris, and held the paper up before him. Harris stared at it, memorizing the map. Louie then ran the paper to the garbage so they'd have no evidence of the theft. Harris drew a perfect rendering of the map, showed it to the other captives, then destroyed it. The map confirmed that the Allies were closing in on Japan.

In July, the scuttlebutt in camp was that the Americans were attacking the critical island of Saipan, in the Mariana Islands, south of mainland Japan. A spindly new captive was hauled in, and everyone eyed him as a source of information, but the guards kept him isolated and forbade the veterans from speaking to him. When the new man was led to the bathhouse, Louie saw his chance. He snuck behind the building and looked in an open window. The captive was standing naked, holding a pan of water and washing as the guard stood by. Then the guard stepped away to light a cigarette.

"If we've taken Saipan, drop the pan," Louie whispered.

The pan clattered to the floor. The captive picked it up, dropped it again, then did it a third time. The guard rushed back in, and the captive pretended that the pan had accidentally slipped.

Louie hurried to his friends and announced that Saipan had fallen. At the time of their capture, the American bomber with the longest range was the B-24. Because the Liberator didn't have the range to make the three-thousand-mile round-trip between Saipan and Japan's home islands, the captives must have believed that winning Saipan was only a preliminary step to establishing an island base within bomber range of mainland Japan. They didn't know that the AAF had introduced a new bomber, one with tremendous range. From Saipan, the Japanese mainland was already within reach.

The guards and officials were increasingly agitated. Sasaki had long crowed about the inevitability of Japan's victory, but now he buddied up to the captives, telling Louie of his hatred of former prime minister and war architect Hideki Tojo. He began to sound like he was rooting for the Allies.

As they considered the news on Saipan, Louie and the others had no idea what horrors were attending the Allied advance. That same month, American forces turned on Saipan's neighboring isle, Tinian, where the Japanese held five thousand Koreans, conscripted as laborers. Apparently afraid that the Koreans would join the enemy if the Americans invaded, the Japanese employed the kill-all policy. They murdered all five thousand Koreans.

At night, as they lay in their cells, the captives began hearing an unsettling sound, far in the distance. It was the scream of air-raid sirens. They listened for bombers, but none came.

———

As summer stretched on, conditions in Ofuna declined. The air was clouded with flies, lice hopped over scalps, and wiggling lines of fleas ran the length of the seams in Louie's shirt. Louie spent his days and nights scratching and slapping, and his skin, like that of everyone else, was speckled with angry bite marks. The Japanese offered a rice ball to the man who killed the most flies, inspiring a cutthroat swatting competition and hoarding of flattened corpses. Then, in July, the men were marched outside and into a canal to bail water into rice paddies. When they emerged at the day's end, they were covered in leeches. Louie had six on his chest alone. The men became frantic, begging the guards for their cigarettes. As they squirmed around, jabbing at the leeches with cigarettes, one of the guards looked down at them.

"You should be happy in your work," he said.

On August 5, a truck bearing the month's rations arrived. As Fitzgerald watched, camp officials stripped it nearly clean. Curley announced that the rations were again being cut, blaming it on rats. Fitzgerald noted in his diary that after officials were done "brown bagging" their way through the seventy pounds of sugar allotted to the captives, one teacup of sugar remained. On August 22, a truck backed up to the kitchen door, and the captive kitchen workers were told to leave. Fitzgerald went to the *benjo,* from which he could see the kitchen. He saw sacks of food being piled into the truck, which then left camp. "Someone must be opening up a store and really getting set up in business," he wrote.

The beatings went on. The Quack was especially feral. One day, Louie saw some Japanese dumping fish into the trough in which the captives washed their hands and feet. Told to wash the fish, Louie walked up and peered into the trough. The fish were putrid and undulating with maggots. As he recoiled, the Quack saw him, pounded over, and punched him a dozen times. That night, the same fish was ladled into Louie's bowl. Louie wouldn't touch it. A guard jabbed him behind the ear with a bayonet and forced him to eat it.

And then there was Gaga. Something about this affectionate little duck, perhaps the fact that he was beloved to the captives, provoked the guards. They tortured him mercilessly, kicking him and hurling him around. Then one day, in full view of the captives, Shithead opened his pants and violated the bird. Gaga died. Of all the things he witnessed in war, Louie would say, this was the worst.

Louie's mind fled Ofuna and carried him home. He hadn't seen his family in two years. He thought of the little white house, Virginia and Sylvia, his father and dear, devoted Pete. Most poignant were his memories of his mother. Fred Garrett had told Louie that he'd been given up for dead. Louie couldn't bear the thought of what this news must have done to his mother.

It was the accumulation of so much suffering, the tug of memory, and the conviction that the Japanese wouldn't let them leave Ofuna alive that led Louie to listen to the nearby planes and wonder if they could be a way out. Examining the fence, he, Tinker, and Harris concluded that it might be possible to get around the guards and over the barbed wire. The thought hooked all three of them. They decided to make a run for it, commandeer a plane, and get out of Japan.

At first, their plans hit a dead end. They'd been brought in blindfolded and had ventured out of camp only briefly, to irrigate the rice paddies, so they knew little about the area. They didn't know where the airport was, or how they'd steal a plane. Then a kind guard inadvertently helped them. Thinking that they might enjoy looking at a book, he gave them a Japanese almanac. Harris cracked it open and was immediately rapt. The book was full of detailed information on Japan's ports, the ships in its harbors and the fuels they used, and the distances between cities and landmarks. It was everything they needed to craft an escape.

In hours spent poring over the book, they shaped a plan. They discarded the plane idea in favor of escape by boat. Just a few miles to the east was the port of Yokohama, only there was nowhere to go from there. But if they crossed Japan to the western shore, they could get to a port that would offer a good route to safety.

They'd go on foot. Harris plotted a path across the island, a walk of about 150 miles. It would be dangerous, but Harris's earlier experience of hiking all over the Bataan Peninsula gave them confidence. Once at a port, they'd steal a powerboat and fuel, cross the Sea of Japan, and flee into China. Given that Louie had drifted two thousand miles on a hole-riddled raft with virtually no provisions, a few hundred miles on the Sea of Japan in a sturdy powered boat seemed manageable. Tinker, who'd been captured more recently than Harris and Louie, had the most current knowledge of which areas of China were occupied by the enemy. He worked out a route that they hoped would steer them clear of the Japanese.

They counted on finding safe harbor in China. In 1942, America had launched its first and, until recently, only bombing raid on Japan's home islands. The raid had used B-25s flown, perilously, off an aircraft carrier, under command of Lieutenant Colonel Jimmy Doolittle. After bombing Japan, some of the Doolittle crews had run out of gas and crashed or bailed out over China. Civilians had hidden the airmen from the Japanese, who'd ransacked the country in search of them. Harris, Tinker, and Louie had heard rumors that the Japanese had retaliated against Chinese civilians for sheltering the Doolittle men, but didn't know the true extent of it. The Japanese had murdered an estimated quarter of a million civilians.

There was one problem that the men didn't know how to overcome. When they stood near the guards, it was impossible not to notice how much the Americans differed from typical Japanese people, and not simply in facial features. The average Japanese soldier was five foot three. Louie was five foot ten, Tinker six feet, Harris even taller. Hiking across Japan, they'd be extremely conspicuous. China might be welcoming, but in Japan, it would be foolish to assume that they'd find friendly civilians. After the war, some POWs would tell of heroic

Japanese civilians who snuck them food and medicine, incurring ferocious beatings from guards when they were caught. But this behavior
was not the rule. POWs led through cities were often swarmed by civilians, who beat them, struck them with rocks, and spat on them. If
Louie, Harris, and Tinker were caught, they would almost certainly be
killed, either by civilians or by the authorities. Unable to remedy the
height difference, they decided to move only at night and hope for the
best. If they were going to die in Japan, at least they could take a path
that they and not their captors chose, declaring, in this last act of life,
that they remained sovereign over their own souls.

As the plan took shape, the prospective escapees walked as much as
possible, strengthening their legs. They studied the guards' shifts, noting
that there was a patch of time at night when only one guard watched the
fence. Louie stole supplies for the journey. His barber job gave him access to tools, and he was able to make off with a knife. He stole miso
paste and rice. He gathered bits of loose paper that flitted across the
compound, to be used for toilet paper, and every strand of loose string
he could find. He stashed all of it under a floorboard in his cell.

For two months, the men prepared. As the date of escape neared,
Louie was filled with what he called "a fearful joy."

Just before the getaway date, an event occurred that changed everything. At one of the POW camps, a prisoner escaped. Ofuna officials
assembled the men and issued a new decree: Anyone caught escaping
would be executed, and for every escapee, several captive officers
would be shot. Louie, Tinker, and Harris suspended their plan.

————

With the escape off, Louie and Harris channeled their energy into the
captive information network. At the beginning of September, a captive
saw a newspaper lying on the Quack's desk. There was a war map
printed in it. Few things were more dangerous than stealing from the
Quack, but given the threat of mass executions upon an Allied invasion, the captives were willing to do almost anything to get news. Only
one man had the thieving experience for a job this risky.

For several days, Louie staked out the Quack's office, peeking in
windows to watch him and the guards. At a certain time each day,
they'd go into the office for tea, walk out together to smoke, then return. The length of their cigarette break never varied: three minutes.
This was Louie's only window of opportunity, and it was going to be a
very, very close call.

With Harris in place, Louie loitered by the Quack's office, waiting for his moment. The Quack and the guards stepped out, cigarettes in hand. Louie crept around the side of the building, dropped onto all fours so that he wouldn't be seen through the windows, and crawled into the office. The newspaper was still there, sitting on the desk. Louie snatched the paper, stuck it under his shirt, then crawled back out, rose to his feet, and walked to Harris's cell, striding as quickly as he could without attracting attention. He opened the paper and showed it to Harris, who stared at it for several seconds. Then Louie crammed it under his shirt again and sped back to the Quack's office. His luck had held; the Quack and the guards were still outside. He went back down on all fours, hurried in, threw the paper on the desk, and fled. No one had seen him.

At the barracks, Harris pulled out a strip of toilet paper and a pencil and drew the map. The men all looked at it. Memories later differed as to the subject of the map, but everyone recalled that it showed Allied progress. Harris hid the map among his belongings.

In the late afternoon of September 9, Harris was sitting in a cell with another captive, discussing the war, when the Quack swept into the doorway. Harris hadn't heard him coming. The Quack noticed something in Harris's hand, stepped in, and snatched it. It was the map.

The Quack studied the map; on it, he saw the words "Philippine" and "Taiwan." He demanded that Harris tell him what it was; Harris replied that it was idle scribbling. The Quack wasn't fooled. He went to Harris's cell, ransacked it, and found, by his account, a trove of hand-drawn maps—some showing air defenses of mainland Japan—as well as the stolen newspaper clipping and the dictionary of military terms. The Quack called in an officer, who spoke to Harris, then left. Everyone thought that the issue was resolved.

That night, the Quack abruptly called all captives into the compound. He looked strange, his face crimson. He ordered the men to do push-ups for about twenty minutes, then adopt the Ofuna crouch. Then he told Harris to step forward. Louie heard the marine whisper, "Oh my God. My map."

The men who witnessed what followed would never blot it from memory. Screeching and shrieking, the Quack attacked Harris, kicking him, punching him, and clubbing him with a wooden crutch that he took from an injured captive. When Harris collapsed, his nose and shins streaming blood, the Quack ordered other captives to hold him

Harris's handmade
Japanese-English
dictionary, discovered
by Sueharu Kitamura,
"the Quack."
*Courtesy of
Katherine H. Meares*

The Quack.
Courtesy of Louis Zamperini

William Harris.
*Courtesy of
Katherine H. Meares*

up, and the beating resumed. For forty-five minutes, perhaps an hour, the beating went on, long past when Harris fell unconscious. Two captives fainted.

At last, raindrops began to patter over the dirt, the Quack, and the body beneath him. The Quack paused. He dropped the crutch, walked to a nearby building, leaned against its wall, and slid languidly to the ground, panting.

As the guards dragged Harris to his cell, Louie followed. The guards jammed Harris in a seated position against a wall, then left. There Harris sat, eyes wide open but blank as stones. It was two hours before he moved.

Slowly, in the coming days, he began to revive. He was unable to feed himself, so Louie sat with him, helping him eat and trying to speak with him, but Harris was so dazed that he could barely communicate. When he finally emerged from his cell, he wandered through camp, his face grotesquely disfigured, his eyes glassy. When his friends greeted him, he didn't know who they were.

Three weeks later, on the morning of September 30, 1944, the guards called the names of Zamperini, Tinker, Duva, and several other men. The men were told that they were going to a POW camp called Omori, just outside of Tokyo. They had ten minutes to gather their things.

Louie hurried to his cell and lifted the floorboard. He pulled out his diary and tucked it into the folds of his clothing. At a new camp, a body search would be inevitable, so he left his other treasures for the next captive to find. He said good-bye to his friends, among them Harris, still floating in concussed misery. Sasaki bid Louie a friendly farewell, offering some advice: If interrogated, stick to the story he'd told on Kwajalein. A few minutes later, after a year and fifteen days in Ofuna, Louie was driven from camp. As the truck rattled out of the hills, he was euphoric. Ahead of him lay a POW camp, a promised land.

Twenty-three

Monster

I T WAS LATE MORNING ON THE LAST DAY OF SEPTEMBER 1944. Louie, Frank Tinker, and a handful of other Ofuna veterans stood by the front gate of the Omori POW camp, which sat on an artificial island in Tokyo Bay. The island was nothing more than a sandy spit, connected to shore by a tenuous thread of bamboo slats. Across the water was the bright bustle of Tokyo, still virtually untouched by the war. Other than the patches of early snow scattered over the ground like hopscotch squares, every inch of the camp was an ashen, otherworldly gray, reminding one POW of the moon. There were no birds anywhere.

They were standing before a small office, where they'd been told to wait. In front of them, standing beside the building, was a Japanese corporal. He was leering at them.

He was a beautifully crafted man, a few years short of thirty. His face was handsome, with full lips that turned up slightly at the edges, giving his mouth a faintly cruel expression. Beneath his smartly tailored uniform, his body was perfectly balanced, his torso radiating power, his form trim. A sword angled elegantly off of his hip, and circling his waist was a broad webbed belt embellished with an enormous metal buckle. The only incongruities on this striking corporal were his

Mutsuhiro Watanabe, "the Bird." *National Archives*

hands—huge, brutish, animal things that one man would liken to paws.

Louie and the other prisoners stood at attention, arms stiff, hands flat to their sides. The corporal continued to stare, but said nothing. Near him stood another man who wore a second lieutenant's insignia, yet hovered about the lower-ranking corporal with eager servility. Five, perhaps ten minutes passed, and the corporal never moved. Then, abruptly, he swept toward the prisoners, the second lieutenant scurrying behind. He walked with his chin high and his chest puffed, his gestures exaggerated and imperious. He began to inspect the men with an air of possession—looking them over, Louie thought, as if he were God himself.

Down the line the corporal strode, pausing before each man, raking his eyes over him, and barking, "Name!" When he reached Louie, he stopped. Louie gave his name. The corporal's eyes narrowed. Decades after the war, men who had looked into those eyes would be unable to shake the memory of what they saw in them, a wrongness that elicited a twist in the gut, a prickle up the back of the neck. Louie dropped his eyes. There was a rush in the air, the corporal's arm swinging, then a fist thudding into Louie's head. Louie staggered.

"Why you no look in my eye?" the corporal shouted. The other men in the line went rigid.

Louie steadied himself. He held his face taut as he raised his eyes to the corporal's face. Again came the whirling arm, the jarring blow into his skull, his stumbling legs trying to hold him upright.

"You no look at me!"

This man, thought Tinker, *is a psychopath.*

———

The corporal marched the men to a quarantine area, where there stood a rickety canopy. He ordered the men to stand beneath it, then left.

Hours passed. The men stood, the cold working its way up their sleeves and pant legs. Eventually they sat down. The morning gave way to a long, cold afternoon. The corporal didn't come back.

Louie saw a wooden apple box lying nearby. Remembering his Boy Scout friction-fire training, he grabbed the box and broke it up. He asked one of the other men to unthread the lace from his boot. He fashioned a spindle out of a bamboo stick, fit it into a hole in a slat from the apple box, wound the bootlace around the spindle, and began alternately pulling the ends, turning the spindle. After a good bit of work, smoke rose from the spindle. Louie picked up bits of a discarded *tatami* mat, laid them on the smoking area, and blew on them. The mat remnants whooshed into flames. The men gathered close to the fire, and cigarettes emerged from pockets. Everyone got warmer.

The corporal suddenly reappeared. "*Nanda, nanda!*" he said, a word that roughly translates to "What the hell is going on?" He demanded to know where they'd gotten matches. Louie explained how he had built the fire. The corporal's face clouded over. Without warning, the corporal slugged Louie in the head, then swung his arm back for another blow. Louie wanted to duck, but he fought the instinct, knowing from Ofuna that this would only provoke more blows. So he stood still, holding his expression neutral, as the second swing connected with his head. The corporal ordered them to put the fire out, then walked away.

Louie had met the man who would dedicate himself to shattering him.

———

The corporal's name was Mutsuhiro Watanabe.* He was born during World War I, the fourth of six children of Shizuka Watanabe, a lovely and exceptionally wealthy woman. The Watanabes enjoyed a privileged life, having amassed riches through ownership of Tokyo's Takamatsu Hotel and other real estate and mines in Nagano and Manchuria. Mutsuhiro, whose father, a pilot, seems to have died or left the family when Mutsuhiro was relatively young, grew up on luxury's lap, living in beautiful homes all over Japan, reportedly waited on by servants and swimming in his family's private pool. His siblings knew him affectionately as Mu-cchan.

After a childhood in Kobe, Mutsuhiro attended Tokyo's prestigious Waseda University, where he studied French literature and cultivated an infatuation with nihilism. In 1942, he graduated, settled in Tokyo, and took a job at a news agency. He worked there for only one month; Japan was at war, and Mutsuhiro was deeply patriotic. He enlisted in the army.

Watanabe had lofty expectations for himself as a soldier. One of his older brothers was an officer, and his older sister's husband was commander of Changi, a giant POW camp in Singapore. Attaining an offi-

———

* In POW memoirs, Watanabe's first name is almost always listed as Matsuhiro. Official documents confirm that the correct spelling was Mutsuhiro.

cer's rank was of supreme importance to Watanabe, and when he ap-
plied to become an officer, he probably thought that acceptance was his
due, given his education and pedigree. But he was rejected; he would be
only a corporal. By all accounts, this was the moment that derailed
him, leaving him feeling disgraced, infuriated, and bitterly jealous of
officers. Those who knew him would say that every part of his mind
gathered around this blazing humiliation, and every subsequent action
was informed by it. This defining event would have tragic consequences for hundreds of men.

Corporal Watanabe was sent to a regiment of the Imperial Guards
in Tokyo, stationed near Hirohito's palace. As the war hadn't yet come
to Japan's home islands, he saw no combat. In the fall of 1943, for unknown reasons, Watanabe was transferred to the military's most igno-
minious station for NCOs, a POW camp. Perhaps his superiors wanted
to rid the Imperial Guards of an unstable and venomous soldier, or perhaps they wanted to put his volatility to use. Watanabe was assigned to
Omori and designated the "disciplinary officer." On the last day of November 1943, Watanabe arrived.

Even prior to Watanabe's appearance, Omori had been a trying place.
The 1929 Geneva Convention, which Japan had signed but never rati-
fied, permitted detaining powers to use POWs for labor, with restric-
tions. The laborers had to be physically fit, and the labor couldn't be
dangerous, unhealthy, or of unreasonable difficulty. The work had to
be unconnected to the operations of war, and POWs were to be given
pay commensurate with their labor. Finally, to ensure that POW officers had control over their men, they could not be forced to work.

Virtually nothing about Japan's use of POWs was in keeping with
the Geneva Convention. To be an enlisted prisoner of war under the
Japanese was to be a slave. The Japanese government made contracts
with private companies to send enlisted POWs to factories, mines,
docks, and railways, where the men were forced into exceptionally arduous war-production or war-transport labor. The labor, performed
under club-wielding foremen, was so dangerous and exhausting that
thousands of POWs died on the job. In the extremely rare instances in
which the Japanese compensated the POWs for their work, payment
amounted to almost nothing, equivalent to a few pennies a week. The
only aspect of the Geneva Convention that the Japanese sometimes respected was the prohibition on forcing officers to work.

Like almost every other camp, Omori was a slave camp. For ten to eleven hours a day, seven days a week, Omori's enlisted POWs did backbreaking labor at shipyards, railyards, truck-loading stations, a sandpit, and a coalyard. Men had to be on the verge of death to be spared; minimum fever levels for exemption were 40 degrees Celsius, or 104 degrees Fahrenheit. The labor was extremely grueling; according to POW Tom Wade, each man at the Tokyo railyards lifted a total of twenty to thirty *tons* of material a day. Probably because Omori was used as a show camp where prisoners were displayed for the Red Cross, the men were "paid" ten yen per month—less than the price of a pack of cigarettes—but they were permitted to spend it only on a tiny selection of worthless goods at a camp canteen, so the money came right back to the Japanese.

Compounding the hardship of Omori was the food situation. The rations were of better quality than those at Ofuna but were doled out in only slightly larger quantities. Because officers weren't enslaved, they were allowed only half the ration given to slaves, on the justification that they needed fewer calories. Along with rice, the men received some vegetables, but protein was almost nonexistent. About once a week, someone would push a wheelbarrow into the camp, bearing "meat." Because a wheelbarrow's worth was spread over hundreds of men, a serving amounted to about a thimble-sized portion; it consisted of things like lungs and intestines, assorted dog parts, something the POWs called "elephant semen," and, once, a mystery lump that, after considerable speculation, the men decided was a horse's vagina.

Just as at Ofuna, beriberi and other preventable diseases were epidemic at Omori. Because rations were halved for sick men who were unable to work, the ill couldn't recover. Men harrowed by dysentery— "the *benjo* boogie"—swallowed lumps of coal or burnt sticks to slow the digestive waterfall. Many men weighed less than ninety pounds.

The only saving grace of Omori, prior to November 1943, had been the attitude of the Japanese personnel, who weren't nearly as vicious as those at Ofuna. The prisoners gave them nicknames, including Hog-jaw, Baby Dumpling, Bucktooth, Genghis Khan, and Roving Reporter; one unfortunate officer, wrote POW Lewis Bush, wore puffy pants and "walked as though he was always bursting to go to the lavatory," prompting the men to call him Lieutenant Shit-in-Breeches. There were a few rogues and one or two outright loons, but several camp employees were friendly. The rest were indifferent, enforcing the rules with blows but at least behaving predictably. Relatively speaking, Omori wasn't known for violence. When Watanabe came, all that changed.

He arrived bearing candy and cigarettes for the POWs. He smiled and made pleasant conversation, posed for photographs with British officers, and spoke admiringly of America and Britain. For several days, he raised not a ripple.

On a Sunday morning, Watanabe approached some POWs crowded in a barracks doorway. A POW named Derek Clarke piped up, "Gangway!" to clear a path. That one word sent Watanabe into an explosion. He lunged at Clarke, beat him until he fell down, then kicked him. As Bush tried to explain that Clarke had meant no harm, Watanabe drew his sword and began screaming that he was going to behead Clarke. A Japanese officer stopped the attack, but that evening Watanabe turned on Bush, hurling him onto a scalding stove, then pummeling and kicking him. After Bush went to bed, Watanabe returned and forced him to his knees. For three hours, Watanabe besieged Bush, kicking him and hacking off his hair with his sword. He left for two hours, then returned again. Bush expected to be murdered. Instead, Watanabe took him to his office, hugged him, and gave him beer and handfuls of candy and cigarettes. Through tears, he apologized and promised never to mistreat another POW. His resolution didn't last. Later that night, he picked up a kendo stick—a long, heavy training sword—and ran shrieking into a barracks, clubbing every man he saw.

Watanabe had, in Bush's words, "shown his hand." From that day on, both his victims and his fellow Japanese would ponder his violent, erratic behavior and disagree on its cause. To Yuichi Hatto, the camp accountant, it was simply madness. Others saw something calculating. After Watanabe attacked Clarke, POW officers who had barely noticed him began looking at him with terror. The consequence of his outburst answered a ravening desire: Raw brutality gave him sway over men that his rank did not. "He suddenly saw after he hit a few men that he was feared and respected for that," said Wade. "And so that became his style of behavior."

Watanabe derived another pleasure from violence. According to Hatto, Watanabe was a sexual sadist, freely admitting that beating prisoners brought him to climax. "He did enjoy hurting POWs," wrote Hatto. "He was satisfying his sexual desire by hurting them."

A tyrant was born. Watanabe beat POWs every day, fracturing their windpipes, rupturing their eardrums, shattering their teeth, tearing one man's ear half off, leaving men unconscious. He made one officer sit in a shack, wearing only a *fundoshi* undergarment, for four days in winter. He tied a sixty-five-year-old POW to a tree and left him there for days. He ordered one man to report to him to be punched in the face every night for three weeks. He practiced judo on an appendectomy patient. When gripped in the ecstasy of an assault, he wailed and howled, drooling and frothing, sometimes sobbing, tears running down his cheeks. Men came to know when an outburst was imminent: Watanabe's right eyelid would sag a moment before he snapped.

Very quickly, Watanabe gained a fearsome reputation throughout Japan. Officials at other camps began sending troublesome prisoners to Watanabe for "polishing," and Omori was dubbed "punishment camp." In the words of Commander Maher, who'd been transferred from Ofuna to become the ranking Omori POW, Watanabe was "the most vicious guard in any prison camp on the main island of Japan."

Two things separated Watanabe from other notorious war criminals. One was the emphasis that he placed on emotional torture. Even by the standards of his honor-conscious culture, he was unusually consumed by his perceived humiliation, and was intent upon inflicting the same pain on the men under his power. Where men like the Quack were simply goons, Watanabe combined beatings with acts meant to batter men's psyches. He forced men to bow at pumpkins or trees for hours. He ordered a clergyman POW to stand all night saluting a flagpole, shouting the Japanese word for "salute," *keirei;* the experience left the man weeping and out of his mind. He confiscated and destroyed POWs' family photographs, and brought men to his office to show them letters from home, then burned the unopened letters in front of them. To ensure that men felt utterly helpless, he changed the manner in which he demanded to be addressed each day, beating anyone who guessed wrong. He ordered men to violate camp policies, then attacked them for breaking the rules. POW Jack Brady summed him up in one sentence. "He was absolutely the most sadistic man I ever met."

The other attribute that separated Watanabe from fellow guards was his inconsistency. Most of the time, he was the wrathful god of Omori. But after beatings, he sometimes returned to apologize, often in tears. These fits of contrition usually lasted only moments before the shrieking and punching began again. He would spin from serenity to raving madness in the blink of an eye, usually for no reason. One POW recalled seeing him gently praise a POW, fly into a rage and beat the POW unconscious, then amble to his office and eat his lunch with the placidity of a grazing cow.

When Watanabe wasn't thrashing POWs, he was forcing them to be his buddies. He'd wake a POW in the night and be "nice as pie," asking the man to join him in his room, where he'd serve cookies and talk about literature. Sometimes he'd round up anyone in camp who could play an instrument or sing, bring them to his room, and host a concert. He expected the men to respond as if they adored him, and at times, he seemed to honestly believe that they did.

Maybe he held these gatherings because they left the POWs feeling more stressed than if he were consistently hostile. Or maybe he was just lonely. Among the Japanese at Omori, Watanabe was despised for his haughtiness, his boasts about his wealth, and his curtness. He made a great show of his education, droning on about nihilism and giving pompous lectures on French literature at NCO meetings. None of his colleagues listened. It wasn't the subject matter; it was simply that they loathed him.

Perhaps this is why he turned to POWs for friendship. The tea parties, wrote Derek Clarke, were "tense, sitting-on-the-edge-of-a-volcano affairs." Any misstep, any misunderstood word might set Watanabe off, leaving him smashing teapots, upending tables, and pounding his guests into oblivion. After the POWs left, Watanabe seemed to feel humiliated by having had to force friendship from lowly POWs. The next day he would often deliver a wild-eyed whipping to the previous night's buddies.

Like any bully, he had a taste for a particular type of victim. Enlisted men usually received only the occasional slapped face; officers were in for unrelenting cruelty. Among those officers, a few were especially irresistible to him. Some had elevated status, such as physicians, chaplains, barracks commanders, and those who'd been highly successful in civilian life. Others he resented because they wouldn't crawl before him. These he singled out and hunted with inexhaustible hatred.

From the moment that Watanabe locked eyes with Louie Zamperini, an officer, a famous Olympian, and a man for whom defiance was second nature, no man obsessed him more.

Twenty-four

Hunted

AFTER A DAY SPENT SHIVERING IN OMORI'S QUARANTINE area, Louie was led into the main body of the camp, an enormous compound crowded with some nine hundred prisoners. He wandered down a long row of barracks until he found the one to which he was assigned. As he walked in, several POWs came forward to greet him. One of them slipped a cup of piping hot tea into his chilled hands. A Scottish prisoner approached, carrying a spoon and a bulging sock. He dipped the spoon into the sock and ladled out two heaping teaspoons of sugar into Louie's cup. To any POW, sugar was a treasure of incalculable value, and Louie couldn't understand how this man could have acquired an entire sock full of it.

As he sipped his tea, Louie was introduced to two barracks commanders, British lieutenant Tom Wade and American lieutenant Bob Martindale, who began filling him in on Omori. They spoke about the corporal who had attacked him at the gate. His name was Watanabe, they said, but Louie should never refer to him by his real name. Such was Watanabe's paranoia that he often hid outside the barracks, trying to catch men speaking of him so he could beat them for it. The men referred to him by a host of nicknames, including the Animal, the Big Flag, Little Napoleon, and, most often, the Bird, a name chosen because it carried no negative connotation that could get the POWs beaten.

It was the Bird's favorite pastime to send guards bursting into a barracks ahead of him, screaming *Keirei!* He would then race in to choose his victim. Sitting far from the door didn't ensure safety; the Bird loved to leap through open windows. Men were told to always be ready, speak of him only in whispers, and agree in advance on a subject to switch to if the Bird ran into the room demanding to be told what they were talking about. Men were advised to say that they were speaking of sex, because the subject interested and distracted him.

The Omori barracks were arranged in two lines separated by a central avenue. At the avenue's end stood the Bird's office, placed so that the corporal could see the entire avenue through his large front window. To get anywhere in camp, other than the *benjos* behind the barracks, POWs had to step into the Bird's view. One of his demands was that men salute not only him but his window. He often left the office vacant and hid nearby, baseball bat in hand, ready to club men who failed to salute the window.

Among the POWs, there was an elaborate sentry system to monitor the Bird's movements. When he was in his office, men would say, "The Animal is in his cage." When he was out, they'd say, "The Animal is on the prowl." "Flag's up!" meant that the Bird was coming. Men were so attuned to the Bird's presence that they instantly recognized the clopping sound his clogs made in the sand. The sound usually triggered a stampede to the *benjos,* where the Bird seldom went.

As he absorbed the advice on coping with the Bird, Louie learned something else that surely sank his heart. He had thought that since this was a POW camp, he would be able to write home to let his family know he was alive. Once, Omori POWs had been allowed to write letters, but no longer. The Bird didn't allow it.

When new POWs arrived at Omori, they were registered with the Red Cross, and word of their whereabouts was forwarded to their governments, then their families. But Omori officials didn't register Louie. They had special plans for him, and were apparently hiding him. In the absence of Louie's name on a Red Cross roster, the American government had no reason to believe that he was alive, and Louie's family was told nothing.

For Louie, the shared lessons about the Bird did no good. No sooner had Louie stepped outside than the Bird found him, accused him of an imaginary infraction, and attacked him in a wild fury. The next day came another beating, and the next, another. Though there were hundreds of POWs in camp, this deranged corporal was fixated on Louie, hunting the former Olympian, whom he would call "number one prisoner." Louie tried to conceal himself in groups of men, but the Bird always found him. "After the first few days in camp," Louie said, "I looked for him like I was looking for a lion loose in the jungle."

When Louie woke each morning, the first thing that he thought of was the Bird. He'd look for the corporal through morning *tenko*, roll call, farting at the emperor, and forcing down rations. After breakfast, the enlisted men were assembled into work parties and marched away. With the camp population drastically diminished by the exodus, Louie had no crowds to hide in. The Bird was on him immediately.

The one good thing about being an officer in Omori was that one was exempt from slave labor, albeit at the painful cost of half of the standard ration. But soon after Louie's arrival, the Bird called out the officers and announced that from now on, they'd labor at the work sites alongside the enlisted men. When a man protested that this violated international law, the Bird swung his kendo stick straight into the man's head. The Bird approached the next man, who also said he wouldn't work. Again the kendo stick banged down. Louie was the third man. Trying to avoid getting his head cracked open, he blurted out a compromise idea. They'd love to work within the camp, he said, making it a better place.

The Bird paused. He seemed to feel that as long as he forced the officers to work, he was winning. He sent them into a shack and ordered them to stitch up leather ammunition pouches, backpacks, and equipment covers for the Japanese military. Louie and the other men were kept there for about eight hours a day, but they worked only when the Bird was around, and even then, they deliberately stitched the leather improperly.

The Bird's next move was to announce that from now on, the officers would empty the *benjos*. Eight *benjos* were no match for nine hundred dysenteric men, and keeping the pits from oozing over was a tall order. Louie and the other officers used "honey dippers"—giant ladles—to spoon waste from the pits into buckets, then carried the buckets to cesspits outside the camp. The work was nauseating and degrading, and when heavy rains came, the waste oozed out of the

cesspits and back into camp. To deprive the Bird of the pleasure of seeing them miserable, the men made a point of being jolly. Martindale
created the "Royal Order of the *Benjo*." "The motto," he wrote, "was
unprintable."

As the officers finished each day of abuse, honey-dipping, and errant
sewing, the enlisted slaves were driven back to camp. The first time
Louie saw them return, he learned where that sock of sugar had come
from.

At the work sites, Omori's POWs were waging a guerrilla war. At
the railyards and docks, they switched mailing labels, rewrote delivery
addresses, and changed the labeling on boxcars, sending tons of goods
to the wrong destinations. They threw fistfuls of dirt into gas tanks and
broke anything mechanical that passed through their hands. Forced to
build engine blocks, American Milton McMullen crafted the exteriors
well enough to pass inspection but fashioned the interiors so the engines would never run. POWs loading at docks "accidentally" dropped
fragile items, including a large shipment of wine and furniture en route
to a Nazi ambassador. (The broken furniture was sent on; the wine was
decanted into POW canteens.) Coming upon the suitcases of the German envoy, POWs shredded the clothes, soaked them in mud and oil,
and repacked them with friendly notes signed "Winston Churchill."
They drank huge quantities of tea and peed profusely on nearly every
bag of rice they loaded. And in one celebrated incident, POWs loading
heavy goods onto a barge hurled the material down with such force
that they sank the barge, blocking a canal. After a Herculean effort was
put into clearing the sunken barge and bringing in a new one, the
POWs sank it, too.

Emboldened by the thought that he was probably going to die in
Japan and, thus, had nothing to lose, McMullen joined several other
POWs in committing an act that was potentially suicidal. While enslaved at a railyard, they noticed that a group of track workers had ne-
glected to put their tools away. When their guard became absorbed in
wooing a pretty girl, the POWs sprinted from their stations, snatched
up the tools, dashed over to a section of track, wrenched the pins and
bolts out, and rushed back to their work. The guard, still talking to the
girl, noticed nothing. A switch engine chugged in, pulling several boxcars. The engine hit the sabotaged strip, the rails shot out from under
it, and the entire train tipped over. No one was hurt, but the Japanese

were frantic. They looked to the POWs, who kept working, their faces devoid of expression. The Japanese began screaming accusations at one another.

As dangerous as these acts were, for the POWs, they were transformative. In risking their necks to sabotage their enemy, the men were no longer passive captives. They were soldiers again.

What the POWs couldn't sabotage, they stole. They broke into shipping boxes, tapped bottles, lifted storage room doors off their hinges, raided ships' galleys, and crawled up factory chutes. Scottish POWs who worked in the Mitsubishi food warehouse ran the most sophisticated operation. When the Japanese took their shoe sizes for work boots, the men asked for boots several sizes too big. They knitted special socks, some four feet long, and hoarded hollow bamboo reeds. Once at the sites, they leaned casually against sugar sacks, stabbed the reeds in, then ran the reeds into the socks, allowing sugar to pour through the reeds until the socks were full. Others tied up their pant cuffs, stuck the reeds in their waistbands, and filled their pants with sugar. Each load was deposited in a secret compartment in the latrine, to be retrieved at day's end.

Each evening, Louie saw the slaves tramping back in, their clothes packed with booty. The critical moment came when inspection was called. Men would deftly pass contraband, or the men bearing it, around during the searches, while the guards' backs were turned. McMullen would hide fish in his sleeves; when patted down, he'd hold his arms up and grip the fish tails so they wouldn't slide out. The biggest trick was hiding the POWs who arrived fall-down drunk after chugging down any alcohol that they couldn't smuggle. The drunken men were shuffled into the center of the lineup, their shoulders pinched between the shoulders of sober men, so that they wouldn't pitch face forward into the guards.

When the men were safely in the barracks, Louie watched them unpack themselves. Under the men's clothes, sugar-filled socks hung from necks or arms, dangled under armpits and down pant legs, in the necks of turtleneck sweaters, in false pockets, under hats. Two-foot-long salmon would emerge from under shirts. Louie once saw a thief pull three cans of oysters from a single boot. Legs would be swaddled in tobacco leaves. One American built a secret compartment in his canteen, filling the bottom with stolen alcohol while the top, upon inspection, yielded only water.

Men were caught all the time, and when they were, all the men of the work party were beaten with fists, bats, and rifle butts. But the men were fed so little and worked so hard that they felt they had to steal to survive. They set up a "University of Thievery," in which "professors"— the most adept thieves—taught the art of stealing. The final exam was a heist. When men were caught stealing, POW officers suggested that the culprits be transferred to sites that didn't carry food. The Japanese agreed, and the POW officers then replaced the inept thieves with University of Thievery alumni.

Though Louie, as an officer, had no opportunity to steal, he was quickly integrated into the thieving system, rolling tobacco leaves for drying and putting them up in secret "wall safes" to cure. Once the leaves were properly aged, Louie would return to shave them into smokable shreds.

Thanks to the stealing, a black market with a remarkable diversity of goods flourished in camp. One group stole all the ingredients for a cake, only to discover, upon baking it, that the flour was actually cement. Because there were so many men, there wasn't a lot of loot to go around, but everyone benefited in some way. Whenever the thieves had something extra, they gave it to Louie, who still wasn't managing to gain weight. A few times, they even smuggled him smoked oysters. Louie devoured them and tiptoed to the fence to pitch the cans into Tokyo Bay.

Stolen food, especially the Scots' sugar, was the camp currency, and the "sugar barons" became the rich men of Omori, even hiring assistants to do their laundry. The Scots drove hard bargains, but they also donated one-quarter of the loot to sick POWs. One night, when he found Frank Tinker deathly ill, Louie waited for the guards to pass, snuck to the Scots' barracks, and told them that Tinker was in trouble. The Scots sent Louie back to Tinker with a load of sugar, no charge. Tinker would later say that Louie's sugar run "saved my soul." According to Martindale, Tinker wasn't the only man saved. Deaths from illness and malnutrition had once been commonplace, but after the thievery school was created, only two POWs died, one from a burst appendix. And in a place predicated on degradation, stealing from the enemy won back the men's dignity.

As the weeks passed, the Bird didn't relent in his attacks on Louie. The corporal sprang upon him randomly, every day, pounding his face and head. Any resistance from Louie, even shielding his face, would inspire the Bird to more violence. Louie could do nothing but stand there, staggering, as the Bird struck him. He couldn't understand the corporal's fixation on him, and was desperate for someone to save him.

During one of the Bird's attacks, Louie saw the camp commander, Kaname Sakaba, step out of his office and look toward him. Louie felt relief, thinking that now that Sakaba had seen this abuse of a POW by a lowly corporal, here at a show camp, he'd put a stop to it. But Sakaba watched indifferently, then walked back inside. Subsequent beatings, of Louie and of others, were no different. Other Japanese officers watched, some looking on approvingly, others looking dismayed. Sometimes, when they issued orders, they allowed the Bird, a mere corporal, to overrule them right to their faces.

According to camp accountant Yuichi Hatto, this strange situation was the result of a wrinkle in rank. Sakaba was ravenous for promotion. The appearance of order in his camp and the productivity of its slaves furthered his interests, and Watanabe's brutality was his instrument. While it is unknown whether Sakaba ordered Watanabe to abuse POWs, he obviously approved. According to Hatto, some camp employees were offended by Watanabe's treatment of POWs, but because those acts pleased Sakaba, the Bird was untouchable, even by those who outranked him. In consequence, the Bird flaunted his impunity and virtually ran the camp. He viewed the POWs as his possessions, and he sometimes attacked other Japanese who interacted with them. Watanabe was, said Hatto, "not a mere guard, but an absolute monarch of POWs at Omori."

Some Japanese, including Hatto, tried to help POWs behind Watanabe's back. No one did more than Private Yukichi Kano, the camp interpreter. When sick men were taken off work duty, losing half their rations, Kano found them easy jobs to keep them officially "at work" so they could eat enough to get well. When he saw prisoners violating the rules by eating vegetables in the garden area, or pocketing mussels at low tide outside the camp, he talked the guards into looking the other way. In winter, he hung blankets along the infirmary walls and scrounged up charcoal to heat the rooms. He snuck sick men away from the sadistic Japanese doctor and into the hands of a POW who was a physician. "There was a far braver man than I," wrote POW Pappy Boyington, winner of the Medal of Honor. Kano's "heart was being torn out most of the time, a combination of pity for the ignorance and brutality of some of his own countrymen and a complete understanding of the suffering of the prisoners." But for Louie, the Bird's pet project, Kano could do nothing.

When Louie saw Red Cross officials being taken on a carefully staged tour of camp, he thought that help had finally arrived. But to his dismay, the Bird tailed the officials and stood by, listening intently, as POWs answered the officials' questions about life in camp. No POW was foolish enough to answer truthfully, knowing the retribution that would follow. Louie had no choice but to keep his mouth shut.

Louie was on his own. As the attacks continued, he became increasingly angry. His experience in childhood, when bullies had sent him home bloody every day, was repeating itself. His interior world lit up with rage, and he couldn't hide it.

Each time the Bird lunged for him, Louie found his hands drawing into fists. As each punch struck him, he imagined himself strangling the Bird. The Bird demanded that Louie look him in the face; Louie wouldn't do it. The Bird tried to knock Louie down; Louie wobbled but wouldn't fall. In his peripheral vision, he could see the Bird looking furiously at his clenched fists. Other prisoners warned Louie that he had to show deference or the Bird would never stop. Louie couldn't do it. When he raised his eyes, all that shone in them was hate. To Watanabe, whose life was consumed with forcing men into submission, Louie's defiance was an intolerable, personal offense.

More and more now, the POWs could hear air-raid sirens echoing across the bay, from Tokyo. They were all false alarms, but they raised the prisoners' hope. Louie searched the empty sky and hoped that the bombers would come before the Bird put an end to him.

At half past six Greenwich mean time on Wednesday, October 18, 1944, a program called *Postman Calls* began its evening airing on Radio Tokyo. It was one of twelve propaganda programs conducted in English and broadcast to Allied troops. The broadcasters were POWs known as "propaganda prisoners," usually working under threat of execution or beating.

This evening, the program made an announcement: "This is the postman calling California and Mrs. Louise Zamperini, 2028 Gramercy Street, Torrance, California. Here is a message from her son, First Lieutenant Louis Silvie Zamperini, now interned in the Tokyo camp. 'My darling family, I am uninjured and in good health. I miss you all tremendously and dream of you often. Praying that you are all in good health and hope to see you again someday. Love to all relatives and friends. Hold my belongings and money for me. Love, Louis.' "

A few miles away at Omori, Louie knew nothing of the broadcast. The Japanese had written it themselves or forced a propaganda prisoner to do so.

The broadcast wasn't aired in America, but in the town of Claremont, South Africa, a man named E. H. Stephan either picked up the signal on shortwave radio or received a report of it. Stephan worked for a service that monitored broadcasts and sent news of POWs to family members. He filled out a card with information about the broadcast. Louie, the card said, was a POW in an Axis camp.

Stephan stapled a transcript of the radio message to the card. He addressed it using the contact information typed in the message, misunderstood as Louise Vancerini, 2028 Brammersee Street, Terence, California. He dropped the card in the mail.

Thanks to the mistaken address and the severe delays of the wartime mail, the card would wander the world for months. In January 1945, it would turn up in Trona, a crossroads in the California desert. It would be the end of January, nearly three and a half months after the broadcast, when someone in Trona would pick up the letter, scribble *try Torrance* on the outside, and mail it on.

Twenty-five

B-29

ON ONE OF THE LAST DAYS OF OCTOBER 1944, LOUIE pushed a wheelbarrow over the Omori bridge, through the village at the bridge's end, and into Tokyo. With him were another POW and a guard; they'd been ordered to pick up meat for the POW rations. Louie had been in Japan for thirteen months, but this was the first time that he had passed, unblindfolded, into the society that held him captive.

Tokyo was bled dry. There were no young men anywhere. The war had caused massive shortages in food and goods, and the markets and restaurants were shuttered. The civilians were slipshod and unbathed. Everyone knew that the Americans were coming, and the city seemed to be holding its breath. Teams of children and teenagers were shoveling out slit trenches and tearing down buildings to make firebreaks.

Louie, the other POW, and the guard arrived at a slaughterhouse, where their wheelbarrow was filled with horse meat. As they pushed it back toward Omori, Louie looked up at a building and saw graffiti scrawled over one wall. It said, *B Niju Ku*. The first character was simple enough, the English letter *B*. Louie knew that *niju* meant twenty and *ku* meant nine, though he didn't know that *ku* carried another meaning: pain, calamity, affliction. Louie walked the wheelbarrow into

Omori, wondering what "B twenty-nine" referred to, and why someone would write it on a wall.

———

At ten minutes to six on the morning of November 1, 1944, a wondrous American plane lifted off a runway on Saipan. Its size boggled the imagination: 99 feet long, 141 feet from wingtip to wingtip, almost 30 feet high at the tail, and weighing 120,000 pounds or more loaded, it dwarfed the famously huge B-24. Powered by four 2,200-horsepower engines—each engine almost twice as powerful as each of those of the B 24—it could rocket across the sky at up to 358 miles per hour and carry giant bomb loads. A B-24 didn't have a prayer of making it from Saipan to Japan's home islands and back. This plane could do it. It was the B-29 Superfortress, and it would bring down Japan.

The bomber, soon to be named *Tokyo Rose* as a mocking homage to the women who broadcast Japanese propaganda, was piloted by Captain Ralph Steakley. That morning, he flew his plane north. The plane split the air nearly six miles up. Above was a sky of intense blue; below, sliding over the horizon, came Japan.

B-29s had been used a handful of times over Japan, in raids launched from China, beginning four and a half months earlier. Largely because of the difficulty of supplying the Chinese bases and flying the vast distances between those bases and Japan, the missions had been ineffective. But to the Japanese, the swift leviathans were terrifying, inspiring the graffiti that Louie had seen. Three weeks after the first China-based raid, Saipan had been captured, and American plans had shifted to launching B-29s from there. Steakley's was the first run from Saipan to Tokyo, which hadn't seen an American plane since the Doolittle raid in 1942. His plane carried not bombs but cameras: Steakley was mapping the path for the B-29s that would follow his. At noon, the plane reached the city.

Louie was standing in a group of POWs, doing calisthenics on the orders of the guards, when a siren began sounding. The guards, as usual during alerts, shooed the men into the barracks. The POWs were used to the sirens, which had always been false alarms, so the alert caused little concern.

In the barracks, the men peered out the windows. Something was different; the guards were gaping at the sky as if, wrote Bob Martindale, "they were looking for the Messiah." Then there was a glint above, a finger pointing urgently, and a crush of POWs bolting for the door. Running into the compound with his face skyward, Louie saw a sliver of radiant white light high over Tokyo, contrails curling behind it like twisting spines. "Oh God, God, an American plane!" someone shouted. The guards looked stricken. Martindale heard them speaking to each other in high agitation. One phrase stood out: "*B niju ku.*"

Louie, like all the POWs, had no idea what kind of plane this was. Then a POW who'd just been captured said that it was a new American bomber called a B-29. A cheer rang out. Men began shouting, "B-29! B-29!" The bomber was the most beautiful thing that Louie had ever seen.

Across the bay, masses of civilians stood in the streets, looking at the sky. As the plane passed into the civilians' view, Frank Tinker heard the people shouting, sounds that blended into a roar. Louie glanced toward the south end of camp. The Bird was standing just outside his office, motionless and expressionless, watching the plane.

"It was not their Messiah," Martindale wrote, "but ours."

The bomber was flying at perfect liberty. Steakley guided it in a series of straight runs over the city as his crewmen snapped photographs. Below, the guards began pursuing the elated POWs, trying to force them back into the barracks. The men shushed each other, fearing that they'd be beaten for celebrating. The clamor died down. Louie stood with the other men and watched the bomber, occasionally darting between barracks to avoid the guards.

Steakley flew over Tokyo for more than an hour. No Japanese planes or guns engaged him. Finally, as he turned back for Saipan, a Zero banked up for his tail, followed briefly, then turned away.

Newspapers were relatively easy to come by in Omori. Slave laborers snuck them in, and each day, at his work site, Milton McMullen gave a Korean truck driver a bag of stolen rice in exchange for a small English-language paper, which McMullen smuggled into camp in his boot. For the POWs, the papers were inexhaustibly amusing. Though the Japanese press covered the European theater accurately, it was notorious for distorting the news of the Pacific war, sometimes absurdly. Louie once read a story about a Japanese pilot who ran out of ammunition in a dogfight and downed his opponent with a rice ball.

On the day after the B-29 flyover, the coverage wore a similar stripe. "Paper says, 'Lone enemy B-29 visits Tokyo area,' " wrote POW Ernest Norquist in his diary. "It said it came from the Mariana Island group, flew over the city and 'was drive off' [sic] without dropping a single bomb. I laughed as I read the words 'driven off' for neither the anti-aircraft fire nor the Zeros had come within miles of that great big beautiful bird." Louie saw another headline that said the bomber had FLED IN CONSTERNATION.

The plane had simply crossed over Tokyo, but everyone in Japan, captive and free, knew what it meant. Every morning, the Omori POWs were assembled and ordered to call out their number in Japanese. After November 1, 1944, the man assigned number twenty-nine would sing out "Niju ku!" at the top of his lungs. "Not even bayonet prods," wrote Wade, "could wipe the smiles from the POW faces now."

Louie wasn't smiling for long. The B-29, and what it portended, fed the Bird's vitriol. One day Louie was in his barracks, sitting with friends far in the rear, out of sight of the door, in case the Bird came in. As the men passed around a cigarette rolled in toilet paper, two guards banged in, screaming "Keirei!" Louie leapt up in tandem with the other men. In bounded the Bird.

For several seconds, the Bird looked around. He took a few steps into the room, and Louie came into his view. The corporal rushed down the barracks and halted before Louie. He wore the webbed belt that Louie had seen on him his first day in Omori. The buckle was several inches square, made of heavy brass. Standing before Louie, the Bird jerked the belt off his waist and grasped one end with both hands.

"You come to attention last!"

The Bird swung the belt backward, with the buckle on the loose end, and then whipped it around himself and forward, as if he were performing a hammer throw. The buckle rammed into Louie's left temple and ear.

Louie felt as if he had been shot in the head. Though he had resolved never to let the Bird knock him down, the power of the blow, and the explosive pain that followed, overawed everything in him. His legs seemed to liquefy, and he went down. The room spun.

Louie lay on the floor, dazed, his head throbbing, blood running from his temple. When he gathered his wits, the Bird was crouching over him, making a sympathetic, almost maternal sound, a sort of *Awwww*. He pulled a fold of toilet paper from his pocket and pressed it gently into Louie's hand. Louie held the paper to his temple.

"Oh, it stop, eh?" the Bird said, his voice soft.

Louie pulled himself upright. The Bird waited for him to steady himself. The soothing voice and the offer of the paper for his wound were revelations to Louie: There was compassion in this man. The sense of relief was just entering his mind when the buckle, whirling around from the Bird's swinging arms, struck his head again, exactly where it had hit before. Louie felt pain bursting through his skull, his body going liquid again. He smacked into the floor.

———

For several weeks, Louie was deaf in his left ear. The Bird continued to beat him, every day. As his attacker struck him, Louie bore it with clenched fists and eyes blazing, but the assaults were wearing him down. The sergeant began lording over his dream life, coming at him and pounding him, his features alight in vicious rapture. Louie spent hour after hour in prayer, begging for God to save him. He lost himself in fantasies of running through an Olympic stadium, climbing onto a podium. And he thought of home, tormented by thoughts of what his disappearance must have done to his mother. He longed to write to her, but there was no point. Once, a Japanese officer had announced that men could write home, and everyone in camp penned letters to their parents, wives, children, and steady girls. When the Bird learned of it, he called in Commander Maher, handed him the letters, and forced him to burn them.

One day in mid-November, Louie was sitting in his barracks when the Bird walked in and approached him, accompanied by two Japanese strangers. Louie expected a beating, but instead, the strangers were friendly. They told Louie that they were producers from Radio Tokyo and that they had something they thought he'd like to see. They handed Louie a piece of paper. Louie looked at it: It was a transcript of an NBC radio broadcast announcing his death. The transcript was real. Louie's death declaration, delivered in June, had reached the American media on November 12, that same week.

The Radio Tokyo men wanted Louie to come to their studio to announce that he was alive on the *Postman Calls* show. They wanted Louie to do this, they said, for his sake and that of his suffering family. He was free to write his own message. Louie didn't trust them, and gave them no answer. They told him to take a day to think about it. Louie consulted Martindale, who told him that several POWs had made such broadcasts, and as long as Louie didn't read propaganda, there was no harm in accepting.

So Louie said yes. The Radio Tokyo men brought him pen and paper, and he set to work. Knowing that his family might not believe that it was really he, he added details that he hoped would convince them. To ensure that his message got through, he decided to speak positively about his captors. He included the names of other POWs who feared that their families thought they were dead, and also mentioned Bill Harris, whom he'd last seen a month and a half earlier, at Ofuna. He opted not to mention Phil. He hadn't seen the pilot for eight months, and didn't know if he was still alive.

Louie was driven to the Radio Tokyo studio. The producers greeted him as if he were a beloved friend. They read his speech and gave it a hearty approval. It would be taped for broadcast two days later. The producers planned to use that evening's broadcast to tease the audience, then wait before presenting his voice to the world, proof that they were telling the truth.

Louie was taken to the microphone and given his cue. He read his message, to the pleasure of the producers. As the officials prepared to drive him back to Omori, Louie went to a producer who had been especially kind. He said that there was a man in camp named Watanabe who was beating the POWs. The producer seemed concerned and told Louie that he'd see what he could do.

In San Francisco at half past two on the morning of November 18, 1944, a young woman named Lynn Moody was alone in the Office of War Information, working the graveyard shift. Across the hall in the Federal Communications Commission station, one of her colleagues was listening to Japanese radio and typing up broadcasts for review by propaganda analysts. Moody was bored, so she crossed the hall to say hello. The colleague asked if Moody could fill in while she took a break.

Moody slipped on the earphones and began typing. The show airing was *Postman Calls*. As she typed, Moody was startled to hear a name that she knew well: Louis Zamperini. Moody was a member of the USC class of 1940, and Louie was an old friend. The announcer was speaking about the October 18 message that had been broadcast, supposedly from Louie, but in fact written without Louie's knowledge.

Giddy with excitement, Moody typed, placing unclear words within parentheses:

> Exactly one month ago we broadcast a message. This message over the same station, same program, "Postman Calls," was from First Lieutenant Louis (Silvie) Zamperini, United States Army Air Corps. Recently a news report has been brought to our attention in which it is stated that First Lieutenant Louis Zamperini is listed as dead by the United States War Department. According to the report, Lieutenant Zamperini was reported missing in action in the South Pacific in May, 1943. The apparently uninformed source of this item is a broadcasting station in California quoting the War Department of the United States of America. We hope we can rectify this mistake on someone's part by saying that Louis Zamperini is alive and well as a prisoner of war here in Tokyo.
>
> This is one of the many examples of the men missing in action erroneously reported and later being established as a lie. The last war was full of such instances and much suffering and heartaches could have been avoided by the transmittal of reliable information to the parties concerned regarding the whereabouts of men (in such cases); It is one of the purposes of this program to alleviate this condition and furnish speedy, reliable and authentic message service to the relatives and friends of men interned in prisoner of war camps throughout Japan. We sincerely hope Louis' mother is listening in tonight or will be informed of what we say.
>
> Long will Louis Zamperini's name live in our memories. Those of us from the regions of Southern California well recall the days that Louis was breaking all records in the mile run. His unbroken national interscholastic mile record stands as a challenge to the aspirants of the (Ginger Cup). We followed closely Zamperini's efforts in 1936 Olympic games held in Berlin, Germany. His opponents and some of the foremost in the country speak highly of him. He has run against such names as (Bensig) and Cunningham. The same personality that so endeared him to us as he raced against time on the tracks of the world is not dead but very much alive and with us yet. We regret the unhappiness that must have accompanied the news of his reported death but hope that the efforts of his fellow prisoners of war on "Postman Calls" will (atone) in some small way for the error.

So chin up, Mrs. Louis Zamperini of (Torrance) California, Louis is here; the same old Louis, cheerful, sportsmanlike, the idol of all our Southern California fans and graduates. You might pass the glad tidings along, Mrs. Zamperini, for we know all the lovers of the (spiked shoe) sport will b [*sic*] glad to hear this. Louis is not on the track anymore an [*sic*] for that we are sorry. He will be missed there. Louis is neither missing nor dead as has been reported and for that we are more than glad. It makes us very happy indeed to have performed this service for our prisoners and relatives and it is out [*sic*] earnest wish that no other such instances of this information will be forthcoming. We hope this little group of prisoners connected with "Postman Calls" program can be of further service in the future. That's what we're here for, so keep on listening, Mrs. Zamperini, and don't mention it; the pleasure is all ours.

Moody typed as fast as she could, making a string of typos in her exhilaration. About an hour later, the FCC woman came back. "I practically danced around the room telling her about it," Moody later wrote.

Down the coast in Torrance, the Zamperinis were coping with the aftermath of the public announcement of Louie's death. After a package came bearing Louie's Purple Heart, a letter arrived concerning his life insurance payout, $10,000. Louise deposited the money in the bank but didn't spend any of it. When Louie came home, she declared, it would be his. And after the news of Louie's death broke, the film director Cecil B. DeMille showed up to do a radio interview with the family for the Sixth War Bond Drive. Sylvia and Louise were given scripts that called for them to speak of Louie as if he were dead. Out of politeness, the Zamperinis read the scripts as written.

Somewhere in all of this, a deliveryman came, bearing a bouquet of flowers for Sylvia. It was an anniversary gift from her husband, Harvey, now manning a tank gun in Holland. A few days later she got a telegram: Harvey had been wounded. The telegram said nothing of what his injuries were, or how serious. Sylvia waited, knotted with anxiety. Finally, a letter arrived, composed by Harvey and dictated to a nurse from his hospital bed. His tank had been hit and had burst into flames. He had escaped, but his hands and face were burned. Of all the terrible scenarios that had run through Sylvia's mind, fire was the one thing that she'd never imagined. Harvey was, after all, a firefighter. Exhausted and barely able to eat, Sylvia crept through November, haunted by nightmares and growing ever more gaunt.

————

On November 20, Lynn Moody, still in high spirits over the broadcast about Louie two days before, was back working the midnight-to-eight shift. At two-thirty A.M., one of the FCC transcribers yelled to her to come quickly.

Moody ran in, put on the earphones, and listened. It was *Postman Calls* again. "Hello, America," the announcer began, "this is the postman calling and bringing a special message as promised earlier in tonight's program to Mrs. Louis Zamperini, 2028 Gramercy Street, Torrance, California. We hope Mrs. Zamperini is listening in tonight for we have a real treat for her. Her son has come down to the studio especially to send her this message of reassurance after the erroneous report of a few days ago by the United States War Department, that he was officially given up as dead and missing. We assure Mrs. Zamperini that such is not the case. The next voice heard will be that of First Lieutenant Louis Helzie [*sic*] Zamperini, United States Air Force, now interned in the Tokyo camp. Go right ahead, Lieutenant Zamperini."

A young man's voice came across the airwaves. Moody knew the instant she heard it: It was Louie.

Hello mother and father, relatives and friends. This is your Louie talking. Through the courtesy of the authorities here I am broadcasting this personal message to you.

This will be the first time in two and one half years that you will have heard my voice. I am sure it sounds the same to you as it did when I left home.

I am uninjured and in good health and can hardly wait until the day we are together again. Not having heard from you since my most abrupt departure, I have been somewhat worried about the condition of the family, as far as health is concerned. I hope this message finds all of you in the best of health and good spirits.

I am now interned in the Tokyo prisoners' camp and am being treated as well as can be expected under war time conditions. The camp authorities are kind to me and I have no kick coming.

Please write as often as you can and in doing so, send me snapshots of everyone. In my lonesome hours nothing would be more appreciated than to look at pictures of the family.

Before I forget it, Dad, I would be very pleased if you would keep my guns in good condition so we might do some good hunting when I return home.

Mother Sylvia and Virginia, I hope you will keep up your wonderful talents in the kitchen. I often visualize those wonderful pies and cakes you make.

Is Pete still able to pay you his weekly visits from San Diego? I hope he is still near home.

Give my best to Gorton, Harvey, Eldon and Henry and wish them the best of care. I send my fondest love to Sylvia, Virginia and Pete and hope they are enjoying their work at the present. I miss them very much.

Since I have been in Japan I have run into several of my old acquaintances. You will probably remember a few of them.

The tall Marine, William Harris, from Kentucky is here and enjoying good health. Lorren Stoddard Stanley Maneivve and Peter Hryskanich are the same. You must remember William Hasty from Bishopville? We have been rooming together for the past two months. He is looking fine.

I know that you have taken care of my personal belongings and saving long ago. You have no doubt received the rest of my belongings from the Army.

Hello to Bob Lewellyn and all of my home town friends. Before closing I wish you a merry Xmas and a Happy New Year.

Your loving son, Louie

Later that day, the phone rang at the Zamperinis' house. The caller was a woman from the nearby suburb of San Marino. She said that she'd been listening to her radio when the station had aired an intercepted broadcast of an American prisoner of war speaking on Japanese radio. The broadcast had been scratchy and indistinct, but she was sure that she had heard the name right. The POW she had heard, she said, was Louie.

The Zamperinis were shocked and wary. The woman was a stranger, and they were afraid that she was a prankster. Sylvia and Louise asked for her address and drove to her house. The woman told them everything she had heard. Sylvia and Louise thanked her and left. They believed the woman, but they didn't know if they could believe the broadcast itself. It could easily have been faked. "I was thinking, 'Could it be true? Could it be true?' " Sylvia recalled.

After Sylvia and Louise got home, a Western Union telegram arrived from the provost marshal general. It read, FOLLOWING ENEMY PROPAGANDA BROADCAST FROM JAPAN HAS BEEN INTERCEPTED. Below were Louie's words, as typed by Moody. The telegram ended with a disclaimer: PENDING FURTHER CONFIRMATION THIS REPORT DOES NOT ESTABLISH HIS STATUS AS A PRISONER OF WAR.

Messages began pouring in, from friends and strangers all over the country, telling the Zamperinis of the broadcast, which had been intercepted and re-aired on several stations. And Louie's uncle Gildo Dossi called from Wilmington, Iowa. He had clicked on his radio and heard a voice that he felt certain was that of his nephew.

The messages relaying the content of the broadcast were varied, but a common thread ran through several of them: a request that they take care of Louie's guns. Louie had grown up hunting, shooting rabbits in the fields around Torrance and on the Cahuilla Indian Reservation, and he was especially careful with his guns. To the Zamperinis, this was the fingerprint, the detail that the Japanese could not have known. Louise and Sylvia dissolved in tears, then began shouting with joy.

Pete picked up the phone, dialed Payton Jordan's number, and shouted three words into the receiver:

"Payt! *He's alive!*"

Twenty-six

Madness

THE RADIO TOKYO MEN WERE BACK AT OMORI, SMILING. What a lovely voice Louie had, what a brilliant job he had done. How about another broadcast?

As long as he wrote his own copy, Louie saw no reason to decline. He composed another message to his family, then rode with the producers to Tokyo. When he reached the studio, the producers announced a change of plans. They didn't need the message he'd written; they had one all ready. They handed Louie a sheet of paper. This is what it said, exactly as written:

Well, believe it or not . . . I guess I'm one of those "Lucky guys", or maybe, I dunno, maybe I'm really unlucky . . . Anyway . . . here's me, Louis Zamperini, age 27, hometown Los Angeles, California, good ole United States of America speaking. What I mean by lucky is that I'm still alive and healthy . . . Yes, and it's a funny thing . . . I've heard and also saw with my own eyes that I'm washed-up that is I was reported to have died in combat. . . . Yes, one of those who died gallantry [*sic*] fighting for the cause . . . I think the official report went something like this . . . 'First Lieutenant Louis S. Zamperini, holder of the national inter-scholastic mile record, is, listed as dead by the War Department . . . The former University of Southern California miler was reported missing in action in the South Pacific in May 1943' . . . Well, what do you know? . . . Boy. . . . that's rich. . . . Here I am just as alive as I could be. . . . but hell I'm supposed to be dead. . . . Yeah and this reminds me of another fellow who's in the same boat as me or at least he was. . . . Anyway he told me that he was officially reported as 'killed in action' but in reality was a prisoner-of-war. . . . After several months he received a letter from his wife in which she told him that she had married again since she thought he was dead . . . Of course, she was astonished to hear that he was safe and held in an internment camp. . . . She however, consolated him by saying that she was willing to divorce again or marry him once again when he gets home. . . . Boy, I really feel sorry for a fellow like that.and the blame lies with the official who allow such unreliable rports [*sic*] . . . . After all the least they can do is to let the folks back home know just where theri boy are [*sic*] . . .

Anyway thats not my worry but I hope the folks back home are properly notified of the fact that I am alive and intend to stay alive . . . It's certainly a sad world when a fellow can't even be allowed to live, I mean when a fellow is killed off by a so-called 'official report. . . . How about that? . . .

Louie was aghast. He had long wondered why he'd been spared from execution on Kwajalein, after the nine marines had been killed, and why he'd been subjected to the will-weakening torment of Ofuna yet not interrogated, even though everyone else had been. At last, the Japanese had made their intentions clear. On Kwajalein, after Louie's execution had been ordered, an officer had persuaded his superiors to keep Louie alive to make him into a propaganda tool. A famous American Olympian, he'd reasoned, would be especially valuable.* The Japanese had probably sent Louie to the crucible of Ofuna, then to Omori under the Bird, to make his life in camp unbearable so he'd be willing to do anything, even betray his country, to escape it. They had hidden him from the world, keeping his name off Red Cross rosters, and waited until his government had publicly declared his death before

---

* Phil had no such potential usefulness but was probably spared because his execution would have made Louie less likely to cooperate.

announcing that he was alive. In doing so, they hoped to embarrass America and undermine American soldiers' faith in their government.

Louie refused to read the statement. Still smiling, the producers asked him to join them on a little tour. They brought him to a cafeteria and served him a delicious American-style meal, then took him to a private living area that had beds with mattresses and sheets. If Louie would make the broadcast, the producers said, he could live here, and he'd never have to see Omori again. Finally, Louie was introduced to a group of men, Australians and Americans. These men, the producers said, were helping them make broadcasts. As Louie held out his hand, the propaganda prisoners dropped their eyes to the floor. Their faces said it all; if Louie agreed to make this broadcast, he would be forced into a life as his enemy's propagandist.

Louie was taken back to the studio and urged to do the broadcast. He refused. The smiles evaporated; the faces hardened. The producers ordered him to do it. He said no. The producers left the room to meet in private.

Louie was alone in the studio. In front of him were several copies of the message that they wanted him to deliver. He slid his hand through a tear in his pocket, snagged a copy, and pulled it into his coat. The producers returned.

"Okay," one of them said. "I think you go to punishment camp."

Omori was called a punishment camp, but the producers were clearly referring to some other place. For Louie, any camp had to be better than Omori, because the Bird wouldn't be there. The producers gave him one last chance to change his mind. He did not.

Louie was dumped back at Omori. The Bird was waiting for him, glowing with renewed hatred. His beatings resumed, with intensified vigor. Maybe Louie was being punished for refusing to make the broadcast, or maybe the producer to whom Louie had appealed for help had told the Bird of Louie's accusations. Louie stood his ground, took his beatings with rebellion boiling in him, and waited to be shipped to "punishment camp." And like all the other POWs, he watched the sky, praying that the promise of that first B-29 would be fulfilled.

In the early afternoon on Friday, November 24, the Tokyo sirens began to howl. From the sky came an immense shivering sound. The POWs looked up. There, so high that they appeared to be gleaming slits in the sky, were acres and acres of B-29s, one hundred and eleven of them, flying toward an aircraft factory on the rim of the city. Caught in what would later be called the jet stream, the planes were streaking along at speeds approaching 445 miles per hour, almost 100 miles per hour faster than they were built to fly. The Americans had arrived.

"It was a cold, clear, sunny day," wrote POW Johan Arthur Johansen, who was at a slave site at the time. "The planes were shining

A B-29 over Japan. *Associated Press*

like silver in the sunshine against the blue sky overhead . . . It was a beautiful sight which lift[ed] our spirit right up to the sky." Men began yelling, "Drop the bombs!" and "Happy landings!" and "Welcome back!" The guards stared up, so awed by the planes that they didn't seem to hear the men shouting.

At Omori, the camp accountant, Yuichi Hatto, was standing with a group of POWs. As they watched, a lone Japanese fighter raced toward the planes, then abruptly, startlingly, flew straight into a bomber, the smaller plane shattering and raining down on Tokyo Bay. The bomber began falling, white smoke twirling from it. A single parachute puffed from its side, and one of the POWs cried, "One safe! Safe!" The English word caught in Hatto's ear; he had heard it used only in baseball games. The bomber hit the water, killing all aboard. The lone survivor, under his parachute, wafted over Tokyo as gently as a dandelion seed. As the man sank into the city, Hatto had a sick feeling, thinking of what would happen to that airman when he reached the ground. The other bombers flew on. A few minutes later, there was distant booming.

As the fall stretched on, B-29s crossed over Omori nearly every day, sometimes a lone plane, sometimes vast continents of aircraft. On sunny days, the men stood out and watched them; on cloudy days, they only heard them, a growl above the gray. In Tokyo, the sirens sang so incessantly that the POWs began sleeping through them.

Eighty-one bombers went over on November 27. On the drizzly night of November 29–30, the prisoners were awakened by two incendiary raids on Tokyo's industrial areas. Explosions were heard far away, and the POWs could see licks of fire on the mainland, the last gasps of the 2,773 structures that burned that night. Civilians began streaming over the bridge and camping outside Omori's walls in hopes of escaping the bombs.

One day that fall, Louie stood outside, watching Japanese fighters turning lupine circles around a crowd of B-29s. The battle was so high that only the giant, shining bombers were consistently visible; the fighters, tiny in contrast, flickered in and out of view as the sunlight caught them. Every little while, there was a sharp, brief burst of light alongside the bombers. To Louie, it looked like firecrackers. It was the fighters, gunned by the B-29s, blowing up. The bombers flew on, imperious. The Bird watched the scene with a stricken face. *"Hikoki dame,"* he said. *"Hikoki dame."* Japan's planes, he was lamenting, were no good.

Every B-29 that beat a path over Tokyo wound the Bird tighter. He hounded the POWs with endless inspections, prohibited smoking, singing, and card playing, and outlawed religious services. He slapped one officer across the face repeatedly for five minutes, made him stand at attention, coatless, for four hours in the cold, then ordered him to clean the *benjos* for two hours a day for two weeks. He beat a kitchen worker with a spoon the size of an oar. He pawed through the men's belongings, confiscating personal papers and photographs of loved ones, deeming much of it "suspicious" and destroying it. He was seized with paranoia. "You win war, and you make all Japanese like black slaves!" he shouted at a POW. He hauled Martindale to his office, ac-

B-29 Superfortresses. *Associated Press*

cused him of plotting to burn down a barracks, and beat him so energetically, with fists and a kendo stick, that he overturned all of the furniture.

In December, the Bird left camp for several days, and Omori was
briefly peaceful. But on the night before the Bird was slated to return,
the POWs were jarred from their sleep to hear him charging through
camp in a driving rainstorm, yelling that it was a fire drill. When the
designated firefighters assembled under the freezing downpour, the
Bird punched several of them in the face, ran through barracks shouting and punching other men, then ordered every man in camp to line
up outside. When Louie and the others did as told, the Bird drew his
sword, swung it around, and screamed orders and invectives. For two
hours, the Bird forced the men to pump water on imaginary fires, beat
out phantom blazes with brooms, and run in and out of buildings "rescuing" food and documents.

As December progressed, the Bird's mania deepened. He rounded
up the officers and hounded them across the bridge and into Tokyo, on
the pretense of retrieving firewood from bombed-out houses. Troughs
of water for firefighting had been set along the streets, and as the men
marched, the Bird leapt upon one, drew his sword, and screamed

"*Keirei!*" The men saluted him, and the Bird, lost in a fantasy, stood on his roost in an absurdly exaggerated troop-reviewing pose that reminded Tom Wade of Mussolini. Civilians gathered and began cheering. After the POWs had passed, the Bird jumped down, ran ahead, and hopped onto another trough, shouting, striking his pose, and demanding salutes. Over and over he repeated the farce, driving the men on for miles.

When the bombs were falling, the Bird would snap, running through camp with his sword in the air, wailing at the men, foam flying from his mouth, lips peeled back in a wicked rictus, eyelid drooping, face purple. During at least two bombings, he prevented the POWs from seeking cover in the trenches. In one incident, he ran the POWs outside, stood them at attention, and ordered the guards to aim their rifles at them. With bombs booming, the Bird raced up and down the line of terrified POWs, swinging his sword over their heads.

Every escalation in the bombing brought a parallel escalation in the Bird's attacks on Louie. He sped around camp in search of the American, fuming and furious. Louie hid, but the Bird always found him. Three or four times a week, the Bird launched himself at Louie in what Frank Tinker would call his "death lunge," coming at him with fists flying, going for his face and head. Louie would emerge dazed and bleeding. He was more and more convinced that Watanabe wouldn't stop until he was dead.

Louie began to come apart. At night, the Bird stalked his dreams, screeching, seething, his belt buckle flying at Louie's skull. In the dreams, the smothered rage in Louie would overwhelm him, and he'd find himself on top of his monster, his hands on the corporal's neck, strangling the life from him.

———

As Louie suffered through December, some three hundred miles away, his former pilot was wasting away in a filthy, unheated barracks in the Zentsuji POW camp. Phil had been transferred to Zentsuji the previous August, joining one-legged Fred Garrett, who'd been transferred from Ofuna.

Though Ofuna interrogators had spoken of Zentsuji as a "plush" reward, the camp was no such place. The prisoners' diet was so poor that the men wandered the compound, ravenous, pulling up weeds and eating them. Their only drinking water came from a reservoir fed by runoff from rice paddies fertilized with human excrement, and to avoid dying of thirst, the POWs had to drink it, leaving 90 percent of them afflicted with dysentery. In one barracks room, men lost an average of fifty-four pounds over eighteen months. An officer estimated that twenty men fainted each day. Almost everyone had beriberi, and some men went blind from malnutrition. On the last day of November, they buried an American who had starved to death.

There was one blessing at Zentsuji. Phil was permitted to send brief messages home on postcards. He wrote one after another. They were mailed, but got snarled in the postal system. The fall waned and another Christmas approached, and Phil's family received none of them.

A year and a half had passed since Phil had disappeared. His family remained in limbo, having heard nothing about him since his plane had gone down. In November, they had learned about Louie's broadcast. The news had been tantalizing, but frustrating. Louie had mentioned other servicemen who were with him, but the names had been obscured by static, and the transcript hadn't conveyed them with certainty. Had Louie mentioned Allen?

On a Friday night in December 1944, the telephone rang in Kelsey Phillips's home. On the line was a major from the adjutant general's office at the War Department. Probably through the Red Cross, the department had received news from Zentsuji. Allen was alive.

Kelsey was jubilant. She asked the major to cable her husband and her son's fiancée, and in Washington, Cecy got the news she had awaited for so long. The fortune-teller had said that Allen would be found before Christmas. It was December 8. Overcome with elation, Cecy called her brother to shout the news, quit her job, dashed through her apartment throwing clothes and pictures of Allen into a suitcase, and hopped a plane back to Indiana to wait for her fiancé to come home.

Four days before Christmas, a card from Allen, written in October, finally reached home. "Dear Folk: Hope you all are well and am looking forward to being home with you. I hope we can go rabbit hunting before the season closes Dad. Give my love to Cecy Martha and Dick. Happy birthday dad." Kelsey pored over the precious slip of paper, comforted by the familiar lines of her son's handwriting. Chaplain Phillips, now stationed in France, got the news on Christmas Eve. "Words really cannot describe the way I feel," he wrote to his daughter. "I am in an altogether new world now. I can think of nothing more wonderful. It is a real touch of all that heaven means."

In a letter officially confirming that Allen was a POW, the Phillipses were asked not to speak publicly about the fact that Allen had been discovered alive. Kelsey would henceforth heed this request, but the letter had reached her too late; by the morning after the War Department's call, the news was already all over town, and stories about Allen's survival were in the local papers. The Zamperinis, who had received a similar letter stating that the War Department now believed that Louie's broadcast had been real, were also asked not to speak of it publicly. The War Department probably didn't want it known that they had erroneously declared two airmen dead, especially as the Japanese were exploiting this fact.

Kelsey was allowed to send one cable to her son, and she filled the other days writing letters to him. On December 14, she wrote to Louise Zamperini. As relieved as Kelsey was for Allen, there was heaviness in her heart. Of all of the men on *Green Hornet,* only Louie and Allen had been found. Hugh Cuppernell's mother was so demoralized that she could no longer bear to write to the other mothers. Sadie Glassman, mother of the belly gunner, Frank Glassman, had written to Louise, asking if she had heard anything about Frank. "Even though we have heard nothing," she wrote, "the fact that you might know something makes us feel as though there might be a little hope."

"It is difficult to rejoice outwardly (though I do in my heart) when I think of the other mothers whom I have learned to love, and realize how keenly they feel the loss that is theirs," Kelsey wrote to Louise. "How my heart goes out to them and I shall write them every one."

As Christmas neared, Louie faltered. Starvation was consuming him. The occasional gifts from the thieves helped, but not enough. What was most maddening was that ample food was so near. Twice that fall, Red Cross relief packages had been delivered for the POWs, but instead of distributing them, camp officials had hauled them into storage and begun taking what they wanted from them.* They made no effort to hide the stealing. "We could see them throwing away unmistakable wrappers, carrying bowls of bulk cocoa and sugar between huts and even trying to wash clothes with cakes of American cheese," wrote Tom Wade. The Bird was the worst offender, smoking Lucky Strike cig-

---

* After the war, the head of the Tokyo area camps would admit that he had ordered the distribution of Red Cross parcels to Japanese personnel.

arettes and openly keeping Red Cross food in his room. From one delivery of 240 Red Cross boxes, the Bird stole forty-eight, more than five hundred pounds of goods.

Toward the end of December, the Bird ordered all of the men to the compound, where they found a truck brimming with apples and oranges. In all of his time as a POW, Louie had seen only one piece of fruit, the tangerine that Sasaki had given him. The men were told that they could take two pieces each. As the famished men swarmed onto the pile, Japanese photographers circled, snapping photos. Then, just as the men were ready to devour the fruit, the order came to put it all back. The entire thing had been staged for propaganda.

On Christmas Eve, some Red Cross packages were finally handed out. Louie wrote triumphantly of it in his diary. His box, weighing some eleven pounds, contained corned beef, cheese, pâté, salmon, butter, jam, chocolate, milk, prunes, and four packs of Chesterfields. All evening long, the men of Omori traded goods, smoked, and gorged themselves.

That night, there was another treat, and it came about as the result of a series of curious events. Among the POWs was a chronically unwashed, ingenious, and possibly insane kleptomaniac named Mansfield. Shortly before Christmas, Mansfield broke into the storehouse—slipping past seven guards—and made off with several Red Cross packages, which he buried under his barracks. Discovering his cache, guards locked him in a cell. Mansfield broke out, stole sixteen more parcels, and snuck them back into his cell. He hid the contents of the packages in a secret compartment he'd fashioned himself, marking the door with a message for other POWs: *Food, help yourself, lift here.* Caught again, he was tied to a tree in the snow without food or water, wearing only pajamas, and beaten. By one account, he was left there for ten days. Late one night, when Louie was walking back from the *benjo,* he saw the camp interpreter, Yukichi Kano, kneeling beside Mansfield, draping a blanket over him. The next morning, the blanket was gone, retrieved before the Bird could see it. Eventually, Mansfield was untied and taken to a civilian prison, where he flourished.

The one good consequence of this event was that in the storehouse, Mansfield had discovered a Red Cross theatrical trunk. He told other POWs about it, and this gave the men the idea of boosting morale by staging a Christmas play. They secured the Bird's approval by stroking his ego, naming him "master of ceremonies" and giving him a throne at the front of the "theater"—the bathhouse—outfitted with planks perched on washtubs to serve as a stage. The men decided to put on a musical production of *Cinderella,* written, with creative liberties, by a British POW. Frank Tinker put his operatic gifts to work as Prince Leander of Pantoland. The Fairy Godmother was played by a mountainous cockney Brit dressed in a tutu and tights. Characters included Lady Dia Riere and Lady Gonna Riere. Louie thought it was the funniest thing he'd ever seen. Private Kano translated for the guards, who sat in the back, laughing and clapping. The Bird gloried in the limelight, and for that night, he let Louie and the others be.

At Zentsuji, Christmas came to Phil and Fred Garrett. Some POWs scrounged up musical instruments and assembled in the camp. Before seven hundred starving men, they played rousing music as the men sang along. They ended with the national anthems of England, Holland, and the United States. The Zentsuji POWs stood together at attention in silence, thinking of home.

After Christmas, the Bird abruptly stopped attacking the POWs, even Louie. He paced about camp, brooding. The men watched him and wondered what was going on.

Several times that year, a dignitary named Prince Yoshitomo Tokugawa had come to camp. A prominent and influential man, reportedly a descendant of the first shogun, Tokugawa was touring camps for the Japanese Red Cross. At Omori, he met with POW Lewis Bush, who told him about the Bird's cruelty.

The Bird was suspicious. After Tokugawa first visited, the Bird forbade Bush from speaking to him again. When the prince returned, Bush defied the Bird, who beat him savagely as soon as the prince left. Tokugawa kept coming, and Bush kept meeting with him. The Bird slugged and kicked Bush, but Bush refused to be cowed. Deeply troubled by what he heard, Tokugawa went to the war office and the Red Cross and pushed to have something done about Watanabe. He told Bush that he was encountering resistance. Then, just before the New Year, the prince at last succeeded. The Bird was ordered to leave Omori.

Tokugawa's victory was a hollow one. Officials made no effort to take the Bird out of contact with POWs. They simply ordered his transfer to a distant, isolated camp, where he'd have exactly the same sway over prisoners, without the prying eyes of the prince and the Red Cross. Ensuring that no censure of Watanabe was implied, Colonel Sakaba promoted him to sergeant.

The Bird threw himself a good-bye party and ordered some of the POW officers to come. The officers dashed around camp to gather stool samples from the greenest dysentery patients, mixed up a ferocious gravy, and slathered it over a stack of rice cakes. When they arrived at the party, they presented the cakes to the Bird as a token of their affection. While the men lavished the Bird with lamentations on how they'd miss him, the Bird ate heartily. He seemed heartbroken to be leaving.

Later that day, Louie looked out of the barracks and saw the Bird standing by the gate in a group of people, shaking hands. All of the POWs were in a state of high animation. Louie asked what was happening, and someone told him that the Bird was leaving for good. Louie felt almost out of his head with joy.

If the rice cakes performed as engineered, they didn't do so quickly. The Bird crossed the bridge onto the mainland, looking perfectly well. At Omori, the reign of terror was over.

Twenty-seven

Falling Down

AT OMORI, LIFE BECAME IMMEASURABLY BETTER. PRIVATE Kano quietly took over the camp, working with Watanabe's replacement, Sergeant Oguri, a humane, fair-minded man. The Bird's rules were abolished. Someone got into the Bird's office and found a pile of mail sent to the POWs by their families. Some of the letters had been in his office for nine months. The letters were delivered, and the POWs were finally allowed to write home. "Trust you're all in good health and in the highest of spirits, not the kind that comes in bottles," Louie wrote in one letter to his family. "Tell Pete," he wrote in another, "that when I'm 50, I'll have more hair on my head than he had at 20." The letters, like so many others, languished in the glacial mail system, and wouldn't make it to America until long after the war's end.

Two weeks into 1945, a group of men, tattered and bent, trudged over the bamboo bridge and into Omori. Louie knew their faces: These were Ofuna men. Commander Fitzgerald was with them. The Omori prisoners told him that he was the luckiest man in Japan. A vicious tyrant called the Bird had just left.

Among the new POWs, Louie spotted Bill Harris, and his heart fell. Harris was a wreck. When Louie greeted him, his old friend looked at him vaguely. He was hazy and distant, his mind struggling for purchase on his thoughts.

The beating the Quack had delivered to Harris in September 1944 hadn't been the last. On November 6, apparently after Harris was caught speaking, the Quack had pounced on him again, joining several guards in clubbing him into unconsciousness. Two months later, Harris had been beaten once more, for stealing nails to repair his torn shoes, which he was trying to nurse through a frigid winter. He had asked the Japanese to give him some, but they had refused.

The Omori POW doctor examined Harris gravely. He told Louie that he thought the marine was dying.

That same day, Oguri opened the storehouse and had the Red Cross boxes handed out. Giving his box to Harris was, Louie would say, the hardest and easiest thing he ever did. Harris rallied.

Since his refusal to become a propaganda prisoner, Louie had been waiting to be shipped to punishment camp. While the Bird had badgered him, he had awaited his fate with equanimity. Now that the Bird was gone, and Harris was here with Louie's other friends, Louie wanted to stay. He met every day with dread, awaiting his transfer.

––––

The B-29s kept coming. Sirens sounded several times a day. Rumors eddied around camp: Manila had been captured, Germany had fallen, the Americans were about to charge the Japanese beaches. Louie, like a lot of POWs, was worried. Frightened by the bombing, the guards were increasingly jumpy and angry. Even guards who had once been amiable were now hostile, lashing out without reason. As the assaults on Japan intensified and the probability of invasion rose, the Japanese seemed to view the POWs as threatening.

Among the American forces, a horrifying piece of news had just surfaced. One hundred and fifty American POWs had long been held on Palawan Island, in the Philippines, where they'd been used as slaves to construct an airfield. In December, after American planes bombed the field, the POWs were ordered to dig shelters. They were told to build the entrances only one man wide.

On December 14, an American convoy was spotted near Palawan. The commander of the Japanese 2nd Air Division was apparently sure that the Americans intended to invade. It was the scenario for which

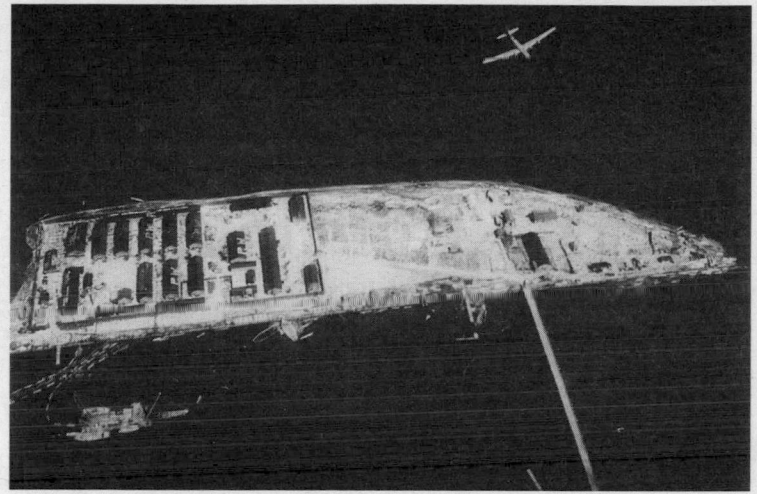

A B-29 over the Omori POW camp. *Raymond Halloran*

the kill-all order had been written. That night, the commander sent a radio message to Palawan: "Annihilate the 150 prisoners."

On December 15 on Palawan, the guards suddenly began screaming that there were enemy planes coming. The POWs crawled into the shelters and sat there, hearing no planes. Then liquid began to rain onto them. It was gasoline. The guards tossed in torches, then hand grenades. The shelters, and the men inside, erupted in flames.

As the guards cheered, the POWs fought to escape, some clawing their own fingertips off. Nearly all of those who broke out were bayoneted, machine-gunned, or beaten to death. Only eleven men escaped. They swam across a nearby bay and were discovered by inmates at a penal colony. The inmates delivered them to Filipino guerrillas, who brought them to American forces.

That night, the Japanese threw a party to celebrate the massacre. Their anticipation of an American landing turned out to be mistaken.

Sleet was falling over Omori as February 16 dawned. At seven-fifteen, Louie and the other POWs had just finished a breakfast of barley and soup when the sirens piped up. Commander Fitzgerald looked at his friends. He knew that this would probably not be B-29s, which would have had to fly all night to reach Japan so early. It was probably carrier aircraft: His navy must be near. A few seconds later, the room was shaking. The men bolted for the doors.

Louie ran out into a crashing, tumbling world. The entire sky was swarming with hundreds of fighters, American and Japanese, rising and falling, streaming bullets at one another. Over Tokyo, lines of dive-bombers bellied down like waves slapping a beach, slamming bombs into the aircraft works and airport. As they rose, quills of fire came up under them. Louie was standing directly underneath the largest air battle yet fought over Japan.

The guards fixed their bayonets and ordered the POWs back inside. Louie and the others filed into the barracks, waited for the guards to rush off to censure someone else, then stole out. They ran behind a barracks, climbed the camp fence, and hung there, resting their elbows on the top. The view was electrifying. Planes were sweeping over every corner of the sky, and all around, fighters were dropping into the water.

One dogfight riveted Louie's attention. An American Hellcat hooked up with a Japanese fighter and began chasing it. The Japanese fighter turned toward the city and dove low over the bay, the Hellcat right behind it. The two planes streaked past the camp, the Japanese fighter racing flat out, the Hellcat's guns firing. Several hundred POWs watched from the camp fence, their eyes pressed to knotholes or their heads poking over the top, hearts leaping, ears roaring. The fighters were so close that Louie could see both pilots' faces. The Japanese fighter crossed over the coast, and the Hellcat broke away.

All told, fifteen hundred American planes and several hundred Japanese planes flew over the POWs that day. That night, the city was bathed in red fires. The following day, back the planes came. By the end of February 17, more than five hundred Japanese planes, both on the ground and in the air, had been lost, and Japan's aircraft works had been badly hit. The Americans had lost eighty planes.

Seven days later, the hammer fell. At seven in the morning, during a heavy snowstorm, sixteen hundred carrier-based planes flew past Omori and bombed Tokyo. Then came B-29s, 229 of them, carrying incendiary bombs. Encountering almost no resistance, they sped for the industrial district and let their bombs fall. The POWs could see fire dancing over the skyline.

———

On the last day of February, Louie and the other officers were called into the compound. Fifteen names were called, among them Zamperini, Wade, Tinker, Mead, and Fitzgerald. They were told that they were being transferred to a camp called 4B, also known as Naoetsu. Louie greeted the news with bright spirits. Wherever he was going, he would be joined by almost all of his friends.

On the evening of March 1, the chosen men gathered their belongings and donned overcoats that had been distributed the day before. Louie said good-bye to Harris. He would never see him again.

The Naoetsu-bound men climbed aboard a truck, which bore them into Tokyo. Watching the air battle over the city had been exhilarating, but when the men saw the consequences, they were shocked. Whole neighborhoods had been reduced to charred ruins, row after row of homes now nothing but black bones. In the rubble, Louie noticed something shining. Standing in the remains of many houses were large industrial machines. What Louie was seeing was a small fragment of a giant cottage industry, war production farmed out to innumerable private homes, schools, and small "shadow factories."

Louie and the other transferring POWs were driven to the railway station and put on a train. They rode all night, moving west, into a snowy landscape. As they rode on, the snow became deeper and deeper.

At about nine A.M. on March 2, the train drew up to Naoetsu, a seaside village on the west coast of Japan. Led to the front of the station, the POWs stared in amazement; the snow rose up some fourteen feet overhead. Climbing up a stairway cut into the drifts, they found themselves in a blindingly white world, standing atop a snow mountain that buried the entire village. "It was as if a giant frosted cake were sitting in the town," Wade wrote. The snow was so deep that residents had dug vertical tunnels to get in and out of their homes. The contrast to fire-blackened Tokyo was jarring.

Pulling their baggage along on sleighs, the POWs began the mile-and-a-quarter walk to camp. It was windy and bitterly cold. Fitzgerald, who had a badly infected foot, had the most difficulty. His crutches poked deep in the snow and wouldn't hold his weight.

The prisoners crossed a bridge and saw the Sea of Japan. Just short of it, cornered against the Ara and Hokura rivers, was the Naoetsu POW camp, almost entirely obscured by snow. Louie and the others trudged into the compound and stopped before a shack, where they were told to stand at attention. They waited for some time, the wind frisking their clothes.

At last, a door thumped open. A man rushed out and snapped to a halt, screaming *"Keirei!"*

It was the Bird.

Louie's legs folded, the snow reared up at him, and down he went.

Twenty-eight

Enslaved

LOUIE WOULD REMEMBER THE MOMENT WHEN HE SAW THE Bird as the darkest of his life. For the Bird, it was something else. He beamed like a child on his birthday. He seemed certain that the POWs were overjoyed to see him.

Fitzgerald forked forward on his crutches and assumed the duties of senior POW. The Bird announced that just as at Omori, he was in command, and that the men must obey. He said that he would make this camp just as Omori had been under his tenure.

Ringing with shock, Louie picked himself up and hiked through the snow to the barracks, a two-story building on the edge of a small cliff that dropped straight down to the frozen Hokura River. The three hundred residents, mostly Australians, were shrunken down to virtual stick figures. Most were wearing the tropical-weight khakis in which they'd been captured, and which, thanks to years of uninterrupted wear, were so ragged that one civilian likened them to seaweed. The wind, scudding off the sea, whistled through cracks in the walls, and there were so many holes in the roof that it snowed indoors. The whole building was visibly infested with fleas and lice, and rats trotted through the rooms. The beds were planks nailed into the walls; the mattresses were loose rice straw. Everywhere, there were large gaps in the floor; the POWs had pulled up the floorboards and burned them in an effort to survive temperatures that regularly plunged far below zero.

Stacked against one wall were dozens of small boxes, some of which had broken open and spilled gray ash onto the floor. These were the cremated remains of sixty Australian POWs—one in every five prisoners—who had died in this camp in 1943 and 1944, succumbing to pneumonia, beriberi, malnutrition, colitis, or a combination of these. Relentless physical abuse had precipitated most of the deaths. In a POW camp network that would resonate across history as a supreme example of cruelty, Naoetsu had won a special place as one of the blackest holes in the Japanese Empire. Of the many hells that Louie had known in this war, this place would be the worst.

Louie lay on his plank and tried to ready himself for what Naoetsu would bring. As he fell asleep that night, halfway around the globe the world's best runners were gathering for a track meet at Madison Square Garden. The promoters had renamed the marquee event in tribute to Louie, who was still believed dead by virtually everyone outside of his family. When the Zamperinis heard of it, they were upset: The race was to be called the Louis S. Zamperini Memorial Mile. Out of respect for the family, the name was changed to the Louis S. Zamperini

POWs at Naoetsu. *Australian War Memorial, negative number 6033201*

Invitational, but that did little to lift the spirits of those involved. Marty Glickman, who'd been on the 1936 Olympic team with Louie, watched the race with tears streaming down his face.

The race was won by Jim Rafferty, America's best miler. His time was 4:16.4, four seconds slower than the time Louie had clocked on the sand of Oahu just before climbing aboard *Green Hornet*.

———

The first weeks Louie spent in Naoetsu were almost lethally cold. Each night of shivering in his bed of straw ended abruptly before dawn, when he was shouted awake and forced outside for *tenko* in deep snow, howling wind, and darkness. By day, he huddled with Tinker, Wade, and his other friends in patches of sunlight, trying in vain to keep warm. He was soon nursing a cough, fever, and flulike symptoms, and the Naoetsu slop did nothing to help his body recover. The rations, which were halved for officers, rarely varied from millet or barley and boiled seaweed, plus a few slices of vegetable. The drinking water, which the POWs had to haul in on sleds, was yellow and reeked. Seeing the guards smoking American cigarettes, the POWs knew that the Red Cross was sending relief packages, but the prisoners got nothing.

Watanabe was the same fiend that he'd been at Omori, prompting the Aussies to nickname him "Whatabastard." He held a far lower rank than Naoetsu's commander, an elfin man sporting an abbreviated mustache as an apparent homage to Hitler, but the commander deferred to the Bird, just as the officers at Omori had done. And here, the Bird had recruited a henchman, an eggplant-shaped man named Hiroaki Kono, who trailed Watanabe around camp, assaulting men with the intensity, wrote Wade, of "a roaring Hitlerian animal."

Louie's transfer to Naoetsu, into the grip of the Bird, had been no coincidence. Watanabe had handpicked him and the others to come to this camp, which was short on officers. According to Wade, each chosen man had a skill or history that would make him useful. Al Mead, who had helped save Louie from starvation at Ofuna, had headed Omori's cookhouse; Fitzgerald had been a ranking officer; Wade had been a barracks commander; and so on. The only man with no such history was Louie. Wade believed that the Bird had chosen Louie simply because he wanted to torment him.

Wade was right. From almost the moment that Louie walked into camp, the Bird was on him, slapping him, punching him, and berating him. Other POWs were shocked at how the sergeant pursued Louie, attacking him, remembered one POW, "just for drill." Louie took his beatings with as much defiance as ever, provoking the Bird to ever more violent attacks. Once again in his tormenter's clutches, Louie descended back into a state of profound stress.

And yet, by virtue of his rank, Louie was fortunate. Naoetsu was a factory village that generated products critical to the war effort, and all of its young workers had gone to war. The POWs were here to take their place. Each day, the enlisted POWs waded through the snow to labor in a steel mill, a chemical factory, the port's coal and salt barges, or a site at which they broke rocks for mineral extraction. The work was extraordinarily arduous and often dangerous, and shifts went on day and night, some for eighteen hours. In the hikes back from this slave labor, men were so rubber-legged that they tumbled into snow crevasses and had to be dragged out.

Each morning and night, Louie saw the enlisted men rambling in from their slave shifts, some completely obscured by coal soot, some so exhausted that they had to be carried into the barracks. The Japanese literally worked men to death at Naoetsu. Louie had much to bear, but at least he didn't have this.

———

Winter faded. The river ice gave way to flowing water, and houses emerged where only snow had been. When the drifts in the compound melted, a pig miraculously appeared. All winter, he'd been living below the POWs in a snow cavern, sustained by bits of food dropped to him by an Australian. Louie looked at him in wonder. The animal's skin had gone translucent.

With the ground thawed, the Bird announced that he was sending the officers to work as farm laborers. Though this violated the Geneva Convention's prohibition on forcing officers to labor, Fitzgerald now knew what life in camp with the Bird was like. Work on the farm would keep the officers out of the Bird's path for hours every day, and couldn't be anything like the backbreaking labor done by the enlisted men. Fitzgerald raised no protest.

Each morning, Louie and the rest of the farming party assembled before the barracks, attended by a civilian guard named Ogawa. They loaded a cart with *benjo* waste—to be used as fertilizer, as was customary in Japan—then yoked themselves to the cart like oxen and pulled it to and from the farm. As they picked their way along the road, sometimes darting off to try to steal a vegetable from a field while Ogawa's back was turned, Japanese farmers came out to stare at them, probably the first Westerners they'd ever seen. Louie looked back at the wan, stooped old men and women. The hardships of this war were evident on their blank, weary faces and from their bodies, winnowed for want of food. A few children scampered about, raising their arms in imitation of surrender and mocking the prisoners. There were no young adults.

The walk, six miles each way, was a tiring slog, but the work, planting and tending potatoes, was relatively easy. Ogawa was a placid man, and though he carried a club, he never used it. The plot had a clean well, a relief after the stinking camp water, and Ogawa let the men drink all they wished. And because they were now working outside the camp, the officers were granted full rations. Though those rations were dwindling as Japan's fortunes fell, a full bowl of seaweed was better than half a bowl of seaweed.

April 13 was a bright day, the land bathed in sunshine, the sky wide and clear. Louie and the other officers were scattered over the potato plot, working, when the field suddenly went still and the men turned their faces to the sky. At the same moment, all over Naoetsu, labor at the outdoor work sites halted as the POWs and guards gazed up. High overhead, something was winking in the sunlight, slender ribbons of white unfurling behind it. It was a B-29.

It was the first Superfortress to cross over Naoetsu. The Omori officers had seen hundreds of B-29s over Tokyo, but for the Australians, who'd been hidden in this village since 1942, this was their first glimpse of the bomber.

Followed by innumerable eyes, some hopeful and some horrified, the B-29 made a slow arc from one horizon to the other, following the coastline. No guns shot at it; no fighters chased it. It dropped no bombs, passing peacefully overhead, but its appearance was a telling sign of how far over Japan the Americans were now venturing, and how little resistance the Japanese could offer. As all of Naoetsu watched, the plane slid out of view, and its contrails dissolved behind it.

The POWs were elated; the Japanese were unnerved. At the work sites, the prisoners hid their excitement behind neutral faces to avoid provoking the guards, who were unusually tense and hostile. On the walk back to camp that evening, the prisoners absorbed a few swipes with a club, but their mood remained merry. When they reached the gates, the Bird was waiting for them.

Roosevelt, he said, was dead.

The men deflated. The Bird sent them into the barracks.

A few days later, Ogawa made a little joke to the Bird, teasing him about how his POW officers were lazy. Ogawa meant no harm, but the remark sent the Bird into a fury. He shouted for the farm workers to line up before him, then began berating them for their indolence. He stormed and frothed, seeming completely deranged.

Finally, he screamed his punishment: From now on, all officers would perform hard labor, loading coal on barges. If they refused, he would execute every one of them. One look at the Bird told Fitzgerald that this was an order he could not fight.

Early the next morning, as the officers were marched off to labor, the Bird stood by, watching them go. He was smiling.

———

It was a short walk into slavery. The officers were taken to the riverbank and crowded onto a barge, which was heaped with coal destined for the steel mill. Six men were given shovels; Louie and the rest were given large baskets and told to strap them to their backs. Then, on the guards' orders, the shovelers began heaving coal into each man's basket. As a cubic foot of loose coal can weigh as much as sixty pounds, the bearers were soon staggering. Once the baskets were full, the bearers were ordered to lug the loads off the barge and up the shore to a railroad car, where they wobbled up a narrow, steep ramp, dumped the coal into the car, and returned to have their baskets refilled.

All day the men shoveled and hauled. The guards kept the basket men moving at a rapid clip. By the time the guards finally let them stop, the men were utterly exhausted; by Wade's estimate, over the course of the day, each basket bearer had carried well over four tons of coal.

So began a daily routine. Each time the men finished clearing one barge, they were pushed aboard another, and the hauling went on, punishing their bodies and numbing their minds. Somewhere along the way, as he and the others bent under their burdens and plodded along, Tom Wade began reciting poetry and speeches. Louie and the other slaves shoveled and walked in time with Shakespeare's soliloquies, with Churchill's vow to fight in the fields and in the streets and in the hills, with Lincoln's last full measure of devotion.

The barges were eventually empty, but the officers' life in slavery had only just begun. In a mass of POWs, Louie was herded onto another of the barges, which was pulled by a tugboat into the Sea of

Japan. About three-quarters of a mile out, the barge drew alongside an anchored coal ship and stopped, the sea heaving under it, water spraying over the deck. Standing before the prisoners, a guard gestured to a net slung over the side of the ship. Jump from the barge onto the net, he said, then climb up onto the ship's deck.

The POWs were appalled. On the tossing sea, the two vessels were pitching up and down, crashing together and rolling apart, and the net was a rapidly moving target. If the men mistimed their jumps, they'd be caught between the crafts as they collided or thrown into the water as they gapped apart. The men balked, but the guards forced them forward, and the POWs began jumping. Louie, as scared as everyone else, sprang across and climbed clear.

He was hustled into the ship's hold. Before him stood a giant dome of coal and, beside it, a large hanging net. As he was given a shovel, the guards suddenly teemed around him, screaming at him to get to work. Louie jammed his shovel into the coal and began piling it into the net.

Hour after hour, Louie stooped over his shovel in a churning cloud of black dust. The guards turned circles around him and the others, shouting and cracking them with clubs and kendo sticks. They pushed the POWs at such a frenzied pace that the laborers never had a moment to straighten their backs. Clubbed and badgered, Louie shoveled so frantically that the men alongside him whispered to him to slow down. At last, in the evening, the work was halted. The POWs were taken back to shore and dropped there, so caked in coal that they were virtually indistinguishable.

Every morning, the men were sent back to take up their shovels again. Every night, they dragged back into camp, a long line of blackened ghosts trudging into the barracks and falling onto their bunks, weary to their bones, spitting black saliva. There was just one bathtub in camp, and its water was almost never changed. The one other place to bathe was a vat at the steel mill, but the guards marched the POWs there for baths only once every ten days. Unwilling to brave the camp tub, the coal-labor men lived in a patina of soot, waiting to go to the mill. Eventually, Wade felt so befouled that he had someone shave the coal-clotted hair from his head. "It was an act of expiation," he wrote.

Day after day, Louie shoveled. Occasionally, he was switched from coal to industrial salt; the work was just as taxing, and the salt liquefied in his sweat and ran down his back, burning fissures in his skin. Fitzgerald labored alongside his men and tangled with the foremen to protect them. Once, during a nonstop fourteen-hour shift, he ordered the POWs to stop and told the foreman that he wouldn't let his men work until they were fed. After much argument, the overseers brought the men a single, huge ball of rice, then sent them back to work.

Tragedy was inevitable, and Louie was there when it happened. He was standing on the barge, awaiting his turn to jump to the ship, when the man ahead of him mistimed his leap, thudding into the side of the ship just as it collided with the barge. Crushed between the vessels, the man crumpled onto the barge. The guards hardly paused, pushing Louie to make his jump. While the rest of the POWs tramped past him, the injured man was left where he lay. Louie never learned if he survived.

The slave labor at Naoetsu was the kind of work that swallowed men's souls, but the prisoners found ways to score little victories, so essential to their physical and emotional survival. Most of the work sites offered nothing to sabotage, but stealing was epidemic. On the barges, men would wait until the operator stepped away, then sprint into the galley and stuff all the food they could find into their clothes. The lunch boxes of the civilian guards kept vanishing; an overseer's pack of cigarettes, set down while he turned away, would be gone when he turned back. The POWs would pinch anything they could, often items they had no need for, risking a beating or worse for something as useless as a pencil box. The box itself was nothing; the theft of it was everything.

Because the POW diet was severely deficient in sodium, leaving many men crippled by muscle cramps and other ailments, the men developed a system for stealing and processing salt. As they worked, the men on the salt barges would secrete handfuls of salt in their pockets. In its raw form, the salt was inedible, so the barge men would carry it up to camp and slip it to the POWs assigned to the steel mill. These men would hide the salt in their clothing and carry it to the mill, wait until the guard wasn't looking, then drop lumps of it into canteens filled with water. At day's end, they'd hang the canteens on the sides of a coal-fire vat. By morning, the water would be boiled away, leaving only edible salt residue, a treasure beyond price.

While in the *benjo* one day, Louie looked through a knothole and noticed that a grain sack was resting against it, in a storage room on the other side of the wall. Remembering the thieving techniques of the Scots at Omori, he left the *benjo*, searched the camp, and found a pile of discarded bamboo reeds, which were hollow. He took one and, when the guards weren't watching, sharpened the end. That night, he put on his camp-issued pajamas, which were fitted with strings around the ankles. He pocketed his bamboo reed, pulled his ankle strings as tight as he could, and headed to the *benjo*. Once inside, he jammed one end of the reed through the knothole hard enough to pierce the grain sack, then put the other end into his pajama fly. The grain—rice—poured through the reed and into his pants. When he had about five pounds in each leg, Louie pulled the reed out.

Louie walked out of the *benjo*, moving as naturally as a man could with ten pounds of rice in his pajamas. He strolled past the barracks guards and climbed the ladder to the second floor, where Commander Fitzgerald awaited him, a blanket spread before him. Louie stepped onto the blanket, untied his pant legs, and let the rice spill out, then hurried back to his bunk. Fitzgerald quickly folded up the blanket, then hid the rice in socks and secret compartments he had made under the wall panels. After memorizing the guards' routines, Louie and Fitzgerald would wait for a time when the guards left the building, then dig out the rice, rush it to the building stove, boil it in water, and scoop it into their mouths as rapidly as they could, sharing it with a few others. They never got more than about a tablespoon of rice per man, but the accomplishment of outwitting their slaveholders was nourishment enough.

In Naoetsu's little POW insurgency, perhaps the most insidious feat was pulled off by Louie's friend Ken Marvin, a marine who'd been captured at Wake Atoll. At his work site, Marvin was supervised by a one-eyed civilian guard called Bad Eye. When Bad Eye asked Marvin to teach him English, Marvin saw his chance. With secret delight, he began teaching Bad Eye catastrophically bad English. From that day forward, when asked, "How are you?," Bad Eye would smilingly reply, "What the fuck do you care?"

Disaster struck Louie one day that spring, on the riverbank. He'd been transferred back to hauling and was hunched under a basket, lugging a heavy load of salt from a barge to a railroad car. He carried his basket up the riverbank, then began the perilous walk up the railcar ramp. As he made his way up, a guard stepped onto the top of the ramp and started down. As they passed, the guard threw out his elbow, and Louie, top-heavy under the basket, fell over the side. He managed to get his legs under him before he hit the ground, some four feet down. One leg hit before the other. Louie felt a tearing sensation, then scorching pain in his ankle and knee.

Louie couldn't bear any weight on the leg. Two POWs supported him while he hopped back to camp. He was removed from barge duty, but this was hardly comforting. Not only would he now be the only officer trapped in camp with the Bird all day, but his rations would be cut in half.

Louie lay in the barracks, ravenous. His dysentery was increasingly severe, and his fevers were growing worse, sometimes spiking to 104 degrees. To get his rations restored, he had to find work that he could do on one leg. Spotting an abandoned sewing machine in a shed, he volunteered to tailor the guards' clothes in exchange for full rations. This kept him going for a while, but there was soon no one left to tailor for, and his rations were halved again. Such was his desperation that he went to the Bird and begged for work.

The Bird savored his plea. From now on, he said, Louie would be responsible for the pig in the compound. The job would earn him full rations, but there was a catch: Louie was forbidden to use tools to clean the pig's sty. He'd have to use his hands.

All his life, Louie had been fastidious about cleanliness, so much so that in college he had kept Listerine in his car's glove compartment so he could rinse his mouth after kissing girls. Now he was condemned to crawl through the filth of a pig's sty, picking up feces with his bare hands and cramming handfuls of the animal's feed into his mouth to save himself from starving to death. Of all of the violent and vile abuses that the Bird had inflicted upon Louie, none had horrified and demoralized him as did this. *If anything is going to shatter me,* Louie thought, *this is it.* Sickened and starving, his will a fraying wire, Louie had only the faint hope of the war's end, and rescue, to keep him going.

Twenty-nine

Two Hundred and Twenty Punches

AT ELEVEN-THIRTY ON THE MORNING OF MAY 5, 1945, THE sound of four massive engines broke the silence over Naoetsu. A B-29 was turning circles over the village. Sirens sounded, but in the steel mill, the foreman ignored them, and the POWs continued working the furnaces. Then there was a sudden, enormous crash, and it began snowing very hard inside the mill.

It wasn't snow, but a tremendous quantity of dust falling from the rafters. Something had shaken the mill violently. The foreman announced that the sound had only been a transformer blowing up, and kept the men working.

A moment later, a worker ran in and said something urgently to the foreman. The Japanese dropped everything and sprinted out, abandoning the POWs as they ran for the air-raid shelters on the beach. Gathering that only a B-29 could make the foreman run like that, the panicked POWs crowded together in a small room, praying that they wouldn't get hit.

They didn't. The B-29's bombs missed the plant, blowing gaping holes in a field nearby. It took an hour for everyone, captive and free, to calm down. The guards did their best to impress the POWs with the incompetence of American airmen, taking them on a crater tour to show how badly the bomber had missed, but they were spooked. There was much more to this raid than a couple of holes in a farmer's field, and everyone knew it. For the POWs, kept in ignorance of the Pacific war's progression, this raid, and the growing number of B-29 sightings over the village, raised a dazzling possibility. If the Americans were turning their efforts toward a lone steel mill in a place as obscure as Naoetsu, had the B-29s already destroyed the big strategic cities?

The answer came ten days later. Four hundred new POWs tramped through the gates and halted in the compound. The Bird leapt onto a perch over them and delivered his standard harangue:

"You must be sober! You must be sincere! You must work for earnest! You must obey! I have spoken."

"Who the hell is Ernest?" muttered a POW.

When the Bird was finished, the four hundred new men wedged into the barracks with the three hundred old ones, and the *benjos* ranneth over. The new men said they'd come from slave camps in the huge cities of Kobe, a matrix of war production, and Osaka, Japan's biggest port. Weeks before, B-29s had swept over those cities in gleaming, three-hundred-plane swarms, showering them in fire. Large swaths of Kobe and Osaka had been burned to the ground. Of no use to Japan in razed cities, the POWs had been shipped to Naoetsu to be reenslaved for the empire. The new men had one other piece of news: Germany had fallen. The whole weight of the Allies was now thrown against Japan.

That month, the Bird's presence at Naoetsu became sporadic. On top of his duty at Naoetsu, he'd been named disciplinary officer for Mitsushima, a camp in the mountains. He arrived there with his trademark flourish, bursting through a door and shouting, "*Nanda!*" at a group of startled POW officers, demanding to know what they were doing. Immediately, he set to beating the officers day and night. The POWs there called him "the Knob."

The Bird was so vicious at Mitsushima that the POW officers soon concluded that they had to kill him to save themselves. Conspirators formed "murder squads" set on drowning the Bird or hurling him from a cliff. Whenever the Bird was in camp, they stalked him, but he seemed to be on to them, moving about with armed guards. Meanwhile, two POW physicians, Richard Whitfield and Alfred Weinstein, hatched a plan to poison the Bird with massive doses of atropine and morphine.

Again the Bird eluded them: The day after the doctors formed their plan, the Bird had the pharmacy medications locked up.

Whitfield devised a new plan. Preparing a bottle of saline solution and glucose to serve as a culture medium, he mixed in stool samples from two patients infected with amoebic and bacillary dysentery, tossed in three flies, then stored the bottle next to his skin for several days to incubate the pathogens. He and Weinstein delivered it to the POW cook, who poured it onto the Bird's rice for the better part of a week. To their amazement, the Bird didn't get sick, so the doctors mixed up a new dose, using the stools of six ill POWs. This time, they hit the jackpot.

In two days, the Bird was violently ill, completely incapacitated with rocketing diarrhea and a 105-degree fever. Weinstein found him in his room, crying and "whimpering like a child." The Bird ordered Weinstein to cure him. Weinstein gave him what he said were sulfa pills. Suspicious, the Bird made Weinstein take some of the pills himself. Weinstein took them, knowing that all that was in them was aspirin and baking soda. The Bird lost fifteen pounds in one week. Weinstein urged him to eat his rice.

With the Bird out of the way, the men and even the guards were, wrote Weinstein, "almost hysterically childish" in their delight. But the Bird seemed unmurderable. After ten days, his fever broke. He returned to Naoetsu to take out his rage on the officers and Louie.

By June, Louie's leg was healed enough to bear his weight, and he was sent back to shovel coal and salt. He was growing ever sicker, and his dysentery never eased. When he appealed for rest while burning up with fever, the Bird refused him. His temperature was only 103, he said; you go to work. Louie went.

One day that month, Louie, Tinker, and Wade were shoveling on a barge when the foreman discovered that fish had been stolen from the galley. The foreman announced that if the thieves didn't turn themselves in, he'd report the theft to the Bird. During a lunch break, the innocent men persuaded the culprits to confess. When the men walked into camp that night, the foreman told the Bird anyway, as he suspected that more men had been in on the theft.

The Bird called for the work party to line up before him and ordered the thieves to stand before the group. He then walked down the line, pulling out Wade, Tinker, Louie, and two other officers and making them stand with the thieves. He announced that these officers were

responsible for the behavior of the thieves. His punishment: Each enlisted man would punch each officer and thief in the face, as hard as
possible.

The chosen men looked at the line of enlisted men in terror: there
were some one hundred of them. Any man who refused to carry out the
order, the Bird said, would meet the same fate as the officers and
thieves. He told the guards to club any men who didn't strike the chosen men with maximum force.

The enlisted men had no choice. At first, they tried to hit softly, but
the Bird studied each blow. When a man didn't punch hard enough, the
Bird would begin shrieking and clubbing him, joined by the guards.
Then the errant man would be forced to hit the victim repeatedly until
the Bird was satisfied. Louie began whispering to each man to get it
over with, and hit hard. Some of the British men whispered, "Sorry,
sir," before punching Wade.

For the first few punches, Louie stayed on his feet. But his legs soon
began to waver, and he collapsed. He pulled himself upright, but fell
again with the next punch, and then the next. Eventually, he blacked
out. When he came to, the Bird forced the men to resume punching
him, screaming, "*Next! Next! Next!*" In Louie's whirling mind, the
voice began to sound like the tramping of feet.

The sun sank. The beating went on for some two hours, the Bird
watching with fierce and erotic pleasure. When every enlisted man had
done his punching, the Bird ordered the guards to club each one twice
in the head with a kendo stick.

The victims had to be carried to the barracks. Louie's face was so
swollen that for several days he could barely open his mouth. By
Wade's estimate, each man had been punched in the face some 220
times.

———

June 1945 became July. Every day, a single B-29 crossed over Naoetsu,
so high that only the contrails gave it away. The men called it "the
Lone Ranger." Every night, bombers passed over in strength, forests of
planes brushing over the village. To the POWs, they were a beautiful
sight, "all lit up," wrote POW Joe Byrne, "as if they were going to a
picnic." Throughout each day and night, the air-raid sirens kept kicking in. Sometimes, at night, the men could hear soft booming in the
darkness.

Louie was sick and demoralized. He lay on his plank, daydreaming about the Olympics, holding them before himself as a shining promise, a future for which to endure an unbearable present. He prayed ceaselessly for rescue. His nightmares of his battles with the Bird were hellish, unbearable. His hope was dimming. In his barracks one day, a man dragged in from slave work, looking spent. He lay down, asked to be awakened for dinner, and went still. At chowtime, Louie kicked his foot. The man didn't move. He was dead. He was young, like everyone else, and hadn't even looked sick.

The food situation was increasingly dire. In the spring, with the import of the Kobe and Osaka POWs, the camp population had more than doubled, but the rations had not. Now the rations were smaller still, usually consisting of nothing but seaweed. When a famished prisoner tried to get food from civilians, the Bird broke his jaw. Several POW officers appealed to the authorities for meat; to withhold it, they said, violated international law. After this appeal, two guards left camp and returned with a dog, reportedly the only one left in Naoetsu. The next morning, a bell rang, and Louie walked into the compound. There, impaled on a post facing the POWs, was the dog's skinned head. A few minutes later, the men were served breakfast. In the bowls were the remains of the dog.

As summer stretched on and the rations dwindled, Louie and the other POWs began looking toward winter with dread. They were told that both their rations and the barracks heating fuel were going to be cut more come winter, and might be halted altogether. Many of the men were already so thin and sick that they were, wrote one, "hanging on from day to day." Few POWs, in Naoetsu or anywhere else, thought they'd live to see another spring. At Omori, someone made up a slogan: "Frisco dive in '45 or stiff as sticks in '46."

There was a worry more pressing yet. Even in isolated Naoetsu, it was obvious to the POWs that the Japanese empire was staggering. Watching B-29s crossing over with impunity, they knew that Japan's air defenses had been gutted, and that the Americans were very close. The civilians that they saw were in shocking condition: The limbs of the adults were grotesquely swollen from beriberi; the children were emaciated. The POWs were so disturbed by the obvious famine among the civilians that they stopped stealing at the work sites. It was clear to them that Japan had long ago lost this war.

But Japan was a long way from giving in. If a massively destructive air war would not win surrender, invasion seemed the only possibility.

POWs all over the country were noticing worrisome signs. They saw women holding sharpened sticks, practicing lunges at stacks of rice straw, and small children being lined up in front of schools, handed wooden mock guns, and drilled. Japan, whose people deemed surrender shameful, appeared to be preparing to fight to the last man, woman, or child.

Invasion seemed inevitable and imminent, both to the POWs and to the Japanese. Having been warned of the kill-all order, the POWs were terrified. At Borneo's Batu Lintang POW camp, which held two thousand POWs and civilian captives, Allied fighters circled the camp every day. A civilian warned POW G. W. Pringle that "the Japanese have orders no prisoners are to be recaptured by Allied forces. All must be killed." Villagers told of having seen hundreds of bodies of POWs in the jungle. "This then is a forerunner of a fate which must be ours," wrote Pringle in his diary. A notoriously sadistic camp official began speaking of his empathy for the POWs, and how a new camp was being prepared where there was ample food, medical care, and no more forced labor. The POWs knew it was a lie, surely designed to lure them into obeying an order to march that would, as Pringle wrote, "afford the Japs a wonderful opportunity to carry out the Japanese Government order to 'Kill them all.'"

Pringle was right. In the camp office sat written orders, drawn up by the commander and approved by central military authorities, for all captives to be "liquidated" on September 15. Women and children would be poisoned; civilian men would be shot; the sick and disabled would be bayoneted. The five hundred POWs would be marched twenty-one miles into the jungle, shot, and burned.

At Omori, Japanese kitchen workers, as well as some soldiers, told the POWs that plans for their destruction had been set. The POWs would be turned loose, on the excuse that the guards were needed to defend Japan, and when the men stepped onto the bridge, the guards would mow them down with machine guns. The POW officers met to discuss it, but couldn't come up with any way to prevent it or defend themselves.

At camps across Japan, things looked just as ominous. Machine guns and barrels of accelerant were brought in. Metal dog tags were confiscated, in an apparent effort to comply with the stipulation that those executing POWs "not . . . leave any traces." Prisoners were ordered to dig tunnels and caverns, and at a number of camps, friendly guards warned POWs that mines, ditches, and tunnels were going to be used as death chambers.

That summer, at Phil and Fred Garrett's camp, Zentsuji, officials suddenly announced that they were separating the Americans from the other POWs. The officials said that the Americans were being moved to a pleasant new camp, for their safety. The men were loaded onto a train and taken across Japan, through sad rivers of refugees. Peeking past the drawn window blinds, they saw razed cities. The air smelled of burned bodies.

After dark, they reached a remote area. The men were told to begin walking up a nearly impassable trail, winding up the side of a mountain. In a crashing rainstorm, they hiked for hours, through forest, over boulders, and through ravines, climbing so high that the surrounding mountains were capped in snow in summer. Garrett, his stump still unhealed, labored on his crutches, and the Japanese wouldn't allow anyone to help him. Men began fainting from exhaustion, but the Japanese drove the group on, allowing no rest stops. Drenched to the skin, the POWs limped up the path for eleven miles, leaving a trail of discarded possessions as they tried to lighten their loads.

At two in the morning, high on the mountain, Phil, Garrett, and the other POWs reached a collection of wooden shacks in a rocky clearing. Too exhausted to stand in formation, they collapsed. They were told that this was their new camp, Rokuroshi. No one explained why the POWs had been taken so far from anywhere and anyone, to a place that appeared uninhabitable. The POW physician, Hubert Van Peenen, looked about him, considered their situation, and came to a conclusion: *This is the place of our extermination.*

At Naoetsu that summer, camp officials began speaking of their concern that the POWs could be injured in air raids. For this reason, the officials said, the prisoners were soon going to be taken into the mountains, where they'd be safe. Away from their officers, the guards told a different story, telling the POWs that the army had issued orders to kill them all in August. This might have been dismissed as a lie, but that July, a civilian worker known for his sympathy for POWs warned a prisoner that an execution date had been set. The date he gave was the same as one that had reportedly been mentioned to prisoners in at least two other camps.

All of the Naoetsu POWs, the civilian said, would be killed on August 22.

Thirty

The Boiling City

N O ONE IN NAOETSU WAS SLEEPING. B-29S CROSSED OVER
every night, and the air-raid sirens wailed for hours on end,
competing with the roar of the planes. The sound of them, and the
sight of endless flocks of planes soaring unopposed over Japan, sent the
Bird ever deeper into madness.

During the raids, the POWs were ordered to stay in the barracks
with the lights out. Once the planes had passed, the Bird would bound
in, ordering the Americans outside. He and his henchman, Kono, would
pace back and forth, shouting and swinging clubs, kendo sticks, or rifles. On some nights, the Bird would shove the men into two lines, facing one another, and order them to slap each other's faces. Sometimes he
and Kono would make them stand with their arms over their heads for
two to three hours at a time, or force them into the Ofuna crouch,
pounding them when they faltered. During one beating, Louie was
clubbed on his previously injured ankle, leaving it so painful that he
could barely walk. And on at least one of these nights, the Bird beat
Louie to unconsciousness.

Louie's job as pig custodian was over. Barge loading had also been canceled; Allied planes had sunk so many Japanese ships that none came

or went from Naoetsu anymore. Louie was back on half rations. Limping, sick, and hungry, he begged the Bird for work so he could get full rations again. The Bird brought him a paper-thin gray goat that appeared to be on the brink of death.

"Goat die, you die," the Bird said.

Louie had nothing to secure the goat with, and no pen to put him in. His friend Ken Marvin stole a rope from his work site and brought it to him. Louie tied the goat to a pole and began nursing him, giving him water and grain. At night he tied him inside a grain shack. The goat only got sicker.

One morning, the Bird ordered Louie to come before him. He said that the goat had gotten loose, broken into a grain bin, and gorged himself. The animal was deathly ill, and it was Louie's fault. Louie knew that his knot had been secure. If the goat had gotten loose, someone had untied him. The goat died.

Terrified of retribution, Louie tried to hide from the Bird, but his dysentery was becoming very serious. Risking being seen by the Bird, he went to the camp doctor to plead for medication. The Bird ran him down, demanding to know if he had received permission to approach the doctor. Louie said no.

The Bird marched Louie away from the doctor's shack, passing Tinker and Wade, who'd been ordered to work outside. Out in the compound, the Bird halted. Lying on the ground before them was a thick, heavy wooden beam, some six feet long. Pick it up, the Bird said. With some effort, Louie hoisted it up, and the Bird ordered him to lift it high and hold it directly over his head. Louie heaved the beam up. The Bird called a guard over. If the prisoner lowers his arms, the Bird told him, hit him with your gun. The Bird walked to a nearby shack, climbed on the roof, and settled in to watch.

Louie stood in the sun, holding up the beam. The Bird stretched over the roof like a contented cat, calling to the Japanese who walked by, pointing to Louie and laughing. Louie locked his eyes on the Bird's face, radiating hatred.

Several minutes passed. Louie stood, eyes on the Bird. The beam felt heavier and heavier, the pain more intense. The Bird watched Louie, amused by his suffering, mocking him. Wade and Tinker went on with their work, stealing anxious glances at the scene across the compound. Wade had looked at the camp clock when Louie had first lifted the beam. He became more and more conscious of how much time was passing.

Five more minutes passed, then ten. Louie's arms began to waver and go numb. His body shook. The beam tipped. The guard jabbed Louie with his gun, and Louie straightened up. Less and less blood was reaching his head, and he began to feel confused, his thoughts gauzy, the camp swimming around him. He felt his consciousness slipping, his mind losing adhesion, until all he knew was a single thought: *He cannot break me.* Across the compound, the Bird had stopped laughing.

Time ticked on, and still Louie remained in the same position, conscious and yet not, the beam over his head, his eyes on the Bird's face, enduring long past when his strength should have given out. "Something went on inside of me," he said later. "I don't know what it was."

There was a flurry of motion ahead of him, the Bird leaping down from the roof and charging toward him, enraged. Watanabe's fist rammed into Louie's stomach, and Louie folded over in agony. The beam dropped, striking Louie's head. He flopped to the ground.

When he woke, he didn't know where he was or what had happened. He saw Wade and some other POWs, along with a few guards, crouched around him. The Bird was gone. Louie had no memory of the last several minutes, and had no idea how long he'd stood there. But Wade had looked at the clock when Louie had fallen.

Louie had held the beam aloft for thirty-seven minutes.

———

On the night of August 1, sirens sounded and the village shook. In the barracks, the POWs looked out and saw wave after wave of Superfortresses. In the skies over Japan that night, America was staging by far the biggest air raid, by tonnage, of World War II: 836 B-29s, bearing more than 6,100 tons of bombs, incendiaries, and mines. The POWs working the factory night shifts ran for the beach shelters, but the planes bypassed Naoetsu. In Nagaoka, forty miles away, civilians looked up and thought it was raining. The rain was napalm.

With the bombers sweeping overhead, the Bird stormed into the barracks and shouted for all Americans to get out. As the men lined up in the compound, the Bird and Kono picked up their kendo sticks, walked behind them, and began smashing them over their heads. Men started falling. When Louie went down, the Bird crouched over him, clubbing him. Woozy, Louie lay there as the Bird and the sirens screamed.

At dawn the sirens went silent. The POWs on the beach came out of the shelters. In the compound, the Bird and Kono went still. Louie stumbled to his feet and looked to the northeast. The edge of the world was glowing; Nagaoka was burning down.

That same night, B-29s showered leaflets over thirty-five Japanese cities, warning civilians of coming bombings and urging them to evacuate. The Japanese government ordered civilians to turn the leaflets in to authorities, forbade them from sharing the warnings with others, and arrested anyone with leaflets in their possession. Among the cities listed on the leaflets were Hiroshima and Nagasaki.

———

That night was a turning point for Louie. The next morning, his dysentery was suddenly extremely severe. He was dangerously dehydrated and beginning to have trouble eating. Each day he was thinner, weaker.

Every day and night, the B-29s raked over the sky and the Bird rampaged through camp. He attacked Ken Marvin, knocked him unconscious, roused him with a bucket of water to his face, told him to take care of his health, then knocked him out again. While Louie hid upstairs on his bunk, sick with fever, he saw the Bird and Kono beat two sick POWs until they acquiesced to the Bird's order to lick excrement from their boots. On another day, Louie looked across the compound to see the Bird and Kono standing before a line of POWs, holding a confiscated book on boxing and taking turns punching the prisoners.

Louie was walking in the compound when the Bird collared him and dragged him to the overflowing *benjo* pit. After pulling over several men, the Bird forced Louie and the others down on their stomachs, on top of the waste pits, and ordered them to do push-ups. Louie was just barely able to hold his body clear of the pit. Others were not so fortunate. When the exhausted men failed to push themselves all the way up, the Bird pressed the butt of his rifle to their heads and ground their faces into the waste.

Then came the day that Louie had been dreading. He was standing outside, filling a tub of water, when the Bird barked at him to come over. When Louie arrived, the Bird looked wrathfully at him and gestured toward the water.

"Tomorrow I'm going to drown you."

Louie spent a day gripped with fear, looking for the Bird, thinking about the tub of water. When the Bird found him, he was terrified.

"I have changed my mind," the Bird said. Then he lunged at Louie and began punching him in the face, alternating right and left fists in a violent ecstasy. As abruptly as he had started, he stopped. Suddenly serene, he let go of Louie.

"I will drown you tomorrow," he said.

The Bird strolled away. His face wore the same soft languor that Louie had seen on the face of the Quack after he beat Harris at Ofuna. It was an expression of sexual rapture.

———

Louie could take no more. He joined about a dozen officers in a secret meeting. By the time they parted, they had a plan to kill the Bird.

The plan was simple. The men would leap onto the Bird and pull him to the top floor of the barracks, overlooking the drop to the Hokura River. There, they would lash him to a large rock and shove him out the window. When he struck the water below, the rock would carry him under. He would never draw another breath.

The officers divvied up the tasks involved in the killing. A group of men would figure out how to overpower the Bird, who was quite fit and would be difficult to subdue. Several of the biggest POWs would find a heavy but portable rock and, out of view of the guards, hoist it up the ladders and roll it to the window. Louie was tasked with stealing enough strong rope to lash the rock to the Bird.

Louie couldn't find a rope long enough to tie a man to a boulder. He began stealing shorter lengths of rope, secreting them away, then tying them together with his strongest Boy Scout knots. Meanwhile, the rock crew found a large boulder, big enough to drown the Bird and several other men. Somehow, they got it into the compound, into the barracks, and up the ladder without discovery. They positioned it by the window. When Louie had finally stolen enough rope, he tied it into one long line. It was looped around the rock, a dangling end lying ready to be wound around the Bird's body. Louie then prepared for the second phase of the plan. He had volunteered to be one of the men to capture the Bird, drag him up, and throw him to his death.

As the conspirators planned, the Bird entered the barracks. If the rock was then in place, he either didn't see it or didn't recognize what it was there for. He dug through the men's possessions. Under the *tatami* mat of an English officer, he found a piece of paper on which were listed the crimes of each of the Japanese officials. When the Bird looked up, he saw the man sneering at him.

The Bird was spooked. He believed that he saw the POWs glaring murderously at him. They had never looked at him in this way before.

He knew that Japan was losing the war, and that when the end came, the Americans would try him. These POWs would accuse him of crimes, and the Americans would surely sentence him to death. No one, he knew, would defend him, and that fact left him angry and panicked. He was going to have to go to extreme measures to save himself.

Next to a window near which the Bird passed each day, the rock and rope sat ready. From the barracks window, it was a long plunge to the water.

At a quarter to three on the morning of August 6, 1945, a B-29 skipped off Runway Able on Tinian Island. At the yoke was Paul Tibbets, a veteran bomber pilot. The plane headed north, toward Japan. The mission was so secret that Tibbets carried cyanide capsules for all of the crewmen, to be used if they crashed and were captured.

As the day's first light walked over the Pacific, the plane rose toward its bombing altitude, more than thirty thousand feet. Two crewmen climbed into the bomb bay. There sat a twelve-foot-long, nine-thousand-pound bomb called Little Boy. The men dropped to their hands and knees and crawled around the bomb, pulling out test plugs and replacing them with firing plugs. Little Boy was armed.

Crossing the Inland Sea, Tibbets saw a city ahead. A scout plane flying over it radioed back in code: The weather was clear. They wouldn't have to bypass this city and pursue the alternate targets. Tibbets spoke over the interphone:

"It's Hiroshima."

The plane passed the coastline and crossed over the city. Tibbets turned the plane west, then ordered his crew to don shaded goggles. Below, he saw a T-shaped bridge, the target. Tibbets surrendered control of the plane to the Norden bombsight, and the bombardier lined up on the bridge.

At 8:15.17, the bomb slipped from the plane. Tibbets turned the plane as hard as he could and put it into a dive to gain speed. It would take forty-three seconds for the bomb to reach its detonation altitude, a little less than two thousand feet. No one knew for sure if, in that brief time, the bomber could get far enough away to survive what was coming.

One of the crewmen counted seconds in his head. When he hit forty-three, nothing happened. He didn't know that he had been counting too quickly. For an instant, he thought the mission had failed.

Exactly as the thought crossed his mind, the sky over the city ripped open in a firestorm of color and sound and felling wind. A white light, ten times the intensity of the sun, enveloped the plane as the flash and sound and jolt of it skidded out in all directions. The tail gunner, looking out the back of the plane through his goggles, thought that the light had blinded him. Tibbets's teeth began tingling, and his mouth filled with a taste of lead. He would later be told that it was the metal in his fillings resonating with the radioactivity of the bomb. He looked ahead and saw the entire sky swirling in pink and blue. Next to him, the copilot scribbled two words in his diary: *MY GOD!*

Behind him, the tail gunner's vision cleared and he saw an eerie shimmering warp in the air over the city, ripping toward them at one thousand feet per second. "Here it comes!" he said. The shock wave slammed into the plane, pitching the men into the air and back down again. In confusion, someone yelled, "Flak!" Then a second wave, a consequence of the force of the explosion hitting the ground and then ricocheting upward, smacked them, and the plane heaved again.

At POW Camp 10-D, on the far side of the mountains by Hiroshima, prisoner Ferron Cummins felt a concussion roll down from the hills, and the air warmed strangely. He looked up. A fantastically huge, roiling cloud, glowing bluish gray, swaggered over the city. It was more than three miles tall. Below it, Hiroshima was boiling.

Thirty-one

The Naked Stampede

THE NAOETSU POWS KNEW THAT SOMETHING BIG HAD happened. The guards paced around with stricken faces. Civilians walked past the camp, eyes dazed, hands in fists. A guard said something to Louie that stuck in his head: Hiroshima had been hit by cholera. The city was shut down, he said, and no one could come or go.

At one of the work sites, a civilian told a different story: One American bomb, he said, had destroyed an entire city. The POWs thought that he must have meant one raid with many bombs, but the man kept repeating that it was *one* bomb. He used a word that sounded like "atomic." The word was unfamiliar, and no one knew how one bomb could wipe out a city. Tom Wade got hold of a newspaper. Something the paper called an "electronic bomb" had been dropped, and many people had died. The POWs didn't know what to make of it.

At Omori, the shaken camp commander gathered the POWs. "One plane came over," he said, "and a whole city disappeared." He asked if anyone knew what weapon could do such a thing. No one had an answer.

On August 9, Nagasaki, like Hiroshima, disappeared.

Uneasy days passed. Everything in Naoetsu remained the same, and day and night, the POWs were still sent to labor in Japan's war pro-

Nagasaki, August 9, 1945.
Nagasaki Atomic Bomb Museum/epa/Corbis

duction factories. Clearly, something catastrophic had happened, but Japan had not given in.

For the POWs, time had all but run out. It was now approaching mid-August, and the kill-all policy loomed. Even if Japan surrendered, many POWs believed that the guards would kill them anyway, either out of vengeance or to prevent them from testifying to what had been done to them. Indeed, an Omori interrogator had told Commander Fitzgerald that the Japanese had plans to kill the POWs in the event that they lost the war.

With officials talking about taking them to a new camp in the hills, the POWs believed that the Japanese planned to dump their bodies in a mountain forest, where no one would ever find them. They discussed defending themselves, but they had no answers to twenty-five guards with rifles. Escape, too, was impossible; the camp was cornered against the sea and two rivers, and with no way to get boats for seven hundred prisoners, the only route out was toward the village, where the sickly, weak men would be caught easily. They were fish in a barrel.

Louie lingered in his bunk, fading, praying. In his nightmares, he and the Bird fought death matches, the Bird trying to beat him to death, Louie trying to strangle the life from the sergeant. He'd been staying as far as he could from the Bird, who had been whipping about camp like a severed power line, but the sergeant always hunted him down.

Then, abruptly, the violence stopped. The Bird had left camp. The guards said that he had gone to the mountains to ready the promised new camp for the POW officers. The August 22 kill-all death date was one week away.

On August 15, Louie woke gravely ill. He was now having some twenty bloody bowel movements a day. After the month's weigh-in, he didn't record his weight in his diary, but he did note that he'd lost six kilos, more than thirteen pounds, from a frame already wasted from starvation. When he gripped his leg, his fingers sank in, and the imprints remained for long after. He'd seen too many men die to be ignorant of what this meant: beriberi.

In late morning, after the night work crews had dragged in and the day crews had headed off, Louie crept out of the barracks. With the Bird away, it was safer to walk in the open. Crossing the compound, Louie saw Ogawa, his overseer at the potato field. Ogawa had always been an innocuous man, one of the few Japanese whom Louie had never had reason to fear. But when he saw Louie, Ogawa yanked out his club and struck Louie in the face. Louie reeled in astonishment, his cheek bleeding.

A few minutes later, at noon, the compound was suddenly, eerily silent. The Japanese were all gone. At the same moment, in the factory mess halls, the POWs looked up from their bowls and realized that they were alone. The guards had left.

In camp, Tinker walked through the compound. Passing the guardroom, he glanced inside. There were the guards, crowded around a radio in rapt attention, listening to a small, halting Japanese voice. Something of great importance was being said.

At the factories, at half past one, the guards reappeared and told the POWs to get back to their stations. As Ken Marvin returned to his station, he found his overseers sitting down. One of the Japanese told him that there was no work. Looking around, Marvin spotted Bad Eye, the one-eyed civilian guard he'd been teaching incorrect English, and asked him why there was no work. Bad Eye replied that there was no electricity. Marvin looked up; all of the light bulbs were burning. He turned quizzically to Bad Eye and told him that the lights were on. Bad Eye said something in Japanese, and Marvin wasn't sure he understood. Marvin found a friend fluent in Japanese, pulled him into the room, and asked Bad Eye to repeat what he'd said.

"The war is over."

Marvin began sobbing. He and his friend stood together, bawling like children.

The workers were marched back to camp. Marvin and his friend hurried among the POWs, sharing what Bad Eye had said, but not one of their listeners believed it. Everyone had heard this rumor before, and each time, it had turned out to be false. In camp, there was no sign that anything had changed. The camp officials explained that the work had been suspended only because there had been a power outage. A few men celebrated the peace rumor, but Louie and many others were anticipating something very different. Someone had heard that Naoetsu was slated to be bombed that night.

The POWs couldn't sleep. Marvin lay on his bunk, telling himself that if they were sent to work in the morning, Bad Eye's story must have been false. If they weren't, maybe the war was over. Louie hunkered down, miserably ill, waiting for the bombers.

No B-29s flew over Naoetsu that night. In the morning, the work crews were told that there was no work and were dismissed.

Upstairs, Louie began vomiting. As he bobbed in a fog of nausea, someone came to his bunk and handed him five letters. They were from Pete, Sylvia, and his parents, all written many months earlier. Louie tore open the envelopes, and out came photographs of his family. It was the first that Louie had seen or heard of them in nearly two and a half years. He clutched his letters and hung on.

The POWs were in a state of confusion; the guards would tell them nothing. A day passed with no news. When night fell, the men looked over the countryside and saw something they'd never seen before. The village was illuminated in the darkness; the blackout shades all over Naoetsu had been taken down. As a test, some of the POWs removed the shades on the barracks windows. The guards ordered them to put the shades back up. If the war had ended, the guards were going to considerable lengths to hide this fact from the POWs. The kill-all date was five days away.

The next day, Louie was sicker still. He examined his feeble body and scrawled sad words in his diary: "Look like skeleton. feel weak."

The Bird reappeared, apparently back from preparing whatever lay in store for the POWs in the mountains. He looked different, a shade of a mustache darkening his lip. Louie saw him step into his office and close the door.

———

On August 17, at Rokuroshi POW camp on the frigid summit of a Japanese mountain, a telephone rang.

Phil, Fred Garrett, and more than 350 other Rokuroshi POWs were shivering through summer inside the barracks, trying to survive on a nearly all-liquid diet. In this extremely remote, deathly quiet camp, the lone telephone hardly ever rang, and the POWs noticed it. A few minutes later, the Japanese commander hurried out of camp and down the mountain.

For some time, the Rokuroshi prisoners had been racked with tension. All summer, the sky had been scratched with vapor trails. One night in July, the men had looked from the barracks to see the whole southern horizon lit up in red, generating light so bright that the men could read by it. On August 8, the guards had begun nailing the barracks doors shut. Then, on August 15, the guards had suddenly become much more brutal, and the POWs' workload, breaking rocks on a hillside, had been intensified.

After the commander left, something troubling happened. The guards began bringing the POWs out of the barracks and dividing them into small groups. Once they had the men assembled, they herded them out of camp and deep into the mountain forest, heading nowhere. After pushing the men onward through the trees for some time, the guards led the men back to camp and into the barracks. Later, the walks were repeated. No explanation was given. The guards seemed to be inuring the men to this strange routine in preparation for something terrible.

———

On August 20, a white sky stretched out over Naoetsu, heavy and threatening. There was a shout in the compound: All POWs were to assemble outside. Some seven hundred men tramped out of the barracks and formed lines before the building. The little camp commander, gloves on his hands and a sword on his hip, stepped atop the air-raid spotter's platform, and Kono climbed up beside him. The commander spoke, and Kono translated.

"The war has come to a point of cessation."

There was no reaction from the POWs. Some believed it, but kept silent for fear of reprisal. Others, suspecting a trick, did not. The commander went on, becoming strangely solicitous. Speaking as if the POWs were old friends, he voiced his hope that the prisoners would help Japan fight the "Red Menace"—the Soviet Union, which had just seized Japan's Kuril Islands.

With the commander's speech finished and the POWs waiting in suspicious silence, Kono invited the POWs to bathe in the Hokura River. This, too, was odd; the men had only rarely been allowed to go in the river. The POWs broke from their lines and began hiking down to the water, dropping clothes as they walked. Louie dragged along after them, peeled off his clothes, and waded in.

All over the river, the men scattered, scrubbing their skin, unsure what was happening. Then they heard it.

It was the growl of an aircraft engine, huge, low, and close. The swimmers looked up, and at first saw nothing but the overcast sky. Then, there it was, bursting from the clouds: a torpedo bomber.

As the men watched, the bomber dove, leveled off, and skimmed over the water, its engine screaming. The POWs looked up at it. The bomber was headed straight toward them.

In the instant before the plane shot overhead, the men in the water could just make out the cockpit and, inside, the pilot, standing. Then the bomber was right over them. On each side of the fuselage and on the underside of each wing, there was a broad white star in a blue circle. The plane was not Japanese. It was American.

The plane's red code light was blinking rapidly. A radioman in the water near Louie read the signals and suddenly cried out:

"Oh! The war is over!"

In seconds, masses of naked men were stampeding out of the river and up the hill. As the plane turned loops above, the pilot waving, the POWs swarmed into the compound, out of their minds with relief and rapture. Their fear of the guards, of the massacre they had so long awaited, was gone, dispersed by the roar and muscle of the bomber. The prisoners jumped up and down, shouted, and sobbed. Some scrambled onto the camp roofs, waving their arms and singing out their joy to the pilot above. Others piled against the camp fence and sent it crashing over. Someone found matches, and soon, the entire length of fence was burning. The Japanese shrank back and withdrew.

In the midst of the running, celebrating men, Louie stood on wa-

vering legs, emaciated, sick, and dripping wet. In his tired mind, two
words were repeating themselves, over and over.

I'm free! I'm free! I'm free!

Down on the riverbank, a battered Australian POW named Matt Clift
sat at the water's edge. His eyes were on the torpedo bomber, which
was swooping overhead, alternately crossing over the river, then the
camp. As Clift watched, something flitted out of the cockpit, trailing a
long yellow ribbon. It carried through the air westward, directly
toward the river. Clift stood up, leaned over the water, and reached out
so far that he was on the verge of falling in. The object, a little wooden
packet, dropped right into his hands. Regaining his balance with the
treasure in his grasp, Clift had a delightful thought: *Chocolate!* His
heart filled with gratitude for the "damn good bloke" of a pilot above.

Clift spent some time trying to twist the packet open, and at some
point realized, to his crushing disappointment, that it wasn't chocolate.
When he finally got it open, he found a handwritten message inside:

OUR TBFS* HAVEN'T BEEN ABLE TO GET THROUGH THIS STUFF
TODAY. WILL LEAD THEM BACK TOMORROW WITH FOOD AND
STUFF. LT. A. R. HAWKINS, VF-31, FPO BOX 948, LUFKIN, TEXAS.[†]

Before he flew off, Hawkins dropped two gifts: a candy bar with a
bite taken out of it and a twenty-count packet of cigarettes with one
missing. Fitzgerald had the candy bar sliced into seven hundred slivers,
and each man licked a finger, dabbed it on his bit of chocolate, and put
it in his mouth. Louie's portion was the size of an ant. Then Fitzgerald
had the men form nineteen circles, each of which received one cigarette. Each man got one delectable puff.

Another American plane thrummed over, and a man fell out of it.
Down and down he fell, and his parachute didn't open. Everyone
gasped. Then they realized that it wasn't a man; it was a pair of pants,
stuffed full of something, the waist and leg holes tied shut.

---

* Torpedo bombers.
† The TBF pilot, Ray Hawkins, was a legend. In World War II, he shot down fourteen Japanese planes, making him an ace nearly three times over, and was
  awarded three Navy Crosses. He went on to fly in the Korean War, then became
  a Blue Angels flight leader. He was the first man to eject from a jet at supersonic
  speed. He survived.

The officers retrieved the pants, and Louie stood among them as the waist was opened. Inside, sitting atop a pile of goods, was an American magazine. On the cover was a photograph of an impossibly voluminous bomb cloud. The men fell silent, piecing together the rumors of one giant bomb vaporizing Hiroshima and the abrupt end to the war.

Below the magazine were cartons of cigarettes and candy bars, and very soon, the compound was littered with wrappers and naked, skinny, smoking men. In a pocket, Fitzgerald found a letter belonging to the pants' owner. The man had been busy: He had a wife in California and a girlfriend in Perth.

The rock still sat at the foot of the barracks window, Louie's rope tied around it. But the conspirators were too late; the Bird was nowhere to be found. Sometime that day, or perhaps the day before, he had taken off his uniform, picked up a sack of rice, slipped into the Naoetsu countryside, and vanished.

Thirty-two

Cascades of Pink Peaches

O N AUGUST 22, PHIL AND FRED GARRETT SAT IN THE Rokuroshi POW camp, wondering what was happening. Isolated on their chilly mountain, the POWs had been told nothing of the momentous events of recent days. All they knew was that the camp commander had been gone for five days, and in his absence, the guards had been leading the POWs on ominous walks through the forest.

That afternoon, the Japanese commander slogged back up the mountain, looking wilted. He walked into the barracks and approached the ranking American, Lieutenant Colonel Marion Unruh.

"The emperor has brought peace to the world," he said.

The commander surrendered his sword to Unruh, who gathered his men and told them that the war was over. The POWs immediately gathered for a thanksgiving service. They were told that they must not seek revenge; they were officers and gentlemen, and they were to behave that way.

The POWs promptly threw a party to end all parties. They demolished the camp fence and built a gigantic pile of wood, described by one POW as fifty feet tall. They asked the Japanese interpreter if he could get them *sake*, and a barrel full of it soon arrived. The men jacked the lid off the barrel, imbibing began, the pile of wood was set on fire, an

POWs celebrate the war's end. *Naval History and Heritage Command*

Alabaman transformed a huge can into a drum, and inebriated men began dancing. A conga line of crazy drunk POWs wrapped around camp and through the barracks, and one partier did a striptease, flinging off his clothes to reveal an emphatically unattractive body. The revelry, which went on all night, was so riotous that one man marveled at the fact that all the POWs were still alive when the sun came up.

The following day, the hungover POWs walked down the mountain to the nearest villages. They found mostly ghost towns. The civilians had seen the bonfire, abandoned their homes, and fled. The POWs hiked back up and waited for help to come.

At Naoetsu, most of the guards stayed in camp, their haughtiness replaced by gushing obsequiousness. There was almost no food and no tobacco. Fitzgerald went to the Japanese commander three times a day to demand more food, and was rejected each time. POWs left camp in search of something to eat. Someone came back with a cow. Someone else herded in pigs. It wasn't enough. Fitzgerald wrote a dispatch to the Swiss consul in Tokyo, telling of the terrible conditions in camp and asking for immediate help, but the Japanese commander refused to send it. Livid, Fitzgerald threatened to inform the American forces about the commander's behavior, but the commander still refused.

At about ten in the morning on August 26, six days after the war's end was announced in Naoetsu, Fitzgerald was just stepping out of the commander's office when a crowd of American fighter planes, sent from the carrier *Lexington,* shot overhead and began circling. The POWs charged outside, yelling. They hastily cleared an area, fetched some white lime, and painted two giant words on the ground: FOOD SMOKES. Messages dropped from the cockpits. The planes had been hauling emergency supplies to POW camps but had exhausted their loads. The pilots promised that food would soon come.

Unable to feed the POWs, the pilots did the next best thing, putting on a thirty-minute air show while the prisoners shouted their approval. Fitzgerald stood among his men, moved by their joyful upturned faces. "Wonderful?" wrote J. O. Young in his diary. "To stand cheering, crying, waving your hat and acting like a damn fool in general. No one who has not spent all but 16 days of this war as a Nip prisoner can really know what it means to see 'Old Sammy' buzzing around over the camp."

The fighters had a persuasive effect on the Japanese commander. He called for Fitzgerald, complained that Fitzgerald had not behaved "like a gentleman," and accused him of bluffing when he had threatened to tell the American forces about him.

"I meant every word I said," Fitzgerald replied.

Ninety minutes later, Japanese trucks drove into camp, and out came rations, biscuits, and canned fruit.

That afternoon, more planes from the *Lexington* flew over, and sea bags began thumping down all over camp. The POWs ran for their lives. One man, leaping from a fence to avoid getting clobbered, broke his ankle. One bag missed the camp altogether, splashing down in the river. The POWs ventured out, tore into the bags, and split up the loot. Each man received half a tin of tangerines, one pack of hardtack, two cigarettes, and a bit of candy. Someone waded into the river to grab the errant bag, and in it found magazines and a newspaper. Concerned that the food dropped wasn't nearly adequate, Fitzgerald told someone to write 700 PWS HERE on the ground.

As the men ate, they passed around the magazines and peeled through the soaked pages. The fighting, they learned, had ended on August 15; the small voice that Wade had heard on the radio in the guardroom that day had been that of Emperor Hirohito, announcing the cessation of hostilities. This meant that for five days—seven in the case of Rokuroshi—the Japanese had deceived the POWs to hide the fact that the war was over. Given all the signs that a massacre had been imminent, it seems likely that the commanders had been awaiting instruction on whether or not to carry it out, and had wanted to keep the men docile in case the answer was affirmative.

Three days after the fighters flew over, the Americans sent in the big boys: six B-29s, the words *Food for POWs* scrawled down the wing of one of them. The bomb bay doors parted and pallets poured out, swinging under red, white, and blue parachutes. The first load hit the compound. Others fell over the rice paddies, pursued by hundreds of gleeful living skeletons. One canister bore a message written in chalk: BOMBED HERE IN MAY 45 — SORRY I MISSED. BILLY THE KID. RHODE ISLAND NEW YORK. Boxes fell all over the landscape. Some civilians pulled them into their homes and hid them. Others, though in great hardship themselves, dragged them into camp.

The cargo banged down and boxes broke open. Cascades of pink peaches spilled over the countryside. A vegetable crate exploded, and the sky rained peas. A box dragged down the power lines in Naoetsu. Another harpooned the guardhouse. Louie and Tinker just missed being totaled by a giant drum full of shoes that they never saw coming. It shot through the *benjo* roof, landing on an unfortunate Australian, whose leg was broken, and a Yank from Idaho, whose skull was fractured, fortunately not fatally. The Idahoan had been fasting all day in hopes that care packages would begin falling and he could gorge himself on American food instead of seaweed. To prevent further disaster, someone ran onto the road and wrote DROP HERE.

An orgy of eating and smoking commenced. Men crammed their stomachs full, then had seconds and thirds. Louie opened a can of condensed split pea soup and shoveled it into his mouth, too hungry to add water. J. O. Young and two friends drank two *gallons* of cocoa. The food kept falling. So much of it showered down that Fitzgerald asked a man to go out on the road and make sure that whoever had written 700 PWS HERE hadn't accidentally added a zero.

At nightfall, the eating stopped. Men upended by swollen stomachs drifted off to sleep with no air raids, no *tenkos,* no Bird. Louie lay among them, swaddled in an American parachute that he had dragged in from the rice paddy.

"'Tis about 6 p.m., and I'm lying here in blissful misery just as all POWs have sat around and dreamed about throughout this internment, in short so full of chow that it's hard to even breath [*sic*]," J. O. Young wrote in his diary. "As four years prisoners . . . there is no such thing as being satisfied after eating. You either don't have enough, or as we are all now so darn full you're in misery."

"There's just one thing left to say as we bunk down for the night," he continued, "an [*sic*] that it's wonderful to be Americans and free men, and it's a might [*sic*] hard job even now to realize we're free men."

On the morning of September 2, a B-29 known as *Ghost Ship* traced the long thread of beach marking the coast of western Japan. The plane had earned its moniker when an air traffic controller, unable to see five-foot, seven-inch pilot Byron Kinney in the cockpit, had exclaimed, "There's nobody in that plane! It must be a ghost ship!" In a briefing on Guam the afternoon before, Kinney had been told that he'd be carrying supplies to a remote POW camp called Naoetsu.

Louie was in the compound alone when *Ghost Ship* dipped under the clouds, skimmed the rice paddy, dropped its first load, and began a long circle for a second drop. Hearing the bomber, sleepy men shuffled out of the barracks and began running into the drop zone. Louie saw the plane coming back and began trying to alert the men. As he descended, Kinney saw POWs scattered over the paddy, looking "dirty, ragged and haggard," and a lone man trying to pull them back. He aborted the drop and circled again. By the time he returned, Louie had cleared the paddy. The second drop rolled out.

Kinney turned the plane again, descended very low over camp, and

B-29 pilot Byron Kinney shot this photograph on his final pass over Naoetsu on September 2, 1945. The Naoetsu POW camp is straight ahead, on the far side of the bridge. The large barracks from which Louie and other officers planned to throw the Bird to his death is faintly visible, at the confluence of the two rivers.
Byron Kinney

dipped his wings. Louie stood under him in a crowd of POWs, waving his shirt. Kinney was so low that he and Louie saw each other's smiling faces. "We could almost hear their cheers as we passed over the last time," Kinney wrote. "They looked so happy. It touched my heart. I felt perhaps we were the hand of Providence reaching out to those men. I was very thankful I had gone."

As *Ghost Ship* sailed off, one of Kinney's crewmen piped the radio over the interphone. On came General Douglas MacArthur's voice, broadcasting from the deck of the USS *Missouri* in Tokyo Bay. Standing with MacArthur was Bill Harris. He'd been rescued from Omori and brought to the ship to occupy a place of honor. Alongside the Americans stood Japanese officials, there to sign surrender documents.

In its rampage over the east, Japan had brought atrocity and death on a scale that staggers the imagination. In the midst of it were the prisoners of war. Japan held some 132,000 POWs from America, Britain, Canada, New Zealand, Holland, and Australia. Of those, nearly

36,000 died, more than one in every four.* Americans fared particularly badly; of the 34,648 Americans held by Japan, 12,935—more than 37 percent—died.† By comparison, only 1 percent of Americans held by the Nazis and Italians died. Japan murdered thousands of POWs on death marches, and worked thousands of others to death in slavery, including some 16,000 POWs who died alongside as many as 100,000 Asian laborers forced to build the Burma-Siam Railway. Thousands of other POWs were beaten, burned, stabbed, or clubbed to death, shot, beheaded, killed during medical experiments, or eaten alive in ritual acts of cannibalism. And as a result of being fed grossly inadequate and befouled food and water, thousands more died of starvation and easily preventable diseases. Of the 2,500 POWs at Borneo's Sandakan camp, only 6, all escapees, made it to September 1945 alive. Left out of the numbing statistics are untold numbers of men who were captured and killed on the spot or dragged to places like Kwajalein, to be murdered without the world ever learning their fate.

In accordance with the kill-all order, the Japanese massacred all 5,000 Korean captives on Tinian, all of the POWs on Ballale, Wake, and Tarawa, and all but 11 POWs at Palawan. They were evidently about to murder all the other POWs and civilian internees in their custody when the atomic bomb brought their empire crashing down.

On the morning of September 2, 1945, Japan signed its formal surrender. The Second World War was over.

———

For Louie, these were days of bliss. Though he was still sick, wasted, and weak, he glowed with euphoria such as he had never experienced. His rage against his captors was gone. Like all the men around him, he felt flush with love for everyone and everything.

Only the thought of the Bird gave him pause. A few days earlier, Louie would have bound and killed him without remorse. Now the vengeful urge no longer had sure footing. The Bird was gone, his ability to reach Louie—physically, at least—extinguished. At that moment, all Louie felt was rapture.

Forgiveness coursed through all of the men at Naoetsu. POWs

———

* Japan also held more than 215,000 POWs from other countries and untold thousands of forced laborers. Their death rates are unknown.
† There has been some confusion concerning American POW statistics. The figures above, compiled by Charles Stenger, PhD, in a comprehensive study of POW statistics for the Veterans Administration, appear to be definitive.

doled out supplies to civilians and stood in circles of children, handing out chocolate. Louie and other POWs brought food and clothing to the guards and asked them to take it home to their families. Even Kono was spared. Ordered to stay in camp, he holed up in his office for eleven days, so afraid of retribution that he never once came out. When a POW opened the door, Kono gasped and ran to a corner. A few days before, he might have met with reprisal, but today, there was no such spirit. The POWs left him alone.*

There was only one act of vengeance in the camp. When a particularly hated guard appeared in the galley, a POW grabbed him by the collar and the seat of the pants and threw him out the door with such force that he sailed over the riverside drop-off and into the Hokura River. The POWs never saw him again.

The pallets didn't stop falling. After a few days of B-29 visits, food, medicine, and clothing were piling up everywhere. The officers distributed the food as soon as it landed, and every man was entombed in goodies. Eventually someone climbed on the roofs and wrote: NO MORE—THANKS. ANY-NEWS?

Gorging brought consequences. Digestive systems that had spent years scraping by on two or three cups of seaweed per day were overwhelmed. Naoetsu became a festival of rapid-fire diarrhea. The *benjo* lines wound everywhere, and men unable to wait began dropping their pants and fertilizing Japan wherever the spirit moved them. Then they went right back to happy feasting.

All over Japan, B-29s continued pouring food down on POWs. More than one thousand planes saturated the landscape with nearly forty-five hundred tons of Spam and fruit cocktail, soup, chocolate, medicine, clothing, and countless other treasures. At Omori, Bob Martindale had taken over the hateful little office where the Bird had sat before his picture window, hunting men. He was there when an enormous box sailed out of the sun, hit the ground just outside the window, and exploded, obliterating the Bird's office in a cataclysm of American cocoa powder. Martindale stumbled out, caked head to toe in cocoa, but otherwise uninjured.

---

* Kono put on civilian clothes, fled camp, wrote his mother to say he was killing himself, then took a false name and moved to Niigata. A year later, he was recognized on a wanted poster and arrested. Convicted of abusing POWs, he was sentenced to life at hard labor.

Everyone in camp was eager to get home, but radio messages sent out by the occupying forces stated that POWs should remain in camps for the time being. Fitzgerald was told that an evacuation team would come to Naoetsu on September 4 to oversee the POWs' transport to Yokohama, and then home. So the POWs settled in to wait, eating, smoking, resting, eating, celebrating, swimming, and eating more. Louie ate voraciously, got stronger, and expanded exponentially, his face and body bloating from water retention.

Louie did his best to clean himself up, starting with his muslin shirt, which he'd worn every day since the morning he had climbed into *Green Hornet*. A beloved brother to him, it was torn, faded, and stained with coal dust, and Louie's handwritten name was now nearly invisible on its breast pocket. Louie boiled it in a pot to kill the lice and fleas, then scrubbed it to get the coal out.

POWs fanned out over the countryside. Men carried air-dropped items into town, where they met cautiously friendly civilians and traded their goods for shaves, haircuts, and souvenirs. They knocked on doors, offering to trade air-dropped food and tobacco for fresher fare. Inside the houses, they saw large industrial machines, just as Louie had seen in the ruins of Tokyo. Tinker found a Victrola in camp, then went to town and bought a gift for Louie, a recording of Gustave Charpentier's *Impressions d'Italie*. The POWs broke into the store-house and found some fifteen hundred Red Cross boxes. Several men discovered a brothel and came back to camp with sinners' grins. Ken Marvin and a friend borrowed kids' bikes and pedaled the roads, discovering what a beautiful place they'd been in all this time. Coming upon a public bath full of civilians, Marvin jumped right in with them, scrubbing himself clean for the first time since his last shower on Wake Atoll in December 1941. "My God!" he remembered. "Just like a smorgasbord!"

September 4 arrived. The evacuation team never showed up. More than two weeks had passed since the TBF had flown over the river and blinked out the message that the war was over, and Commander Fitzgerald, like all of the men in camp, was sick of waiting. He asked Marvin and another man to don MP badges and walk with him to the train station. When they got there, Fitzgerald asked a Japanese station official to arrange for a ten-carriage train to be there the next day. The official refused, and was plenty obnoxious about it.

Commander John Fitzgerald had been in Japanese custody since

April 1943. For two and a half years, he'd been forced to grovel before sadists and imbeciles as he tried to protect his men. He'd been starved, beaten, and enslaved, given the water cure, had his fingernails torn out. He was done negotiating. He hauled back and punched the station official, to the delight of Ken Marvin. The next morning, the train was there, right on time.

Early on the morning of September 5, Louie packed up his diary, the record from Tinker, and his letters from home, and stepped down the barracks ladder for the last time. In the compound, the POWs were congregating in joyful anticipation. Everyone carried what few possessions they had, and the British Commonwealth soldiers held the white boxes bearing the remains of the sixty Aussies who had died in camp. Determined to leave this indecent place with dignity, the men assembled behind flags of their nations. Then, together, they passed through the camp gate and marched up the road, toward wives and sweethearts and children and Mom and Dad and home.

As he walked over the bridge, Louie glanced back. Some of the guards and camp officials stood in the compound, watching them go. A few of the sickest POWs remained behind, awaiting transport the next day. Fitzgerald stayed with them, unwilling to leave until the last of his men was liberated.* Louie raised his arm and waved the war good-bye. He crossed over the bridge, and the camp passed out of view.

As the train pushed off for Yokohama, the POWs' last sight of Naoetsu was a broken line of Japanese, the few civilian guards and camp staffers who had been kind to them, standing along the side of the track. Their hands were raised in salute.

---

* When Fitzgerald got home, he would be honored with the Navy Cross and the Silver Star for his heroism in combat and in the POW camp.

Thirty-three

Mother's Day

THE NAOETSU POWS HAD CONTROL OF THE TRAIN. AT EVERY town on the line, the train squealed to a stop and the men piled off, then piled back on, laden with liberated *sake* and whatever else they could steal. The journey went on, *sake* coursed through skinny bodies, and the men grew rowdier. A lieutenant stood up and, with solemn officiousness, warned the men to behave themselves. He didn't want anyone falling off the train, he said.

At about three in the afternoon, the train stopped and began backing up. Just as the lieutenant had feared, a man had gone overboard. As the train rolled backward, the errant POW came into view. It was the lieutenant himself, at least three sheets to the wind. He was lucky. All afternoon, drunken POWs staggered off the train, but the train didn't stop for them. They had to find their own way.

From the top of Japan to the bottom, trains packed with POWs snaked toward Yokohama. Men pressed their faces to the windows to catch their first glimpse of what all of those B-29s had done. Once-grand cities were now flat, black stains, their only recognizable feature a gridwork of burned roads, passing nothing, leading nowhere.

At the first sight of the destruction of their enemy, the POWs cheered. But after the first city there was another, then another, city after city razed, the survivors drifting about like specters, picking through the rubble. The cheering died away. On Louie's train, the silence came as they passed through Tokyo. A week after Louie had left Omori, sixteen square miles of Tokyo, and tens of thousands of souls, had been immolated by B-29s.

A few of the trains slipped past Hiroshima. Virtually every POW believed that the destruction of this city had saved them from execution. John Falconer, a survivor of the Bataan Death March, looked out as Hiroshima neared. "First there were trees," he told historian Donald Knox. "Then the leaves were missing. As you got closer, branches were missing. Closer still, the trunks were gone and then, as you got in the middle, there was nothing. Nothing! It was beautiful. I realized this was what had ended the war. It meant we didn't have to go hungry any longer, or go without medical treatment. I was so insensitive to anyone else's human needs and suffering. I know it's not right to say it was beautiful, because it really wasn't. But I believed the end probably justified the means."

At seven that evening, the Naoetsu train entered bombed-out Yokohama and stopped at the station.

"Welcome back, boys."

"Before me in immaculate khaki uniform and cap stood an American girl with a magazine-cover smile, faultless makeup and peroxide blonde hair," wrote Tom Wade. "After three and a half years in prison camp, I had been liberated by the great American blonde!"

The POWs were soon blissfully enveloped in Red Cross nurses, some of whom cried at the sight of them. Perhaps the women weren't all beautiful, but to Ken Marvin, they looked like goddesses.

Someone spotted a mess hall, and a charge ensued. In the midst of it stood a journalist, Robert Trumbull. He called out, asking if anyone had a story to tell. As he hurried past, Frank Tinker told him to talk to Louie Zamperini, gesturing toward his friend.

"Zamperini's dead," said Trumbull, who thought that the man in question didn't even look like the famous runner. He asked Louie if he could prove his identity. Louie pulled out his wallet. The Japanese had cleaned out the main folds, but in a hidden pocket he'd tucked eight dollars, the cartoon that had gotten him and Phil beaten up, and a USC football admission pass inscribed with his name.

Trumbull was astonished. He took Louie aside and began asking questions, and Louie recounted his entire saga. He omitted one detail: For the sake of Mac and his family, he said nothing of how the chocolate had been lost. Phil would do the same, saying that the chocolate had gone overboard. When Louie finished, Trumbull asked him to summarize what he had endured. Louie stood silently.

"If I knew I had to go through those experiences again," he finally said, "I'd kill myself."

The next morning, Louie was taken to an airfield to be flown to Okinawa, where many POWs were being collected before being sent home. Seeing a table stacked with K rations, he began cramming the boxes under his shirt, brushing off an attendant who tried to assure him that he didn't have to hoard them, as no one was going to starve him anymore. Looking extremely pregnant, Louie boarded his plane.

Somewhere in the bustle, he'd been separated from his friends. There had been no good-byes. By seven that morning, he was airborne—leaving Japan, he hoped, forever.

At Okinawa, a staff sergeant named Frank Rosynek stood by the airfield, watching transport planes come in. He was with Louie's old outfit, the 11th Bomb Group, which was now stationed on Okinawa, and he had come to the airfield to welcome the POWs. "They were a pathetic looking bunch: mostly skin and bones, clad in rags with makeshift footwear, and nervous," he wrote. He walked among them, listening to their stories, marveling at how they savored the mess hall grub, watching them tear up over photographs of wives and steady girls who, they hoped, hadn't given them up for dead.*

Rosynek's CO asked him to come to the debriefing of a POW from the 11th. When Rosynek arrived, he saw three officers sitting before a drawn, unshaven POW in sun-bleached clothes. The officers were staring at the POW as if in shock. The colonel told Rosynek that the man was Louis Zamperini, and that he had disappeared some two and a half years earlier. Everyone in the bomb group had thought he was dead. Rosynek was incredulous. It had been his job to write next-of-kin

---

* One POW's worst nightmare came true. Upon liberation, he was told by a reporter that his wife, believing him dead, had just married his uncle. When she learned that her first husband was alive, the woman immediately had her new marriage annulled and got the Associated Press to deliver a message to her lost husband: "I love only you, Gene. Please forgive me."

letters for lost men, and he had probably written to Zamperini's mother, but he no longer remembered. There had been so many such letters. Not one of those men had turned up alive, until now.

It was probably sometime later that day when the dead man walked into the 11th Bomb Group's quarters. Jack Krey, who had packed up Louie's belongings on Oahu, captured the reaction to news of Louie's reappearance: "Well, I'll be damned."

It wasn't the reunion that Louie had anticipated. Most of these men were strangers to him. Many of his friends, he learned, were dead. Two hundred and twenty-five men from the 11th had gone missing and were presumed dead, including twenty-six from Louie's 42nd squadron. Many more had been killed in action. Of the sixteen rowdy young officers who had shared the pornographic palace on Oahu, only four—Louie, Phil, Jesse Stay, and Joe Deasy—were still alive. Louie and Phil had vanished in the Pacific. Deasy had gone home with tuberculosis. Only Stay had completed his forty-mission tour of duty. He'd seen five planes on his wing go down, with every man killed, and yet somehow, the sum total of damage to his bombers was one bullet hole. He'd gone home in March.

Someone brought Louie the August 15 issue of the *Minneapolis Star-Journal*. Near the back was an article entitled "Lest We Forget," discussing athletes who had died in the war. More than four hundred amateur, professional, and collegiate athletes had been killed, including nineteen pro football players, five American League baseball players, eleven pro golfers, and 1920 Olympic champion sprinter Charlie Paddock, whom Louie had known. There on the page with them, Louie saw his own picture and the words "great miler . . . killed in action in the South Pacific."

The Okinawa mess hall was kept open around the clock for the POWs, who couldn't stop eating. Louie headed straight for it, but was stopped at the door. Because the Japanese had never registered him with the Red Cross, his name wasn't on the roster. As far as the mess was concerned, Louie wasn't a POW. He encountered the same problem when trying to get a new uniform to replace the pants and shirt that he had worn every day since May 27, 1943. Until the snafu was straightened out, he had to subsist on candy bars from Red Cross nurses.

Soon after Louie's arrival, he was sent to a hospital to be examined. Like most POWs, in gorging day and night, he had gained weight ex-

Louie in Okinawa. On his
right hand is the USC class ring
that caught in the wreckage of
his plane as it sank.
Courtesy of Louis Zamperini

tremely rapidly; he now weighed 143 pounds, just seventeen pounds
under his weight at the time of the crash. But thanks to dramatic water
retention, it was a doughy, moon-faced, muscleless weight. He still had
volatile dysentery and was as weak as a blade of grass. He was only
twenty-eight, but his body, within and without, was etched with the
trauma of twenty-seven months of abuse and deprivation. The physicians, who knew what Louie had once been, sat him down to have a
solemn talk. After Louie left the doctors, a reporter asked him about
his running career.

"It's finished," he said, his voice sharp. "I'll never run again."

The Zamperinis were on edge. Since Louie's crash, his only message to
make it to America had been his radio broadcast ten months earlier.
The letters that he had written after the Bird had left Omori had not arrived. Other than the War Department's December confirmation that
Louie was a POW, no further word from or about him had come. The
papers were full of stories about the murder of POWs, and families
couldn't rest easy. The Zamperinis contacted the War Department, but
the department had nothing to tell. Sylvia kept writing to Louie, telling
him of all they would do when he came home. "Darling, we will take
the best of care for you," she wrote. "You shall be 'King Toots,'—
anything your heart desires—(yes, even red heads and all)." But she,
like the rest of the family, was scared. Pete, living in his officer's quarters in San Diego, kept calling home to see if news had come. The answer was always no.

On the morning of September 9, Pete was startled awake by a hand on his shoulder, shaking him vigorously. He opened his eyes to see one of his friends bending over him with a huge smile. Trumbull's story had appeared in the *Los Angeles Times*. The headline said it all: ZAMPERINI COMES BACK FROM DEAD.

In a moment, Pete was on his feet, throwing on his clothes. He bolted for a telephone and dialed his parents' number. Sylvia picked up. Pete asked if she had heard the news.

"Did you hear the news?" she repeated back to him. "Did I! Wow!" Pete asked to speak to his mother, but she was too overcome to talk.

Louise and Virginia rushed to church to give thanks, then raced home to prepare the house. As she stood in Louie's room, dusting his running trophies, Louise blinked away tears, singing out, "He's on the way home. He's on the way home."

"From now on," she said, "September 9 is going to be Mother's Day to me, because that's the day I learned for sure my boy was coming home to stay."

"What do you think, Pop?" someone asked Louie's father.

"Those Japs couldn't break him," Anthony said. "My boy's pretty tough, you know."

———

Liberation was a long time coming for Phil and Fred at Rokuroshi. After the August 22 announcement of the war's end, the POWs sat there, waiting for someone to come get them. They got hold of a radio, and on it they heard chatter from men liberating other camps, but no one came for them. They began to wonder if anyone knew they were there. It wasn't until September 2 that B-29s finally flew over Rokuroshi, their pallets hitting the rice paddies with such force that the men had to dig them out. The POWs ate themselves silly. One man downed twenty pounds of food in a single day, but somehow didn't get sick.

That afternoon, an American navy man dug through his belongings and pulled out his most secret and precious possession. It was an American flag with a remarkable provenance. In 1941, just before Singapore had fallen to the Japanese, an American missionary woman had given it to a British POW. The POW had been loaded aboard a ship, which had sunk. Two days later, another British POW had rescued the flag from where it lay underwater and slipped it to the American navy man, who had carried it through the entire war, somehow hiding it from the Japanese, until this day. The POWs pulled down the Japanese flag and ran the Stars and Stripes up the pole over Rokuroshi. The men stood before it, hands up in salutes, tears running down their faces.

On September 9, Phil, Fred, and the other POWs were finally trucked off the mountain. Arriving in Yokohama, they were greeted with pancakes, a band playing "California, Here I Come," and a general who broke down when he saw them. The men were escorted aboard a ship for hot showers and more food. On September 11, the ship set off for home.

When news of the Trumbull story reached Indiana, Kelsey Phillips's telephone began ringing, and friends and reporters flocked onto her front porch. Remembering the War Department's request that she not speak publicly of her son's survival, Kelsey kept a smiling silence, awaiting official notification that Allen had been released from the POW camp. It wasn't until September 16 that the War Department telegram announcing Allen's liberation reached her. It was followed by a phone call from her sister, who delivered a message from Allen that had passed from person to person from Rokuroshi to Yokohama to San Francisco to New Jersey to Indiana: He was free. Allen's friends went downtown and bought newspapers, spread them out on someone's living room floor, and spent the morning reading and crying.

As she celebrated, Kelsey thought of what Allen had written in a letter to her. "I would give anything to be home with all of you," the letter said, "but I'm looking forward to the day—whenever it comes."

"That day," Kelsey rejoiced, "has come."

On Okinawa, Louie was having a grand time, eating, drinking, and making merry. When he was given orders to fly out, he begged a doctor to arrange for him to stay a little longer, on the grounds that he didn't want his mother to see him so thin. The doctor not only agreed to have Louie "hospitalized," he threw him a welcome-back-to-life bash, complete with a five-gallon barrel of "bourbon"—alcohol mixed with Coke syrup, distilled water, and whatever else was handy.

More than a week passed, bombers left with loads of POWs, and still Louie stayed on Okinawa. The nurses threw him another party, the ersatz bourbon went down easy, and there was a moonlit jeep ride with a pretty girl. Along the way, Louie discovered that a delightful upside to being believed dead was that he could scare the hell out of people. Learning that a former track recruiter from USC was on the island, he asked a friend to tell the recruiter that he had a college running prospect who could spin a mile in just over four minutes. The recruiter eagerly asked to meet the runner. When Louie appeared, the recruiter fell over backward in his chair.

On September 17, a typhoon hit Okinawa. Louie was in a tent when nature called, sending him into the storm to fight his way to an outhouse. He was on the seat with his pants down when a wind gust shot the outhouse over an embankment, carrying Louie in it. Dumped in the mud under a downpour, Louie stood up, hitched up his pants, got broadsided by another gust, and fell over. He crawled through the mud, "lizarding his way," as he put it, up the hill. He had to bang on the hospital door for a while before someone heard him.

The next morning dawned to find planes flipped over, ships sunk, tents collapsed. Louie, covered in everything that a somersault inside an outhouse will slather on a man, was finally willing to leave Okinawa. He got an enlisted man to pour water over his head while he soaped off, then went to the airfield. When he saw the plane that he was to ride in, he felt a swell of nausea. It was a B-24.

The first leg of the journey, to the Philippine city of Laoag, went without incident. On the second flight, to Manila, the plane was so overloaded with POWs that it nearly crashed just after takeoff, dipping so low that seawater sprayed the POWs' legs through gaps in the bomb bay floor.* But the bomber made it to Manila, where Louie got passage out on a transport plane. He sat in the cockpit, telling the pilot his story, from the crash to Kwajalein to Japan. As Louie spoke, the pilot dropped the plane down over an island and landed. The pilot asked Louie if he'd ever seen this place before. Louie looked around at a charred wasteland, recognizing nothing.

"This is Kwajalein," said the pilot.

This *couldn't* be Kwajalein, Louie thought. In captivity, glimpsing the island through gaps in his blindfold, or when being hustled to interrogation and medical experimentation, he'd seen a vast swath of intense green. Now, he couldn't find a single tree. The fight for this place had ripped the jungle off the island. Louie would long wonder if kindhearted Kawamura had died here.

Someone told him that there was, in fact, one tree still standing.

---

* Louie was luckier than he knew. Another transport crashed on takeoff, in part because several Dutch POWs had overloaded the plane by packing aboard a large cache of GI shoes that they intended to sell back home. Everyone on the plane died. Another POW transport was lost over the ocean.

They borrowed a jeep and drove over to see it. Staring at Kwajalein's last tree, with food in his belly, no blindfold over his eyes, no one there to beat him, Louie felt as if he were in the sweetest of dreams.

On he went to Hawaii. Seeing the condition of the POWs, American authorities had decided to hospitalize virtually all of them. Louie was checked into a Honolulu hospital, where he found himself rooming with Fred Garrett. It was the first time that Louie had slept on a mattress, with sheets, since the first days after his capture. He was given a new uniform and captain's bars, having been promoted during his imprisonment, as most army POWs were. Trying on his new clothes, he pulled off his beloved muslin shirt, set it aside, and forgot about it. He went downtown, then remembered the shirt and returned to retrieve it. It had been thrown away. He was heartbroken.

Louie and Fred hit the town. Seemingly everyone they met wanted to take them somewhere, feed them, buy them drinks. On a beach, they made a spectacle of themselves when Fred, feeling emasculated by the pity over his missing leg, flung away his crutches, hopped over to Louie, and tackled him. The wrestling match drew a crowd of offended onlookers, who thought that an able-bodied soldier was beating up a helpless amputee. Swinging around Hawaii, getting drunk, knocking heads with Fred, Louie never left himself a moment to think of the war. "I just thought I was empty and now I'm being filled," he said later, "and I just wanted to keep being filled."

That October, Tom Wade walked off a transport ship in Victoria, Canada. With a multitude of former POWs, he began a transcontinental rail journey that became a nonstop party, including eight impromptu weddings. "I must have kissed a thousand girls crossing the continent," Wade wrote to Louie, "and when I walked through the train with lipstick all over my face after the first station, I was the most popular officer on the train." In New York, he was taken aboard the *Queen Elizabeth* to sail for England. He snuck down the gangway, necked with a Red Cross girl, and stole back aboard toting a box of Hershey bars. When he reached England, he discovered that the local women preferred Yank and Canadian soldiers to Brits. "I decided to do something about it," he wrote. "I sewed a couple of extra patches and oddments on to my uniform, nobody was any wiser, and stormed them. I did all right."

On October 16, Russell Allen Phillips, wearing his dress uniform and captain's bars, stepped off a train in Indiana. He'd been gone for four years. His mother, his sister, and a throng of friends were there. A telegram had come from his father, who was soon to return from Europe: THANK THE LORD GREAT DAY HAS ARRIVED. WELCOME HOME MY SON. There, too, was the woman whose image had sustained him. Cecy was in his arms at last.

At Kelsey's house in Princeton, they sat Allen down on the front steps, and he grinned while they snapped his picture. When they got the print back, someone wrote one word on it: *Home!*

Four weeks later, in a wedding ceremony officiated by Reverend Phillips at Cecy's parents' house, the hero finally got the girl. Allen had

Russell Allen Phillips arrives at his mother's house.
On the back of this photo, someone wrote, "Home!"
Courtesy of Karen Loomis

no car, so he borrowed one from a friend. Then, as he had promised in a letter so long ago, he ran away with Cecy to a place where no one would find them.

⸻

Pete was so anxious to see Louie that he could hardly bear it. The fighting had ended in mid-August, it was now October, and still Louie was hospital-hopping far from home. Then Pete learned that Louie was finally stateside, transferred from Hawaii to San Francisco's Letterman General Hospital. As soon as he got the news, Pete went AWOL. He bummed a ride to San Francisco on a navy plane, hitched his way to

Letterman, and walked in. At the front desk, he called Louie's room. A minute later, Louie bounded into the lobby.

Each felt startled by the sight of the other. Pete had expected Louie to be emaciated and was surprised to find him looking almost portly. Louie was disturbed to see how the years of worry had depleted his brother. Pete was gaunt, and he'd gone largely bald. The brothers fell together, eyes shining.

Pete and Louie spent several days together in San Francisco while doctors finally cured Louie of his dysentery. After reading the Trumbull article, Pete had worried that Louie might be severely traumatized, but as the two laughed and kidded each other, his fears faded. Louie was as upbeat and garrulous as ever. Once, when a group of reporters shuffled in to interview Louie, they crowded around Pete, assuming that of the two men, this haggard one had to be the POW.

On a drizzling October day, the army sent a banged-up B-25 to San Francisco to bring Louie home. Pete, still AWOL, went aboard with his brother. The plane lifted off and rose over the clouds into a shining blue morning. Scared to death of flying, Pete tried to distract himself from the plane's rattles and groans by staring out over a carpet of bright clouds, the upside of the rainstorm. He felt as if he could step from the plane and walk on them.

Over Long Beach, they sank back into the rain and landed. There, bursting from army cars, were their mother and father, and Sylvia and Virginia. The moment the plane stopped, Louie jumped down, ran to his sobbing mother, and folded himself around her.

"*Cara mamma mia,*" he whispered. It was a long time before they let go.

Louie's homecoming, Long Beach Airport. Foreground, left to right: Virginia, Sylvia, Louise, and Louie. *Courtesy of Louis Zamperini*

PART

V

Thirty-four

The Shimmering Girl

O N AN OCTOBER AFTERNOON, LOUIE STEPPED OUT OF AN army car and stood on the lawn at 2028 Gramercy Avenue, looking at his parents' house for the first time in more than three years.

"This, this little home," he said, "was worth all of it."

As his parents and siblings filed into the house, Louie paused, overcome by a strange uneasiness. He had to push himself to walk up the steps.

The house was done up top to bottom for his homecoming. The surface of the dining room table was a traffic jam of heaping dishes. Three years' worth of Christmas and birthday presents sat ready for opening. There was a cake with *Welcome Home Louie* inscribed in the icing. In the garage sat Louie's beige Plymouth convertible, just as he had left it.

The family ringed around Louie, babbling, eager to look at him and touch him. Anthony and Louise smiled, but there was a cast to their eyes, a tension that had never been there before. What Louie didn't see was the rash on his mother's hands. As soon as Louise had learned that her son was coming home, the rash had vanished. Nothing, not even a scar, remained. She would never tell Louie about it.

After dessert, the family sat and talked. They spoke easily, as they always had. No one asked about prison camp. Louie volunteered a little about it, and to everyone's relief, it seemed to carry little emotion for him. It seemed that he was going to be just fine.

Sylvia had a surprise for Louie. Lynn Moody, the woman who had transcribed Louie's broadcast, had arranged for a recording of it to be sent to the Zamperinis. The family treasured the record, which had given them proof that he was alive. Knowing nothing of the circumstances in which the broadcast had been made, Sylvia was eager to share it with Louie. As he sat nearby, relaxed and cheerful, she dropped the record on the turntable. The broadcast began to play.

Louie was suddenly screaming. Sylvia turned and found him shaking violently, shouting, "*Take it off! Take it off! I can't stand it!*" As Sylvia jumped up, Louie swore at the voice, yelling something about propaganda prisoners. Sylvia snatched up the record, and Louie yelled at her to break it. She smashed it and threw it away.

Louie fell silent, shivering. His family stared at him in horror.

Louie walked upstairs and lay down on his old bed. When he finally drifted off, the Bird followed him into his dreams.

The same man was on many other minds that fall. On ships docked at Yokohama, in tents in Manila, and in stateside hospitals, former POWs were telling their stories. Investigators, gathering affidavits on war criminals, sat by as men told of abuses and atrocities that pushed the bounds of believability. As the stories were corroborated again and again, it became clear that these events had been commonplace in camps throughout Japan's empire. In interview after interview, former POWs mentioned the same name: Mutsuhiro Watanabe. When Wade wrote that name on his statement, his interviewer exclaimed, "*Not* the same Watanabe! We've got enough to hang him six times already."

"Sit back and take it easy," Wade replied. "There's lots more to come."

On September 11, General MacArthur, now the supreme commander of Allied powers in occupied Japan, ordered the arrest of forty war-crimes suspects. While thousands of men would be sought later, this preliminary list was composed of those accused of the worst crimes, including list-topper Hideki Tojo, mastermind of Pearl Harbor and the man on whose orders POWs had been enslaved and starved, and Masaharu Homma, who was responsible for the Bataan Death March.* On the list with them was Mutsuhiro Watanabe.

———

The Bird had left Naoetsu in a panic, and without a plan. According to Watanabe family accounts, he fled to the village of Kusakabe, where his mother and other relatives were living. About a week and a half after Mutsuhiro's arrival, his aunt found him out drinking and told him that she'd just heard a radio broadcast naming him as a war-crimes suspect. Mutsuhiro decided to make a run for it. He apparently told his mother that he was leaving to visit a friend's tomb, then took his little sister aside and told her that he had to escape, but asked her not to tell his mother. As Mutsuhiro was preparing to go, his little sister gave him a deck of playing cards, to be used for fortune-telling.

Wearing his uniform with the insignia torn off, Mutsuhiro packed a trunk with food and clothing and lugged it to a car. He drove to the rail station and walked onto the first train he saw, without checking its destination. He hoped it would take him to someplace distant and obscure, but the train reached its terminus only two towns down the line, at the metropolis of Kofu. He got off, wandered the station, then lay down and slept.

In the morning, he meandered around Kofu. Somewhere in the city, he passed a radio and heard his name listed among those wanted for war crimes. To learn that he was being sought was no surprise, but he was shocked to hear his name listed alongside that of Tojo. If his case was considered comparable to that of Tojo, he thought, arrest would mean execution.

At all costs, he vowed, he wouldn't let himself fall into the hands of the Americans. He resolved to disappear forever.

———

As Mutsuhiro fled, the hunt for him began. Though they were now operating under the orders of their former enemies, the Japanese police

---

* Tojo was found in his home that day, sitting in a chair, blood gushing from a self-inflicted bullet wound in his chest. Whispering "*Banzai!*" and saying he'd rather die than face trial, Tojo was given a pint of American blood plasma, then taken to a hospital. When he recovered, he was housed at Omori, sleeping in Bob Martindale's bunk. He complained about lice and bedbugs. He was tried, sentenced to death, and, in 1948, hanged. He and 1,068 other convicted war criminals were later honored in Tokyo's Yasukuni Shrine, memorializing Japanese who died in the service of the emperor.

worked swiftly and energetically to round up war-crimes suspects. The Watanabe case was no exception. After finding nothing at Mutsuhiro's last known address, police appeared at his mother's door in Kusakabe. Shizuka Watanabe told them that her son had been there, but had left. They had missed him by three days. Shizuka suggested that he might seek refuge with his sister Michiko, who lived in Tokyo. She'd soon be visiting Michiko, she said, and if she found Mutsuhiro there, she'd urge him to turn himself in.

The police seized on the lead. Shizuka gave them an address for Michiko, and they converged on it. Not only was there no Michiko there, there was no house. Every home in the neighborhood had burned long ago, in the firebombing.

Shizuka was now the focus of suspicion. On her regular visits to Tokyo, she always stayed with Michiko, and given that she was scheduled to do so that very week, she surely knew that her daughter's home had burned down. Shizuka's misdirection of the detectives may have been an honest mistake—Michiko had moved to a home down the same road, so the only change in the address was the door number—but the police began to suspect that she knew where her son was. On September 24, the police arrested her. If she knew anything, she let nothing slip. She was released.

The police were a long way from giving up. Two detectives began tailing Shizuka and often came into her home to question her. Her monetary transactions were tracked, and her landlord was regularly questioned. Mutsuhiro's other relatives were investigated, questioned, and sometimes searched. Police intercepted all of the family's incoming and outgoing mail. They even had a stranger deliver a fake letter, apparently making it appear to be from Mutsuhiro, in hopes of getting the family to betray his whereabouts.

Widening the hunt, the police investigated Mutsuhiro's former army roommates. The home of his Omori commander was searched and put under surveillance. Mutsuhiro's photograph was distributed throughout police ranks in the Tokyo metropolitan area and four prefectures. Every police station in Nagano Prefecture, where a Watanabe family mine was located, conducted special searches. Detectives went through Mutsuhiro's academic records and searched for his teachers and classmates, going back to his childhood. They even got hold of a love letter from a girl who had asked Mutsuhiro if he'd marry her.

They found only two leads. A former soldier told them that Mutsuhiro had spoken of his intention to flee to Fukuoka Prefecture to be a farmer. The soldier thought that Mutsuhiro would hide with a friend named Yo. Police found Yo, questioned and investigated him, and questioned people in his neighborhood. It was a dead lead. Meanwhile, a detective at Mitsushima found a man who'd seen Mutsuhiro in August. The man said that Mutsuhiro had left, claiming to be headed for Tokyo, at the war's end. But Mutsuhiro had gone to Kusakabe; there was no evidence that he'd gone to Tokyo. He may have seeded his acquaintances with false information to misdirect his pursuers.

There was one other possible clue. The man at Mitsushima mentioned something he had overheard Mutsuhiro say: He would rather kill himself than be captured. It seemed no idle threat; that fall, during a roundup of suspected war criminals, there was a wave of suicides among those sought. Perhaps the Bird was already dead.

While investigators combed Japan for Mutsuhiro, prosecutors were inundated with some 250 POW affidavits concerning his actions in camps. These would be distilled into an 84-count indictment. Even with each count stated with maximum brevity, in single spacing, the indictment stretched over eight feet of paper. It would reflect only a tiny fraction of the crimes that POWs said Watanabe had committed; Louie's accusations of myriad attacks would make up only one count. Investigators believed that they had far more evidence than they needed to have Watanabe convicted and put to death. But nothing could go forward. The Bird was still at large.

As his tormenter disappeared into darkness, Louie was pulled into blinding light. With his Odyssean saga featured in newspapers, magazines, and radio shows, he was a national sensation. Two thousand people wrote him letters. Press photographers tailed him. His attempts to sleep were invariably interrupted by a ringing phone. Strangers teemed around him, pushing for news on what he'd do next. Everyone wanted him to tell his story. The War Department booked him on a speaking tour, and he was inundated with speaking invitations that usually came with an award, making them impossible to decline. In his first weeks home, staying with his parents, he gave ninety-five speeches and made countless radio appearances. When he went to dinner clubs, the managers begged him to regale the guests. For Louie, all of the attention was drenching, a great noise, overpowering.

When Payton Jordan first saw Louie again, he was reassured by his old friend's familiar impish grin and the springy cadence of his speech. But when Louie spoke of the war, Jordan sensed something rustling just behind his eyes, a clamoring emotion pent up in a small space. He spoke not with anger or anguish but with bewilderment. Sometimes he'd pause and drift off, a troubled expression on his face. "It was like he got hit real hard," Jordan recalled, "and he was trying to shake it off."

Louie was struggling more than Jordan or anyone else knew. He was beginning to suffer bouts of suffocating anxiety. Each time he was asked to stand before a crowd and shape words around his private horror, his gut would wring. Every night, in his dreams, an apparition would form in his head and burn there. It was the face of the Bird, screaming, "*Next! Next! Next!*"

Very early one morning, Louie tiptoed from his room without telling anyone where he was going, slid into his Plymouth, put his foot on the gas, and didn't stop until he was high in the mountains. He spent the day walking among the trees, thinking of his dead friends and his own survival, drawing from the wilderness the peace that it had given him since his boyhood summer on the Cahuilla reservation. The moment he nosed the car back in the driveway, the whirling began again.

Shortly after returning home, Louie found himself sitting in the audience at a gala held by the *Los Angeles Times*, which was giving him an award. Louie forked through his dinner, waiting for his name to be announced, apprehensive over having to relive his ordeal before all these people. Drinks were set before him, and he sipped them and felt his nerves unwinding. By the time he rose to speak, he was in a haze, and he rambled on for much too long. When he got back to his seat, he felt relieved. The alcohol had brought him a pleasant numbness.

One day not long after, as he sat at breakfast and fretted over the prospect of another speech, he broke out a bottle of Canadian Club whiskey and poured a shot into his coffee. That gave him a warm feeling, so he had another shot. It couldn't hurt to have a third. The whiskey floated him through that speech, too, and so began a routine. A flask became his constant companion, making furtive appearances in parking lots and corridors outside speaking halls. When the harsh push of memory ran through Louie, reaching for his flask became as easy as slapping a swatter on a fly.

———

One afternoon in the middle of March 1946, Louie was at a bar at the Deauville Club in Miami Beach, chatting up a stewardess. He had just completed the latest of many surreal liberation experiences, traveling to New York to fire the starting gun for Madison Square Garden's Zamperini Invitational Mile, the race conceived to honor him when almost everyone thought he was dead. After the race, he'd come to Miami Beach for the two weeks of R&R awarded to returning servicemen. A USC classmate, Harry Read, had accompanied him.

Across the room, a door opened. Louie glanced up. Flitting into the club was an arrestingly beautiful young woman, her hair a tumble of blondness, her body as quick and gracile as a deer's. Those who knew her spoke of a shimmer about her, an incandescence. Louie drank in one long look and, he later told Sylvia, had the astounding thought that he had to marry this girl.

The next day, Louie and Harry returned to the club, vaulted the fence surrounding its private beach, and spread their towels near a pair of sunbathing women. When one of the women turned, Louie saw that it was the beauty from the bar. He was hesitant to speak to her, afraid that he'd come off as a wolf, but Harry charged right in, regaling the women with Louie's history. When Harry mentioned the 1938 NCAA Championships, when rival runners had spiked Louie's legs, the pretty woman stopped him. She said that when she was twelve, her mother had taken her to a theater to see Errol Flynn in *Robin Hood,* and there she'd watched a newsreel showing the NCAA mile winner and his bandaged legs. The sight had stuck in her mind.

Her name was Cynthia Applewhite, and she was a few weeks past her twentieth birthday. Louie spoke with her for a while, and the two discovered that they had geography in common; as a child, she had lived near Torrance. She seemed to like him, and he thought her bright and lively and so beautiful. When they parted, Louie grumbled something about how she probably wouldn't want to see him again. "Maybe," she said playfully, "I want to see you again."

Louie wasn't the first guy to be felled by Cynthia. Dense forests of men had gone down at the sight of her. She was dating two guys at once, both named Mac, and each Mac was trying to outlast the other. Since the Macs had Cynthia booked for every evening, Louie asked her for a daytime date, to go fishing. Showing up in blue jeans rolled up to the knee, she took up a fishing pole, smiled gaily for photographs, and braved seasickness with cheer. When Louie asked if he could take her out again, she said yes.

Cynthia Applewhite, on the day after Louie met her.
Courtesy of Louis Zamperini

They seemed an unlikely pair. Cynthia was wealthy and pedigreed; she'd been educated in private schools, then an elite finishing academy. But for all of her polishing, she was not a buttoned-up girl. A friend would remember her as *"different"*—passionate and impulsive. At thirteen, when her family lived in New York State, she developed such a fever for Laurence Olivier that, unbeknownst to her parents, she hopped a train to Manhattan to see him in *Wuthering Heights*. At sixteen, she was drinking gin. She dressed in bohemian clothes, penned novels, painted, and yearned to roam forgotten corners of the world. She was habitually defiant and fearless, and when she felt controlled, as she often did, she could be irresistibly willful. Mostly, she was bored silly by the vanilla sort of boys who trailed her around, and by the stodgy set in Miami Beach.

Along came Louie. Here was someone exotic, someone who answered her yearning for adventure, understood her fiercely independent personality, and was from nowhere near Miami Beach. She was impressed with this older man, introducing him with his full name, as if he were a dignitary. On one of their first dates, he raced her through his hotel, snatching up toilet paper rolls and streaming them down the side of the building, earning the hotel manager's wrath and Cynthia's exhilaration. She gave up the Macs, and she and Louie swept around Miami.

At the end of March, just before he was to leave for his speaking tour, Louie led Cynthia onto a beach and confessed that he was in love with her. Cynthia replied that she thought she loved him but wasn't sure. Louie was undiscouraged. Before their walk was done, he had talked her into marrying him. They had known each other for less than two weeks.

After Louie left, Cynthia broke the news to her parents. The Applewhites were alarmed that their daughter was flinging herself into marriage with a twenty-nine-year-old soldier whom she'd known for just days. Cynthia couldn't be swayed, so Mrs. Applewhite refused to give her money to fly to California to get married. Cynthia vowed to get the money somehow, either by borrowing it or, in defiance of her mother, getting a job.

Louie wrote to Cynthia almost every day, and every morning at ten-thirty, he sat waiting for the mailman to bring him a pink envelope from Cynthia. Though the letters were adoring on both sides, they reveal how little the two knew about each other. Cynthia had no idea that Louie was losing his emotional equilibrium. From Harry, she knew a little about his time as a POW, but Louie had said almost nothing. In his letters, the closest he came to addressing it was to joke that he hoped that she'd go easy on rice and barley in her cooking. On one of their dates, Louie had gotten very drunk, but he had apologized and curbed himself from then on. Louie's drinking may have struck Cynthia as harmless, but it was in fact a growing problem. In critical ways, she was engaged to a stranger.

Louie seemed to be aware that in marrying her, he was asking more of her than she knew, and he frequently warned her of how much she was taking on. Still, he wanted a wedding as soon as possible. "We have got to set a date early in June," he wrote in mid-April, "or I'll just go plain crazy." Soon after, he wrote that they had to marry in May. She told him that she'd help him forget his past, and he grasped her promise as a lifeline. "If you love me enough," he wrote back, "I'll have to forget it. How much can you love?"

———

As Cynthia worked on her parents, Louie went into wedding overdrive. He tracked down reception sites, invitations, a caterer, and a jeweler. He found the Church of Our Savior, which Cynthia had attended as a child. He bought a used Chevy convertible and overhauled it to impress Cynthia. Trying to make a new man of himself, he quit drinking and smoking. He took terminal leave from the air force, meaning that he formally ended active duty but would still wear his uniform and draw pay until his accumulated leave ran out in August, at which point he'd become a captain in the Air Force Reserve. He began a low-paying job at the Warner Brothers studios, teaching actors how to ride horses.

What he didn't have was a proper place to live. Because Los Angeles was teeming with repatriated soldiers, inexpensive housing was all but impossible to find, so Louie was still living with his parents. Cynthia wrote of how badly she wanted a home of her own, but Louie, in some distress, wrote back to explain that he didn't have the money. The best he could do was to move into the house that Harry Read shared with his mother and promise Cynthia that he'd do whatever he could to earn enough money for a home. He bought an air mattress for Cynthia; he'd sleep on the floor. After POW camp, he said, he didn't mind sleeping on floors.

The Applewhites' opposition to the marriage, the pressure to make a good life for Cynthia, and his black memories left Louie taut with stress. He had little appetite. He was emerging from years in which the only constants were violence and loss, and his letters show how much he feared something terrible befalling Cynthia. He clung to the thought of her as if, at any moment, she might be torn from his hands.

He was especially worried about her parents' views of him. He felt certain that they objected to him personally, finding his Italian ethnicity and middle-class origins repellent. He wrote earnest letters to her father, trying to win him over. When he kept seeing the same car parked by the Reads' house, he became convinced that it was a detective hired by Cynthia's father. According to Cynthia's brother, Ric, his parents had no objection to Louie, only to a hasty marriage. As for the spying, Ric said, such an act would be unlike his easygoing father, and would have made no sense, as Mr. Applewhite liked Louie. Right or wrong,

Louie's suspicions illustrated how sensitive he was to the idea that he was unworthy of Cynthia. Perhaps it wasn't the Applewhites he was trying to convince.

Six months after returning from Japan, Louie began to feel a familiar pull. It had just been announced that the summer Olympic Games, which hadn't been held since 1936, were set to return. They'd be held in London in July 1948. Louie's bad leg felt passably sound, and he finally felt healthy. He began testing himself with long hikes, borrowing a dog for company. The leg felt sturdy, the body strong. July of '48 was more than two years away. Louie began training.

In May, Cynthia and her parents made a deal. Cynthia could visit Louie, on the condition that they not marry until the fall, in a ceremony at the Applewhite mansion. Cynthia threw her clothes into a suitcase and went to the airport. As she left, her brother Ric felt a pang of worry. He was afraid that his young sister, dashing off to be with a man she hardly knew, might be making an enormous mistake.

At Burbank Airport on May 17, a plane stopped on the tarmac, the stairway unfolded, and Louie bounded up the steps to embrace Cynthia, then squired her home to meet his family. The Zamperinis fell for her, just as Louie had.

Driving away after the visit, Louie sensed that Cynthia was drawing backward. Maybe during the visit there had been a word or a look that hinted at all she didn't know, or maybe impulsive decisions made in the fog of lovesickness were becoming real. Whatever it was, Louie thought he was losing her. He lost his temper and abruptly said that maybe they should call off the engagement. Cynthia panicked, and they argued, overwrought. When they calmed down, they made a decision.

On Saturday, May 25, the same day that the papers quoted Louie as saying he'd marry Cynthia at the summer's end, Louie and Cynthia drove to the Church of Our Savior, where the Zamperinis were waiting. He wore his dress uniform; she wore a simple off-white suit. One of Louie's college buddies walked Cynthia down the aisle, and Louie and Cynthia said their vows. There had been no time to bake a wedding cake, so Pete's birthday cake, made by Sylvia the day before, did double duty.

Suspecting that Louie's friends would pull wedding night pranks, the newlyweds stole off to an obscure hotel, and Cynthia called home.

Her announcement prompted an explosion. Cynthia hung on the phone all evening, crying, while her mother, who'd gone to great effort to plan a fall wedding, bawled her out. Louie sat by, listening as his bride was excoriated for marrying him, trying in vain to get her to hang up. Eventually he picked up a bottle of champagne, popped it open, drank it dry, and went to sleep by himself.

Thirty-five

Coming Undone

FROM ACROSS THE ROOM, THEY LOOKED LIKE THREE OR-
dinary men. It was an evening in the latter half of 1946, and Louie
sat at a table in the Florentine Gardens, a dinner club in Hollywood,
with Cynthia nestled near him. Phil and Cecy had come from Indiana
for a visit, and Fred Garrett had motored across town to join them for
dinner. Phil and Louie were grinning at each other. The last time they'd
been together was March of '44, when Phil was being shipped out of
Ofuna and neither man knew if he'd live to see the other again.

The men smiled and talked. Fred, who was soon to become an air
traffic controller, had a new prosthetic leg. In a festive mood, he
bumped out to the dance floor to show the room that he could still cut
a rug. Phil and Cecy were about to move to New Mexico, where Phil
would open a plastics business. Louie and Cynthia were glowing from
their honeymoon, spent sharing a sleeping bag in Louie's beloved
mountains, where Cynthia, for all her finishing schools, had proven
game for getting dirty. Louie was running again, full of big plans, as
garrulous and breezy as he'd been before the war. As the men leaned together for photographs, all that they had been through seemed forgotten.

Sometime amid the laughing and conversation, a waiter set a plate in front of Fred. On it, beside the entrée, was a serving of white rice. That was all it took. Fred was suddenly raving, furious, hysterical, berating the waiter and shouting with such force that his face turned purple. Louie tried to calm him, but Fred was beyond consolation. He had come completely undone.

The waiter hurried the rice away and Fred pulled himself together, but the spell was broken. For these men, nothing was ever going to be the same.

At the end of World War II, thousands of former prisoners of the Japanese, known as Pacific POWs, began their postwar lives. Physically, almost every one of them was ravaged. The average army or army air forces Pacific POW had lost sixty-one pounds in captivity, a remarkable statistic given that roughly three-quarters of the men had weighed just 159 pounds or less upon enlistment. Tuberculosis, malaria, dysentery, malnutrition, anemia, eye ailments, and festering wounds were widespread. At one chain of hospitals, doctors found a history of wet beriberi in 77 percent of POWs and dry beriberi in half. Among Canadian POWs, 84 percent had neurologic damage. Respiratory diseases, from infections and exposure to unbreathable air in factories and mines, were rampant. Men had been crippled and disfigured by unset broken bones, and their teeth had been ruined by beatings and years of chewing grit in their food. Others had gone blind from malnutrition. Scores of men were so ill that they had to be carried from camps, and it was common for men to remain hospitalized for many months after repatriation. Some couldn't be saved.

The physical injuries were lasting, debilitating, and sometimes deadly. A 1954 study found that in the first two postwar years, former Pacific POWs died at almost four times the expected rate for men of their age, and continued to die at unusually high rates for many years. The health repercussions often lasted for decades; a follow-up study found that twenty-two years after the war, former Pacific POWs had hospitalization rates between two and eight times higher than former European POWs for a host of diseases.

As bad as were the physical consequences of captivity, the emotional injuries were much more insidious, widespread, and enduring. In the first six postwar years, one of the most common diagnoses given to hospitalized former Pacific POWs was psychoneurosis. Nearly forty years after the war, more than 85 percent of former Pacific POWs in one study suffered from post-traumatic stress disorder (PTSD), characterized in part by flashbacks, anxiety, and nightmares. And in a 1987 study, eight in ten former Pacific POWs had "psychiatric impairment," six in ten had anxiety disorders, more than one in four had PTSD, and nearly one in five was depressed. For some, there was only one way out: a 1970 study reported that former Pacific POWs committed suicide 30 percent more often than controls.

All of this illness, physical and emotional, took a shocking toll. Veterans were awarded compensation based on their level of disability, ranging from 10 percent to 100 percent. As of January 1953, one-third of former Pacific POWs were categorized as 50 to 100 percent disabled, nearly eight years after the war's end.

These statistics translated into tormented, and sometimes ruined, lives. Flashbacks, in which men reexperienced their traumas and were unable to distinguish the illusion from reality, were common. Intense nightmares were almost ubiquitous. Men walked in their sleep, acting out prison camp ordeals, and woke screaming, sobbing, or lashing out. Some slept on their floors because they couldn't sleep on mattresses, ducked in terror when airliners flew over, or hoarded food. One man had a recurrent hallucination of seeing his dead POW friends walking past. Another was unable to remember the war. Milton McMullen couldn't stop using Japanese terms, a habit that had been pounded into him. Dr. Alfred Weinstein, who had infected the Bird with dysentery at Mitsushima, was dogged by urges to scavenge in garbage cans.* Huge numbers of men escaped by drinking. In one study of former Pacific POWs, more than a quarter had been diagnosed with alcoholism.

Raymond "Hap" Halloran was a navigator who parachuted into Tokyo after his B-29 was shot down. Once on the ground, Halloran was beaten by a mob of civilians, then captured by Japanese authorities, who tortured him, locked him in a pig cage, and held him in a

---

* Returning home to the postwar housing shortage, Weinstein took out a $600,000 loan, built an apartment complex in Atlanta, and offered the 140 family units to veterans at rents averaging less than $50 per month. "Priorities: 1) Ex-POWs; 2) Purple Heart Vets; 3) Overseas Vets; 4) Vets; 5) Civilians," read his ad. ". . . We prefer Ex-GI's, and Marines and enlisted personnel of the Navy. Ex–Air Corps men may apply if they quit telling us how they won the war." His rule banning KKK members drew threatening phone calls. "I gave them my office and my home address," Weinstein said, "and told them I still had the .45 I used to shoot carabau [water buffalo] with."

burning horse stall during the firebombings. They stripped him naked and him on display at Tokyo's Ueno Zoo, tied upright in an empty tiger cage so civilians could gawk at his filthy, sore-encrusted body. He was starved so severely that he lost one hundred pounds.

After liberation and eight months in a hospital, Halloran went home to Cincinnati. "I was not the same 19-year-old Raymond whose mother kissed him goodbye that fall morning in 1942," he wrote. He was intensely nervous and wary of anything approaching him from behind. He couldn't sleep with his arms covered, fearing that he'd need to fight off attackers. He had horrific nightmares, and would wake running in his yard, shouting for help. He avoided hotels because his screaming upset other guests. More than sixty years after the war, he was still plagued by "poor inventory control," keeping eight pillows and six clocks in his bedroom, buying far more clothes and supplies than he'd ever need, and stockpiling bulk packages of food. And yet Halloran was fortunate. Of the five survivors of his crew, two drank themselves to death.*

Some former POWs became almost feral with rage. For many men, seeing an Asian person or overhearing a snippet of Japanese left them shaking, weeping, enraged, or lost in flashbacks. One former POW, normally gentle and quiet, spat at every Asian person he saw. At Letterman General Hospital just after the war, four former POWs tried to attack a staffer who was of Japanese ancestry, not knowing that he was an American veteran.

Troubled former POWs found nowhere to turn. McMullen came out of Japan racked by nightmares and so nervous that he was barely able to speak cogently. When he told his story to his family, his father accused him of lying and forbade him to speak of the war. Shattered and deeply depressed, McMullen couldn't eat, and his weight plunged back down to ninety pounds. He went to a veterans' hospital, but the doctors simply gave him B_{12} shots. As he recounted his experiences to a military official, the official picked up a phone and began talking with someone else. After two years, McMullen got his feet under him again, but he would never really recover. Sixty years after VJ Day, his dreams

---

* As Halloran parachuted over Tokyo, the Zero that had shot him down sped toward him, and Halloran was certain that he was going to be strafed, as so many falling airmen were. But instead of firing, the pilot saluted him. After the war, Halloran and that pilot, Isamu Kashiide, became dear friends.

still carried him back to the camps. Recounting his war experiences was so painful that it would leave him off-kilter for weeks.

The Pacific POWs who went home in 1945 were torn-down men. They had an intimate understanding of man's vast capacity to experience suffering, as well as his equally vast capacity, and hungry willingness, to inflict it. They carried unspeakable memories of torture and humiliation, and an acute sense of vulnerability that attended the knowledge of how readily they could be disarmed and dehumanized. Many felt lonely and isolated, having endured abuses that ordinary people couldn't understand. Their dignity had been obliterated, replaced with a pervasive sense of shame and worthlessness. And they had the caustic knowledge that no one had come between them and tragedy. Coming home was an experience of profound, perilous aloneness.

For these men, the central struggle of postwar life was to restore their dignity and find a way to see the world as something other than menacing blackness. There was no one right way to peace; every man had to find his own path, according to his own history. Some succeeded. For others, the war would never really end. Some retreated into brooding isolation or lost themselves in escapes. And for some men, years of swallowed rage, terror, and humiliation concentrated into what Holocaust survivor Jean Améry would call "a seething, purifying thirst for revenge."

———

The honeymoon in the mountains had been Cynthia's idea. Louie loved her for being so sporting, and for choosing something so dear to his heart. "You must look about you and remember what the trees + hills, streams + lakes look like," he wrote to her before their wedding. ". . . I will see you among them for life." Drifting off beside Cynthia each night, Louie still saw the Bird lurking in his dreams, but the sergeant hung back as if cowed, or perhaps just waiting. It was the closest thing to peace that Louie had known since *Green Hornet* had hit the water.

The drive back to Los Angeles carried them from the great wide open to the confines of Harry Read's mother's house. Cynthia was uncomfortable living there, and Louie wanted to give her the home she dreamed of. He needed to find a career, but was unprepared to do so. Having left USC a few credits short, he had no college degree, a critical asset in a job market glutted with veterans and former war production workers. Like many elite athletes, he had focused on his sport through-

Cynthia Zamperini on her honeymoon.
Courtesy of Louis Zamperini

out his school years and had never seriously contemplated life after running. Now nearly thirty, he had no idea what to do for a living.

He made no effort to find a real career or a nine-to-five, salaried job. His celebrity drew people into his orbit, many of them hawking ventures in which he could invest his life insurance payoff, which he'd been allowed to keep. He went to military-surplus sales, bought Quonset huts, and resold them to movie studios. He did the same with iceboxes, then invested in a telephone technology. He turned respectable profits, but each investment quickly ran its course. He did, however, earn a steady enough income to rent an apartment for himself and Cynthia. It was only a tiny place in a low-rent quarter of Hollywood, but Cynthia did her best to make it homey.

At the end of his first day in the new apartment, Louie slid into bed, closed his eyes, and fell into a dream. As always, the Bird was there, but he was no longer hesitant. The sergeant towered over Louie, the belt flicking from his hand, lashing Louie's face. Every night, he returned, and Louie was helpless once again, unable to flee him or drive him away.

Louie threw himself into training. His long hikes became runs. His strength was coming back, and his dodgy leg gave him no pain. He took it slowly, thinking always of London in '48. He was aiming for the 1,500 meters, and assured himself that if he couldn't make it, he'd return to the 5,000, or even the steeplechase. But without extending himself, he began clocking miles in 4:18, just two seconds slower than the winning time of the Zamperini Invitational that he'd seen in March. He was coming all the way back.

But running wasn't the same. Once he had felt liberated by it; now it felt forced. Running was joyless, but Louie had no other answer to his internal turmoil. He doubled his workouts, and his body answered.

One day, with Cynthia standing by, holding a stopwatch, Louie set off to see how fast he could turn two miles. Early on, he felt a pulse of pain dart across his left ankle, just where it had been injured at Naoetsu. He knew better than to keep pushing, but pushing was all he knew now. As he completed the first mile, barbs of pain were crackling through his ankle. On he went, running for London.

Late in his last lap, there was an abrupt slicing sensation in his ankle. He half-hopped to the line and collapsed. His time was the fastest two-mile run on the Pacific coast in 1946, but it didn't matter. He was unable to walk for a week, and would limp for weeks more. A doctor confirmed that he had disastrously exacerbated his war injury. It was all over.

Louie was wrecked. The quest that had saved him as a kid was lost to him. The last barricade within him fell. By day, he couldn't stop thinking about the Bird. By night, the sergeant lashed him, hungry and feral. As the belt whipped him, Louie would fight his way to his attacker's throat and close his hands around it. No matter how hard he squeezed, those eyes still danced at him. Louie regularly woke screaming and soaked in sweat. He was afraid to sleep.

He started smoking again. There seemed no reason not to drink, so each evening, he swigged wine as he cooked, leaving Cynthia sitting through dinner with a tipsy husband. Invitations to clubs kept coming, and now it seemed harmless to accept the free drinks that were always offered. At first he drank just beer; then he dipped into hard liquor. If he got drunk enough, he could drown the war for a time. He soon began drinking so much that he passed out, but he welcomed it; passing out saved him from having to go to bed and wait for his monster. Unable to talk him into giving it up, Cynthia stopped going out with him. He left her alone each night while he went out to lose the war.

Rage, wild, random, and impossible to quell, began to consume him. Once he harassed a man for walking too slowly on a crosswalk in front of his car, and the man spat at him. Louie gunned the car to the curb, jumped out, and, as Cynthia screamed for him to stop, punched the man until he fell to the ground. On another day, when a man at a bar accidentally let a door swing into him, Louie chested up to him and provoked an embarrassing little scuffle that ended with Louie grinding the man's face in the dirt.

His mind began to derail. While sitting at a bar, he heard a sudden, loud sound, perhaps a car backfiring. Before he knew it, he was on the floor, cringing, as the bar fell silent and the patrons stared. On another night, he was drinking, his mind drifting, when someone nearby yelled something while joking with friends. In Louie's mind, it was *"Keirei!"* He found himself jumping up, back straight, head up, heart pounding, awaiting the flying belt buckle. In a moment the illusion cleared and he saw that, again, everyone in the bar was looking at him. He felt foolish and humiliated.

One day Louie was overcome by a strange, inexplicable feeling, and suddenly the war was all around and in him, not a memory but the actual *experience*—the glaring and grating and stench and howl and terror of it. In a moment he was jerked back out again, confused and frightened. It was his first flashback. After that, if he caught a glimpse of blood or saw a tussle in a bar, everything would reassemble itself as prison camp, and the mood, the light, the sounds, his own body, would all be as they were, inescapable. In random moments, he felt lice and fleas wriggling over his skin when there was nothing there. It only made him drink harder.

Cynthia urged Louie to get help, so he went, reluctantly, to see a counselor at a veterans' hospital. He spoke of the war and the nightmares, and came home feeling as turbulent as when he'd left. After two or three sessions, he quit.

One day he opened a newspaper and saw a story that riveted his attention. A former Pacific POW had walked into a store and seen one of his wartime captors. The POW had called the police, who'd arrested the alleged war criminal. As Louie read the story, all of the fury within him converged. He saw himself finding the Bird, overpowering him, his fists bloodying the face, and then his hands locking about the Bird's neck. In his fantasy, he killed the Bird slowly, savoring the suffering he caused, making his tormentor feel all of the pain and terror and helplessness that he'd felt. His veins beat with an electric urgency.

Louie had no idea what had become of the Bird, but he felt sure that if he could get back to Japan, he could hunt him down. This would be his emphatic reply to the Bird's unremitting effort to extinguish his humanity: *I am still a man.* He could conceive of no other way to save himself.

Louie had found a quest to replace his lost Olympics. He was going to kill the Bird.

Thirty-six

The Body on the Mountain

IT WAS THE FIRST WINTER AFTER THE WAR. AN AGED POLICE officer trudged through a village high in the mountains of Japan's Nagano Prefecture, knocking on doors, asking questions, and moving on. The Ministry of Home Affairs, frustrated at the failure to track down Mutsuhiro Watanabe, was renewing its effort, sending out photographs of and reports on the fugitive to every police chief in Japan. Chiefs were under orders to report twice a month on their progress. Police officers conducted searches and interrogations nearly every day. In one prefecture alone, 9,100 officers were involved in the search for him. The officer in Nagano was part of this effort.

It was around noon when he reached the largest house in the village, home to a farmer and his family. Someone answered the door, and the family, thinking that he was a census taker, invited him in. Inside, the policeman found an old, portly farmer, the farmer's wife, and their live-in laborer. As the laborer prepared a plate of pickles and a cup of tea, a traditional offering to visitors, the officer pulled out a photograph of Watanabe, dressed in his sergeant's uniform. Did they recognize the man? None of them did.

The officer left, moving on to a neighbor. He had no idea that the fugitive he was seeking had just been standing right in front of him, holding a plate of pickles.

The Bird had come to Nagano Prefecture the previous September, after having fled his brother's home, then Kofu. Reaching the hot springs resort community of Manza Spa, he'd checked into an inn. He chose an alias, Saburo Ohta, a common name unlikely to attract notice or dwell in anyone's memory. He had a mustache, which he'd begun growing in the last days of the war. He told people that he was a refugee from Tokyo whose relatives were all dead, a story that, in postwar Japan, was as common as white rice. He vowed to live by two imperatives: silence and patience.

Manza was a good choice, trafficked by crowds in which Watanabe could lose himself. But he soon began to think that he'd be better hidden in the prefecture's remote mountain regions. He met the old farmer and offered himself as a laborer in exchange for room and board. The farmer took him to his home in the rural village, and Watanabe settled in as a farmhand.

Each night, lying on a straw mat on the farmer's floor, Watanabe couldn't sleep. All over Japan, war-crimes suspects had been captured, and were now imprisoned, awaiting trials. He'd known some of these men. They'd be tried, sentenced, some executed. He was free. On the pages on which he poured out his emotions about his plight, Watanabe wrote of feeling guilty when he thought of those soldiers. He also mulled over his behavior toward the POWs, describing himself as "powerful" and "strict when requesting [POWs] to obey the rules." "Am I guilty?" he wrote. He didn't answer his question, but he also expressed no remorse. Even as he wrote of his gratitude for the humanity of the farmer who had taken him in, he couldn't see the parallel with himself and the helpless men who had fallen into his hands.

The radio in the farmer's house was often on, and each day, Watanabe listened to reports on fugitive war-crimes suspects. He scanned the faces of his hosts as the stories aired, worried that they'd suspect him. The newspapers, too, were full of articles on these fugitives, described as "enemies of human beings." The pronouncements wounded Watanabe's feelings. It seemed to him outrageous that the Allies, who "would not forgive," would oversee trials of Japanese. God alone, he felt, was qualified to judge him. "I wanted to cry out," he wrote, " 'That's not fair!' "

The tension of living incognito wore on him. He was especially wary of the farmer's wife, whose gaze seemed to convey suspicion. Sleep came so reluctantly that he had to work himself to exhaustion to bring it on. He brooded on the question of whether or not he should surrender.

One night, as the evening's fire died in the hearth, Watanabe came to the farmer and told him who he was. The farmer listened, his eyes fixed on the fire, his tongue clicking against his false teeth.

"People say to control your mouth, or it brings evil," the farmer said. "You should be careful of your speech."

He said nothing else and turned away.

———

As the Bird hid, other men who had abused POWs were arrested, taken to Sugamo Prison, in Tokyo, and tried for war crimes. Roughly 5,400 Japanese were tried by the United States and other nations; some 4,400 were convicted, including 984 given death sentences and 475 given life in prison.* More than 30 Ofuna personnel were convicted and sentenced to a total of roughly 350 years in prison. The thieving cook, Tatsumi "Curley" Hata, was sentenced to twenty years. Masajiro "Shithead" Hirayabashi, who'd beaten countless prisoners and killed Gaga the duck, was given four years. Commander Kakuzo Iida, "the Mummy," was sentenced to death for contributing to the deaths of five captives. Also convicted was Sueharu Kitamura—"the Quack"—who had mutilated his patients, bludgeoned Harris, and contributed to the deaths of four captives, including one who was carried from Ofuna at the war's end, hours from death, crying out *"Quack"* over and over again. Kitamura was sentenced to hang.

Kaname Sakaba, the Omori commander, was given a life sentence. Of the men from Naoetsu, six civilian guards were tried, convicted, and hanged. Seven Japanese soldiers were also convicted: two were hanged, four given life imprisonment with hard labor, and one given twenty years.

The police found Jimmie Sasaki working as a liaison between the Japanese navy and the occupying forces. Ever a fabulist, he told investigators that Ofuna interrogators were "always kind to prisoners," that he'd never seen a prisoner abused, and that prisoners rarely complained. In questioning, the truth about his position at Ofuna finally

* Some death sentences were later commuted; 920 men were eventually executed.

emerged. He had not been the chief interrogator, bearing a rank equal to admiral, that he had claimed to be; he'd been only a low-ranking interpreter. This man of ever-shifting allegiances tried to shift them again, speaking of his debt to America and asking if someone could get him a job with the U.S. Army. Instead of a job, he received an indictment, charged with ordering the abuse of several captives, including one who'd been starved and tortured to death. Though the trial testimony seemed to raise enormous doubt as to his guilt, Sasaki was convicted and ultimately sentenced to six years of hard labor.

And so the strange and twisting war journey of Louie's onetime friend ended in Sugamo Prison, where he was a model prisoner, tending a vegetable garden and a grove of trees. Who Jimmie Sasaki really was—whether artful spy and willing instrument in Japan's machine of violence or something more innocent—remains a mystery.

Of the postwar stories of the men who ran the camps in which Louie had lived, the saddest was that of Yukichi Kano, the Omori private who'd risked everything to protect the POWs and had probably saved several prisoners' lives. Just after the war's end was announced, Kano came upon a group of drunken guards stumbling toward the barracks, swords drawn, determined to hack some captured B-29 men to death. Kano and another man planted themselves in the guards' path and, after a brief scuffle, stopped them. Kano was a hero, but when the Americans came to liberate the camp, two of them tried to rip the insignia off his uniform. Bob Martindale stepped in and gave the Americans a furious dressing-down. Fearing that Kano might be mistakenly accused of war crimes, Martindale and several other POW officers wrote a letter of commendation for him before they went home.

It did no good. Kano was arrested and jailed as a suspected war criminal. Why he was fingered remains unclear. He was mentioned in many POW affidavits and, in every one, was lauded for his kindness. Perhaps the explanation was that his last name was similar to those of two vicious men, Tetsutaro Kato, an Omori official said to have kicked a POW nearly to death, and Hiroaki Kono, the Bird's acolyte at Naoetsu. Months passed, and Kano languished in prison, frightened and humiliated. He was neither charged nor questioned. He wrote a plaintive letter asking authorities to investigate him so his name could be cleared. "Cross my heart," he wrote, "I have not done anything wrong."

In the winter of 1946, Kano was finally cleared, and MacArthur ordered his release. Kano moved to Yokohama and worked for an import-export business. He missed his POW friends, but for years, he didn't try to contact them. "I thought I should refrain from writing them," he wrote to Martindale in 1955, "as my letter might make them to remind up the hard days in Omori, which, I am sure, they would like to forget." Sometime later, he died of cancer.

In the mountain village where he was known as Saburo Ohta, Watanabe waited out a bitter winter. The visit from the policeman shook him. After the policeman left, the farmer's wife eyed Watanabe with what seemed to be recognition. When night fell, Watanabe lay awake, mulling capture and execution.

When summer came, Watanabe was asked to attend the farmer's son as he toured the country, selling leather straps. The tour would take them through major cities where Watanabe was surely being sought, but he was living on the good graces of the farmer and had to accept. Watanabe donned glasses to obscure his features and headed off, filled with trepidation.

They went to the busy port cities of Akita and Niigata. No one gave Watanabe a second look. As his fear of being discovered eased, he began enjoying himself. The conversation in the cities was dominated by the war, and everyone had an opinion about the conduct of Japanese soldiers, especially those accused of war crimes. People talked of how the hunt for suspected war criminals was being conducted. Watanabe listened intently.

Being out in society made him long to see his family. He thought of how his mother would now be in Tokyo, on her regular summer visit to his sister Michiko's home. The yearning was overpowering. Watanabe took out the fortune-telling cards that his little sister had given him and dealt himself a hand. The cards told him that if he went to his family, he'd be safe. On a sweltering day at the height of the summer of 1946, he boarded a train for Tokyo.

His timing couldn't have been worse. The winter's push to find Watanabe had yielded no clues, and the police were again doubling their efforts. A newly discovered photograph of Watanabe had been copied and distributed, along with a report that described him as a man "known to have perversions" who might be found "wherever there are loose women." Since Japanese citizens were required to register changes of address, police were ordered to pore over registries in search of men traveling alone. They were instructed to monitor transactions at ration boards and prowl post offices, train and bus stations, taxi stands, ferry landings, mines, black market outlets, dive hotels and lodging houses, and any businesses that might attract a man fluent in French. Probably inspired by the clue that Watanabe might have committed suicide, police moved to investigate all unnatural and unusual deaths since November 1945, especially those in which the deceased person was unidentified. As a homesick Watanabe journeyed out of hiding and into Tokyo, he was walking into the manhunt.

Shizuka Watanabe was sitting in Michiko's house with two of her other children when the front door swung open and in walked Mutsuhiro. The room fell silent as the startled family members looked at Mutsuhiro and then at one another. Mutsuhiro, emotionally overwhelmed and dizzy from the midday heat, wavered, afraid he would faint. Michiko came in and saw her brother. The family broke into celebration.

For two hours, Mutsuhiro sat with his family, sipping drinks and listening to them tell of being arrested, questioned, followed, and searched. He said nothing of where he'd been, believing that his family would fare better if they didn't know. As time passed, the family members grew anxious, afraid that the detectives would catch them. They'd been there just two days previously. At two o'clock, Shizuka warned Mutsuhiro that it was the time of day when the detectives usually came to search. Mutsuhiro reassured them that the playing cards had told him that all would be well.

There was shuffling outside. The detectives had arrived. The Watanabes sprang up. Someone tossed Mutsuhiro's belongings into a closet. Someone else snatched up the cups and dumped them in the sink. Mutsuhiro raced into a tearoom and shut the door. Behind him, he heard footfalls as a group of detectives entered the room that he had just left. He heard them questioning his mother and sister, telling them that if they caught Mutsuhiro, he'd be treated well.

The detectives were just feet away, on the other side of the door. His heart racing, Mutsuhiro tried to decide whether to run or to conceal himself here. The room was tiny, scattered with pillows, but there was a closet. Ever so slowly, he inched open the closet's sliding door and squeezed inside. He decided not to close the door, fearing that it would make noise. He stood there, a hand clasped over his mouth to smother the sound of his breathing.

The door opened. A detective looked in. "You have plenty of room," he said to the family. There was a pause as he looked about. If the detective turned his eyes toward the closet, he'd see Mutsuhiro. "It is tidy," the detective said. The door closed. The detectives left.

Mutsuhiro had wished to stay overnight, but the close call changed his mind. He told his mother that he'd try to see her again in two years. Then he left, walking back, he wrote, "into the lonesome world."

Watanabe returned to the village. The farmer's son, unable to make a go of his leather strap sales, opened a coffee shop in the village. Watanabe became his waiter.

The farmer approached Watanabe with a proposition. Arranged marriage was still common in Japan, and the farmer had found a match for him. Watanabe was tempted; he was lonely and unhappy, and liked the idea of marrying. But marriage while in his predicament seemed impossible. He said no.

The young woman eventually came to him. When the farmer's son fell ill, she paid him a visit, and Watanabe, curious, went into the sick-room to see her. He raised the subject of the novel that the farmer's son was reading, thinking that, he wrote, "if she liked books, she must understand the mind and hardship of human life." In his notes about the meeting, he didn't say if she possessed that understanding, but he did seem to like her and thought she would be "a good house-keeper." Part of him seemed to want to fall for her, and he believed that love "could save my daily life."

The woman was taken with the attractive waiter, and began lingering in the coffee shop to be near him. He kept his identity secret from her. She began telling her parents about him in hopes of winning their blessing for a wedding. After brooding on her, Watanabe decided that he had to end the relationship. All he told her was that he had "a burden which would make her unhappy."

With that, he broke with the tenuous existence that he had created in the village. He quit his job and left. He wandered onto a stretch of the Nagano grassland along the Chikuma River and took a job as a cowherd. His inability to control the willful animals exasperated him. He was despondent. At sunset, he lifted his eyes to the majestic Asama

volcano, watching a ribbon of smoke unspooling from her upper
reaches, the cattle grazing below.

———

In Japan's Okuchichibu Mountains stands the holy peak of Mitsumine,
its sides fleeced in forest, its summit ornamented with an ancient
shrine. In the fall of 1946, two bodies were found amid the hollows
and spines of the mountain, a pistol lying with them. One was a man,
the other a woman. No one knew who they were.

The police went to Shizuka Watanabe and asked her and her family
to accompany them to the mountain. The Watanabes were driven up to
Mitsumine and, with the help of guides, taken to the bodies. Shizuka
looked down at the lifeless form of the young man.

Japanese newspapers ran the sensational story: Mutsuhiro Watanabe, one of Japan's most wanted men, was dead. He and a woman,
probably a lover, had killed themselves.

Thirty-seven

Twisted Ropes

LOUIE KNEW NOTHING OF THE DEATH OF THE BIRD. WHEN the bodies were found on Mount Mitsumine, he was in Hollywood, falling to pieces. He was drinking heavily, slipping in and out of flashbacks, screaming and clawing through nightmares, lashing out in fury at random moments. Murdering the Bird had become his secret, fevered obsession, and he had given his life over to it. In a gym near his apartment, he spent hours slamming his hatred into a punching bag, preparing his body for the confrontation that he believed would save him. He walked around every day with murder in his head.

Throughout 1947 and 1948, Louie jumped headlong into scheme after scheme to raise the money to get back to Japan. When Cynthia's brother Ric visited, he found Louie encircled by fawners and hangers-on, all trying to exploit him. One of them talked Louie into investing $7,000 in a plan to purchase and resell earthmoving equipment in the Philippines, promising to double his money. Louie signed the check, and that was the last he saw of either the investor or his money. He formed a Tahitian passenger-boat company in partnership, but creditors took the boat. A deal to found a movie production company in Egypt met a similar end. He even considered working as a mercenary bombardier in an attempted coup in a small Caribbean country, and was still thinking it over when the coup was called off. He and a partner made a verbal agreement with Mexican officials, giving them sole authority to issue fishing licenses to Americans. As his partner drove down to ink the deal, a truck hit him head-on, and the deal died with him. Each time Louie got some money together, it was lost in another failed venture, and his return to Japan had to be put off still longer.

Drinking granted him a space of time in which to let it all go. Slowly, inexorably, he'd gone from drinking because he wanted it to drinking because he needed it. In the daytime, he kept sober, but in the evenings, as the prospect of sleep and nightmares loomed, he was overcome by the need. His addiction was soon so consuming that when he and Cynthia went to Florida to visit her family, he insisted on bringing home so much liquor that he had to take out his Chevy's back seat to fit it all in.

He had become someone he didn't recognize. One night at a bar on Sunset Boulevard, he parked himself on a stool, drank all evening, and wound up stinking drunk. A man passed behind him, ushering his date past. Louie swung around, reached out, and groped the woman's bottom. The next thing Louie knew, he was on his feet, outside, being half-carried by a friend. His jaw was thumping with pain, and his friend was chewing him out. He slowly came to understand that the woman's boyfriend had knocked him unconscious.

On another night, he left Cynthia at home and went to a restaurant in Hollywood with two friends from his running days. Sometime in the early evening, after drinking what he would remember as only a single beer, he felt oddly light and excused himself to step outside. Then time broke into disconnected segments. He was in his car, driving, with no idea where he was or how he'd gotten there. He wove through the streets, disoriented, and came into a hilly neighborhood of mansions and broad lawns. His head spun round and round. He stopped the car and rolled out. There was a tree in front of him, and he relieved himself against it.

When he turned back for his car, he couldn't find it. He stumbled along in a soupy darkness and mental fog, searching in vain for something familiar. He walked all night long, scared, lost, and vainly grasping at lucidity.

As sunrise lit up his surroundings, he realized that he was standing in front of his apartment building. Opening the door, he saw Cynthia, frantic with worry. He toppled into bed. When he woke up and dressed,

Cynthia Zamperini.
Frank Tinker

he had no memory of the night before, and couldn't understand why the heels of his new shoes were worn down. He went outside and looked around, but he couldn't find his car, so he called the police and reported it stolen. Two days later, the police called to tell him that they'd found the car in a wealthy neighborhood in the Hollywood Hills. He went up to where they had found it, and memories of his night came back to him, carrying the ethereal quality of a nightmare.

Cynthia pleaded with Louie to stop drinking. It did no good.

The further Louie fell, the less he could hide it. Ric Applewhite noticed that he was manically germophobic, washing his hands over and over again, and each time, scouring the faucet and handles on the sink. Some of Louie's friends spoke to him about his drinking, but their words had no impact. When Payton Jordan saw Louie, he recognized that he was in trouble, but couldn't get him to talk about it. Pete, too, was worried about Louie, but knew only of his financial woes. He had no idea that Louie had slid into alcoholism, or that he had hatched a wild scheme to kill a man.

Cynthia was distraught over what her husband had become. In public, his behavior was frightening and embarrassing. In private, he was often prickly and harsh with her. She did her best to soothe him, to no avail. Once, while Louie was out, she painted their dreary kitchen with elaborate illustrations of vines and animals, hoping to surprise him. He didn't notice.

Wounded and worried, Cynthia couldn't bring Louie back. Her pain became anger, and she and Louie had bitter fights. She slapped him and threw dishes at him; he grabbed her so forcefully that he left her bruised. Once he came home to find that she had run through a room, hurling everything breakable onto the floor. While Cynthia cooked dinner during a party on a friend's docked yacht, Louie was so snide to her, right in front of their friends, that she walked off the boat. He chased her down and grabbed her by the neck. She slapped his face, and he let her go. She fled to his parents' house, and he went home alone.

Cynthia eventually came back, and the two struggled on together. His money gone, Louie had to tap a friend for a $1,000 loan, staking his Chevy convertible as collateral. The money ran out, another investment foundered, the loan came due, and Louie had to turn over his keys.

When Louie was a small child, he had tripped and fallen on a flight of stairs while hurrying to school. He had gotten up, only to stumble and fall a second time, then a third. He had risen convinced that God himself was tripping him. Now the same thought dwelt in him. God, he believed, was toying with him. When he heard preaching on the radio, he angrily turned it off. He forbade Cynthia from going to church.

In the spring of 1948, Cynthia told Louie that she was pregnant. Louie was excited, but the prospect of more responsibility filled him with guilt and despair. In London that summer, Sweden's Henry Eriksson won the Olympic gold medal in the 1,500 meters. In Hollywood, Louie drank ever harder.

No one could reach Louie, because he had never really come home. In prison camp, he'd been beaten into dehumanized obedience to a world order in which the Bird was absolute sovereign, and it was under this world order that he still lived. The Bird had taken his dignity and left him feeling humiliated, ashamed, and powerless, and Louie believed that only the Bird could restore him, by suffering and dying in the grip of his hands. A once singularly hopeful man now believed that his only hope lay in murder.

The paradox of vengefulness is that it makes men dependent upon those who have harmed them, believing that their release from pain will come only when they make their tormentors suffer. In seeking the Bird's death to free himself, Louie had chained himself, once again, to his tyrant. During the war, the Bird had been unwilling to let go of Louie; after the war, Louie was unable to let go of the Bird.

One night in late 1948, Louie lay in bed with Cynthia beside him. He descended into a dream, and the Bird rose up over him. The belt un-

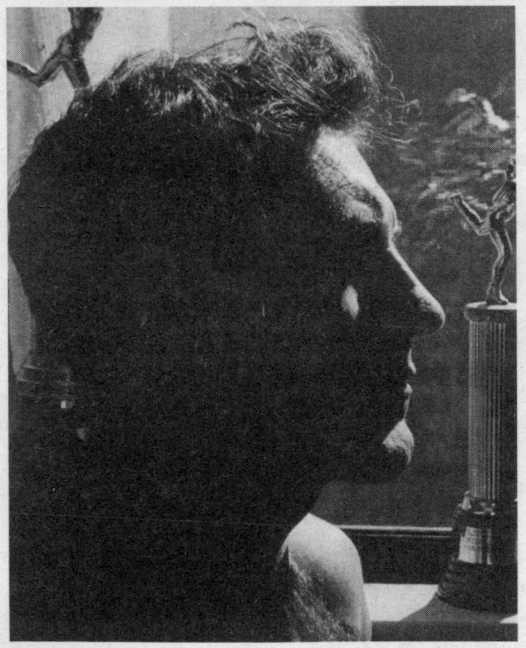

Louie, after the war.
Frank Tinker

furled, and Louie felt the buckle cracking into his head, pain like lightning over his temple. Around and around the belt whirled, lashing Louie's skull. Louie raised his hands to the Bird's throat, his hands clenching around it. Now Louie was on top of the Bird, and the two thrashed.

There was a scream, perhaps Louie's, perhaps the Bird's. Louie fought on, trying to crush the life out of the Bird. Then everything began to alter. Louie, on his knees with the Bird under him, looked down. The Bird's shape shifted.

Louie was straddling Cynthia's chest, his hands locked around her neck. Through her closing throat, she was screaming. Louie was strangling his pregnant wife.

He let go and leapt off Cynthia. She recoiled, gasping, crying out. He sat in the dark beside her, horrified, his nightclothes heavy with sweat. The sheets were twisted into ropes around him.

Little Cynthia Zamperini, nicknamed Cissy, was born two weeks after Christmas. Louie was so enraptured that he wouldn't let anyone else hold her, and did all the diapering himself. But she couldn't cleave him from alcoholism or his murderous obsession. In the sleepless stress of caring for a newborn, Louie and Cynthia fought constantly and furiously. When Cynthia's mother came to help, she wept at the sight of the apartment. Louie drank without restraint.

One day Cynthia came home to find Louie gripping a squalling Cissy in his hands, shaking her. With a shriek, she pulled the baby away. Appalled at himself, Louie went on bender after bender. Cynthia had had enough. She called her father, and he sent her the money to go back to Miami Beach. She decided to file for divorce.

Cynthia packed her things, took the baby, and walked out. Louie was alone. All he had left was his alcohol and his resentment, the emotion that, Jean Améry would write, "nails every one of us onto the cross of his ruined past."

On the other side of the world, early one evening in the fading days of 1948, Shizuka Watanabe sat on the lower floor of a two-story restaurant in Tokyo's Shinjuku district. Outside, the street was lively with shoppers and diners. Shizuka faced the door, watching the blur of faces drifting past.

It was there that she saw him. Just outside the door, gazing in at her amid the passersby, was her dead son.

Thirty-eight

A Beckoning Whistle

F OR SHIZUKA WATANABE, THE MOMENT WHEN SHE SAW HER son must have answered a desperate hope. Two years earlier, she'd been driven up a mountain to see a dead man who looked just like Mutsuhiro. Everyone, even her relatives, had believed it was he, and the newspapers had announced Mutsuhiro's suicide. But Shizuka had felt a trace of doubt. Perhaps she'd registered the same sensation that Louise Zamperini had felt when Louie was missing, a maternal murmur that told her that her son was still alive. She apparently said nothing of her doubts in public, but in secret, she clung to a promise that Mutsuhiro had made when he had last seen her, in Tokyo in the summer of '46: On October 1, 1948, at seven P.M., he'd try to meet her at a restaurant in the Shinjuku district of Tokyo.

While she waited for that day, others began to question whether Mutsuhiro was really dead. Someone looked up the serial number on his army sidearm and found that it was different from that of the gun found beside the body. Mutsuhiro could easily have used another weapon, but an examination of the body had also found some features that seemed different from those of the fugitive. The detectives couldn't rule out Watanabe as the dead man, but they couldn't confirm definitively that it was he. The search for him resumed, and the police descended again on the Watanabes.

Tailed almost everywhere she went, her mail searched, her friends and family interrogated, Shizuka endured intense scrutiny for two years. When October 1, 1948, came, she went to the restaurant, apparently eluding her pursuers. There was her son, a living ghost.

The sight of him brought as much fear as joy. She knew that in appearing in public, standing in full view of crowds of people who had surely all heard of the manhunt for him, he was taking a huge risk. She spoke to him for only a few minutes, standing very close to him, trying to restrain the excitement in her voice. Mutsuhiro, his face grave, questioned her about the police's tactics. He told her nothing about where he was living or what he was doing. Concerned that they would attract attention, mother and son decided to part. Mutsuhiro said that he'd see her again in two years, then slipped out the door.

The police didn't know of the meeting, and continued to stalk Shizuka and her children. Everyone who visited them was tailed and investigated. Each time Shizuka ran errands, detectives trailed behind her. After she left each business, they went in to question those who had dealt with her. Shizuka was frequently interrogated, but she answered questions about her son's whereabouts by referring to the suicides on Mount Mitsumine.

More than a year passed. Shizuka heard nothing from her son, and the detectives found nothing. Everywhere there were rumors about his fate. In one, he had fled across the China Sea and disappeared in Manchuria. One had him shot by American GIs; another had him being struck and killed by a train after an American soldier tied him to the track. But the most persistent stories ended in his suicide, by gunshot, by *hara-kiri* in front of the emperor's palace, by a leap into a volcano. For nearly everyone who had known him, there was only one plausible conclusion to draw from the failure of the massive search.

Whether Shizuka believed these rumors is unknown. But in his last meeting with her, Mutsuhiro had given her one very troubling clue: I will meet you in two years, he had said, *if I am alive.*

In the second week of September 1949, an angular young man climbed down from a transcontinental train and stepped into Los Angeles. His remarkably tall blond hair fluttered on the summit of a remarkably tall head, which in turn topped a remarkably tall body. He had a direct gaze, a stern jawline, and a southern sway in his voice, the product of a childhood spent on a North Carolina dairy farm. His name was Billy Graham.

At thirty-one, Graham was the youngest college president in America, manning the helm at Northwestern Schools, a small Christian Bible school, liberal arts college, and seminary in Minneapolis. He was also the vice president of Youth for Christ International, an evangelical organization. He'd been crisscrossing the world for years, plugging his faith. The results had been mixed. His last campaign, in the Pennsylvania coal town of Altoona, had met with heckling, meager attendance, and a hollering, deranged choir member who had had to be thrown out of his services, only to return repeatedly, like a fly to spilled jelly. So much coal dust had billowed through the town that Graham had left it with his eyes burning and bloodshot.

That September, in a vacant parking lot on the corner of Washington Boulevard and Hill Street in Los Angeles, Graham and his small team threw up a 480-foot-long circus tent, set out sixty-five hundred folding chairs, poured down acres of sawdust, hammered together a stage the size of a fairly spacious backyard, and stood an enormous replica of an open Bible in front of it. They held a press conference to announce a three-week campaign to bring Los Angelenos to Christ. Not a single newspaper story followed.

At first, Graham preached to a half-empty tent. But his blunt, emphatic sermons got people talking. By October 16, the day on which he had intended to close the campaign, attendance was high and growing. Graham and his team decided to keep it going. Then newspaper magnate William Randolph Hearst reportedly issued a two-word order to his editors: "Puff Graham." Overnight, Graham had adoring press coverage and ten thousand people packing into his tent every night. Organizers expanded the tent and piled in several thousand more chairs, but it was still so overcrowded that hundreds of people had to stand in the street, straining to hear Graham over the traffic. Film moguls, seeing leading-man material, offered Graham a movie contract. Graham burst out laughing and told them he wouldn't do it for a million bucks a month. In a city that wasn't bashful about sinning, Graham had kicked off a religious revival.

Louie knew nothing of Graham. Four years after returning from the war, he was still in the Hollywood apartment, lost in alcohol and plans to murder the Bird. Cynthia had returned from Florida, but was staying only until she could arrange a divorce. The two lived on in grim coexistence, each one out of answers.

One day that October, Cynthia and Louie were walking down a hallway in their building when a new tenant and his girlfriend came out of an apartment. The two couples began chatting, and it was at first a pleasant conversation. Then the man mentioned that an evangelist named Billy Graham was preaching downtown. Louie turned abruptly and walked away.

Cynthia stayed in the hall, listening to the neighbor. When she returned to the apartment, she told Louie that she wanted him to take her to hear Graham speak. Louie refused.

Cynthia went alone. She came home alight. She found Louie and told him that she wasn't going to divorce him. The news filled Louie with relief, but when Cynthia said that she'd experienced a religious awakening, he was appalled.

Louie and Cynthia went to a dinner at Sylvia and Harvey's house. In the kitchen after the meal, Cynthia spoke of her experience in Graham's tent, and said that she wanted Louie to go listen to him. Louie soured and said he absolutely wouldn't go. The argument continued through the evening and into the next day. Cynthia recruited the new neighbor, and together they badgered Louie. For several days, Louie kept refusing, and began trying to dodge his wife and the neighbor, until Graham left town. Then Graham's run was extended, and Cynthia leavened her entreaties with a lie. Louie was fascinated with science, so she told him that Graham's sermons discussed science at length. It was just enough incentive to tip the balance. Louie gave in.

———

Billy Graham was wearing out. For many hours a day, seven days a week, he preached to vast throngs, and each sermon was a workout, delivered in a booming voice, punctuated with broad gestures of the hands, arms, and body. He got up as early as five, and he stayed in the tent late into the night, counseling troubled souls.

Graham's weight was dropping, and dark semicircles shadowed his eyes. At times he felt that if he stopped moving, his legs would buckle, so he took to pacing his pulpit to keep himself from keeling over. Once, someone brought a baby to him, and he asked whose child she was. He'd been away from home for so long that he didn't recognize his own daughter. He longed to end the campaign, but the success of it made him sure that Providence had other wishes.

When Louie and Cynthia entered the tent, Louie refused to go farther forward than the back rows. He sat down, sullen. He would wait out this sermon, go home, and be done with it.

The tent was hushed. From someplace outside came a high, beckoning sound. Louie had known that sound since his boyhood, when he'd lain awake beside Pete, yearning to escape. It was the whistle of a train.

———

When Graham appeared, Louie was surprised. He'd expected the sort of frothy, holy-rolling charlatan that he'd seen preaching near Torrance when he was a boy. What he saw instead was a brisk, neatly groomed man two years younger than himself. Though he was nursing a sore throat and asked that his amplifier be turned up to save his voice, Graham showed no other sign of his fatigue. He asked his listeners to open their Bibles to the eighth chapter of John.

> Jesus went unto the mount of Olives. And early in the morning he came again into the temple, and all the people came unto him; and he sat down, and taught them. And the scribes and Pharisees brought unto him a woman taken in adultery; and when they had set her in the midst, They say unto him, Master, this woman was taken in adultery, in the very act. Now Moses in the law commanded us, that such should be stoned: but what sayest thou? This they said, tempting him, that they might have to accuse him. But Jesus stooped down, and with his finger wrote on the ground, as though he heard them not. So when they continued asking him, he lifted up himself, and said unto them, He that is without sin among you, let him first cast a stone at her. And again he stooped down, and wrote on the ground. And they which heard it, being convicted by their own conscience, went out one by one, beginning at the eldest, even unto the last: and Jesus was left alone, and the woman standing in the midst. When Jesus had lifted up himself, and saw no one but the woman, he said unto her, Woman, where are those thine accusers? hath no man condemned thee? She said, No man, Lord. And Jesus said unto her, Neither do I condemn thee: go, and sin no more.*

———

* From the King James version.

Louie was suddenly wide awake. Describing Jesus rising from his knees after a night of prayer, Graham asked his listeners how long it had been since they'd prayed in earnest. Then he focused on Jesus bending down, his finger tracing words in the sand at the Pharisees' feet, sending the men scattering in fear.

"What did they see Jesus write?" Graham asked. Inside himself, Louie felt something twisting.

"Darkness doesn't hide the eyes of God," Graham said. "God takes down your life from the time you were born to the time you die. And when you stand before God on the great judgment day, you're going to say, 'Lord I wasn't such a bad fellow,' and they are going to pull down the screen and they are going to shoot the moving picture of your life from the cradle to the grave, and you are going to hear every thought that was going through your mind every minute of the day, every second of the minute, and you're going to hear the words that you said. And your own words, and your own thoughts, and your own deeds, are going to condemn you as you stand before God on that day. And God is going to say, 'Depart from me.' "*

Louie felt indignant rage flaring in him, a struck match. *I am a good man,* he thought. *I am a good man.*

Even as he had this thought, he felt the lie in it. He knew what he had become. Somewhere under his anger, there was a lurking, nameless uneasiness, the shudder of sharks rasping their backs along the bottom of the raft. There was a thought he must not think, a memory he must not see. With the urgency of a bolting animal, he wanted to run.

Graham looked out over his audience. "Here tonight, there's a drowning man, a drowning woman, a drowning man, a drowning boy, a drowning girl that is out lost in the sea of life." He told of hell and salvation, men saved and men lost, always coming back to the stooped figure drawing letters in the sand. Louie grew more and more angry and more and more spooked.

"Every head bowed and every eye closed," said Graham, offering a traditional invitation to repentance, a declaration of faith, and absolution. Louie grabbed Cynthia's arm, stood up, and bulled his way from the tent.

---

* Excerpts taken from "The Only Sermon Jesus Ever Wrote," sermon by Billy Graham, © 1949 Billy Graham Evangelistic Association. Used with permission. All rights reserved. Author's transcription from audio recording.

Somewhere in the city, a siren began a low wail. The sound, rising and falling slowly, carried through the tent, picked up by the microphone that was recording the sermon.

That night, Louie lay helpless as the belt whipped his head. The body that hunched over him was that of the Bird. The face was that of the devil.

———

Louie rose from his nightmares to find Cynthia there. All morning Sunday, she tried to coax him into seeing Graham again. Louie, angry and threatened, refused. For several hours, Cynthia and Louie argued. Exhausted by her persistence, Louie finally agreed to go, with one caveat: When Graham said, "Every head bowed, every eye closed," they were leaving.

Under the tent that night, Graham spoke of how the world was in an age of war, an age defined by persecution and suffering. Why, Graham asked, is God silent while good men suffer? He began his answer by asking his audience to consider the evening sky. "If you look into the heavens tonight, on this beautiful California night, I see the stars and can see the footprints of God," he said. ". . . I think to myself, my father, my heavenly father, hung them there with a flaming fingertip and holds them there with the power of his omnipotent hand, and he runs the whole universe, and he's not too busy running the whole universe to count the hairs on my head and see a sparrow when it falls, because God is interested in me . . . God spoke in creation."*

Louie was winding tight. He remembered the day when he and Phil, slowly dying on the raft, had slid into the doldrums. Above, the sky had been a swirl of light; below, the stilled ocean had mirrored the sky, its clarity broken only by a leaping fish. Awed to silence, forgetting his thirst and his hunger, forgetting that he was dying, Louie had known only gratitude. That day, he had believed that what lay around them was the work of infinitely broad, benevolent hands, a gift of compassion. In the years since, that thought had been lost.

Graham went on. He spoke of God reaching into the world through miracles and the intangible blessings that give men the strength to out-

* Excerpts taken from "Why God Allows Christians to Suffer and Why God Allows Communism to Flourish," sermon by Billy Graham, © 1949 Billy Graham Evangelistic Association. Used with permission. All rights reserved. Author's transcription from audio recording.

last their sorrows. "God works miracles one after another," he said. ". . . God says, 'If you suffer, I'll give you the grace to go forward.' "

Louie found himself thinking of the moment at which he had woken in the sinking hull of *Green Hornet,* the wires that had trapped him a moment earlier now, inexplicably, gone. And he remembered the Japanese bomber swooping over the rafts, riddling them with bullets, and yet not a single bullet had struck him, Phil, or Mac. He had fallen into unbearably cruel worlds, and yet he had borne them. When he turned these memories in his mind, the only explanation he could find was one in which the impossible was possible.

What God asks of men, said Graham, is faith. His invisibility is the truest test of that faith. To know who sees him, God makes himself unseen.

Louie shone with sweat. He felt accused, cornered, pressed by a frantic urge to flee. As Graham asked for heads to bow and eyes to close, Louie stood abruptly and rushed for the street, towing Cynthia behind him. "Nobody leaving," said Graham. "You can leave while I'm preaching but not now. Everybody is still and quiet. Every head bowed, every eye closed." He asked the faithful to come forward.

Louie pushed past the congregants in his row, charging for the exit. His mind was tumbling. He felt enraged, violent, on the edge of explosion. He wanted to hit someone.

As he reached the aisle, he stopped. Cynthia, the rows of bowed heads, the sawdust underfoot, the tent around him, all disappeared. A memory long beaten back, the memory from which he had run the evening before, was upon him.

Louie was on the raft. There was gentle Phil crumpled up before him, Mac's breathing skeleton, endless ocean stretching away in every direction, the sun lying over them, the cunning bodies of the sharks, waiting, circling. He was a body on a raft, dying of thirst. He felt words whisper from his swollen lips. It was a promise thrown at heaven, a promise he had not kept, a promise he had allowed himself to forget until just this instant: *If you will save me, I will serve you forever.* And then, standing under a circus tent on a clear night in downtown Los Angeles, Louie felt rain falling.

It was the last flashback he would ever have. Louie let go of Cynthia and turned toward Graham. He felt supremely alive. He began walking.

"This is it," said Graham. "God has spoken to you. You come on."

Cynthia kept her eyes on Louie all the way home. When they entered the apartment, Louie went straight to his cache of liquor. It was the time of night when the need usually took hold of him, but for the first time in years, Louie had no desire to drink. He carried the bottles to the kitchen sink, opened them, and poured their contents into the drain. Then he hurried through the apartment, gathering packs of cigarettes, a secret stash of girlie magazines, everything that was part of his ruined years. He heaved it all down the trash chute.

In the morning, he woke feeling cleansed. For the first time in five years, the Bird hadn't come into his dreams. The Bird would never come again.

Louie dug out the Bible that had been issued to him by the air corps and mailed home to his mother when he was believed dead. He walked to Barnsdall Park, where he and Cynthia had gone in better days, and where Cynthia had gone, alone, when he'd been on his benders. He found a spot under a tree, sat down, and began reading.

Resting in the shade and the stillness, Louie felt profound peace. When he thought of his history, what resonated with him now was not all that he had suffered but the divine love that he believed had intervened to save him. He was not the worthless, broken, forsaken man that the Bird had striven to make of him. In a single, silent moment, his rage, his fear, his humiliation and helplessness, had fallen away. That morning, he believed, he was a new creation.

Softly, he wept.

Thirty-nine

Daybreak

O N A CHILLY FALL MORNING IN 1950, LOUIE WALKED UP a long, level road toward a complex of unadorned buildings. As he approached the archway that marked the entrance to the complex, his whole body tingled. On the arch were painted the words SUGAMO PRISON, and beyond it waited Louie's POW camp guards. At long last, Louie had returned to Japan.

In the year that had passed since he had walked into Billy Graham's tent, Louie had worked to keep a promise. He had begun a new life as a Christian speaker, telling his story all over America. The work brought him modest honoraria and offerings, enough to allow him to pay his bills and buy a $150 used DeSoto, finally replacing the car that he'd lost as loan collateral. He had scraped together just enough money for a down payment on a house, but was still so poor that Cissy's crib was the house's only furniture. Louie did the cooking on a single-coil hot plate, and he and Cynthia slept in sleeping bags next to the crib. They were barely getting by, but their connection to each other had been renewed and deepened. They were blissful together.

In the first years after the war, a journey back to Japan had been Louie's obsession, the path to murdering the man who had ruined him. But thoughts of murder no longer had a home in him. He had come here not to avenge himself but to answer a question.

Louie (right) at Sugamo. *Courtesy of Louis Zamperini*

Louie had been told that all of the men who had tormented him had been arrested, convicted, and imprisoned here in Sugamo. He could speak about and think of his captors, even the Bird, without bitterness, but a question tapped at the back of his mind. If he should ever see them again, would the peace that he had found prove resilient? With trepidation, he had resolved to go to Sugamo to stand before these men.

On the evening before, Louie had written to Cynthia to tell her what he was about to do. He had asked her to pray for him.

—

The former guards, 850 of them, sat cross-legged on the floor of a large, bare common room. Standing at the front of the room, Louie looked out over the faces.

At first he recognized none of them. Then, far in the rear, he saw a face he knew, then another and another: Curley, the Weasel, Kono, Jimmie Sasaki. And there was the Quack, who was petitioning to have his death penalty commuted. As Louie looked at this last man, he thought of Bill Harris.

There was one face missing: Louie couldn't find the Bird. When he asked his escort where Watanabe was, he was told that he wasn't in Sugamo. Over five years, thousands of policemen had scoured Japan in search of him, but they had never found him.

As Louie had been packing to come to Japan, the long-awaited day had arrived in the life of Shizuka Watanabe: October 1, 1950, the day her son had promised to come to her, if he was still alive. He had told her to go to the Shinjuku district in Tokyo, where he would meet her at the same restaurant where they had last seen each other, two years before. At 10:05 that morning, police saw Shizuka climb aboard a train bound for the Shinjuku district. At the restaurant, Mutsuhiro apparently never showed up.

Shizuka went to Kofu and checked into a hotel, staying alone, taking no visitors. For four days, she wandered the city. Then she left Kofu abruptly, without paying her hotel bill. The police went in to question the hotel matron. Asked if Shizuka had spoken of her son, the matron said yes.

"Mutsuhiro," Shizuka had said, "has already died."

In the corner of a sitting room in her house, Shizuka would keep a small shrine to Mutsuhiro, a tradition among bereaved Japanese families. Each morning, she would leave an offering in memory of her son.

In Sugamo, Louie asked his escort what had happened to the Bird. He was told that it was believed that the former sergeant, hunted, exiled and in despair, had stabbed himself to death.

The words washed over Louie. In prison camp, Watanabe had forced him to live in incomprehensible degradation and violence. Bereft of his dignity, Louie had come home to a life lost in darkness, and had dashed himself against the memory of the Bird. But on an October night in Los Angeles, Louie had found, in Payton Jordan's word, "daybreak." That night, the sense of shame and powerlessness that had driven his need to hate the Bird had vanished. The Bird was no longer his monster. He was only a man.

In Sugamo Prison, as he was told of Watanabe's fate, all Louie saw was a lost person, a life now beyond redemption. He felt something that he had never felt for his captor before. With a shiver of amazement, he realized that it was compassion.

At that moment, something shifted sweetly inside him. It was forgiveness, beautiful and effortless and complete. For Louie Zamperini, the war was over.

Before Louie left Sugamo, the colonel who was attending him asked Louie's former guards to come forward. In the back of the room, the prisoners stood up and shuffled into the aisle. They moved hesitantly, looking up at Louie with small faces.

Louie was seized by childlike, giddy exuberance. Before he realized what he was doing, he was bounding down the aisle. In bewilderment, the men who had abused him watched him come to them, his hands extended, a radiant smile on his face.

EPILOGUE

ON A JUNE DAY IN 1954, JUST OFF A WINDING ROAD IN California's San Gabriel Mountains, a mess of boys tumbled out of a truck and stood blinking in the sunshine. They were quick-fisted, hard-faced boys, most of them intimately familiar with juvenile hall and jail. Louie stood with them, watching them get the feel of earth without pavement, space without walls. He felt as if he were watching his own youth again.

So opened the great project of Louie's life, the nonprofit Victory Boys Camp. Beginning with only an idea and very little money, Louie had found a campsite where the bargain-basement rent compensated for the general dilapidation, then talked a number of businesses into donating materials. He'd spent two years manning backhoes, upending boulders, and digging a swimming pool. When he was done, he had a beautiful camp.

Victory became a tonic for lost boys. Louie took in anyone, including one boy so ungovernable that Louie had to be deputized by a sheriff to gain custody of him. He took the boys fishing, swimming, horseback riding, camping, and, in winter, skiing. He led them on mountain hikes, letting them talk out their troubles, and rappelled down cliffs beside them. He showed them vocational films, living for

Louie demonstrates rappelling to his campers. *Courtesy of Louis Zamperini*

the days when a boy would see a career depicted and whisper, "That's what I want to do!" Each evening, Louie sat with the boys before a campfire, telling them about his youth, the war, and the road that had led him to peace. He went easy on Christianity, but laid it before them as an option. Some were convinced, some not, but either way, boys who arrived at Victory as ruffians often left it renewed and reformed.

When he wasn't with his campers, Louie was happily walking the world, telling his story to rapt audiences in everything from grade school classrooms to stadiums. Improbably, he was particularly fond of speaking on cruise ships, sorting through invitations to find a plum voyage, kicking back on the first-class deck with a cool drink in hand, and reveling in the ocean. Concerned that accepting fat honoraria would discourage schools and small groups from asking him to speak, he declined anything over modest fees. He made just enough money to keep Cissy and her little brother, Luke, in diapers, then blue jeans, then college. On the side, he worked in the First Presbyterian Church of Hollywood, supervising the senior center.

Over the years, he received an absurd number of awards and honors. Lomita Flight Strip, which had been renamed Zamperini Field while Louie was languishing in Naoetsu, was rededicated to him not once more, but twice. A plaza at USC was named after him, as was the stadium at Torrance High. In 1980, someone named a great big barge of a racehorse after him, though as a runner, Zamperini was no Zamperini. The house on Gramercy became a historic landmark. Louie was chosen to carry the Olympic torch before five different Games. So many groups would clamor to give him awards that he'd find it difficult to fit everyone in.

His body gave no quarter to age or punishment. In time, even his injured leg healed. When Louie was in his sixties, he was still climbing Cahuenga Peak every week and running a mile in under six minutes. In his seventies, he discovered skateboarding. At eighty-five, he returned

Louie on the torch run for the 1984
Summer Olympics. *Courtesy of Louis Zamperini*

Louie, skateboarding at eighty-one.
Courtesy of Louis Zamperini

to Kwajalein on a project, ultimately unsuccessful, to locate the bodies of the nine marines whose names had been etched in the wall of his cell. "When I get old," he said as he tossed a football on the Kwajalein beach, "I'll let you know." When he was ninety, his neighbors looked up to see him balancing high in a tree in his yard, chain saw in hand. "When God wants me, he'll take me," he told an incredulous Pete. "Why the hell are you trying to help him?" Pete replied. Well into his tenth decade of life, between the occasional broken bone, he could still be seen perched on skis, merrily cannonballing down mountains.

He remained infectiously, incorrigibly cheerful. He once told a friend that the last time he could remember being angry was some forty years before. His conviction that everything happened for a reason, and would come to good, gave him a laughing equanimity even in hard times. In late 2008, when he was about to turn ninety-two, he was moving a slab of concrete on a dolly down a flight of stairs when the dolly wheels broke, sending Louie and the concrete crashing down the steps. He wound up in the hospital with a minor hip fracture and a shattered thumb. As his daughter came down the hospital corridor toward his room, she heard shouts of "Hey Louie!" from the crowd of friends that her father had made among the hospital staff. "I never knew anyone," Pete once said, "who didn't love Louie." As soon as he was out of the hospital, Louie went on a three-mile hike.

———

With the war over, Phil became Allen again. After a brief stint running a plastics business in Albuquerque, he and Cecy moved to his boyhood hometown, La Porte, Indiana, where they eventually took jobs at a junior high, Allen teaching science, Cecy teaching English. They were soon parents to a girl and a boy.

Allen hardly ever mentioned the war. His friends kept their questions to themselves, fearful of treading upon a painful place. Other than the scars on his forehead from the *Green Hornet* crash, only his habits spoke of what he'd been through. After having lived for weeks on raw albatross and tern, he never again ate poultry. He had a curious affinity for eating food directly out of cans, cold. And the onetime king hot dog of his squadron wouldn't go near an airplane. As the jet age overtook America, he stayed in his car. Only many years later, when his daughter lost her husband in an auto accident, did he brave the air to go to her.

He never returned to Japan, and he seemed, outwardly, free of resentment. The closest thing to it was the flicker of irritation that people thought they saw in him when he was, almost invariably, treated as a trivial footnote in what was celebrated as Louie's story. If he was rubbed wrong by it, he bore it graciously. In 1954, when the TV pro-

Allen Phillips with his children, Chris and Karen, bedtime, 1952.
Courtesy of Karen Loomis

gram *This Is Your Life* feted Louie and presented him with a gold watch, a movie camera, a Mercury station wagon, and a thousand dollars, Allen traveled to California to join Louie's family and friends on stage, wearing a neat bow tie and looking at the floor as he spoke. When the group posed together, Allen slipped to the back.

As Allen grew old, he settled into retired life with Cecy. He walked quite a few back nines, changed his rooting interests from the Sox to the Cubs, and spent whole days just sitting in silence. "Dad must have swung a thousand miles on that front porch swing," said his daughter, Karen Loomis. "What he was thinking, I don't know."

In the 1990s, diabetes and heart disease converged on him. In 1998, a few months before he died, he was moved to a nursing home. When the staff learned his war story, they scheduled an event to honor him. It was probably the first time that what he'd done during the war was publicly recognized not simply in reference to Louie, but for its own sake. For the only time in his life, Allen became an open book. As people gathered to listen to his story, spellbound, Karen saw a lovely light come to her father's face. There was, she said, "a little grin underneath."

————

The men who had befriended Louie in captivity found their way back into civilian life. Some flourished; some struggled for the rest of their lives. There was one terrible loss.

Bill Harris ended the war in grand style, plucked from Omori to stand on the *Missouri* as Japan surrendered. His singular intellectual acuity, lost in the beatings from the Quack, returned to him. He went home, fell irretrievably in love with a navy captain's daughter, married her, and became a doting father to two little girls. After leaning toward retirement, he opted to stay with the marines, rising to lieutenant colonel. He and Louie sent letters back and forth, laying plans to see each other one day soon.

In September 1950, Harris was driving down a highway when the police pulled him over. He was being called to command a battalion in Korea and had to leave the next day. Before he left, he told his wife that if his luck went bad, he wouldn't allow himself to be captured again.

Before dawn on December 7, 1950, Harris stood on a frozen Korean mountain with his weary battalion, which had seen such horrendous fighting that it had lost three-quarters of its men. That morning, it was serving as the rear guard for a convoy. As the convoy crossed an open area in the dark, a vast, entrenched Chinese force ambushed it from point-blank range. What Harris did next became Marine Corps legend. He gathered his men and, under murderous fire, led them straight at the Chinese. They took heavy casualties but held the Chinese off long enough for the convoy to escape.

Bill Harris with his daughter Katey in 1950.
He disappeared a few months later.
Courtesy of Katherine H. Meares

When dawn came, no one could find Harris. The last time anyone had seen him, he'd been heading up a road, carrying two rifles. His men searched for hours but found no trace of him. They concluded that he'd again been captured.

For his actions that night, Harris won the Navy Cross, an award second only to the Congressional Medal of Honor. General Clifton

Capes kept the medal in his desk in hopes that Harris would come home to receive it. He would not. Thirty-two-year-old William Harris was never seen again. When America's Korean War POWs were released, none of them reported having seen him. He was simply gone.

Many years later, Harris's family received a box of bones, apparently returned by North Korea. The remains inside were said to match those of Harris, but the reports were so incomplete that the family was never sure if it was really Bill whom they buried in a church cemetery in Kentucky. What actually happened on that morning in 1950 remains unknown.

After the war, Pete married a Kansas City beauty named Doris, had three kids, and devoted his life to the work he'd been born to do. He coached football at Torrance High, winning the league championship, then moved on to Banning High, in Wilmington, to coach track and football. In thirty years of Banning track, he had only one losing season. Coach Zamperini was so beloved that upon his retirement in 1977, he was feted by eight hundred people on the *Queen Mary*.

"I'm retired; my wife is just tired," Pete used to say, and he loved the motto so much that he had it printed on his business cards. But in truth, retirement never really took. At ninety, Pete had the littlest kids in his neighborhood in training, fashioning dumbbells out of old cans, just as his dad had done for Louie. He'd lead the kids onto his sidewalk and cheer them on through sprints, handing out a dime for each race run, a quarter for a personal best.

Pete was more troubled by Louie's war experience than Louie was. In 1992, he served as escort for a group of students on an ocean fishing trip. Though the vessel was a spanking new, ninety-foot ship, the prospect of being at sea terrified Pete. He showed up with a ridiculously comprehensive assortment of safety items, including a heavy-duty plastic bag to use as a flotation device, a floatable flashlight, a six-foot lanyard, a whistle, and a pocketknife, which he imagined flailing at any sharks who tried to eat him. He spent the trip staring ambivalently at the water.

At the end of his life, Pete remained as dedicated to Louie as he'd been in boyhood. He assembled a scrapbook thick with clippings and photographs of Louie's life, and would happily give up his afternoons to talk about his brother, once spending nearly three hours on the phone with a reporter while sitting in a bath towel. At ninety, he still remembered the final times of Louie's races, to the fifth of a second, three-quarters of a century after Louie had run them. Like Payton Jordan, who went on to coach the 1968 U.S. Olympic track and field team, Pete never stopped believing that Louie could have run a four-minute mile long before Roger Bannister became the first man to do it, in 1954. Many decades after the war, Pete was still haunted by what Louie had endured. When describing Louie's wartime ordeal to an audience gathered to honor his brother, Pete faltered and broke down. It was some time before he could go on.

On a May day in 2008, a car pulled to a stop before Pete's house in San Clemente, and Louie stepped out. He had come to say good-bye to his brother; Pete had melanoma, and it had spread to his brain. Their younger sister Virginia had died a few weeks before; Sylvia and Payton Jordan would follow months later. Cynthia, as gorgeous and headstrong as ever, had succumbed to cancer in 2001, drifting off as Louie pressed his face to hers, whispering, "I love you." Louie, declared dead more than sixty years earlier, would outlive them all.

Pete was on his bed, eyes closed. Louie sat beside him. Softly, he began to talk of his life with Pete, tracing the paths they had taken since pneumonia had brought them to California in 1919. The two ancient men lingered together as they had as boys, lying side by side on their bed, waiting for the *Graf Zeppelin*.

Louie spoke of what a feral boy he had once been, and all that Pete had done to rescue him. He told of the cascade of good things that had followed Pete's acts of devotion, and the bountiful lives that he and Pete had found in guiding children. All of those kids, Louie said, "are part of you, Pete."

Pete's eyes opened and, with sudden clarity, rested on the face of his little brother for the last time. He couldn't speak, but he was beaming.

———

In the fall of 1996, in an office in the First Presbyterian Church of Hollywood, a telephone rang. Louie, then a nudge short of eighty, picked up the receiver.

The voice on the telephone belonged to Draggan Mihailovich, a producer for CBS television. The 1998 Winter Olympics had been awarded to Nagano, and Louie had accepted an invitation to run the torch past Naoetsu. Mihailovich was filming a profile of Louie, to be aired during the Olympics, and had gone to Japan to prepare. While chatting with a man over a bowl of noodles, he had made a startling discovery.

Mihailovich asked Louie if he was sitting down. Louie said yes. Mihailovich told him to grab hold of his chair.

"The Bird is alive."

Louie nearly hit the floor.

—

The dead man had walked out of the darkness late one night in 1952. He'd been gone for nearly seven years. Watanabe stepped off a train in Kobe, walked through the city, and stopped before a house with a garden bisected by a stone path. Before his disappearance, his mother had spent part of each year living in this house, but Watanabe had been gone for so long that he didn't know if she came here anymore. He strode about, searching for a clue. Under the gate light, he saw her name.

In all the time in which he'd been thought dead, Watanabe had been hiding in the countryside. He'd spent the previous summer pedaling through villages on a bicycle fitted with a cooler, selling ice cream, envying the children who played around him. When summer had ended, he'd gone back to farm work, tending rice paddies. Then, one day in March 1952, as he read a newspaper, his eyes had paused over a story. The arrest order for suspected war criminals had been lifted. There on the page was his name.

The lifting of the apprehension order was the result of an unlikely turn in history. Immediately after the war, there was a worldwide outcry for punishment of the Japanese who had abused POWs, and the war-crimes trials began. But new political realities soon emerged. As American occupiers worked to help Japan transition to democracy and independence, the Cold War was beginning. With communism wicking across the Far East, America's leaders began to see a future alliance with Japan as critical to national security. The sticking point was the war-crimes issue; the trials were intensely unpopular in Japan, spurring a movement seeking the release of all convicted war criminals. With the pursuit of justice for POWs suddenly in conflict with America's security goals, something had to give.

On December 24, 1948, as the occupation began to wind down, General MacArthur declared a "Christmas amnesty" for the last seventeen men awaiting trial for Class A war crimes, the designation for those who had guided the war. The defendants were released, and some would go on to great success; onetime defendant Nobusuke Kishi, said to be responsible for forcibly conscripting hundreds of thousands of Chinese and Koreans as laborers, would become prime minister in 1957. Though American officials justified the release by saying that it was unlikely that the defendants would have been convicted, the explanation was questionable; more than two dozen Class A defendants had been tried, and all had been convicted. Even in Japan, it was commonly believed that many of the released men were guilty.

Ten months later, the trials of Class B and C defendants—those accused of ordering or carrying out abuse or atrocities—were ended. An army officer named Osamu Satano was the last man tried by the United States. His punishment fit the reconciliatory mood; convicted of beheading an airman, he was sentenced to just five years. In early 1950, MacArthur ruled that war criminals' sentences would be reduced for good behavior, and those serving life sentences would be eligible for parole after fifteen years. Then, in 1951, the Allies and Japan signed the Treaty of Peace, which would end the occupation. The treaty waived the right of former POWs and their families to seek reparations from Japan and Japanese companies that had profited from their enslavement.* Finally, in March 1952, just before the treaty took effect and the occupation ended, the order for apprehension of fugitive war criminals was lifted. Though Watanabe was on the fugitive list, hardly anyone believed that he was still alive.

When he saw the story, Watanabe was wary. Afraid that the police had planted the story as a trap, he didn't go home. He spent much of the spring working as a fishmonger, all the while wondering if he was free. Finally, he decided to sneak back to his mother.

Watanabe rang the bell, but no one answered. He rang again, longer, and heard footfalls on the garden stones. The gate swung open, and there was the face of his youngest brother, whom he hadn't seen

---

* America's War Crimes Acts of 1948 and 1952 awarded each former POW $1 for each day of imprisonment if he could prove that he wasn't given the amount and quality of food mandated by the Geneva Convention, and $1.50 per day if he could prove that he'd been subjected to inhumane treatment and/or hard labor. This made for a maximum benefit of $2.50 per day. Under the Treaty of Peace, $12.6 million in Japanese assets were distributed to POWs, but because America's POWs had already received meager War Crimes Acts payments, first claim on the assets was given to other nations.

since the latter was a boy. His brother threw his arms around him, then pulled him into the house, singing out, "Mu-cchan's back!"

Mutsuhiro Watanabe's flight was over. In his absence, many of his fellow camp guards and officials had been convicted of war crimes. Some had been executed. The others wouldn't be in prison for long. In keeping with the American effort to reconcile with Japan, all of them, including those serving life sentences, would soon be paroled. It appears that even Sueharu Kitamura, "the Quack," was set free, in spite of his death sentence. By 1958, every war criminal who had not been executed would be free, and on December 30 of that year, all would be granted amnesty. Sugamo would be torn down, and the epic ordeals of POWs in Japan would fade from the world's memory.

Watanabe would later admit that in the beginning of his life in exile, he had pondered the question of whether or not he had committed any crime. In the end, he laid the blame not on himself but on "sinful, absurd, insane war." He saw himself as a victim. If he had tugs of conscience over what he'd done, he shrugged them away by assuring himself that the lifting of the fugitive-apprehension order was a personal exoneration.

"I was just in a great joy of complete release and liberation," he wrote in 1956, "that I was not guilty."

———

Watanabe married and had two children. He opened an insurance agency in Tokyo, and it reportedly became highly profitable. He lived in a luxury apartment worth a reported $1.5 million and kept a vacation home on Australia's Gold Coast.

Almost everyone who knew of his crimes believed he was dead. By his own account, Watanabe visited America several times, but he apparently didn't encounter any former POWs. Then, in the early 1980s, an American military officer visiting Japan heard something about the Bird being alive. In 1991, Bob Martindale was told that a Japanese veteran had spotted a man he thought was Watanabe at a sports event. Among the other POWs, few, if any, heard of this. Louie remained in ignorance, convinced that the Bird had killed himself decades earlier.

In the summer of 1995, the fiftieth anniversary of his flight from Naoetsu, Watanabe was seventy-seven years old. His hair had grayed; his haughty bearing had bent. He seemed to be close to concluding his life without publicly confronting his past. But that year, he was at last ready to admit that he had abused men. Perhaps he truly felt guilty.

Perhaps, as he approached his death, he had a troubling sense that he'd be remembered as a fiend and wished to dispel that notion. Or perhaps he was motivated by the same vanity that had consumed him in wartime, and hoped to use his vile history, and his victims, to draw attention to himself, maybe even win admiration for his contrition. That summer, when London *Daily Mail* reporter Peter Hadfield came calling, Watanabe let him in.

Sitting in his apartment, his pawlike hand clutching a crystal wine glass, he finally spoke about the POWs.

"I understand their bitterness, and they may wonder why I was so severe," he said. "But now my feeling is I want to apologize. A deep, deep apology . . . I was severe. Very severe."

He made a fist and waved it past his chin. "If the former prisoners want, I would offer to let them come here and hit me, to beat me."

He claimed that he'd used only his hands to punish POWs, an assertion that would have riled the men who'd been kicked, clubbed with his kendo stick and baseball bat, and whipped in the face with his belt. He said that he'd only been trying to teach the POWs military discipline, and asserted that he'd been acting under orders. "If I had been better educated during the war, I think I would have been kinder, more friendly," he said. "But I was taught that the POWs had surrendered, and this was a shameful thing for them to have done. I knew nothing about the Geneva Convention. I asked my commanding officer about it, and he said, 'This is not Geneva, this is Japan.'

"There were two people inside me," he continued. "One that followed military orders, and the other that was more human. At times I felt I had a good heart, but Japan at that time had a bad heart. In normal times I never would have done such things.

"War is a crime against humanity," he concluded. "I'm glad our prime minister apologized for the war, but I can't understand why the government as a whole doesn't apologize. We have a bad cabinet."

After the interview, a *Daily Mail* reporter tracked down Tom Wade and told him that Watanabe had asked for forgiveness. "I accept his apology and wish him contentment in his declining years," Wade said. "It's no good hanging on to the hatred after so long."

Asked if he'd like to accept Watanabe's offer to let the POWs beat him, Wade said no, then reconsidered.

"I might just have one good blow," he said.

The *Daily Mail* article apparently ran only in England. It wasn't until almost a year later that Louie learned that Watanabe still lived. His first reaction was to say that he wanted to see him.

———

In the decades after the war, the abandoned Naoetsu campsite decayed, and the village residents didn't speak of what had transpired there. Over time, the memory was largely lost. But in 1978, a former POW wrote a letter to teachers at Naoetsu High School, beginning a dialogue that introduced many locals to the tragedy that had taken place in their village. Ten years later, former POW Frank Hole journeyed back to the village, which had joined another village to form Joetsu City. He planted three eucalyptus seedlings outside city hall and gave city leaders a plaque in memory of the sixty Australians who had died in the camp.

As they learned the POWs' stories, Joetsu residents responded with sympathy. Residents formed a group dedicated to building a peace park to honor the dead POWs and bring reconciliation. Among the founding members was Shoichi Ishizuka, a veteran who'd been held as a POW by the Americans and treated so kindly that he referred to the experience as "lucky prison life." When he learned what his Allied counterparts had endured in his own village, he was horrified. A council was formed, fund-raising began, and exhibits were erected in town. If the plan succeeded, Joetsu would become, among the ninety-one cities in Japan in which POW camps once stood, the first to create a memorial to the POWs who had suffered and died there.

Though 85 percent of Joetsu residents donated to the park fund, the plan generated heated controversy. Some residents fought the plan vehemently, calling in death threats and vowing to tear down the memorial and burn supporters' homes. In keeping with the goal of reconciliation, the memorial council sought the participation of relatives of the guards who'd been convicted and hanged, but the families balked, fearing ostracism. To honor the grief of families on both sides of the war, the council proposed creating a single cenotaph for both the POWs and the hanged guards, but this deeply offended the former POWs. At one point, the plan was nearly given up.

Eventually, the spirit of reconciliation prevailed. In October 1995, on the site of the former Naoetsu camp, the peace park was dedicated. The focal point was a pair of statues of angels, flying above a cenotaph in which rested Hole's plaque. In a separate cenotaph a few yards away was a plaque in memory of the eight hanged guards. At the guards' families' request, no names were inscribed on it, only a simple phrase: *Eight stars in the peaceful sky.*

In early 1997, CBS TV's Draggan Mihailovich arrived in Tokyo to search for Watanabe, armed with an address and a phone number. CBS's Japanese bureau chief called the number and reached Watanabe's wife, who said that her husband couldn't speak to them—he was gravely ill and bedridden. Mihailovich had the bureau chief call again to convey his wishes for Watanabe's recovery. His wishes did the trick: Mrs. Watanabe said that her husband had left the country on business and she didn't know when he'd return.

Seeing that he was being dodged, Mihailovich staked out Watanabe's apartment building and office. He waited for hours; Watanabe didn't appear. Just as Mihailovich was losing hope, his cell phone rang. Watanabe had returned the bureau chief's call. Told that the producers had a message from Louis Zamperini, Watanabe had agreed to meet them at a Tokyo hotel.

Mihailovich rented a room at the hotel and set up a camera crew inside. Doubting that Watanabe would agree to a sit-down interview, he rigged his cameraman with a tiny camera inside a baseball cap. At the appointed hour, in walked the Bird.

They sat down in the lobby, and Watanabe ordered a beer. Mihailovich explained that they were profiling Louis Zamperini. Watanabe knew the name immediately. "Six hundred prisoner," he said. "Zamperini number one."

Bob Simon, CBS's on-air correspondent for the story, thought that this would probably be his only chance to question Watanabe, so there in the lobby, he began grilling him about his treatment of Louie. Watanabe was startled. He said something about Zamperini being a good man, and how he—Watanabe—hated war. He said that his central concern had been protecting the POWs, because if they had escaped, civilians would have killed them. Asked why he'd been on the list of most wanted war criminals, he puffed with apparent pride. "I'm number seven," he said. "Tojo number one." Exile, he said, had been very painful for him.

They asked Watanabe if he'd come upstairs for an on-camera interview. Watanabe asked if the interview would air in Japan, and Mihailovich said no. To Mihailovich's surprise, Watanabe agreed.

Upstairs, with cameras rolling, they handed Watanabe a photograph of a youthful Louie, standing on a track, smiling. Simon dug in.

"Zamperini and the other prisoners remember you, in particular, being the most brutal of all the guards. How do you explain that?"

Watanabe's right eyelid began drooping. Mihailovich felt uneasy.

"I wasn't given military orders," Watanabe said, contradicting the assertion he'd made in the 1995 interview. "Because of my personal feelings, I treated the prisoners strictly as enemies of Japan. Zamperini was well known to me. If he says he was beaten by Watanabe, then such a thing probably occurred at the camp, if you consider my personal feelings at the time."

He tossed his head high, jutted out his chin, and directed a hard gaze at Simon. He said that the POWs had complained of "trifle things" and had used epithets to refer to the Japanese. These things, he said, had made him angry. With hundreds of prisoners, he said, he'd been under great pressure.

"Beating and kicking in Caucasian society are considered cruel. Cruel behavior," he said, speaking very slowly. "However, there were some occasions in the prison camp in which beating and kicking were unavoidable."

When the interview was over, Watanabe looked shaken and angry. Told that Zamperini was coming to Japan and wanted to meet him to offer his forgiveness, Watanabe replied that he would see him and apologize, on the understanding that it was only a personal apology, not one offered on behalf of the Japanese military.

As they packed up, Mihailovich had a last request. Would he agree to be filmed walking down the street? This, it seemed, was what Watanabe had come for. He donned his cap, stepped to the sidewalk, turned, and walked toward the camera. He moved just as he had in parades before his captives, head high, chest thrust out, eyes imperious.

One day nine months later, as he prepared to return to Japan to carry the Olympic torch, Louie sat at his desk for hours, thinking. Then he clicked on his computer and began to write.

To Matsuhiro [*sic*] Watanabe,

    As a result of my prisoner of war experience under your unwarranted and unreasonable punishment, my post-war life became a nightmare. It was not so much due to the pain and suffering as it was the tension of stress and humiliation that caused me to hate with a vengeance.

Under your discipline, my rights, not only as a prisoner of war but also as a human being, were stripped from me. It was a struggle to maintain enough dignity and hope to live until the war's end.

The post-war nightmares caused my life to crumble, but thanks to a confrontation with God through the evangelist Billy Graham, I committed my life to Christ. Love replaced the hate I had for you. Christ said, "Forgive your enemies and pray for them."

As you probably know, I returned to Japan in 1952 [*sic*] and was graciously allowed to address all the Japanese war criminals at Sugamo Prison . . . I asked then about you, and was told that you probably had committed Hara Kiri, which I was sad to hear. At that moment, like the others, I also forgave you and now would hope that you would also become a Christian.

Louis Zamperini

He folded the letter and carried it with him to Japan.

The meeting was not to be. CBS contacted Watanabe and told him that Zamperini wanted to come see him. Watanabe practically spat his reply: The answer was no.

When Louie arrived in Joetsu, he still had his letter. Someone took it from him, promising to get it to Watanabe. If Watanabe received it, he never replied.

Watanabe died in April 2003.

———

On the morning of January 22, 1998, snow sifted gently over the village once known as Naoetsu. Louis Zamperini, four days short of his eighty-first birthday, stood in a swirl of white beside a road flanked in bright drifts. His body was worn and weathered, his skin scratched with lines mapping the miles of his life. His old riot of black hair was now a translucent scrim of white, but his blue eyes still threw sparks. On the ring finger of his right hand, a scar was still visible, the last mark that *Green Hornet* had left in the world.

At last, it was time. Louie extended his hand, and in it was placed the Olympic torch. His legs could no longer reach and push as they once had, but they were still sure beneath him. He raised the torch, bowed, and began running.

All he could see, in every direction, were smiling Japanese faces.

There were children peeking out of hooded coats, men who had once worked beside the POW slaves in the steel mill, civilians snapping photographs, clapping, waving, cheering Louie on, and 120 Japanese soldiers, formed into two columns, parting to let him pass. Louie ran through the place where cages had once held him, where a black-eyed man had crawled inside him. But the cages were long gone, and so was the Bird. There was no trace of them here among the voices, the falling snow, and the old and joyful man, running.

ACKNOWLEDGMENTS

"I'll be an easier subject than Seabiscuit," Louie once told me, "because I can talk."

When I finished writing my first book, *Seabiscuit: An American Legend,* I felt certain that I would never again find a subject that fascinated me as did the Depression-era racehorse and the team of men who campaigned him. When I had my first conversation with the infectiously effervescent and apparently immortal Louie Zamperini, I changed my mind.

That conversation began my seven-year journey through Louie's unlikely life. I found his story in the memories of Olympians, former POWs and airmen, Japanese veterans, and the family and friends who once formed the home front; in diaries, letters, essays, and telegrams, many written by men and women who died long ago; in military documents and hazy photographs; in unpublished memoirs buried in desk drawers; in deep stacks of affidavits and war-crimes trial records; in forgotten papers in archives as far-flung as Oslo and Canberra. By the end of my journey, Louie's life was as familiar to me as my own. "When I want to know what happened to me in Japan," Louie once told his friends, "I call Laura."

In opening his world to me, Louie could not have been more gracious. He sat through some seventy-five interviews, answering thousands of questions with neither impatience nor complaint. He was refreshingly honest, quick to confess his failures and correct a few embellished stories that journalists have written about him. And his memory was astounding; nearly every time I cross-checked his accounts of events against newspaper stories, official records, and other sources, his recollections proved accurate to the smallest detail, even when the events took place some eighty-five years ago.

A superlative pack rat, Louie has saved seemingly every artifact of his life, from the DO NOT DISTURB sign that he swiped from Jesse Owens in Berlin to the paper number that he wore as he shattered the interscholastic mile record in 1934. One of his scrapbooks, which covers only 1917 to 1938, weighs *sixty-three* pounds. This he volunteered to send me, surrendering it to my late friend Debie Ginsburg, who somehow manhandled it down to a mailing service. Along with it, he sent several other scrapbooks (fortunately smaller), hundreds of photographs and letters, his diaries, and items as precious as the stained newspaper clipping that was in his wallet on the raft. All of these things were treasure troves to me, telling his story with immediacy and revealing detail. I am immensely grateful to Louie for trusting me with items so dear to him, and for welcoming me into his history.

Pete Zamperini, Sylvia Zamperini Flammer, and Payton Jordan didn't live to see this book's completion, but they played an enormous role in its creation, sharing a lifetime of memories and memorabilia. There were many joys for me in writing this book; my long talks with Pete, Sylvia, and Payton ranked high among them. I also thank Harvey Flammer, Cynthia Zamperini Garris, Ric Applewhite, and the late Marge Jordan for telling me their stories about Louie and Cynthia.

Karen Loomis, the daughter of Russell Allen Phillips and his wife, Cecy, walked me through her family's history and sent her father's wartime love letters to her mother, scrapbooks, photographs, clippings, and her grandmother's memoir. Thanks to Karen, I was able to peer into the life of the quiet, modest pilot known as Phil and uncover the brave and enduring man underneath. Someday I'll make it down to Georgia for long-promised muffins with Karen. My thanks also go to Bill Harris's daughter Katey Meares, who sent family photographs and told me of the father she lost far too soon, remembering him standing on his head in his kitchen to summon giggles from his girls. I also thank

Monroe and Phoebe Bormann, Terry Hoffman, and Bill Perry for telling me about Phil and Cecy.

For the men who endured prison camp, speaking of the war is often a scaring experience, and I am deeply grateful to the many former POWs who shared their memories, sometimes in tears. I shall never forget the generosity of Bob Martindale, Tom Wade, and Frank Tinker, who spent many hours bringing POW camp and the Bird to life for me. Milton McMullen described Omori, the POW insurgency, and the day he knocked over a train. Johan Arthur Johansen told of Omori and shared his extensive writings on POW camp. The late Ken Marvin spoke of the last pancakes he ate on Wake before the Japanese came, Naoetsu under the Bird, and teaching a guard hilariously offensive English. Glenn McConnell spoke of Ofuna, Gaga the duck, and the beating of Bill Harris. The late John Cook told me of slavery at Naoetsu and shared his unpublished memoir. I also send thanks to former POWs Fiske Hanley, Bob Hollingsworth, Raleigh "Dusty" Rhodes, Joe Brown, V. H. Spencer, Robert Cassidy, Leonard Birchall, Joe Alexander, Minos Miller, Burn O'Neill, Charles Audet, Robert Heer, and Paul Cascio, and POW family members J. Watt Hinson, Linda West, Kathleen Birchall, Ruth Decker, Joyce Forth, Marian Tougas, Jan Richardson, Jennifer Purcell, Karen Heer, and Angie Giardina.

Stanley Pillsbury spent many afternoons on the phone with me, reliving his days aboard his beloved *Super Man,* the Christmas raid over Wake, and the moment when he shot down a Zero over Nauru. Frank Rosynek, a born raconteur, sent his unpublished memoir, "Not Everybody Wore Wings," and wrote to me about the bombing of Funafuti and Louie's miraculous return from the dead on Okinawa. Lester Herman Scearce and the late pilots John Joseph Deasy and Jesse Stay told of Wake, Nauru, Funafuti, and the search for the lost crew of *Green Hornet.* Martin Cohn told of squadron life on Hawaii; John Krey told of Louie's disappearance and reappearance. Byron Kinney described the day he flew his B-29 over Louie at Naoetsu and listened to the Japanese surrender as he flew back to Guam. John Weller described the fearfully complex job of a B-24 navigator.

I am deeply indebted to several Japanese people who spoke candidly of a dark hour in their nation's history. Yuichi Hatto, the Omori camp accountant and a friend to POWs, was an indispensable source on the Bird, Omori, and life as a Japanese soldier, answering my questions in writing, in his second language, when we were unable to speak on the telephone. Yoshi Kondo told me about the founding of the Joetsu Peace Park, and Shibui Genzi wrote to me about Japanese life in Naoetsu. Toru Fukubayashi and Taeko Sasamoto, historians with the POW Research Network Japan, answered my questions and pointed me toward sources.

The delightful Virginia "Toots" Bowersox Weitzel, Louie's childhood friend, made me cassette tapes of the most popular songs at Torrance High in the 1930s, narrating them with stories from her days as a school cheerleader. Toots, who passed away just before this book went to press, told of tackling Louie on his sixteenth birthday, cheering him on as he ran the Torrance track with Pete, and playing football with him in front of Kellow's Hamburg Stand in Long Beach. She was the only ninetysomething person I knew who was obsessed with *American Idol*. Olympians Velma Dunn Ploessel and Iris Cummings Critchell vividly described their experiences aboard the USS *Manhattan* and at the Berlin Games. Draggan Mihailovich told me of his remarkable encounter with the Bird. Georgie Bright Kunkel wrote to me about her brother, the great Norman Bright.

––––––

As I traced Louie's path through history, many people went out of their way to help me find information and make sense of it. With the assistance of former USAAF bombardier Robert Grenz, William Darron of the Army Air Forces Historical Association brought a Norden bombsight to my house, set it up in my dining room, put a rolling screen of Arizona beneath it, and taught me how to "bomb" Phoenix. As I worked on my book, Bill was always happy to answer my questions. Gary Weaver of Disabled American Veterans climbed all over a B-24 to film the interior for me; thanks to Gary Sinise for putting me in contact with Mr. Weaver. Charlie Tilghman, who flies a restored B-24 for the Commemorative Air Force, taught me about flying the Liberator.

When I was too ill to get to the National Archives, Peggy Ann Brown and Molly Brose went there for me, wading into voluminous POW and war-crimes records and coming back with some of my most critical material. John Brodkin typed up my citations to save me from my vertigo and climbed on my dining room table to photograph images out of Louie's scrapbook. Nina B. Smith translated POW documents from Norwegian, and Noriko Sanefuji translated my letters to and from Japanese sources. Julie Wheelock transcribed many of my interviews, straining to hear elderly voices taped on my nearly-as-elderly recorder. Gail Morgan of the Torrance High School Alumni Association dug through the school archives in search of photographs of Louie.

I also want to send thanks to Draggan Mihailovich, Christopher Svendsen, and Sean McManus of CBS, who kindly got me permission to view unaired videotape from CBS's 1998 feature on Louie. Roger Mansell's Center for Research, Allied POWs Under the Japanese (http://www.mansell.com/pow-index.html) was a comprehensive source of information on POW camps; thanks also to historian Wes Injerd, who works with Mansell's site. Jon Hendershott, associate editor at *Track and Field News,* helped me decipher confusing 1930s mile records. Paul Lombardo, author of *The One Sure Cure: Eugenics, the Supreme Court and Buck v. Bell,* and Tony Platt, author of *Bloodlines: Recovering Hitler's Nuremberg Laws,* taught me about eugenics. Rick Zitarosa of the Naval Lakehurst Historical Society answered questions about the *Graf Zeppelin.* Janet Fisher of the Northeast Regional Climate Center, Janet Wall of the National Climatic Data Center, and Keith Heidorn, PhD, of the Weather Doctor (http://www.islandnet.com/~see/weather/doctor.htm), answered weather-related questions. Fred Gill, MD, helped me understand Phil's head injury. Charles Stenger, PhD, cleared up my confusion on POW statistics.

Working with Yvonne Kinkaid and Colonel J. A. Saaverda (Ret.) of the Reference Team, Analysis and Reference Division, Air Force Historical Research and Analysis, Bolling Air Force Base, the wonderfully helpful Colonel Frank Trippi (Ret.) unearthed heaps of AAF documents for me. I am also grateful to Lieutenant Colonel Robert Clark, USAF (Ret.), at the Air Force Historical Studies Office, Bolling Air Force Base; Will Mahoney, Eric Van Slander, and Dave Giordano of the National Archives; Cathy Cox and Barry Spink of the Air Force Historical Research Agency, Maxwell Air Force Base; and Carol Leadenham, assistant archivist for reference at the Hoover Institution Archives. I also thank my dear friend Colonel Michael C. Howard, USMC (Ret.), who worked with Captain William Rudich, USN (Ret.), Lieutenant Colonel Todd Holmquist, USMC, Major Heather Cotoia, USMC, Boatswain's Mate Chief Frank Weber, USN (Ret.), and Jim

Heath, PhD, professor emeritus, Portland State University, to find information on Everett Almond, the navigator who was killed by a shark while trying to save himself and his pilot.

Thanks also to Pete Golkin, Office of Communications, National Air and Space Museum; Midge Fischer, EAA Warbirds of America; Patrick Ranfranz, Greg Babinski, and Jim Walsh of the 307th Bomb Group Association; Lieutenant Commander Ken Snyder of the National Naval Aviation Museum; Rich Kolb and Mike Meyer of the Veterans of Foreign Wars; Helen Furu of the Norwegian Maritime Museum; Siri Lawson of WarSailors.com; Phil Gudenschwager, 11th Bomb Group historian; Justin Mack, Web developer, 11th Bomb Group; Bill Barrette, Sugamo historian; Wayne Weber of the Billy Graham Center archives at Wheaton College; Melany Ethridge of Larry Ross Communications; Tess Miller and Heather VanKoughnett of the Billy Graham Evangelistic Association; Shirley Ito, librarian, LA84 Foundation; Victoria Palmer, Georgetown Public Library; Edith Miller, Palo Alto High School; Wayne Wilson, vice president, Amateur Athletic Foundation of Los Angeles; Lauren Walser of *USC Trojan Family* magazine; Cheryl Morris, Alumni Records, Princeton; Parker Bostwick of the *Torrance News Torch;* and Eric Spotts of Torrance High School.

Others who assisted me include my dear friend Alan Pocinki, who has helped me in more ways than I can count; Linda Goetz Holmes, author of *Unjust Enrichment;* Hampton Sides, author of *Ghost Soldiers;* Morton Janklow; Dave Tooley; Karen and Russ Scholar; William Baker, professor emeritus, University of Maine; John Powers of NorthChinaMarines.com; Ken Crothers; Christine Hoffman; Bud Ross; John Chapman; Robin Rowland; Ed Hotaling; Morton Cathro; Chris McCarron; Bob Curran; Mike Brown; Richard Glover; Jim Teegarden of pbyrescue.com; Tom Gwynne of *Wingslip;* Cheryl Cerbone, editor, *Ex-POW Bulletin;* Clydie Morgan, Ex American Prisoners of War; Mike Stone of accident-report.com; Dr. Stanley Hoffman; Kathy Hall; Jim Deasy; Captain Bob Rasmussen, USN (Ret.); Thorleif Andreassen; Janet McIlwain; Gary Staffo; Lynn Gamma; Patrick Hoffman; and Gene Venske.

There are several people to whom I owe special thanks. My brother John Hillenbrand, a longtime private pilot, reviewed the aircraft and flying sections of my book with an extraordinarily careful eye and helped me understand the arcane details of aeronautics. My sister,

Susan Avallon, read and reread the manuscript, offered invariably brilliant suggestions, and talked me through the places that had me stumped. Susan and John, I am so lucky to be your little sister. I also thank *EQUUS* magazine editor Laurie Prinz and my old Kenyon friend Chris Toft, who read my manuscript and gave me insightful suggestions.

The author of the beautifully written *Finish Forty and Home: The Untold Story of B-24s in the Pacific,* Phil Scearce, knows the world of the AAF's Pacific airmen better than any other historian. As I wrote this book, Phil was singularly generous, sharing his voluminous research, directing me to sources, and helping me sort through many a quandary. I am forever in his debt.

I have great gratitude for B 29 navigator and former POW Raymond "Hap" Halloran. As I wrote this book, Hap became my almost daily email correspondent, offering me research help, sharing his photographs, telling of his experiences, sending gifts to cheer my sister's children after their father's death, and simply being my friend. Very few human beings have seen humanity's dark side as Hap has, and yet he is ever buoyant, ever forgiving. Hap's resilient heart is my inspiration.

From the beginning of this project, I worked with two translators in Japan. They did so much more for me than mere translation, teaching me about their culture, helping me to understand the war from the Japanese perspective, and offering their thoughts on my manuscript. Because the war remains a highly controversial issue in Japan, they have asked me not to identify them, but I will never forget what they have done for me and for this book.

If I had a firstborn, I'd owe it to my editor, Jennifer Hershey. Jennifer was infinitely kind and infinitely patient, offering inspired suggestions on my manuscript, making countless accommodations for my poor health, and ushering me from first draft to last. I also thank my spectacularly talented agent, Tina Bennett, who guides me through authordom with a sure and supportive hand, and my former editor, Jon Karp, who saw the promise in this story from the beginning. Thanks also to Tina's assistant, Svetlana Katz, and Jennifer's assistant Courtney Moran.

In the many moments in which I was unsure if I could bring this book to a happy completion, my husband, Borden, was there to cheer me on. He spent long hours at our kitchen table, poring over my manuscript and making it stronger, and, when illness shrank my world to the upper floor of our house, filled that little world with joy. Thank you, Borden, for your boundless affection, for your wisdom, for your faith in me, and for always bringing me sandwiches.

Finally, I wish to remember the millions of Allied servicemen and prisoners of war who lived the story of the Second World War. Many of these men never came home; many others returned bearing emotional and physical scars that would stay with them for the rest of their lives. I come away from this book with the deepest appreciation for what these men endured, and what they sacrificed, for the good of humanity. It is to them that this book is dedicated.

Laura Hillenbrand
May 2010

NOTES

All letters to or from Louis Zamperini, or to or from his family members, as well as diaries, are from the papers of Louis Zamperini, except where noted otherwise.

All letters between Phillips family members, as well as Kelsey Phillips's unpublished memoir "A Life Story," are from the papers of Karen Loomis.

All interviews were conducted by the author, except where noted otherwise. As some seventy-five interviews were conducted with Louis Zamperini, citations of these interviews are not dated.

ABBREVIATIONS

AAFLA	Amateur Athletic Foundation of Los Angeles
AFHRA	Air Force Historical Research Agency
BGEA	Billy Graham Evangelistic Association
HIA	Hoover Institution Archives
NACP	National Archives at College Park, Maryland
NHC	Naval Historical Center
NPN	No publication named
NYT	New York Times
RAOOH	Records of Allied Operational and Occupation Headquarters
RG	Record Group
SCAP	Supreme Commander of Allied Powers

Preface
xvii Raft: "42nd Bombardment Squadron: Addendum to Squadron History," September 11, 1945, AFHRA, Maxwell AFB, Ala.; Louis Zamperini, telephone interview;

Robert Trumbull, "Zamperini, Olympic Miler, Is Safe After Epic Ordeal," *NYT,* September 9, 1945.

xviii Four-minute mile: Charlie Paddock, "Sportorials," April 1938 newspaper article from Zamperini scrapbook, NPN; George Davis, "For Sake of Sport," *Los Angeles Evening Herald and Express,* undated 1938 article from Zamperini scrapbook; George Davis, "Cunningham Predicts Zamperini Next Mile Champ," undated article from Zamperini scrapbook, NPN; Paul Scheffels, "4 Minute Mile Run Is Closer," *Modesto* (Calif.) *Bee,* February 14, 1940.

PART I

Chapter 1: The One-Boy Insurgency

3 *Graf Zeppelin:* Douglas Botting, *Dr. Eckener's Dream Machine: The Great Zeppelin and the Dawn of Air Travel* (New York: Henry Holt, 2001), pp. 146–88; "Zeppelin Shatters Record," *Salt Lake Tribune,* August 11, 1929; "Zeppelin at L.A.," *Modesto News-Herald,* August 26, 1929; "Zep to Sail Tonight for N.Y.," *San Mateo Times,* August 26, 1929; "Graf Zeppelin Bids Adieu and Soars Homeward," *Chillicothe Constitution-Tribune,* August 8, 1929; Louis Zamperini, telephone interview; Peter Zamperini, telephone interview, March 2, 2006; Rick Zitarosa, Navy Lakehurst Historical Society, email interview, April 25, 2006; Lyle C. Wilson, "Eckener Follows Lindbergh Trail on Homeward Trip," *Daily Northwestern* (Oshkosh, Wisc.), August 8, 1929; W. W. Chaplin, "Graf Zeppelin on Long Trail around World," *Jefferson City Post-Tribune,* August 8, 1929; "Big German Zep Starts World Tour," *Moberly* (Mo.) *Monitor-Index,* August 8, 1929; "Zep's Ocean Hop Starts in Midweek," *Salt Lake Tribune,* August 20, 1929; Karl H. Von Wiegand, "Graf Zeppelin Rides Typhoon Trail to Port," *Salt Lake Tribune,* August 20, 1929; Miles H. Vaughn, "Graf Zeppelin Scores Great Hit with Orient," *Billings Gazette,* August 28, 1929; "In the Spotlight of Today's News," *Waterloo* (Iowa) *Evening Courier,* August 26, 1929; "Zeppelin Will Continue Flight Tonight," *Waterloo* (Iowa) *Evening Courier,* August 26, 1929; "Mikado of Japan to Receive 'Graf' Voyagers at Tea," *Waterloo* (Iowa) *Evening Courier,* August 20, 1929; "Stars Playing Hide and Seek with Zeppelin," *Salt Lake Tribune,* August 25, 1929.

4 Hitler's speech: David Welch, *Hitler: Profile of a Dictator* (London: Routledge, 1998), p. 80.

4 "like a huge shark": Botting, p. 180.

4 Looked like monsters: Ibid., p. 181.

4 "fearfully beautiful": Louis Zamperini, telephone interview.

5 Family history: Peter Zamperini, telephone interviews, October 19, 22, 2004.

5 Boyhood stories: Art Rosenbaum, "Zamperini Cheated Death Nine Times," *San Francisco Chronicle* Sporting Green, March 3, 1940; Maxwell Stiles, "Fire Threatened Career of Zamperini as Child," *Los Angeles Examiner,* undated, 1938; Peter Zamperini, telephone interview, October 22, 2004; Louis Zamperini, telephone interviews; Sylvia Flammer, telephone interviews, October 25, 27, 2004; Louis Zamperini, interview by George Hodak, Hollywood, Calif., June 1988, AAFLA.

8 "Pete never got caught": Sylvia Flammer, telephone interview, October 25, 2004.

8 Italians were disliked: Peter Zamperini, telephone interview, October 15, 2004.

9 "You could beat him": Sylvia Flammer, telephone interview, October 25, 2004.

9 "Louie can't stand it": Peter Zamperini, telephone interview, October 17, 2004.

9 Louie's parents: Peter Zamperini, telephone interview, October 15, 2004; Louis Zamperini, telephone interviews; Sylvia Flammer, telephone interviews, October 25, 27, 2004.

10 "You only asked": Peter Zamperini, telephone interview, October 22, 2004.

10 "It was a matter": Sylvia Flammer, telephone interview, October 25, 2004.

11 Louie's troublemaking: Peter Zamperini, telephone interviews, October 15, 17, 19, 22, 2004; Louis Zamperini, telephone interviews; Sylvia Flammer, telephone interviews, October 25, 27, 2004, and March 2, 2006.

11 Improvising meals: Peter Zamperini, telephone interview, October 22, 2004.

11 Unemployment near 25 percent: United States Census Bureau, U.S. Department of Commerce, http://www.census.gov/rochi/www/fun1.html#1900 (accessed September 7, 2009).

11 Eugenics: Paul Lombardo, "Eugenic Sterilization Laws," Dolan DNA Learning Center, Cold Spring Harbor Laboratory, http://www.eugenicsarchive.org (accessed April 13, 2006); Paul Lombardo, email interview, April 13, 2006; Edwin Black, "Eugenics and the Nazis—the California connection," *San Francisco Chronicle*, November 9, 2003; Anthony Platt, professor emeritus, California State University, email interview, April 13, 2006; Anthony Platt, "The Frightening Agenda of the American Eugenics Movement" (remarks made before California Senate Judiciary Committee, June 24, 2003).

11 Infecting patients with tuberculosis: Edwin Black, "Eugenics and the Nazis—the California Connection," *San Francisco Chronicle*, November 9, 2003.

11 Torrance boy threatened with sterilization: Louis Zamperini, telephone interview.

12 He was "bighearted": Peter Zamperini, telephone interview, October 17, 2004.

12 Listening to train: Louis Zamperini, telephone interview.

Chapter 2: Run Like Mad

14 Pete gets Louie's sports ban lifted: Peter Zamperini, telephone interview, October 17, 2004; Louis Zamperini, telephone interviews.

14 Pete's athletic career: "Track Stars Graduate," undated 1934 newspaper article from Zamperini scrapbook, NPN; "Pete Zamperini Sets Record," undated 1934 newspaper article from Zamperini scrapbook, NPN; "Pete Zamperini Goes to USC," undated 1934 newspaper article from Zamperini scrapbook, NPN.

14 First race: Peter Zamperini, telephone interview, October 17, 2004; Louis Zamperini, telephone interviews; Louis Zamperini, interview by George Hodak, Hollywood, Calif., June 1988, AAFLA.

14 Pete hits Louie with stick: Louis Zamperini, telephone interviews; Maxwell Stiles, "Switch Helped Troy Star Learn to Run," undated 1937 newspaper article from Zamperini papers, NPN.

14 Running away, Cahuilla: Louis Zamperini, telephone interviews.

15 Training: Louis Zamperini, telephone interviews; Peter Zamperini, telephone interview, October 17, 2004; Louis Zamperini, interview by George Hodak, Hollywood, Calif., June 1988, AAFLA; Virginia Bowersox Weitzel, telephone interview, February 19, 2005.

16 Cunningham: Mark D. Hersey, "Cunningham Calls It a Career," KU Connection,

April 8, 2002, http://www.kuconnection.org/april2002/people_Glenn.asp (accessed June 7, 2006); Paul J. Kiell, *American Miler: The Life and Times of Glenn Cunningham* (Halcottsville, N.Y.: Breakaway Books, 2006), pp. 21–149.

16 Fall of 1932 training: Peter Zamperini, telephone interview, October 19, 2004; Louis Zamperini, telephone interviews.

17 Louie's stride: Peter Zamperini, telephone interview, October 17, 2004.

17 *"Smooooooth"*: Virginia Bowersox Weitzel, telephone interview, February 19, 2005.

17 Weenie bakes: Virginia Bowersox Weitzel, telephone interview, February 19, 2005.

17 Louie's time improvement: "Louie 'Iron Man' Zamperini," undated 1934 newspaper article from papers of Peter Zamperini, NPN.

17 "Boy!": "Sport Winks," March 10, 1933, NPN, from Zamperini scrapbook.

17 Two-mile race: "Crack Miler of Torrance Takes Distance Event," October 28, 1933, no newspaper named, from Zamperini scrapbook.

17 UCLA race: "Iron Man Zamperini Wins," *Torrance Herald,* December 16, 1933; Peter Zamperini, telephone interview, October 15, 2004; Louis Zamperini, telephone interviews.

Chapter 3: The Torrance Tornado

19 "sadly disheartened": Undated 1934 article from Zamperini scrapbook, NPN.

19 "the boy who doesn't know": Ibid.

19 Southern California Track and Field Championship: "Zamperini Runs Mile in 4m 21⅕," *Los Angeles Times,* May 24, 1934; Peter Zamperini, telephone interview, October 15, 2004; Louis Zamperini, telephone interviews.

20 Interscholastic records: Jon Hendershott, associate editor, *Track and Field News,* email interview, May 6, 2009; "Zamperini Runs Mile in 4m 21⅕," *Los Angeles Times,* May 24, 1934; "Mercersburg's Great Trio," *Fort Wayne Daily News,* June 3, 1916; Bert Dahlgren, "Reedley's Bob Seaman Is Pushed to National Mile Record of 4:21," *Fresno Bee-Republican,* May 30, 1953; "Dobbs Seeks World Mile Record," *Oakland Tribune,* May 3, 1929.

21 "Torrance Tempest": "Louis Zamperini of Torrance," *Los Angeles Times,* December 31, 1934.

21 *Herald* insures legs: Peter Zamperini, telephone interview, July 10, 2006; Louis Zamperini, telephone interview.

21 Top milers peak in mid-twenties: Charlie Paddock, "Spikes," undated 1938 article from Zamperini scrapbook, NPN.

21 Cunningham world record, fastest high school mile, fastest career mile: "History of the Record for the Mile Run," InfoPlease, www.infoplease.com (accessed July 9, 2004); Kiell, pp. 99–126, 266–67.

22 Compton Open preparation: Peter Zamperini, telephone interview, October 15, 2004; Louis Zamperini, telephone interviews; Louis Zamperini, interview by George Hodak, Hollywood, Calif., June 1988, AAFLA.

22 "If you stay": Peter Zamperini, telephone interview, October 15, 2004.

22 "fifteen-minute torture chamber": Louis Zamperini, letter to Louise Zamperini, July 14, 1936.

22 Compton Open: Undated articles from Zamperini scrapbook, no publications named; Peter Zamperini, telephone interview, October 19, 2004; Louis Zamperini,

telephone interviews; Louis Zamperini, interview by George Hodak, Hollywood, Calif., June 1988, AAFLA.

23 Final qualifying race: "Bright of San Francisco Club," undated article from Zamperini scrapbook, NPN.

23 Send-off to Olympic trials: Louis Zamperini, telephone interviews.

23 Heat: Janet Fisher, Northeast Regional Climate Center, Cornell University, email interview, July 7, 2006; Keith Heidorn, PhD, "How Hot Can It Get? The Great Heat Wave of 1936," The Weather Doctor, http://www.islandnet.com/weather/almanac/arc2006/almo6jul.htm (accessed May 1, 2006); Janet Wall, National Climatic Data Center, email interview, July 7, 2006; Louis Zamperini, telephone interviews; "Cooler Weather in the East Is Delayed Again," *Daily Messenger* (Canandaigua, N.Y.), July 13, 1936; William F. McIrath, "Heat Wave Deaths Pass 3,000 Mark," *Dunkirk* (N.Y.) *Evening Observer*, July 15, 1936; Dr. James LuValle, interview by George Hodak, Palo Alto, Calif., June 1988, AAFLA; Malcolm W. Metcalf, interviewed by George A. Hodak, Claremont, Calif., February 1988, AAFLA; Archie F. Williams, interviewed by George A. Hodak, Santa Rosa, Calif., June 1988, AAFLA; Kenneth Griffin, interview by George Hodak, Carlsbad, Calif., August 1988, AAFLA.

23 Race preparations: Louis Zamperini, letter to Pete Zamperini, July 10, 1936.

24 Prerace coverage, "If I have any": Louis Zamperini, letter to Pete Zamperini, July 1936.

24 Lash as unbeatable: Alan Gould, "Two New Records Fall Before Indiana's Lash," *Burlington* (N.C.) *Daily Times-News*, July 4, 1936; Alan Gould, "Lash Tops U.S. Distance Stars on Trail of First Olympic Title," *Kingston* (N.Y.) *Daily Freeman*, June 27, 1936.

24 "made a wreck of me": "Runner Tells," *Torrance Herald*, September 3, 1936.

24 Olympic trial: "Local Boy Runs Dead Heat," *Los Angeles Times*, July 12, 1936; Bob Lwellyn, untitled article, *Torrance Herald*, July 1936; "Twenty Californians," undated article from Zamperini scrapbook, NPN; Louis Zamperini, interview by George Hodak, Hollywood, Calif., June 1988, AAFLA; "Stars Fall in Games but Negro Contingent Shines," *Helena Daily Independent*, July 13, 1936; George Kirksey, "Records Fall, Champions Beaten in Bitter Finals for American Games Team," *Olean* (N.Y.) *Times-Herald*, July 13, 1936; Henry McLemore, "America Sends Strongest Team to the Olympics," *Dunkirk* (N.Y.) *Evening Observer*, July 15, 1936; George T. Davis, "Zamperini Had Confidence in Ability," *Los Angeles Evening Herald and Express*, July 11, 1936; "Torrance Tornado in Dead Heat," *Torrance Herald*, July 16, 1936; Peter Zamperini, letter to Louis Zamperini, July 19, 1936.

25 "you couldn't put a hair": Louis Zamperini, telephone interview, July 10, 2006.

26 "jackass eating cactus": Telegram, Mr. and Mrs. J. O. Bishop to Louis Zamperini, July 14, 1936.

27 Bright's injured feet: "Louie Says He Won," *Torrance Herald*, July 16, 1936; Louis Zamperini, telephone interview.

27 Norman Bright's running: Georgie Bright Kunkel, "My Brother Was a Long-Distance Runner," *West Seattle Herald*, August 21, 2008.

27 Telegrams: Louis Zamperini, letter to Louise Zamperini, July 14, 1936; Zamperini scrapbook; *Torrance Herald*, undated article from Zamperini scrapbook, NPN.

27 "Am I ever happy": Peter Zamperini, letter to Louis Zamperini, July 19, 1936.

27 Youngest distance runner: Bob Lwellyn, untitled article, *Torrance Herald,* July 1936.

Chapter 4: Plundering Germany

28 Stealing: Louis Zamperini, interview by George Hodak, Hollywood, Calif., June 1988, AAFLA.

28 Mustache: Louis Zamperini, Olympic diary, July 22, 1936, entry.

28 "They had nothing on me": Louis Zamperini, telephone interview.

28 Training on ship: Iris Cummings Critchell, telephone interview, September 29, 2005; Iris Cummings Critchell, interviewed by George A. Hodak, Claremont, Calif., May 1988, AAFLA; Velma Dunn Ploessel, telephone interview, June 16, 2005; Louis Zamperini, Olympic diary; Velma Dunn Ploessel, interviewed by George A. Hodak, Downey, Calif., July 1988, AAFLA; Herbert H. Wildman, interviewed by George A. Hodak, Marina del Rey, Calif., October 1987, AAFLA; Arthur O. Mollner, interviewed by George A. Hodak, Westlake Village, Calif., May 1988, AAFLA.

29 Louie had eaten in restaurants only twice: Louis Zamperini, Olympic diary; Louis Zamperini, telephone interview.

29 Food on the *Manhattan:* Louis Zamperini, interview by George Hodak, Hollywood, Calif., June 1988, AAFLA; Archie F. Williams, interviewed by George A. Hodak, Santa Rosa, Calif., June 1988, AAFLA.

30 "Of course, most of this was due," Louie sitting with Jack Torrance: Dr. James LuValle, interview by George Hodak, Palo Alto, Calif., June 1988, AAFLA.

30 Dinner list: Jack Coleman, letter to Louis Zamperini, list and commentary written on back.

30 Weight gain: Kenneth Griffin, interview by George Hodak, Carlsbad, Calif., August 1988, AAFLA; Louis Zamperini, Olympic diary; "First Light Workouts," article in Zamperini scrapbook, July 23, 1936, NPN; Malcolm W. Metcalf, interviewed by George A. Hodak, Claremont, Calif., February 1988, AAFLA.

31 Athletes stealing glasses: Joanna de Tuscan Harding, interviewed by George A. Hodak, Hollywood Hills, Calif., April 1988, AAFLA.

31 *"Wo ist Jesse?":* Dr. James LuValle, interview by George Hodak, Palo Alto, Calif., June 1988, AAFLA.

31 Olympic Village: Arvo Vercamer and Jason Pipes, "The 1936 Olympic Games in Germany," www.feldgrau.com (accessed July 19, 2006); Richard Mandell, *The Nazi Olympics* (Urbana: University of Illinois Press, 1987), pp. 88–92, 138; Louis Zamperini, interview by George Hodak, Hollywood, Calif., June 1988, AAFLA.

31 Japanese feeding deer: "Sports Parade," *Los Angeles Examiner,* July 30, 1936.

31 Storks: Arvo Vercamer and Jason Pipes, "The 1936 Olympic Games in Germany," www.feldgrau.com (accessed July 19, 2006).

31 Owens pursued by fans: Dr. James LuValle, interview by George Hodak, Palo Alto, Calif., June 1988, AAFLA.

31 Drive through Berlin: Mandell, pp. 139–43; Herbert H. Wildman, interviewed by George A. Hodak, Marina del Rey, Calif., October 1987, AAFLA.

31 Gliders: Iris Cummings Critchell, telephone interview, September 29, 2005.

31 Gypsies: "The Facade of Hospitality," U.S. Holocaust Museum, www.ushm.org/museum/exhibit/online/olympics/zcd062.htm (accessed June 16, 2005).

32 Doves: Louis Zamperini, telephone interview; Iris Cummings Critchell, telephone interview, September 29, 2005; Mandell, p. 145.

32 Bulging eyes, Louie versus Finns: "Sport Shorts," undated article in Zamperini scrapbook, NPN.

32 German nationalism: Iris Cummings Critchell, telephone interview, September 29, 2005; Iris Cummings Critchell, interviewed by George A. Hodak, Claremont, Calif., May 1988, AAFLA.

32 *"Don't let them see me!":* Iris Cummings Critchell, telephone interview, September 29, 2005.

32 Qualifying round: "Owens in New Record," *Los Angeles Evening Herald and Express,* August 4, 1936; "Zamperini Is In," *Torrance Herald,* August 6, 1936.

33 "tired as hell": Louis Zamperini, Olympic diary, August 4, 1936, entry.

33 Olympic final: Louis Zamperini, telephone interview; "Finn Star Wins 5,000 Meter Title," *Waterloo Daily Courier,* August 7, 1936; "Archie Williams Wins 400 Meter Title," *Galveston Daily News,* August 8, 1936; "Sweep in Sprints," *Emporia Gazette,* August 7, 1936; "First American," undated article from Zamperini scrapbook, NPN; "Three Americans," undated article in Zamperini scrapbook, NPN; "Brown Skies," *Los Angeles Times,* August 8, 1936; "Sports Parade," *Los Angeles Times,* August 14, 1936; Stuart Cameron, "Finland Wins Clean Sweep in Distance Running by Taking 5000-Meter Finals," *Dunkirk* (N.Y.) *Evening Observer,* August 7, 1936; "Olympic Games Results," *Reno Evening Gazette,* August 7, 1936; "Archie Williams Wins 400 Meter Final," *Chester* (Pa.) *Times,* August 7, 1936; "Williams Victory Gives U.S. Olympic Dash Sweep," *Syracuse* (N.Y.) *Herald,* August 7, 1936; "Dusky Archie: United States Athletes Take One, Two, Three Lead in Olympics Decathlon," *San Antonio Express,* August 8, 1936.

34 Hitler contorting himself: "Cunningham," *Los Angeles Times,* August 8, 1936.

34 Final laps in distance races: Bill Henry, "Bill Henry Says," *Los Angeles Times,* undated; Mandell, p. 40.

35 Meeting Hitler: Louis Zamperini, telephone interview; Louis Zamperini, interview by George Hodak, Hollywood, Calif., June 1988, AAFLA.

35 Flag: "Zamperini Stormed Hitler's Palace—Lived!," undated article from Zamperini papers, NPN; "Bombardier Zamperini Seeks Return Trip to Germany," article from Zamperini papers, August 13, 1942, NPN; "Zamp Will Try Again," article from Zamperini papers, August 13, 1942, NPN; Louis Zamperini, telephone interviews; Louis Zamperini, interview by George Hodak, Hollywood, Calif., June 1988, AAFLA.

37 Lubin sees anti-Semitism: Frank J. Lubin, interviewed by George A. Hodak, Glendale, Calif., May 1988, AAFLA.

37 Anti-Semitic signs, *Der Stürmer*: "The Facade of Hospitality," U.S. Holocaust Museum, www.ushm.org/museum/exhibit/online/olympics/detail.php?content-facade_hospitality_more&lang=en (accessed April 29, 2010).

37 Fürstner kills himself: Mandell, p. 92.

37 Sachsenhausen: "The Facade of Hospitality," U.S. Holocaust Museum, www.ushm.org/museum/exhibit/online/olympics/detail.php?content=facade_hospitality_more&lang=en (accessed April 29, 2010).

37 Homecoming: "Zamperini Home," *Torrance Herald,* September 3, 1936; "Invalid Woman," *Torrance Herald,* undated article from Zamperini scrapbook; "Olympic Games Hero," *Torrance Herald,* September 3, 1936; "Runner Tells," *Torrance Herald,* September 3, 1936; "Cheering Mass," *Torrance Herald,* September 4, 1936; Louis Zamperini, telephone interview; Louis Zamperini, interview by George Hodak, Hollywood, Calif., June 1988, AAFLA.

37 "I didn't only": "Cheering Mass," *Torrance Herald,* September 4, 1936.

37 Plans for 1940: "Runner Tells," *Torrance Herald,* September 3, 1936; Louis Zamperini, telephone interview; Peter Zamperini, telephone interviews, October 15, 17, 19, 22, 2004.

37 Tokyo given 1940 Games: "Tokyo Prepares," article from Zamperini scrapbook, August 1, 1936, NPN.

Chapter 5: Into War

38 Payton Jordan: Payton Jordan, telephone interviews, August 13, 16, 2004.

38 High jumper on her bed: Sylvia Flammer, telephone interviews, October 25, 27, 2004.

38 Pranks: Louis Zamperini, telephone interview.

38 Sasaki: Louis Zamperini, telephone interview; Payton Jordan, telephone interviews, August 13, 16, 2004; Bruce Gamble, *Black Sheep One: The Life of Gregory "Pappy" Boyington* (Novato, Calif.: Presidio, 2000), p. 323; the following Kunichi Sasaki and James Kunichi Sasaki records from RG 331, RAOOH, WWII, 1907–1966, SCAP, Legal Section, Administration Division and Prosecution Division, NACP: Kunichi Sasaki, Isamu Sato, Kazuo Akane, 1945–1948, Investigation and Interrogation Reports; Nakakichi Asoma et al., trial, exhibits, appeal, and clemency files; Nakakichi Asoma et al., 1945–1952, POW 201 File, 1945–1952, Charges and Specifications, 1945–1948.

40 Sasaki's true college record: Harvard, Yale, Princeton, USC registrar archives; inquiries with Degreecheck.com, April 2007.

40 Louie's winning: George Davis, "Fresno Relays Are Next," undated article in Zamperini scrapbook, NPN; "Zamperini Stars," *Los Angeles Examiner,* May 8, 1938; "Zamperini, Day Smash Meet Marks," undated 1938 article in Zamperini scrapbook, NPN.

40 Coach predicts world record: Lee Bastajian, "Trojans Meet Stanford," undated spring 1938 article from Zamperini scrapbook, NPN.

40 Seabiscuit only runner to beat him: Louis Zamperini, telephone interview.

40 Cunningham prediction: George Davis, "Cunningham Predicts Zamperini Next Mile Champ," undated 1938 article from Zamperini scrapbook, NPN.

40 Fastest mile projected to be 4:01.6: Brutus Hamilton, *Amateur Athlete,* February 1935.

40 Louie training on stairs: Louis Zamperini, telephone interview; Louis Zamperini, interview by George Hodak, Hollywood, Calif., June 1988, AAFLA.

41 First four-minute man: Charlie Paddock, "Sportorials," undated April 1938 article from Zamperini scrapbook, NPN; George Davis, "For Sake of Sport," *Los Angeles Evening Herald and Express,* undated 1938 article from Zamperini scrapbook; George Davis, "Cunningham Predicts Zamperini Next Mile Champ," undated article from Zamperini scrapbook, NPN; "History of the Record for the Mile Run,"

InfoPlease, www.infoplease.com (accessed July 9, 2004); Paul Scheffels, "4 Minute Mile Run Is Closer," *Modesto* (Calif.) *Bee,* February 14, 1940.

41 Prerace warning: Louis Zamperini, telephone interview; Payton Jordan, telephone interviews, August 13, 16, 2004; Louis Zamperini, interview by George Hodak, Hollywood, Calif., June 1988, AAFLA.

41 1938 NCAA Championship race: Louis Zamperini, telephone interview; Payton Jordan, telephone interviews, August 13, 16, 2004; "Zamperini's Record Mile Beats Fenske," *Minnesota Journal,* June 18, 1938; Charles Johnson, "Zamperini Sets Mark," *Star Nighthawk,* June 18, 1938; "Mile Record Smashed at Collegiate Meet," *Minneapolis Tribune,* June 18, 1938; Louis Zamperini, interview by George Hodak, Hollywood, Calif., June 1988, AAFLA.

41 Crowd gasps, *Woooo!:* Payton Jordan, telephone interviews, August 13, 16, 2004.

42 Japan drops Olympics, Finland takes over: Relman Morin, "Japan Abandons Olympics Plans," *Appleton* (Wisc.) *Post-Crescent,* July 14, 1938; "Finland Okays Olympic Games," *Lowell* (Mass.) *Sun,* July 19, 1938.

42 Louie's indoor races: "Fenske Outruns Zamperini by Three Yards," *Fresno Bee,* February 18, 1940; "Fenske Again Beats Best U.S. Milers," *Oakland Tribune,* February 18, 1940; "Fenske's Brilliant Millrose Victory Stamps Him 'King of Milers,'" *Nebraska State Journal* (Lincoln), February 5, 1940; Paul Scheffels, "4 Minute Mile Run Is Closer," *Modesto* (Calif.) *Bee,* February 14, 1940.

42 Indoor versus outdoor records: Jon Hendershott, associate editor, *Track and Field News,* email interview, May 6, 2009; Wally Donovan, *A History of Indoor Track and Field* (El Cajon, Calif.: Edward Jules Co., 1976), p. 294; "History of the Record for the Mile Run," InfoPlease, www.infoplease.com (accessed July 9, 2004).

43 Japan's economic plight, ambitions, preparations: David James, *The Rise and Fall of the Japanese Empire* (London: George Allen and Unwin, 1951), pp. 6–17, 119–27, 168, 173; Iris Chang, *The Rape of Nanking: The Forgotten Holocaust of World War II* (London: Penguin Books, 1998), pp. 25–38.

43 "There are superior": John W. Dower, *War Without Mercy: Race and Power in the Pacific War* (New York: Pantheon Books, 1993), p. 217.

43 "plant the blood": Ibid., p. 277.

43 Military-run schools, soldier training: Chang, pp. 29–32, 57; James Bradley, *Flyboys* (New York: Little, Brown, 2003), pp. 34–36.

43 "Imbuing violence": Chang, p. 218.

44 Stadium partially collapsed: Lon Jones, "War Cheats Trojans: Olympic Chances Lost," *Los Angeles Examiner,* February 28, 1940.

44 Lehtinen gives medal: "Lauri Lehtinen," All Experts, http://en.allexperts.com/e/l/la/lauri_lehtinen.htm (accessed September 11, 2009).

44 Bright, Cunningham enlist: Kiell, pp. 320–21; Georgie Bright Kunkel, "My Brother Was a Long Distance Runner," *West Seattle Herald,* August 21, 2008.

45 Jittery and airsick: Louis Zamperini, letter to Virginia Zamperini, April 10, 1941; Louis Zamperini, telephone interview.

45 Candy bars: Louis Zamperini, telephone interview.

46 Informant's report: Letters between J. Edgar Hoover and Brigadier General Sherman Miles, October–November 1941, FBI, acquired from Department of the Army, United States Army Intelligence and Security Command, Freedom of Information/Privacy Office, Fort George G. Meade, Md.

46 Notes from police officer: Notes by Captain Ernie Ashton, Torrance police detective, written alongside a passage on Sasaki in Ashton's copy of Zamperini's 1956 autobiography, *Devil at My Heels,* from papers of Louis Zamperini.

46 Sasaki in Washington: The following Kunichi Sasaki and James Kunichi Sasaki records from RG 331, RAOOH, WWII, 1907–1966, SCAP, Legal Section, Administration Division and Prosecution Division, NACP: Kunichi Sasaki, Isamu Sato, Kazuo Akane, 1945–1948, Investigation and Interrogation Reports; Nakakichi Asoma et al., trial, exhibits, appeal, and clemency files; Nakakichi Asoma et al., 1945–1952, POW 201 File, 1945–1952, Charges and Specifications, 1945–1948.

46 Hoover orders probe: Letters between J. Edgar Hoover and Brigadier General Sherman Miles, October–November 1941, Federal Bureau of Investigation, acquired from Department of the Army, United States Army Intelligence and Security Command, Freedom of Information/Privacy Office, Fort George G. Meade, Md.

46 Pilot over Hawaii: Mitsuo Fuchida and Masatake Okumiya, *Midway: The Battle That Doomed Japan* (Bluejack Books, 2001).

46 Activities on Oahu: William Cleveland, ed., *Grey Geese Calling* (Askov: American Publishing, 1981), p. 203; Stetson Conn, Rose Engelman, and Byron Fairchild, *United States Army in World War II: Guarding the United States and Its Outposts* (Washington, D.C.: Center of Military History, U.S. Army, 1964), p. 191; Clive Howard and Joe Whitley, *One Damned Island After Another: The Saga of the Seventh* (Chapel Hill: University of North Carolina Press, 1946), p. 25; Robert Cressman and J. Michael Wenger, "Infamous Day," Marines in WWII Commemorative Series, http://www.nps.gov/archive/wapa/indepth/extContent/usmc/pcn-190-003116-00/sec3.htm (accessed September 10, 2009).

47 Two planes lost: "Timeline Pearl Harbor," Pearl Harbor Remembered, http://my.execpc.com/~dschaaf/mainmenu.html (accessed April 29, 2010).

47 Man killed during pillow fight, friend sees Japanese plane crash: Cleveland, p. 203.

47 Louie, Pete learn of Pearl Harbor: Louis Zamperini, telephone interview; Peter Zamperini, telephone interview, October 19, 2004.

PART II

Chapter 6: The Flying Coffin

51 Pancakes: Ken Marvin, telephone interview, January 31, 2005.

52 *"Calm!":* William Manchester, *The Glory and the Dream: A Narrative History of America, 1932–1972* (New York: Bantam Books, 1974), p. 258.

52 Eleanor Roosevelt writes Anna: Doris Kearns Goodwin, *No Ordinary Time: Franklin and Eleanor Roosevelt—the Home Front in World War II* (New York: Simon and Schuster, 1994), p. 289.

52 Butler overheard president: Ibid., p. 290.

52 Japanese staffers burning documents: "Japanese Embassy Burns Official Papers," *Wisconsin State Journal* (Madison), December 8, 1941; Manchester, p. 258.

52 Days after December 7: Carl Nolte, "Pearl Harbor Was a Close Thing for the City in 1941," *San Francisco Chronicle,* December 7, 2006; Stanley Pillsbury, telephone interview, August 25, 2004; "Entire City Put on War Footing," *NYT,* December 8, 1941; "U.S. Cities Prove They Can Swing into Action," *Wisconsin State Journal* (Madison), December 8, 1941; Adam Fjell, " 'A Day That Will Live in Infamy':

Buffalo County and the Attack on Pearl Harbor," *Buffalo Tales,* November–December 2002, vol. 25, no. 6; Goodwin, pp. 295–96.

52 Wake's defense: Lieutenant Colonel R. D. Heinl, Jr., USMC, *The Defense of Wake, Marines in World War II: Historical Monograph* (Historical Section, Division of Public Information Headquarters, U.S. Marine Corps, 1947).

53 Men on Wake singing: Ken Marvin, telephone interview, January 31, 2005.

53 Louie's test scores: Certificate of Proficiency, Air Force Preflight School (bombardier, navigator), Ellington Field, from papers of Louis Zamperini.

53 Norden bombsight: William Darron, Army Air Forces Historical Association, Oradell, N.J., interview and bombsight demonstration, courtesy of Robert Grenz, 2004; Louis Zamperini, telephone interview; "Bombardiers' Information File," War Department, Army Air Forces, March 1945.

53 Twice the price of a house: "The Year 1942," The People History, http://www.thepeoplehistory.com/1942.html (accessed September 11, 2009); "The Norden M-1 Bomb Sight," Plane Crazy, http://www.plane-crazy.net/links/nord.htm (accessed September 11, 2009).

55 Ephrata: Sam Britt, Jr., *The Long Rangers, A Diary of the 307th Bombardment Group* (Baton Rouge: Reprint Company, 1990), pp. 4–5.

55 Phillips: Karen Loomis, telephone interview, November 17, 2004; Monroe Bormann, telephone interview, June 7, 2005; Phoebe Bormann, telephone interview, June 7, 2005; Louis Zamperini, telephone interview; Jesse Stay, telephone interviews, July 23, 2004, and March 16, 2005; Kelsey Phillips, "A Life Story," unpublished memoir.

55 Sandblaster: Jesse Stay, telephone interviews, July 23, 2004, and March 16, 2005.

57 Cecy Perry: Karen Loomis, telephone interview, November 17, 2004; Monroe Bormann, telephone interview, June 7, 2005; Phoebe Bormann, telephone interview, June 7, 2005; letters from Russell Phillips to Cecy Perry, 1941–43.

57 Cecy's ring: Russell Allen Phillips, letters to Cecy Perry, March 11, 21, 1942.

57 "I've wished 100 times": Russell Allen Phillips, letter to Cecy Phillips, summer 1942.

58 Phil's bomber crew: Stanley Pillsbury, telephone interviews, August 25, 2004, March 9, 2005, and August 18, 2006; Charles McMurtry, "Liberator, Hit 594 Times, Wings Home Safely," *Richmond News Leader,* May 14, 1943.

58 Harry Brooks's fiancée: "Sergt. H. V. Brooks Served in Pacific," undated article from Phillips scrapbook, NPN.

59 B-24s: Charlie Tilghman, B-24 pilot, Commemorative Air Force, telephone interview, February 14, 2007; Consolidated Aircraft, *Flight Manual: B-24D Airplane (1942), Flight Manual for B-24 Liberator,* Aircraft Manual Series (Appleton, Wisc.: Aviation Publications, 1977); Martin Bowman, *Combat Legend: B-24 Liberator* (Shrewsbury, Eng.: Airlife, 2003); Frederick A. Johnsen, *B-24 Liberator, Rugged but Right* (New York: McGraw-Hill, 1999); Fiske Hanley II, telephone interview, July 30, 2004; Byron Kinney, email interview, April 26, 2007.

59 "it was like sitting": Byron Kinney, email interview, April 26, 2007.

60 Left arms stronger: Stephen E. Ambrose, *The Wild Blue: The Men and Boys Who Flew the B-24s over Germany* (New York: Simon and Schuster, 2001), p. 77.

60 Tails falling off: Johnsen, p. 28.

60 "It's the Flying Coffin": Louis Zamperini, telephone interview.

60 Training: Stanley Pillsbury, telephone interviews, August 25, 2004, March 9, 2005, and August 18, 2006.

61 "I grew a little": Russell Allen Phillips, letter to Cecy Perry, August or September 1942.

61 "I guess you read": E. C. Williams, letter to Louis Zamperini, July 1, 1941.

61 Stateside crash statistics: *Army Air Forces Statistical Digest, World War II*, Office of Statistical Control, December 1945, Tables 213 and 214.

61 Deaths of friends: Russell Allen Phillips, letter to Cecy Perry, October 1942.

62 Phil runs from meeting to write home: Russell Allen Phillips, letter to Cecy Perry, October 7, 1942.

62 Training for crashes: Louis Zamperini, telephone interview; Consolidated Vultee Aircraft Corporation, Service Department, *Emergency Procedure: B-24 Airplane* (San Diego: Consolidated Vultee Aircraft Corporation, 1944), pp. 21–25.

62 "kind of silly": Russell Allen Phillips, television interview, CBS, La Porte, Ind., January 1997.

62 "a damn swell pilot": "Son of Pickett 'Sky Pilot' Pilots Bomber Over Wake I," undated article from Phillips scrapbook, NPN.

62 Phil's B-24: Stanley Pillsbury, telephone interviews, August 25, 2004, March 9, 2005, and August 18, 2006; Louis Zamperini, telephone interview; Russell Allen Phillips, television interview, CBS, La Porte, Ind., January 1997.

63 Phil's dream of Cecy: Russell Allen Phillips, letter to Cecy Perry, August 15, 1942.

63 Phil misses Cecy by three days: Russell Allen Phillips, letter to Cecy Perry, November 2, 1942.

63 B-24 names: "Warpaint Photo Album," Something About Everything Military, http://www.jcs-group.com/military/war1941aaf/warpaint1.html (accessed September 26, 2009).

63 Moznette names plane: Russell Allen Phillips, letter to Kelsey Phillips, February 13, 1943.

63 Phil says plane masculine: Russell Allen Phillips, letter to Cecy Perry, March 25, 1943.

65 Japan's empire: *West Point Atlas for the Second World War, Asia and the Pacific*, map 22.

Chapter 7: "This Is It, Boys"

66 Oahu in 1942: Stanley Pillsbury, telephone interviews, August 25, 2004, March 9, 2005, and August 18, 2006; Cleveland, p. 158.

66 "one sees only about ⅓": Cleveland, p. 158.

66 Barracks: Jesse Stay, "Twenty-nine Months in the Pacific," unpublished memoir.

66 "You kill one": Russell Allen Phillips, letter to Kelsey Phillips, December 8, 1942.

67 "like a dozen dirty": Russell Allen Phillips, letter to Cecy Perry, April 2, 1943.

67 Water fight: Russell Allen Phillips, letter to Cecy Perry, May 12, 1943.

67 Beer fight: Louis Zamperini, telephone interview.

67 Pornography: Russell Allen Phillips, letter to Cecy Perry, December 29, 1942.

68 Greenhouse windows froze: Cleveland, 103.

68 Phil hits pole: Russell Allen Phillips, letter to Cecy Perry, March 27, 1943.

68 Gunnery, bomb scores: Louis Zamperini, war diary, January 20, 30, February 2, and March 21, 1943 entries.

68 Sea search: Stanley Pillsbury, telephone interview, August 27, 2004; Louis Zamperini, war diary, March 14, 1943, entry; Louis Zamperini, telephone interview.

68 Diving over sub: Louis Zamperini, diary, March 14, 1943.

69 Practical jokes: Louis Zamperini, telephone interviews.

70 "kind of daring": Russell Allen Phillips, television interview, CBS, La Porte, Ind., January 1997.

70 Leisure-time activities: Louis Zamperini, telephone interview; Louis Zamperini, war diary, November 1942–May 1943 entries.

72 Wake attack: Louis Zamperini, war diary, December 22–25, 1942, entries; Stanley Pillsbury, telephone interviews, August 25, 27, 2004, March 9, 2005, and August 18, 2006; Louis Zamperini, telephone interview; Jesse Stay, telephone interviews, July 23, 2004, and March 16, 2005; "Son of Pickett 'Sky Pilot' Pilots Bomber over Wake I," undated article from Phillips scrapbook, NPN; Walter Clausen, undated article from Phillips scrapbook, NPN; "Delphi Flyer Is Given Medal for Pacific Bombing," undated article from Phillips scrapbook, NPN; "Former La Porte Youth Helps to Bomb Wake Isle," undated article from Phillips scrapbook, NPN; "Fledglings' Raid on Wake Token of Things to Come," *Berkshire Evening Eagle,* January 2, 1943; *St. Louis Globe,* undated article from Phillips scrapbook, NPN; "Their Raid on Wake Biggest of Year," *Mansfield News-Journal,* January 2, 1943; "Tells of Raid on Wake Island," *Mansfield News-Journal,* January 2, 1943; "Nobody Scared in Raid on Wake Island, Ace Says," *Ada Evening News,* January 2, 1943; Walter Clausen, "Hawaii Fliers Get Jap Planes in Wake Raid," undated article from Phillips scrapbook, NPN; Britt, p. 12; Jesse Stay, "Twenty-nine Months in the Pacific," unpublished memoir.

76 New Year's: Louis Zamperini, war diary, January 1, 1943, entry.

77 STEEL FILLS JAP SOX: Undated article from Phillips scrapbook, NPN.

77 "fled in terror": "Tells of Raid on Wake Island," *Mansfield News-Journal,* January 2, 1943.

77 Japan finished within the year: "U.S. Can Take Care of Japan, Halsey Thinks," *Ada Evening News,* January 2, 1943.

77 "it's a little premature": Russell Allen Phillips, letter to Kelsey Phillips, December 31, 1942.

Chapter 8: "Only the Laundry Knew How Scared I Was"

78 Coxwell's crash: Louis Zamperini, diary, January 8–10, 1943; Missing Air Crew Report No. 16218, Air Force Historical Studies Office, Bolling AFB, Washington, D.C.; Russell Allen Phillips, letter to Kelsey Phillips, February 13, 1943.

79 Buried in Honolulu: American Battle Monuments Commission.

79 Crashes over the past two months: *Army Air Forces Statistical Digest,* Table 64; Louis Zamperini, diary, December 27, 1942, and January 9, 1943; Britt, pp. 10, 13.

79 Crash, loss statistics: *Army Air Forces Statistical Digest,* Tables 100 and 161.

80 In the air corps, 35,946 personnel: *Army Battle Casualties and Nonbattle Deaths in World War II: Final Report, 7 December 1941–31 December 1946,* Department of the Army, Statistical and Accounting Branch, Office of the Adjutant General, p. 7.

80 Disease kills 15,779: *Preventive Medicine in World War II,* vol. IV: *Communicable*

Diseases, Office of Surgeon General, Department of Army, Washington, D.C., 1958, Table 1.

80 In the Fifteenth Air Force, 70 percent of KIA: Mae Mill Link and Hubert A. Coleman, "Medical Support of Army Air Forces in World War II," Office of the Surgeon General, USAF, Washington, D.C., 1955, p. 516.

81 *Super Man* flies into storms: Louis Zamperini, diary, January 1943; Stanley Pillsbury, telephone interview, August 18, 2006.

82 Planes land together, bulldozer: Frank Rosynek, email interview, June 15, 2005.

82 "The takeoff": Frank Rosynek, "Not Everybody Wore Wings," unpublished memoir.

82 Foot on "off" switch: Stanley Pillsbury, telephone interview, August 18, 2006.

83 Plane hits mountain: Louis Zamperini, telephone interview.

83 Inadvertent release of life raft: Britt, p. 13.

83 Navigation difficulties: John Weller, email interview, September 21, 2006; John Weller, "The History and Flight Log, Jeter Crew," unpublished memoir.

83 "We just sat there": Martin Cohn, telephone interview, August 10, 2005.

83 Half of a Zero on B-24 wing: Cleveland, p. 103.

84 Japanese range finders: Louis Zamperini, diary, March 1, 1943.

84 B-24 drops mine into another: Jesse Stay, telephone interviews, July 23, 2004, and March 16, 2005; Cleveland, pp. 130, 137, 181–82.

84 AAF combat deaths: *Army Battle Casualties,* p. 7.

84 Odds of dying: Jesse Stay, telephone interviews, July 23, 2004, and March 16, 2005.

85 Ditching: W. F. Craven and J. L. Cate, eds., *The Army Air Forces in World War II,* vol. XII: *Services Around the World* (Chicago: University of Chicago, 1966), p. 482.

85 Statistics on ditching: Johnsen, p. 29.

86 Death of Almond: John Henry, "Flier Wins 18-Hour Fight with Sharks," *San Antonio Light,* July 13, 1943.

87 Rescue statistics: "Air Sea Rescue 1941–1952," USAF Historical Division, Air University, August 1954, pp. 66–99; Air Force Historical Studies Office, Bolling AFB, Washington, D.C.

87 Half of Catalinas crashed: Craven and Cate, p. 493.

87 September 1942 raft ordeal: Cleveland, p. 237.

88 Raft found off Christmas Island: Katharina Chase, "Unraveling a WWII Mystery," *Defence,* November–December 2006.

88 Rape of Nanking: Chang, pp. 4–104; Yuki Tanaka, *Hidden Horrors: Japanese War Crimes in World War II* (Boulder: Westview, 1996), p. 80.

88 Rumors of Japanese killing on Kwajalein: Louis Zamperini, telephone interview.

89 All but one man choosing to die in crash: John Fitzgerald, POW diary, Papers of John A. Fitzgerald, Operational Archives Branch, NHC, Washington, D.C.

89 Nervous airman: John Joseph Deasy, telephone interview, April 4, 2005.

89 Louie copes: Louis Zamperini, telephone interview; Louis Zamperini, diary, early 1943 entries; Russell Allen Phillips, letters to Cecy Perry, spring 1943.

90 Bracelet, silver dollar: Russell Allen Phillips, letters to Cecy Perry, August 20, 1942, and March 25, 1943.

90 "When I do get": Russell Allen Phillips, letter to Cecy Perry, March 10, 1943.

90 Tradition of drinking booze of lost men: Louis Zamperini, telephone interview.

Chapter 9: Five Hundred and Ninety-four Holes

91 Exploding sharks: Louis Zamperini, telephone interview.

91 Makin, Tarawa missions: Louis Zamperini, telephone interview; Louis Zamperini, diary, February 17, 20, 1943; Stanley Pillsbury, telephone interviews, August 25, 27, 2004, March 9, 2005, August 18, 2006, January 23 and April 21, 2007.

92 Sharks circle: Stanley Pillsbury, telephone interviews, August 25, 27, 2004, March 9, 2005, August 18, 2006, January 23 and April 21, 2007; Louis Zamperini, telephone interview; Louis Zamperini, diary, March 5, 1943; Russell Allen Phillips, letter to Kelsey Phillips, March 5, 1943.

93 Shooting sharks: Louis Zamperini, diary, April 3, 1943.

93 Nauru: Jack D. Haden, "Nauru: A Middle Ground During World War II," Pacific Islands Report, Pacific Islands Development Program/East-West Center for Pacific Islands Studies/University of Hawaii at Manoa, http://166.122.164.43/archive/2000/April/04-03-19.htm (accessed September 13, 2009); Jane Resture, "Nauru: A Short History," http://www.janeresture.com/nauru_history/index.htm (accessed September 13, 2009); Britt, p. 34.

93 Nauru preparations: Stanley Pillsbury, telephone interviews, August 25, 27, 2004, March 9, 2005, August 18, 2006, January 23 and April 21, 2007; Louis Zamperini, telephone interview; Louis Zamperini, diary, April 17, 19, 1943.

93 "We only hope": Louis Zamperini, diary, April 15, 1943

94 Nauru raid: Stanley Pillsbury, telephone interviews, August 25, 27, 2004, March 9, 2005, August 18, 2006, January 23 and April 21, 2007; Louis Zamperini, telephone interview; Louis Zamperini, diary, April 20–22, 1943, and memoranda; Charles McMurtry, "Liberator, Hit 594 Times, Wings Home Safely," *Richmond News Leader*, May 14, 1943; "Catonsville Air Gunner Has 95 Raids to Credit," undated article from Phillips scrapbook, NPN; Russell Allen Phillips, letter to Cecy Perry, May 1, 1943; "Shapleigh Youth, Injured, Credited with Downing Zero," undated article from papers of Stanley Pillsbury, NPN; Cleveland, pp. 257, 349–50; Howard and Whitley, pp. 137–38; Charles P. Arnot, "Bombardier Zamperini Saves Lives in Shell-Riddled Plane," *Oakland Tribune*, May 4, 1943; Charles P. Arnot, "Japanese Phosphate Plants Are Blown Up," *Honolulu Advertiser*, May 1, 1943; "Gen. Landon, Bomber Commander, Tells the Story of Nauru Attack," May 5, 1943, from papers of Louis Zamperini, NPN; "Two Southland Officers Classified as Heroes in South Pacific Dispatches," *Long Beach Press-Telegram*, May 4, 1943; Charles P. Arnot, "Lt. Phillips on Another 'Thriller,' " May 4, 1943, from Phillips scrapbook, NPN; "Brave Flying Son of Pickett Chaplain Bears Charmed Life," May 1943, article from Phillips scrapbook, NPN; "Yank Pilot, Son of Pickett Chaplain, Saves Crewmen," undated article from Phillips scrapbook, NPN; Charles P. Arnot, "Lieut. Phillips Escapes Death on Pacific Raid," undated article from Phillips scrapbook, NPN; "His Toughest Fight: Lou Zamperini, Former Track Star, Aids Five Wounded as Plane Limps Home," undated article from Phillips scrapbook, NPN; Charles P. Arnot, "Track Star in Heroic Role," undated article from Phillips scrapbook, NPN; Charles P. Arnot,

"Raid on Nauru Told in Detail by Eyewitness," undated article from Phillips scrapbook, NPN; "Lou Zamperini Plays Great Role on Bombing Trip," undated article from Phillips scrapbook, NPN; Louis Zamperini, interview by George Hodak, Hollywood, Calif., June 1988, AAFLA; Charles P. Arnot, "Zamperini, S.C. Track Star, in Epic Air Adventure," *Los Angeles Herald Express,* May 4, 1943; Charles P. Arnot, "Track Star Zamperini Hero in Jap Air Fight," *Los Angeles Herald Express,* May 4, 1943.

96   "a volcano-like mass": Charles P. Arnot, "Raid on Nauru Told in Detail by Eyewitness," undated article from Phillips scrapbook, NPN.

97   Eight hundred rounds per minute: "Pistol Packin' Warplanes," *Popular Mechanics,* April 1944, p. 2.

97   *If he'd just:* Stanley Pillsbury, telephone interview, August 26, 2004.

98   *"Ow!":* Ibid.

99   *One more pass:* Louis Zamperini, diary, April 1943, memoranda page.

100   *I have to kill:* Stanley Pillsbury, telephone interview, August 26, 2004.

100   Japanese never retrieved phosphates: Jane Resture, "Nauru: A Short History," http://www.janeresture.com/nauru_history/index.htm (accessed September 13, 2009).

101   Pillsbury's injuries: Stanley Pillsbury, telephone interview, August 26, 2004; Louis Zamperini, telephone interview; Louis Zamperini, diary, April 20–22, 1943, and memoranda page.

101   Manual alternatives to flaps, gear: *Flight Manual: B-24D,* pp. 71–75.

102   standard landing speed: Charlie Tilghman, B-24 pilot, Commemorative Air Force, telephone interview, February 14, 2007; *B-24 Liberator Pilot Training Manual.*

102   B-24 without brakes needed 10,000 feet: Charlie Tilghman, B-24 pilot, Commemorative Air Force, telephone interview, February 14, 2007.

102   "all torn to pieces" Stanley Pillsbury, telephone interview, August 26, 2004.

102   Parachute idea: Stanley Pillsbury, telephone interview, August 26, 2004; Louis Zamperini, telephone interview; Louis Zamperini, diary, April 1943, memoranda page.

103   *Belle of Texas:* Cleveland, pp. 183, 464; 11th Bomb Group (H), *The Gray Geese* (Paducah, Ky.: Turner Publishing, 1996), p. 73.

103   594 holes: Charles McMurtry, "Liberator, Hit 594 Times, Wings Home Safely," *Richmond News Leader,* May 14, 1943.

104   "He didn't make it": Stanley Pillsbury, telephone interview, March 9, 2005.

104   Brooks family informed: "Sergt. H. V. Brooks Served in Pacific," undated article from Phillips scrapbook, NPN.

Chapter 10: The Stinking Six

106   Funafuti bombing: Stanley Pillsbury, telephone interviews, August 25, 27, 2004, March 9, 2005, August 18, 2006, January 23 and April 21, 2007; Louis Zamperini, telephone interview; Louis Zamperini, diary, April 21–23, 1943; John Joseph Deasy, telephone interview, April 4, 2005; Lester Herman Scearce, Jr., telephone interview, March 11, 2005; Jesse Stay, telephone interviews, July 23, 2004, and March 16, 2005; Frank Rosynek, "Not Everybody Wore Wings," unpublished memoir; Frank Rosynek, email interview, June 15, 2005; Russell Allen Phillips, letter to Cecy Perry, May 1, 1943; Cleveland, p. 346; Britt, pp. 36–37; Howard and Whitley, pp. 138–44; Jesse Stay, "Twenty-nine Months in the Pacific," unpublished

memoir; Louis Zamperini, interview by George Hodak, Hollywood, Calif., June 1988, AAFLA.

106 "I looked around": John Joseph Deasy, telephone interview, April 4, 2005.

106 Man runs into ocean: Howard and Whitley, p. 140.

106 Ladd saves natives: Howard and Whitley, p. 139; Philip Scearce, email interview, July 11, 2008.

107 "This feels like it, boys": Howard and Whitley, p. 140.

107 "like animals crying": Ibid., p. 143.

108 "I wasn't only scared": Cleveland, p. 258.

108 Phil's fear: Russell Allen Phillips, letter to Reverend Russell Phillips, May 2, 1943.

108 "seemed like a railroad carload": Frank Rosynek, "Not Everybody Wore Wings," unpublished memoir.

108 "like the whole island": Cleveland, p. 346.

110 Fourteen Japanese bombers: Britt, pp. 36–37.

110 "the Stinking Six": Frank Rosynek, email interview, June 15, 2005.

110 Doctor works on Pillsbury: Stanley Pillsbury, telephone interviews, August 25, 27, 2004, March 9, 2005, August 18, 2006, January 23 and April 21, 2007.

112 "hamburgered": Stanley Pillsbury, telephone interviews, August 25, 27, 2004, March 9, 2005, August 18, 2006, January 23 and April 21, 2007.

112 Lambert's ninety-five missions: "Catonsville Air Gunner Has 95 Raids to Credit," undated article from Phillips scrapbook, NPN.

112 Palmyra, depression, Kualoa: Louis Zamperini, diary, April–May 1943.

112 Francis McNamara: Louis Zamperini, telephone interview; Russell Allen Phillips, television interview, CBS, La Porte, Ind., January 1997.

113 *Green Hornet:* Cleveland, p. 159; Louis Zamperini, telephone interview; Russell Allen Phillips, television interview, CBS, La Porte, Ind., January 1997.

113 Phil meets Smith: George Smith, letter to Cecy Perry, June 19, 1943.

113 Corpening's plane: Missing Air Crew Report 4945, May 26, 1943 (National Archives Microfiche Publication M1380I, Fiche 1767); Missing Air Crew Reports of the U.S. Army Air Forces, 1942–1947; Records of the Office of the Quartermaster General, RG 92; NACP.

Chapter 11: "Nobody's Going to Live Through This"

114 Louie on May 27, 1943: Louis Zamperini, telephone interview.

115 "There was only one ship": Louis Zamperini, diary, May 27, 1943.

115 *If we're not back in a week:* Louis Zamperini, telephone interview.

115 Search preparations: John Joseph Deasy, telephone interview, April 4, 2005; Louis Zamperini, telephone interview; Missing Aircraft Report 4945, Missing Air Crew Reports of the U.S. Army Air Forces, 1942–1947; Records of the Office of the Quartermaster General, RG 92; NACP; "42nd Bombardment Squadron: Addendum to Squadron History," September 11, 1945, AFHRA, Maxwell AFB, Ala.

115 Preparing for takeoff: Louis Zamperini, telephone interview; Russell Allen Phillips, television interview, CBS, La Porte, Ind., January 1997.

116 Planes side by side: Lester Herman Scearce, Jr., telephone interview, March 11, 2005.

116 Phil tells Deasy to go ahead: Kelsey Phillips, "A Life Story," unpublished memoir.

117 Searching: Louis Zamperini, telephone interview; Russell Allen Phillips, television interview, CBS, La Porte, Ind., January 1997.

117 Phil and Cuppernell switch seats: Kelsey Phillips, "A Life Story," unpublished memoir; Louis Zamperini, telephone interview.
117 Engine dies, wrong engine feathered: Louis Zamperini, telephone interview.
118 "Prepare to crash": Louis Zamperini, telephone interview; Russell Allen Phillips, television interview, CBS, La Porte, Ind., January 1997.
118 Plane falls: Ibid.
119 *Nobody's going to live through this*: Louis Zamperini, telephone interview.
119 Louie and Phil's experiences in crash: Louis Zamperini, telephone interview; Russell Allen Phillips, television interview, CBS, La Porte, Ind., January 1997; "42nd Bombardment Squadron: Addendum to Squadron History," September 11, 1945, AFHRA, Maxwell AFB, Ala.; Robert Trumbull, "Zamperini, Olympic Miler, Is Safe After Epic Ordeal," *NYT*, September 9, 1945; Kelsey Phillips, "A Life Story," unpublished memoir; Louis Zamperini, interview by George Hodak, Hollywood, Calif., June 1988, AAFLA; Sandra Provan, "LP Man's Part of Olympics," *La Porte Herald-Argus*, February 18, 1988.

PART III

Chapter 12: Downed

125 Crash aftermath: Louis Zamperini, telephone interview; Russell Allen Phillips, television interview, CBS, La Porte, Ind., January 1997; "42nd Bombardment Squadron: Addendum to Squadron History," September 11, 1945, AFHRA, Maxwell AFB, Ala.; Robert Trumbull, "Zamperini, Olympic Miler, Is Safe After Epic Ordeal," *NYT*, September 9, 1945; Kelsey Phillips, "A Life Story," unpublished memoir; Louis Zamperini, interview by George Hodak, Hollywood, Calif., June 1988, AAFLA; Sandra Provan, "LP Man's Part of Olympics," *La Porte Herald-Argus*, February 18, 1988.
126 "I'm glad it was you": Louis Zamperini, telephone interview.
127 Phil didn't have bracelet, silver dollar: Ibid.
127 Contents of rafts: Ibid.
127 Contents of 1944 rafts: *Emergency Procedure: B-24*, pp. 26–27.
128 "Gibson Girl," Delano Sunstill: Louis Meulstee, "Gibson Girl," Wireless for the Warrior, http://home.hccnet.nl/l.meulstee/gibsongirl/gibsongirl.html (accessed August 8, 2005); Craven and Cate, pp. 486, 491.
128 "We're going to die!": Louis Zamperini, telephone interview.
128 Hours after crash: Louis Zamperini, telephone interview; "42nd Bombardment Squadron: Addendum to Squadron History," September 11, 1945, AFHRA, Maxwell AFB, Ala.; "Mr. Phillips on CBS, Our Hero, Mr. Phillips," undated article from papers of Karen Loomis, NPN; Gene Stowe, "He Shared Raft with Olympian," *South Bend Herald Tribune*, March 2, 1998.
129 Phil shaking, sharks rubbing against rafts: Russell Allen Phillips, television interview, CBS, La Porte, Ind., January 1997.

Chapter 13: Missing at Sea

131 Events on Palmyra: John Joseph Deasy, telephone interview, April 4, 2005; Lester Herman Scearce, Jr., telephone interview, March 11, 2005.
131 Search: John Joseph Deasy, telephone interview, April 4, 2005; Lester Herman

Scearce, Jr., telephone interview, March 11, 2005; "42nd Bombardment Squadron history," AFHRA, Maxwell AFB, Ala.

132 "we kept hoping": Lester Herman Scearce, Jr., telephone interview, March 11, 2005.

132 Chocolate incident: Louis Zamperini, telephone interview. For the sake of Mac and his family, Louie would not tell of the chocolate incident for many years, instead saying either that the chocolate had been eaten early in the journey or that it had been lost to the sea. Phil, too, would protect Mac, saying that the chocolate was lost in the sea.

133 B-25 flies over: Louis Zamperini, telephone interview; Russell Allen Phillips, television interview, CBS, La Porte, Ind., January 1997; "42nd Bombardment Squadron: Addendum to Squadron History," September 11, 1945, AFHRA, Maxwell AFB, Ala.; Robert Trumbull, "Zamperini, Olympic Miler, Is Safe After Epic Ordeal," *NYT*, September 9, 1945; Louis Zamperini, POW diary (entered when Louie began keeping diary, after October 1943). In later years, Zamperini would speak of the B-24 flying over before the B-25, but in all of his early accounts, including the history he gave to his squadron upon repatriation and the diary he kept as a POW, he stated that the B 25 flew over first. In a 2008 interview, he confirmed that his early accounts were correct.

133 B-24 flies over: See note above, about B-25 flying over; also: Louis Zamperini, telephone interview; Russell Allen Phillips, television interview, CBS, La Porte, Ind., January 1997; John Joseph Deasy, telephone interview, April 4, 2005; Lester Herman Scearce, Jr., telephone interview, March 11, 2005; "42nd Bombardment Squadron: Addendum to Squadron History," September 11, 1945, AFHRA, Maxwell AFB, Ala.; Robert Trumbull, "Zamperini, Olympic Miler, Is Safe After Epic Ordeal," *NYT*, September 9, 1945; Louis Zamperini, POW diary, May 30, 1943 entry (entered when Louie began keeping diary, after October 1943).

134 "If we ever looked": Lester Herman Scearce, Jr., telephone interview, March 11, 2005.

135 Smitty sightings: 42nd squadron activity log, May 30, 1943, AFHRA, Maxwell AFB, Ala.

135 "Cuppernell, Phillips, Zamperini": Cleveland, p. 159.

136 Mac snaps: Louis Zamperini, telephone interview.

136 Louie prays: Ibid.

136 Letters home, Zamperinis see Cuppernells: Russell Allen Phillips, letter to Reverend Russell Phillips, May 15, 1943; Russell Allen Phillips, letter to Cecy Perry, May 15, 1943; Peter Zamperini, letter to Louis Zamperini, June 3, 1943; Payton Jordan, telephone interviews, August 13, 16, 2004; Louis Zamperini, letter to Payton Jordan, May 27, 1943.

136 "I sure hope": Reverend Russell Phillips, letter to Martha Heustis, May 6, 1943.

137 Search ends: Lester Herman Scearce, Jr., telephone interview, March 11, 2005.

137 Krey visits cottage: Jack Krey, telephone interview, August 18, 2005.

138 Telegram to Kelsey Phillips: telegram, Adjutant General to Kelsey Phillips, June 4, 1943.

138 Zamperinis react: Sylvia Flammer, telephone interviews, October 25, 27, 2004; Peter Zamperini, telephone interviews, October 15, 17, 19, 22, 2004.

139 "Life of Zamp": George T. Davis, "Zamperini Career Brilliant, Life of Zamp," *Los Angeles Evening Herald and Express*, June 5, 1943.

139 Jordan learns news: Payton Jordan, telephone interviews, August 13, 16, 2004.

139 Louise's hand sores: Sylvia Flammer, telephone interviews, October 25, 27, 2004.

139 Pillsbury and Douglas: Stanley Pillsbury, telephone interviews, August 25, 2004, March 9, 2005, and August 18, 2006.

140 Pillsbury's remainder of war: Ibid.

140 Flag hung: Jack Cuddy, "Flag Hangs in Memory of Zamperini," *Syracuse* (N.Y.) *Herald-Journal*, June 24, 1943.

Chapter 14: Thirst

141 Heat: Louis Zamperini, telephone interview; Robert Trumbull, "Zamperini, Olympic Miler, Is Safe After Epic Ordeal," *NYT,* September 9, 1945.

142 Rain falls, catching water: Louis Zamperini, telephone interview; Russell Allen Phillips, television interview, CBS, La Porte, Ind., January 1997.

143 Phil cold at night: Russell Allen Phillips, television interview, CBS, La Porte, Ind., January 1997.

143 Phil thought birds must have thought them jetsam: Russell Allen Phillips, television interview, CBS, La Porte, Ind., January 1997.

143 Catching albatross: Louis Zamperini, telephone interview.

143 Fishing: "42nd Bombardment Squadron: Addendum to Squadron History," September 11, 1945, AFHRA, Maxwell AFB, Ala.; Louis Zamperini, telephone interview.

144 What more bad luck could they have?: Louis Zamperini, telephone interview.

144 Sniffing wax: Ibid.

144 Phil's thoughts of Rickenbacker: Russell Allen Phillips, television interview, CBS, La Porte, Ind., January 1997; Russell Allen Phillips, letter to Kelsey Phillips, March 10, 1943.

144 Rickenbacker's ordeal: Edward Rickenbacker, "Pacific Mission, Part I," *Life,* January 25, 1943, pp. 20–26, 90–100; Edward Rickenbacker, "Pacific Mission, Part III," *Life,* February 8, 1943, pp. 94–106; Edward Rickenbacker, *Seven Came Through* (Garden City: Doubleday, 1951).

145 Navy men survive on raft in 1942: Robert Trumbull, *The Raft* (New York: Holt, Rinehart and Winston, 1942).

145 Poon Lim: "Tells of 132 Days on Raft," *NYT,* May 25, 1943 (title was incorrect as to number of days); "Poon Lim," Fact Archive, http://www.fact-archive.com/encyclopedia/Poon_Lim (accessed September 15, 2009).

145 Phil thinking of how long they'd been floating: Russell Phillips, television interview, CBS, La Porte, Ind., January 1997.

145 Quizzing: Louis Zamperini, telephone interview; Russell Phillips, television interview, CBS, La Porte, Ind., January 1997.

147 Mac's withdrawal: Louis Zamperini, telephone interview.

147 "If there was one thing left": Russell Phillips, television interview, CBS, La Porte, Ind., January 1997.

147 Phil's faith: Karen Loomis, telephone interview, November 17, 2004.

147 "I had told Al": Reverned Russell Phillips, letter to Martha Heustis, May 6, 1943.

148 Bodies declining: Louis Zamperini, telephone interview.

148 Cannibalism: Neil Hanson, *The Custom of the Sea: A Shocking True Tale of Ship-*

wreck, Murder, and the Last Taboo (New York: John Wiley and Sons, 1999); Nathaniel Philbrick, *In the Heart of the Sea* (New York: Viking, 2000).

149 Cannibalism not considered: Louis Zamperini, telephone interview.

149 Praying, second albatross, catching fish, bandage rotting: Ibid.

150 Dolphins: Louis Zamperini, telephone interview; Russell Allen Phillips, television interview, CBS, La Porte, Ind., January 1997.

150 Hooks on fingers: Louis Zamperini, telephone interview.

151 Catching birds: Louis Zamperini, telephone interview; Russell Allen Phillips, television interview, CBS, La Porte, Ind., January 1997.

151 Lice, chasing rain: Louis Zamperini, telephone interview.

151 Phil overboard: Russell Allen Phillips, television interview, CBS, La Porte, Ind., January 1997.

152 Prayer followed by rain: Louis Zamperini, telephone interview; Louis Zamperini, interview by George Hodak, Hollywood, Calif., June 1988, AAFLA.

Chapter 15: Sharks and Bullets

153 Strafing: Louis Zamperini, telephone interview; Russell Allen Phillips, television interview, CBS, La Porte, Ind., January 1997; "42nd Bombardment Squadron: Addendum to Squadron History," September 11, 1945, AFHRA, Maxwell AFB, Ala.; "Mr. Phillips on CBS, Our Hero, Mr. Phillips," undated article from papers of Karen Loomis, NPN; Robert Trumbull, "Zamperini, Olympic Miler, Is Safe After Epic Ordeal," *NYT*, September 9, 1945; Louis Zamperini, interview by George Hodak, Hollywood, Calif., June 1988, AAFLA; Alberta H. Jones, "La Porte War Hero Takes Part in Zamperini Show," undated article from Phillips scrapbook, NPN; Louis Zamperini, POW diary, June 23, 1943, entry.

156 Phil thinks America will win: "Mr. Phillips on CBS, Our Hero, Mr. Phillips," undated article from papers of Karen Loomis, NPN.

156 Sharks attacking: Louis Zamperini, telephone interview; Kelsey Phillips, "A Life Story," unpublished memoir.

157 Patching: "42nd Bombardment Squadron: Addendum to Squadron History," September 11, 1945, AFHRA, Maxwell AFB, Ala.; Louis Zamperini, telephone interview; Louis Zamperini, interview by George Hodak, Hollywood, Calif., June 1988, AAFLA.

159 Transforming Phil's raft: Louis Zamperini, telephone interview; Russell Allen Phillips, television interview, CBS, La Porte, Ind., January 1997.

159 Estimating distance from land: Louis Zamperini, telephone interview.

Chapter 16: Singing in the Clouds

160 Sharks try to jump into raft: Louis Zamperini, telephone interview.

161 Attempt to catch shark: Louis Zamperini, telephone interview; Russell Allen Phillips, television interview, CBS, La Porte, Ind., January 1997.

163 Great white: Louis Zamperini, telephone interview.

164 Mac asking Louie if he would die: Louis Zamperini, telephone interview; Russell Allen Phillips, television interview, CBS, La Porte, Ind., January 1997; Robert Trumbull, "Zamperini, Olympic Miler, Is Safe After Epic Ordeal," *NYT*, September 9, 1945.

164 Death of Mac: Louis Zamperini, telephone interview; Russell Allen Phillips, television interview, CBS, La Porte, Ind., January 1997.

165 Louie catches fish with lieutenant's pin: Louis Zamperini, telephone interview.

165 Declining bodies: Louis Zamperini, telephone interview; Russell Allen Phillips, television interview, CBS, La Porte, Ind., January 1997.

166 Doldrums: Louis Zamperini, telephone interview.

166 Sharpening intellect: Ibid.

167 Louie hears singing: Ibid.

168 More birds: Russell Allen Phillips, television interview, CBS, La Porte, Ind., January 1997.

168 More planes: "42nd Bombardment Squadron: Addendum to Squadron History," September 11, 1945, AFHRA, Maxwell AFB, Ala.; Louis Zamperini, telephone interview; Robert Trumbull, "Zamperini, Olympic Miler, Is Safe After Epic Ordeal," *NYT,* September 9, 1945.

168 Storm coming: Louis Zamperini, telephone interview.

168 Phil enjoys swells: Russell Allen Phillips, television interview, CBS, La Porte, Ind., January 1997.

168 Sighting island: Louis Zamperini, telephone interview; Russell Allen Phillips, television interview, CBS, La Porte, Ind., January 1997; Louis Zamperini, POW diary, July 12, 1943, entry.

Chapter 17: Typhoon

169 Islands appearing: "42nd Bombardment Squadron: Addendum to Squadron History," September 11, 1945, AFHRA, Maxwell AFB, Ala.; Robert Trumbull, "Zamperini, Olympic Miler, Is Safe After Epic Ordeal," *NYT,* September 9, 1945.

169 Discussing land matter-of-factly: Russell Allen Phillips, television interview, CBS, La Porte, Ind., January 1997; Robert Trumbull, "Zamperini, Olympic Miler, Is Safe After Epic Ordeal," *NYT,* September 9, 1945.

169 Rowing parallel to islands: "42nd Bombardment Squadron: Addendum to Squadron History," September 11, 1945, AFHRA, Maxwell AFB, Ala.

170 Storm hits: "42nd Bombardment Squadron: Addendum to Squadron History," September 11, 1945, AFHRA, Maxwell AFB, Ala.; Louis Zamperini, telephone interview.

170 Catastrophic typhoon: Keith Heidorn, PhD, email interview, March 24, 2008; "Foochow Flooded After Typhoon," *Nevada State Journal* (Reno), July 24, 1943.

170 Smelling land, listening to surf: Louis Zamperini, telephone interview.

170 Waking among islands: "42nd Bombardment Squadron: Addendum to Squadron History," September 11, 1945, AFHRA, Maxwell AFB, Ala.

171 Seeing planes: Ibid.

171 Capture: Louis Zamperini, telephone interview; Russell Allen Phillips, television interview, CBS, La Porte, Ind., January 1997; "42nd Bombardment Squadron: Addendum to Squadron History," September 11, 1945, AFHRA, Maxwell AFB, Ala.; Robert Trumbull, "Zamperini, Olympic Miler, Is Safe After Epic Ordeal," *NYT,* September 9, 1945; Louis Zamperini, interview by George Hodak, Hollywood, Calif., June 1988, AAFLA; Louis Zamperini, POW diary, July 13, 1943, entry.

172 Swatting beard with bayonet, cigarettes burn beards: "42nd Bombardment

Squadron: Addendum to Squadron History," September 11, 1945, AFHRA, Maxwell AFB, Ala.

172 Questioned, taken into custody: Russell Allen Phillips, television interview, CBS, La Porte, Ind., January 1997; "42nd Bombardment Squadron: Addendum to Squadron History," September 11, 1945, AFHRA, Maxwell AFB, Ala.

172 "These are American fliers": Robert Trumbull, "Zamperini, Olympic Miler, Is Safe After Epic Ordeal," *NYT*, September 9, 1945.

172 Weight: Russell Allen Phillips, affidavit, John D. Murphy Collection, HIA, Stanford, Calif.; Russell Allen Phillips, television interview, CBS, La Porte, Ind., January 1997; "42nd Bombardment Squadron: Addendum to Squadron History," September 11, 1945, AFHRA, Maxwell AFB, Ala.; Louis Zamperini, telephone interview; Louis Zamperini, affidavit, November 1, 1945, John D. Murphy Collection, HIA, Stanford, Calif. Notes that Louie made in 1946 state that he weighed 67 pounds, and in later interviews, he would say that he was told that his weight was 30 kilos, 66 pounds. But in at least three interviews given just after repatriation, he was quoted as saying that he had weighed 87 pounds, and in a signed affidavit made immediately after the war, he was quoted as saying that he weighed 79½ pounds. In one interview just after the war, he also said he weighed 79 pounds. Phil's postwar affidavit stated that he weighed about 150 at the time of the crash and 80 at capture. In the CBS interview, Phil stated that he and Louie weighed the same—about 80 pounds—at capture.

173 First meal: "42nd Bombardment Squadron: Addendum to Squadron History," September 11, 1945, AFHRA, Maxwell AFB, Ala.

173 Interviewed about journey: Louis Zamperini, telephone interview.

173 Told that they were in Marshalls: Russell Allen Phillips, television interview, CBS, La Porte, Ind., January 1997; Louis Zamperini, POW diary; Kelsey Phillips, "A Life Story," unpublished memoir; Louis Zamperini, telephone interview. It is unclear which atoll they were told they were on. In one 1945 interview, a 1946 affidavit, and a 1988 interview, Louie stated that they were told that it was Maloelap, but in many other interviews, as well as in the POW diary that he began shortly after his capture, he stated that they were told they were on Wotje. Phil also stated that it was Wotje.

173 Forty-eight bullet holes: Louis Zamperini, telephone interview.

173 *They are our friends:* Russell Allen Phillips, television interview, CBS, La Porte, Ind., January 1997.

173 "After you leave here": Louis Zamperini, telephone interview.

174 Sick on freighter: Louis Zamperini, telephone interview; Russell Allen Phillips, television interview, CBS, La Porte, Ind., January 1997.

174 Conditions on Kwajalein: Louis Zamperini, telephone interview; Russell Allen Phillips, television interview, CBS, La Porte, Ind., January 1997; Louis Zamperini and Russell Allen Phillips, affidavits, John D. Murphy Collection, HIA, Stanford, Calif.; Louis Zamperini, 1946 notes on captive experience; Robert Trumbull, "Zamperini, Olympic Miler, Is Safe After Epic Ordeal," *NYT*, September 9, 1945.

175 NINE MARINES: Tripp Wiles, *Forgotten Raiders of '42: The Fate of the Marines Left Behind on Makin* (Washington, D.C.: Potomac Books, 2007), photo caption.

175 *All I see:* Louis Zamperini, telephone interview.

PART IV

Chapter 18: A Dead Body Breathing

179 Hardtack, tea: Louis Zamperini, telephone interview; "42nd Bombardment Squadron: Addendum to Squadron History," September 11, 1945, AFHRA, Maxwell AFB, Ala.; Louis Zamperini, affidavit, John D. Murphy Collection, HIA, Stanford, Calif.; Robert Trumbull, "Zamperini, Olympic Miler, Is Safe After Epic Ordeal," *NYT,* September 9, 1945.

179 Meeting native: Louis Zamperini, telephone interview.

180 Forced to sleep by waste hole: Ibid.

180 Diarrhea: Louis Zamperini, affidavit, John D. Murphy Collection, HIA, Stanford, Calif.; Louis Zamperini, telephone interview; Louis Zamperini, 1946 notes on captive experience.

181 Boiling water thrown in face: Louis Zamperini, affidavit, John D. Murphy Collection, HIA, Stanford, Calif.; Louis Zamperini, telephone interview; Louis Zamperini, 1946 notes on captive experience.

181 Louie hears singing: Louis Zamperini, telephone interview.

181 Phil's ordeal: Russell Allen Phillips, television interview, CBS, La Porte, Ind., January 1997; Russell Allen Phillips, affidavit, John D. Murphy Collection, HIA, Stanford, Calif.

181 Carving name in wall: Louis Zamperini, telephone interview.

181 "What's going to happen?": Russell Allen Phillips, television interview, CBS, La Porte, Ind., January 1997.

181 Guards' cruelty: Russell Allen Phillips, television interview, CBS, La Porte, Ind., January 1997; Louis Zamperini, telephone interview; "42nd Bombardment Squadron: Addendum to Squadron History," September 11, 1945, AFHRA, Maxwell AFB, Ala.; Louis Zamperini, affidavit, John D. Murphy Collection, HIA, Stanford, Calif.; Robert Trumbull, "Zamperini, Olympic Miler, Is Safe After Epic Ordeal," *NYT,* September 9, 1945.

183 "I was literally": Raymond Halloran, email interview, March 3, 2008.

183 Louie's interrogation: Louis Zamperini, telephone interview; "42nd Bombardment Squadron: Addendum to Squadron History," September 11, 1945, AFHRA, Maxwell AFB, Ala.

183 Women sexually enslaved: Chang, pp. 52–53.

184 "a ruptured octopus": "42nd Bombardment Squadron: Addendum to Squadron History," September 11, 1945, AFHRA, Maxwell AFB, Ala.

184 Phil's interrogation: Louis Zamperini, telephone interview; Russell Allen Phillips, television interview, CBS, La Porte, Ind., January 1997; Russell Allen Phillips, affidavit, John D. Murphy Collection, HIA, Stanford, Calif.

185 Kawamura: Louis Zamperini, telephone interview; Louis Zamperini, interview by George Hodak, Hollywood, Calif., June 1988, AAFLA. Louie would later be unsure if the name was Kawamura or Kawamuda, but the former is almost certainly correct, as it is a common name.

185 Sub men attack: Louis Zamperini, affidavit, John D. Murphy Collection, HIA, Stanford, Calif.; Louis Zamperini, telephone interview.

186 Medical experimentation: Louis Zamperini, telephone interview; Russell Allen Phillips, affidavit, John D. Murphy Collection, HIA, Stanford, Calif.; Louis Zam-

perini, affidavit, John D. Murphy Collection, HIA, Stanford, Calif.; Louis Zamperini, 1946 notes on captive experience.

187 Japanese experiment on captives: Tanaka, pp. 135–65; Gary K. Reynolds, *U.S. Prisoners of War and Civilian American Citizens Captured and Interned by Japan in World War II: The Issue of Compensation by Japan,* Congressional Research Service, December 17, 2002, pp. 19–21.

187 Dengue fever: Louis Zamperini, telephone interview; "42nd Bombardment Squadron: Addendum to Squadron History," September 11, 1945, AFHRA, Maxwell AFB, Ala.; Louis Zamperini, affidavit, John D. Murphy Collection, HIA, Stanford, Calif.; Louis Zamperini, 1946 notes on captive experience.

187 Second round of interrogation: Louis Zamperini, telephone interview.

188 Condemned, then saved from execution: Louis Zamperini, telephone interview; Louis Zamperini, interview by George Hodak, Hollywood, Calif., June 1988, AAFLA.

Chapter 19: Two Hundred Silent Men

189 Attacked on ship: "42nd Bombardment Squadron: Addendum to Squadron History," September 11, 1945, AFHRA, Maxwell AFB, Ala.; Louis Zamperini, affidavit, John D. Murphy Collection, HIA, Stanford, Calif.; Louis Zamperini, telephone interview; Louis Zamperini, 1946 notes on captive experience; Robert Trumbull, "Zamperini, Olympic Miler, Is Safe After Epic Ordeal," *NYT,* September 9, 1945.

190 Sailor knocking on Louie's head, beaten in car: Louis Zamperini, telephone interview.

191 Louie allowed to bathe: Ibid.

191 Meeting Sasaki, "We meet again": Ibid.

192 "unarmed combatants": William R. Gill and Davis P. Newton, "A Compilation of Biographical Source Documents Concerning Major William Herald Walker, U.S. Army Air Force (1919–1945), a Prisoner of War in Japan During World War II," 1999, p. 15.

193 Life in Ofuna: Yuzuru Sanematsu, "A Record of the Aftermath of Ofuna POW Camp," *Shukan Yomiuri,* August 1974, translated from Japanese; William R. Gill and Davis P. Newton, "A Compilation of Biographical Source Documents Concerning Major William Herald Walker, U.S. Army Air Force (1919–1945), a Prisoner of War in Japan During World War II," 1999; "Ofuna: Dolder Rescue Team Report," September 22, 1945, http://www.mansell.com/pow_resources/camplists/tokyo/ofuna/ofuna.html (accessed September 20, 2009); Louis Zamperini, telephone interview; Jean Balch, letter to legal section, prosecution division, SCAP, January 18, 1948; Gamble, p. 321; Affidavit, Arthur Laurence Maher, from Case Docket No. 218: Nakakichi Asoma et al. (vol. II, part 2 of 2 sections, exhibits, 1945–1949), RG 331, RAOOH, WWII, 1907–1966, SCAP, Legal Section, Administration Division (10/02/1945–04/28/1952?), Record of the Trial File, 1945–49, NACP; John A. Fitzgerald, POW diary, Papers of John A. Fitzgerald, Operational Archives Branch, NHC, Washington, D.C.; Gregory Boyington, *Baa Baa Black Sheep* (New York: Bantam, 1977), pp. 251–53; Johan Arthur Johansen, *Krigsseileren,* issues 1–2, 1990, translated from Norwegian by Nina B. Smith; "Main Subject Is on Ofuna POW Camp, February 1946–July 1947" and "Main Subject

Is on Ofuna POW Camp, September 1945–May 1947," RG 331, RAOOH, WWII, 1907–1966, SCAP, Legal Section, Administration Division (10/02/1945–04/28/1952?), Miscellaneous Subject File, NACP; information on Ofuna from the following files on Kunichi Sasaki and James Kunichi Sasaki in RG 331, RAOOH, WWII, 1907–1966, SCAP, Legal Section, Administration and Prosecution Divisions (10/02/1945–04/28/1952?), NACP: Kunichi Sasaki et al., 1945–1948, Investigation and Interrogation Reports; Nakakichi Asoma et al., trial, exhibits, appeal, and clemency files, NACP; Nakakichi Asoma, 1945–1952, POW 201 File, 1945–1952, Charges and Specifications, 1945–1948, NACP; Yuichi Hatto, *Aa, Omori Shuyojo* (Tokyo: Kyoshin Shuppan, 2004), translated from Japanese.

194 "My job": Glenn McConnell, telephone interview, June 8, 2007.

194 "were of such intensity": Affidavit, Glenn McConnell, from files on Sueharu Kitamura, RG 331, RAOOH, WWII, 1907–1966, SCAP, Legal Section, Administration Division (10/02/1945–04/28/1952?), NACP.

194 "Iron must be beaten": Yuichi Hatto, written interview, August 28, 2004.

194 "No strong soldiers": Ibid.

194 "transfer of oppression": Chang, p. 217; Tanaka, p. 204.

195 Japanese view of Westerners, "Anglo-Saxon devils": Shoichi Ishizuka, "About Naoetsu POW Camp," *Gaiko Forum,* June 2006.

195 Japanese view of capture: Yuichi Hatto, *Aa, Omori Shuyojo* (Tokyo: Kyoshin Shuppan, 2004), translated from Japanese; Shoichi Ishizuka, "About Naoetsu POW Camp," *Gaiko Forum,* June 2006.

195 "Have regard for": Shoichi Ishizuka, "About Naoetsu POW Camp," *Gaiko Forum,* June 2006.

195 "the night of a thousand suicides": "Cowra Outbreak, 1944," Fact Sheet 198, National Archives of Australia, http://www.naa.gov.au/about-us/publications/fact-sheets/fs198.aspx (accessed September 23, 2009); Harry Gordon, *Voyage from Shame: The Cowra Breakout and Afterwards* (Brisbane: University of Queensland Press, 1994). While the Cowra incident is sometimes described simply as an escape attempt, the event's authoritative historian, Harry Gordon, describes it as a "mass suicide bid." While some Japanese POWs remained in camp and committed suicide or were killed by other POWs, those who made the breakout run, including hundreds who ran directly at camp machine guns, were trying to force the Australians to kill them. According to one survivor, they carried weapons to "show hostility . . . so they would surely be shot at" and carried implements to use to kill themselves if the Australians didn't kill them. Some who successfully escaped later killed themselves to avoid recapture.

196 Frederick Douglass: Frederick Douglass, *Narrative of the Life of Frederick Douglass* (Cheswold: Prestwick House, 2004), p. 33.

196 Kitamura: Files on Sueharu Kitamura, RG 331, RAOOH, WWII, 1907–1966, SCAP, Legal Section, Administration Division (10/02/1945–04/28/1952?), NACP.

196 Hirose saves POW from beating: Affidavit, Frederick Dewitt Turnbull, from Case Docket No. 216: Katsuo Kohara (Vol. I, Record of Trial–Vol. II, Exhibits) 1945–1949, RG 331, RAOOH, WWII 1907–1966, SCAP, Legal Section, Administration Division (10/02/1945–04/28/1952?), NACP.

196 Child's sympathy for POWs: Lewis Bush, *Clutch of Circumstance* (Tokyo: Okuyama, 1956), p. 184.

196 "The general opinion": Yukichi Kano, "Statement of Yukichi Kano Tokio P.O.W. Camp H.Q. (Omori)," undated, from papers of Robert Martindale.

197 Sympathetic guard assaulted: Boyington, p. 257.

197 Food: John A. Fitzgerald, POW diary, Papers of John A. Fitzgerald, Operational Archives Branch, NHC, Washington, D.C.; Boyington, pp. 270–71; Gamble, p. 328; Louis Zamperini, 1946 notes on captive experience.

197 "We were dying": Jean Balch, "Yorktown Aviator: My Experience as Prisoner of War," www.ussyorktown.com/yorktown/pow.htm (accessed July 1, 2004).

197 Beriberi: Alfred A. Weinstein, *Barbed Wire Surgeon* (New York: Lancer Books, 1965), p. 83; Tom Henling Wade, *Prisoner of the Japanese* (Kenthurst, Australia: Kangaroo, 1994), p. 44; Gamble, p. 324.

198 Tarawa: Gavan Daws, *Prisoners of the Japanese: POWs of World War II in the Pacific* (New York: William Morrow, 1994), p. 278.

198 Ballale: Peter Stone, *Hostages to Freedom* (Yarram, Australia: Oceans Enterprises, 2006).

198 Wake massacre: Daws, p. 279; Major Mark E. Hubbs, "Massacre on Wake Island," Yorktown Sailor, http://www.yorktownsailor.com/yorktown/massacre.html (accessed October 18, 2009).

198 "kill-all" rule and "At such time": Entry from the Journal of the Taiwan POW Camp H.Q. in Taihoku, Aug. 1, 1944, Document 2701, certified as Exhibit O in Document 2687; Numerical Evidentiary Documents Assembled as Evidence by the Prosecution for Use as Evidence Before the International Military Tribunal for the Far East, 1945–1947 (National Archives Microfilm Publication M1690, roll 346, frame 540), RAOOH, WWII, RG 331, NACP.

198 "If there is any fear" (May 1944 order): V. Dennis Wrynn, "American Prisoners of War: Massacre at Palawan," *World War II*, November 1997.

Chapter 20: *Farting for Hirohito*

200 Farting guard: Louis Zamperini, telephone interview.

200 Maher: Affidavit, Arthur Laurence Maher, from Case Docket No. 218: Nakakichi Asoma et al. (vol. II, part 2 of 2 sections, exhibits), 1945–1949), RG 331: RAOOH, WWII, 1907–1966, SCAP, Legal Section, Administration Division (10/02/1945–04/28/1952?), Record of the Trial File, 1945–49; Robert Martindale, *The 13th Mission* (Austin: Eakin, 1998), pp. 109–10.

200 Fitzgerald: John A. Fitzgerald, POW diary, Papers of John A. Fitzgerald, Operational Archives Branch, NHC, Washington, D.C.

201 Harris: Edgar D. Whitcomb, *Escape from Corregidor* (New York: Paperback Library, 1967), pp. 106–59, 284; Katey Meares, email interviews, March 14, 17, 18, 27, 2008.

202 Photographic memory: Louis Zamperini, telephone interview.

202 Sasaki's behavior: Louis Zamperini, telephone interview; Gamble, p. 323; the following records of Kunichi Sasaki and James Kunichi Sasaki, from the NACP, RG 331, RAOOH, WWII, 1907–1966, SCAP, Legal Section, Administration Division and Prosecution Division: Kunichi Sasaki, Isamu Sato, Kazuo Akane, 1945–1948, Investigation and Interrogation Reports; Nakakichi Asoma et al., trial, exhibits, appeal, and clemency files; Nakakichi Asoma et al., 1945–1952, POW 201 File, 1945–1952, Charges and Specifications, 1945–1948.

203 Gaga: Glenn McConnell, telephone interview, June 8, 2007; Boyington, pp. 255–56.

203 "to rest their tortured brains": Boyington, p. 256.

203 Phil doing calisthenics: Russell Allen Phillips, television interview, CBS, La Porte, Ind., January 1997.

203 "I'll never fly again": Louis Zamperini, telephone interview.

203 Maher tells captive to steal: John A. Fitzgerald, POW diary, Papers of John A. Fitzgerald, Operational Archives Branch, NHC, Washington, D.C.

203 Morse code: Louis Zamperini, telephone interview; Johan Arthur Johansen, email interview, March 26, 2005.

204 Louie tells of mother's cooking: Frank Tinker, telephone interview, February 20, 2005; Boyington, p. 271; Tom Wade, telephone interview, January 2, 2005.

204 Guard nicknames: Louis Zamperini, telephone interview; Jean Balch, letter to Legal Section, Prosecution Division, SCAP, January 18, 1948; Boyington, p. 258.

204 Speaking offensively to guards: Boyington, pp. 267–68.

204 Convincing guard that sundial worked at night: Boyington, pp. 264–65.

204 Farting at Hirohito: Louis Zamperini, telephone interview; Gamble, p. 325.

204 POW diary: Louis Zamperini, telephone interview.

205 Guards say they shot Lincoln and torpedoed D.C.: Constance Humphrey, "A Taste of Food from Skies," *Pittsburgh Post-Gazette,* March 29, 1946.

205 Papers stolen during interrogation: John A. Fitzgerald, POW diary, Papers of John A. Fitzgerald, Operational Archives Branch, NHC, Washington, D.C.

206 Fall 1943: Louis Zamperini, telephone interview; Johan Arthur Johansen, *Krigsseileren,* issue 1, 1990, translated from Norwegian by Nina B. Smith.

206 Officials stealing food: Louis Zamperini, telephone interview; Boyington, pp. 290–91.

206 "To give you an idea": John A. Fitzgerald, POW diary, Papers of John A. Fitzgerald, Operational Archives Branch, NHC, Washington, D.C.

207 Smoking: Louis Zamperini, telephone interview.

207 Collapsing at baseball, editor comes to camp: Ibid.

207 Race against a Japanese runner: Louis Zamperini, telephone interview; Louis Zamperini, 1946 notes on captive experience.

207 Asking Sasaki to help, Mead and Duva: Louis Zamperini, telephone interview.

208 Minsaas dies: John A. Fitzgerald, POW diary, Papers of John A. Fitzgerald, Operational Archives Branch, NHC, Washington, D.C.; Johan Arthur Johansen, *Krigsseileren,* issue 2, 1990, translated from Norwegian by Nina B. Smith; Johan Arthur Johansen, email interview, March 26, 2005.

208 "We . . . believed": Johan Arthur Johansen, email interview, March 26, 2005.

208 Christiansen gives coat: Louis Zamperini, telephone interview.

208 Garrett: Louis Zamperini, telephone interview; Fred Garrett, affidavit, John D. Murphy Collection, HIA, Stanford, Calif.

209 Tinker: Frank Tinker, telephone interview, February 20, 2005.

209 Mental clarity of Tinker, Harris: Ibid.

210 Louie's second race: Louis Zamperini, telephone interview.

210 "made me a professional": Ibid.

210 Phil taken away: Russell Allen Phillips, affidavit, John D. Murphy Collection, HIA, Stanford, Calif.

211 Zentsuji said to be good camp: Tom Wade, telephone interview, January 2, 2005.

211 Phil sent to Ashio: Kelsey Phillips, "A Life Story," unpublished memoir.

211 Ashio: Roger Mansell, "Ashio POW Camp," Center for Research, Allied POWs Under the Japanese, http://www.mansell.com/pow_resources/camplists/tokyo/Ashio/ashio_main.html, Palo Alto, Calif. (accessed September 19, 2009).

211 Phil's letter burned: Russell Allen Phillips, letter to Kelsey Phillips, April 1944; Kelsey Phillips, "A Life Story," unpublished memoir.

Chapter 21: Belief

212 Sylvia crying: Sylvia Flammer, telephone interviews, October 25, 27, 2004.

212 Zamperinis coping: Ibid.; Peter Zamperini, telephone interviews, October 15, 17, 19, 22, 2004; Peter Zamperini, letter to Louis Zamperini, June 3, 1943.

213 Louise writes to General Hale: Louise Zamperini, diary notes, July 13, 1943; Louis Zamperini, telephone interview.

214 Louie's trunk arrives: Louise Zamperini, diary notes, October 6, 1943.

215 Gifts for Louie: Louis Zamperini, letter to Edwin Wilber, May 1946.

215 Christmas card for Louie: From papers of Louis Zamperini.

215 "The entire island": *Eastern Mandates* (Washington, D.C.: Center for Military History Publications, 1993), p. 14.

215 Wood slat: Louis Zamperini, telephone interview.

215 Papers on Kwajalein: John Joseph Deasy, telephone interview, April 4, 2005.

216 "I was happy": Ibid.

216 Condolence letter: Henry Rahaley, letter to Reverend and Mrs. Phillips, June 16, 1943.

216 Oak-leaf clusters: Reverend Russell Phillips, letter to Cecy Perry, July 28, 1943.

217 Reverend Phillips's plaque: Reverend Russell Phillips, letter to Martha Heustis, March 17, 1944.

217 "I think I have": Reverend Russell Phillips, letter to Martha Heustis, August 4, 1943.

217 Smitty's letter to Cecy: George Smith, letter to Cecy Perry, June 19, 1943.

218 Cecy moves to D.C., visits fortune-teller: Terry Hoffman, telephone interview, March 6, 2007.

218 "This year sure": Delia Robinson, letter to Louise Zamperini, June 23, 1944.

218 "We thought surely": Mrs. A. J. Deane, letter to Louise Zamperini, June 27, 1944.

218 Death notice: Sylvia Flammer, telephone interviews, October 25, 27, 2004.

219 "None of us": Ibid.

219 Plan to find Louie: Peter Zamperini, telephone interview, October 19, 2004.

Chapter 22: Plots Afoot

220 Escape plot: Louis Zamperini, telephone interview.

220 Rations cut: John A. Fitzgerald, POW diary, Papers of John A. Fitzgerald, Operational Archives Branch, NHC, Washington, D.C.

220 Louie stealing food, starching shirts: Louis Zamperini, telephone interview.

221 Barbering job: Ibid.

222 Official says POWs will be killed: John A. Fitzgerald, POW diary, Papers of John A. Fitzgerald, Operational Archives Branch, NHC, Washington, D.C.

222 Stealing map from Mummy: Louis Zamperini, telephone interview.

222 Getting info about Saipan: Ibid.

223 Sasaki's sudden change: Ibid.

223 Murder on Tinian: Eric Lash, "Historic Island of Tinian," *Environmental Services,* October 2008, vol. 1, 2nd edition; Major General Donald Cook, "20th Air Force Today," *20th Air Force Association Newsletter,* Fall 1998.

223 Infestation, leeches, "You should be happy": John Fitzgerald, POW diary, Papers of John A. Fitzgerald, Operational Archives Branch, NHC, Washington, D.C.; Louis Zamperini, telephone interview.

223 Fitzgerald sees stealing: John Fitzgerald, POW diary, Papers of John A. Fitzgerald, Operational Archives Branch, NHC, Washington, D.C.

224 Putrid fish, Quack beating: Louis Zamperini, telephone interview; Louis Zamperini, 1946 notes on captive experience; Louis Zamperini, interview by George Hodak, Hollywood, Calif., June 1988, AAFLA.

224 Murder of Gaga: Louis Zamperini, telephone interview.

224 Louie thinking of home: Ibid.

225 Plan to escape by boat: Ibid.

225 Doolittle raid: Kennedy Hickman, "World War II: The Doolittle Raid," About.com, http://militaryhistory.about.com/od/aerialcampaigns/p/doolittleraid.htm (accessed October 15, 2009).

225 Kindness of civilians: Boyington, pp. 304–05.

225 Murder of Chinese civilians: Chang, p. 216; Kennedy Hickman, "World War II: The Doolittle Raid," About.com, http://militaryhistory.about.com/od/aerialcampaigns/p/doolittleraid.htm (accessed October 15, 2009).

225 Average Japanese soldier five foot three: "Battle of the Pacific: How Japs Fight," *Time,* February 15, 1943; Tar Shioya, "The Conflict Behind the Battle Lines," *San Francisco Chronicle,* September 24, 1995.

226 Civilians attack POWs: Milton McMullen, telephone interview, February 16, 2005; K. P. Burke, *Proof Through the Night: A B-29 Pilot Captive in Japan—the Earnest Pickett Story* (Salem, Ore.: Opal Creek, 2001), p. 88; Fiske Hanley II, *Accused American War Criminal* (Austin: Eakin, 1997), pp. 68–69.

226 Preparations for escape, "a fearful joy": Louis Zamperini, telephone interview.

226 Suspension of plan: Ibid.

226 Newspaper theft, Harris beating: Ibid.; files on Sueharu Kitamura, RG 331, RAOOH, WWII, 1907–1966, SCAP, Legal Section, Administration Division (10/02/1945–04/28/1952?), NACP; Glenn McConnell, telephone interview, June 8, 2007; John A. Fitzgerald, POW diary, Papers of John A. Fitzgerald, Operational Archives Branch, NHC, Washington, D.C.; Gamble, p. 328.

229 Sasaki's advice: Affidavit, Louis Zamperini, in file of Nakakichi Asoma, 1945–1952, RG 331: RAOOH, WWII, SCAP, Legal Section, Administration Division (10/02/1945–04/28/1952?), Charges and Specifications, 1945–1948, NACP.

Chapter 23: Monster

230 Appearance of Omori: Bush, p. 150.

230 POW likens Omori to the moon: Wade, p. 83.

230 No birds: Ray "Hap" Halloran and Chester Marshall, *Hap's War* (Menlo Park, Calif.: Hallmark, n.d.).

230 Watanabe's appearance: Weinstein, p. 228; Tom Wade, telephone interview, January 2, 2005.

230 Liken to paws: Draggan Mihailovich, email interview, August 3, 2007.

232 Louie meeting Watanabe: Louis Zamperini, telephone interview.

232 *This man:* Frank Tinker, telephone interview, February 20, 2005.

232 Building fire: Louis Zamperini, telephone interview.

233 Watanabe's history: Martindale, pp. 92–93; Wade, pp. 103–04; Yuichi Hatto, written interview, August 28, 2004; James, p. 278; Mutsuhiro Watanabe (Sgt.), vols. 1–3, 1945–1952, POW 201 File 1945–1947, SCAP, Legal Section, Administrative Division, RAOOH, RG 331, NACP; "From Chief of Hyogo Prefectural Police Force," November 21, 1950, report, from papers of Frank Tinker.

234 Japanese sign but don't ratify Geneva Convention: Tanaka, p. 73.

234 Slavery: Martindale, p. 90; Wade, pp. 97–99, 129; Bush, pp. 152–53; Johan Arthur Johansen, *Krigsseileren,* issue 3, 1990, translated from Norwegian by Nina B. Smith.

235 Lifting thirty tons a day: Wade, p. 99.

235 Men paid ten yen per month: Martindale, p. 111.

235 Those who don't work receive half rations: Bush, p. 160.

235 Food at Omori: Martindale, p. 120; Bush, p. 159.

235 Nicknames: Ernest O. Norquist, *Our Paradise: A GI's War Diary* (Hancock, Wisc.: Pearl-Win, 1989), p. 293; Bush, p. 205.

236 Watanabe's first days: Wade, pp. 103–05; Tom Wade, telephone interview, January 2, 2005; Bush, pp. 176–79.

236 Hatto thinks Watanabe mad: Yuichi Hatto, written interview, August 28, 2004.

236 "He suddenly saw": Tom Wade, telephone interview, September 17, 2005.

236 "He did enjoy hurting": Yuichi Hatto, written interview, August 28, 2004.

236 Watanabe's behavior: Mutsuhiro Watanabe (Sgt.), vol. 1, 1945–1952, POW 201 File 1945–1947, SCAP, Legal Section, Administrative Division, RAOOH, RG 331, NACP; Martindale, pp. 95–110, 130, 144–55; Robert Martindale, telephone interview, January 2, 2005; Norquist, pp. 277–79, 283–84; Wade, pp. 103–08; Weinstein, pp. 228–33, 247, 256; Derek (Nobby) Clarke, *No Cook's Tour* (Hereford, Eng.: Authors OnLine, 2005), pp. 114–16; Donald Knox, *Death March: The Survivors of Bataan* (San Diego: Harcourt Brace Jovanovich, 1983), p. 377; James, pp. 277–83.

237 Watanabe's fame: James, p. 278; Affidavit, Arthur Laurence Maher, from files on Mutsuhiro Watanabe (Sgt.), vol. 1, 1945–1952, POW 201 File 1945–1947, SCAP, Legal Section, Administrative Division, RAOOH, RG 331, NACP.

237 "punishment camp": Martindale, pp. 104–05.

237 "the most vicious guard": Affidavit, Arthur Laurence Maher, from files on Mutsuhiro Watanabe (Sgt.), vol. 1, 1945–1952, POW 201 File 1945–1947, SCAP, Legal Section, Administrative Division, RAOOH, RG 331, NACP.

237 "He was absolutely": Knox, p. 379.

238 Beating POW, then becoming placid: Weinstein, p. 230.

238 Forcing men to be his friends: Martindale, pp. 149–50; Clarke, p. 116; Robert Martindale, telephone interview, January 2, 2005.

238 Watanabe despised by guards: Bush, p. 200; Yuichi Hatto, written interview, August 28, 2004.

238 "tense, sitting-on-the-edge-of-a-volcano": Clarke, p. 116.

Chapter 24: Hunted

239 Louie enters main body of Omori: Louis Zamperini, telephone interview.

239 Lessons on avoiding the Bird: Norquist, pp. 278–79; Wade, p. 124; Bush, p. 187; Weinstein, pp. 228–33; Clarke, pp. 114–16; J. Watt Hinson, email interview, July 26, 2004.

240 The Bird's office: Martindale, p. 78.

240 Louie not registered with Red Cross: Louis Zamperini, telephone interview.

240 Attacked every day: Louis Zamperini, telephone interview.

241 "number one prisoner": CBS Television, "48 Hours: Race to Freedom," 1998.

241 "After the first few days in camp": Louis Zamperini, telephone interview.

241 The Bird forces officers to work: Clarke, p. 114; Martindale, p. 97; Louis Zamperini, telephone interview; Weinstein, p. 249.

241 Cleaning *benjos:* Louis Zamperini, telephone interview; Martindale, pp. 99–100; Lewis Bush, p. 186; Clarke, p. 114.

242 "The motto": Martindale, p. 100.

242 Sabotage, stealing: John Fitzgerald, POW diary, Papers of John A. Fitzgerald, Operational Archives Branch, NHC, Washington, D.C.; "42nd Bombardment Squadron: Addendum to Squadron History," September 11, 1945, AFHRA, Maxwell AFB, Ala.; Louis Zamperini, telephone interview; Milton McMullen, telephone interview, February 16, 2005; Martindale, pp. 127–28, 156–72; Wade, pp. 97–99, 129; Bush, p. 161; Johan Arthur Johansen, email interview, March 26, 2005; Weinstein, pp. 243–45; Gloria Ross, "A Singular Man," *Airman,* January 1982; Tom Wade, telephone interview, January 2, 2005.

244 "University of Thievery": Martindale, pp. 168–69.

244 Stealing ingredients for cake: Ibid., p. 128.

244 Louie gets sugar for Tinker: Frank Tinker, telephone interview, February 20, 2005; Louis Zamperini, telephone interview.

244 Only two deaths after school created: Martindale, p. 169.

244 Louie beaten: Louis Zamperini, telephone interview.

245 Sakaba watches beating: Ibid.

245 The Bird holding power over superiors: Norquist, p. 279; Wade, p. 120; Weinstein, p. 255.

245 Watanabe's impunity: Yuichi Hatto, written interview, August 28, 2004.

245 Kind guards: Bush, p. 200; Yuichi Hatto, written interview, August 28, 2004; Boyington, pp. 302–03; Martindale, p. 195; Norquist, p. 288; Gamble, p. 336; Yukichi Kano, "Statement of Yukichi Kano Tokio P.O.W. Camp H.Q. (Omori)," undated, from papers of Robert Martindale.

246 Red Cross inspection: Martindale, p. 123; Louis Zamperini, telephone interview.

246 Louie's defiance: Louis Zamperini, telephone interview.

246 *Postman Calls:* E. Bartlett Kerr, *Surrender and Survival: The Experience of American POWs in the Pacific, 1941–1945* (New York: William Morrow, 1985), pp. 189–90; "The Zero Hour," Glasgow.com, http://www.glasglow.com/e2/th/The_Zero_Hour.html (accessed September 25, 2009).

246 Radio message: E. H. Stephan, postcard to Zamperini family, October 18, 1944.

247 Louie knew nothing of broadcast: Louis Zamperini, telephone interview.

247 Message in Trona: E. H. Stephan, postcard to Zamperini family, October 18, 1944, stamp on card.

Chapter 25: B-29

248 Louie taking wheelbarrow to Tokyo: Louis Zamperini, telephone interview.

248 State of Tokyo: Milton McMullen, telephone interview, February 16, 2005; Bush, pp. 213, 222–23; Weinstein, p. 248.

248 Graffiti: Louis Zamperini, telephone interview.

249 B-29: "Boeing B-29 Superfortress," Military Factory, http://www.militaryfactory .com/aircraft/detail.asp?aircraft_id=82 (accessed October 15, 2009).

249 Steakley's flight: E. Bartlett Kerr, *Flames over Tokyo: The U.S. Army Air Forces' Incendiary Campaign Against Japan, 1941–1945* (New York: Donald I. Fine, 1991), p. 92.

249 Earlier B-29 raids on mainland Japan: Ibid., pp. 57–60, 64–68.

249 B-29 flying over Omori: Louis Zamperini, telephone interview; Tom Wade, telephone interview, September 17, 2005; Frank Tinker, telephone interview, February 20, 2005; Martindale, pp. 166–67; Wade, pp. 138–39; Clarke, p. 147; Robert Martindale, telephone interview, January 2, 2005; Tom Wade, telephone interview, January 2, 2005.

250 "It was not their Messiah": Martindale, p. 176.

250 Smuggling newspapers: Milton McMullen, telephone interview, February 16, 2005.

250 Distortions in Japanese press: Weinstein, p. 242.

250 Plane downed with rice ball: Louis Zamperini, telephone interview.

250 "Lone enemy B-29 visits Tokyo area": Norquist, p. 287.

251 FLED IN CONSTERNATION: Louis Zamperini, telephone interview.

251 "*Niju ku!*": Wade, p. 139.

251 The Bird beats Louie with belt: Louis Zamperini, telephone interview; Robert Trumbull, "Zamperini, Olympic Miler, Is Safe After Epic Ordeal," *NYT*, September 9, 1945.

252 The Bird forces Maher to burn letters: Affidavit, Francis Harry Frankcom, from files on Mutsuhiro Watanabe (Sgt.), vol. 1, 1945–1952, POW 201 File 1945–1947, SCAP, Legal Section, Administrative Division, RAOOH, RG 331, NACP.

252 Radio Tokyo visit: Louis Zamperini, telephone interview; Martindale, pp. 129–30; "42nd Bombardment Squadron: Addendum to Squadron History," September 11, 1945, AFHRA, Maxwell AFB, Ala.

253 Writing radio address: Louis Zamperini, telephone interview.

253 Lynn Moody: Lynn Moody Hoffman, letter to Louis Zamperini, August 14, 1998.

255 DeMille interviews Zamperinis: Sylvia Flammer, telephone interviews, October 25, 27, 2004; "Sixth War Bond Drive," November 19, 1944, interview transcript.

255 Harvey's wounding: Sylvia Flammer, telephone interviews, October 25, 27, 2004.

256 Moody hears new broadcast: Lynn Moody Hoffman, letter to Louis Zamperini, August 14, 1998.

256 Text of address: From papers of Louis Zamperini.

257 Visit with caller from San Marino: Handwritten notes from papers of Louis Zamperini.

257 "I was thinking": Sylvia Flammer, telephone interviews, October 25, 27, 2004.

258 Telegram concerning broadcast: telegram, provost marshal general to Louise Zamperini, undated, from the papers of Louis Zamperini.

258 Uncle hears broadcast: "Louis Zamperini Radio Talk Heard by Uncle," *Des Moines Register*, December 12, 1944.

258 Detail about guns: Sylvia Flammer, telephone interviews, October 25, 27, 2004.

258 "Payt! *He's alive!*": Payton Jordan, telephone interview, August 16, 2004.

Chapter 26: Madness

259 Radio Tokyo men return: Louis Zamperini, telephone interview.

259 Text of new message: From papers of Louis Zamperini.

260 Reason Louie spared from execution: Louis Zamperini, telephone interview; Louis Zamperini, notes from 1950 meeting with Kwajalein officer; Louis Zamperini, interview by George Hodak, Hollywood, Calif., June 1988, AAFLA.

261 Producers encourage Louie: Louis Zamperini, telephone interview; "42nd Bombardment Squadron: Addendum to Squadron History," September 11, 1945, AFHRA, Maxwell AFB, Ala.

261 "Okay": Louis Zamperini, telephone interview.

261 November 24, 1944, raid: Martindale, p. 177; Johan Arthur Johansen, email interview, March 26, 2005; Johan Arthur Johansen, *Krigsseileren*, issue 4, 1990, translated from Norwegian by Nina B. Smith; Tom Wade, telephone interview, January 2, 2005; "Tokyo in Flames After Crippling Superfort Blow," *Ogden Standard Examiner*, November 25, 1944; Kerr, *Flames*, pp. 97–101.

262 "It was a cold": Johan Arthur Johansen, email interview, March 26, 2005.

262 Hatto sees parachuting man: Yuichi Hatto, written interview, August 28, 2004.

263 Sirens: Norquist, pp. 288, 291.

263 November 27 and 29–30 bombings: Ibid., p. 291.

263 Louie watches air battle: Louis Zamperini, telephone interview.

263 *"Hikoki dame"*: Ibid.

263 "You win war": Bush, p. 207.

263 The Bird beats Martindale: Martindale, pp. 180–81.

264 The Bird leaves, then returns for fire drill: Ibid., pp. 152–53; Wade, pp. 140–41.

264 The Bird herds officers into Tokyo: Martindale, pp. 144–45; Wade, p. 141; Affidavit, Francis Harry Frankcom, from files on Mutsuhiro Watanabe (Sgt.), vol. 1, 1945–1952, POW 201 File 1945–1947, SCAP, Legal Section, Administrative Division, RAOOH, RG 331, NACP.

265 The Bird makes men stand at attention: Johan Arthur Johansen, *Krigsseileren*, issue 4, 1990, translated from Norwegian by Nina B. Smith.

265 "death lunge": Frank Tinker, telephone interview, February 20, 2005.

265 Louie's nightmares about the Bird: Louis Zamperini, telephone interview.

265 Zentsuji: Don Wall, *Singapore and Beyond: The Story of the Men of the 2/20 Battalion, Told by the Survivors* (Cowra, Australia: James N. Keady, 1985), pp. 307–09; Affidavit, Major Melvin Miller, from files of "The Mad Quack" (1st Lt.), POW 201 File 1945–1947, SCAP, Legal Section, Administrative Division, RAOOH, RG 331, NACP.

266 Phillipses hear of broadcast: "Lt. Allan Phillips May Be Prisoner in Tokyo," undated article from Phillips scrapbook, NPN.

266 Major from the adjutant general's office calls: "Lt. Allen Phillips Alive as Prisoner of the Japs; Missing Year and a Half," undated article from Phillips scrapbook, NPN.

266 Cecy races home: Terry Hoffman, telephone interview, March 6, 2007.

266 "Words really cannot": Reverend Russell Phillips, letter to Martha Heustis, January 5, 1945.

267 Phillipses asked to keep news secret: Kelsey Phillips, letter to Louise Zamperini, December 15, 1944.

267 Kelsey sad for other mothers: Ibid.

267 "Even though we": Sadie Glassman, letter to Zamperinis, November 18, 1944.

267 "It is difficult": Kelsey Phillips, letter to Louise Zamperini, December 15, 1944.

267 Red Cross packages delivered: Norquist, pp. 282, 290.

267 Official admits to giving packages to Japanese: Martindale, p. 134.

267 "We could see them throwing away": Wade, p. 138.

268 The Bird steals forty-eight packages: Wade, p. 138; Affidavits, Francis Harry Frankcom and Fort Hammond Callahan, from files on Mutsuhiro Watanabe (Sgt.), vol. 1, 1945–1952, POW 201 File 1945–1947, SCAP, Legal Section, Administrative Division, RAOOH, RG 331, NACP.

268 Apples and oranges distributed, taken back: Martindale, p. 187.

268 Louie gets Red Cross package: Louis Zamperini, POW diary.

268 Mansfield: Martindale, pp. 122–23; Norquist, pp. 287–88; Wade, pp. 137–38; Robert Martindale, telephone interview, January 2, 2005.

269 *Cinderella:* Martindale, pp. 189–92; Wade, pp. 143–44; Johan Arthur Johansen, *Krigsseileren,* issue 4, 1990, translated from Norwegian by Nina B. Smith; Clarke, pp. 151–54.

269 Christmas at Zentsuji: Wall, p. 308.

269 Tokugawa comes to Omori: Bush, pp. 183, 198–99; Yuichi Hatto, written interview, August 28, 2004; Report of Lieutenant Lewis Bush, from files on Mutsuhiro Watanabe (Sgt.), vol. 1, 1945–1952, POW 201 File 1945–1947, SCAP, Legal Section, Administrative Division, RAOOH, RG 331, NACP.

270 The Bird promoted: Yuichi Hatto, written interview, August 28, 2004; James, p. 280.

270 Men put feces on Bird's rice cakes: Martindale, pp. 191–92.

270 Louie learns Bird leaving: Louis Zamperini, telephone interview.

Chapter 27: Falling Down

271 Life in camp improves: Louis Zamperini, telephone interview; Martindale, pp. 194–95; Affidavit, Francis Harry Frankcom, from files on Mutsuhiro Watanabe (Sgt.), vol. 1, 1945–1952, POW 201 File 1945–1947, SCAP, Legal Section, Administrative Division, RAOOH, RG 331, NACP.

271 Mail found in the Bird's office: Affidavit, Francis Harry Frankcom, from files on Mutsuhiro Watanabe (Sgt.), vol. 1, 1945–1952, POW 201 File 1945–1947, SCAP, Legal Section, Administrative Division, RAOOH, RG 331, NACP.

271 "Trust you're all": Louis Zamperini, letter to family, January 6, 1945.

271 "Tell Pete": Louis Zamperini, letter to family, January or February 1945.

271 Ofuna arrivals: Louis Zamperini, telephone interview; John A. Fitzgerald, POW diary, Papers of John A. Fitzgerald, Operational Archives Branch, NHC, Washington, D.C.

271 Condition of Harris: Louis Zamperini, telephone interview.

272 Harris's beatings: John A. Fitzgerald, POW diary, Papers of John A. Fitzgerald, Operational Archives Branch, NHC, Washington, D.C.

272 Doctor thinks Harris dying, Louie gives him Red Cross box: Louis Zamperini, telephone interview; Louis Zamperini, POW diary, January 15, 1945, entry.

272 Palawan massacre: Hampton Sides, *Ghost Soldiers: The Epic Account of World War II's Greatest Rescue Mission* (New York: Anchor Books, 2002), pp. 7–17; Kerr, *Surrender*, pp. 212–15; V. Dennis Wrynn, "American Prisoners of War: Massacre at Palawan," *World War II*, November 1997.

273 February 16–17 air raid: Louis Zamperini, telephone interview; John A. Fitzgerald, POW diary, Papers of John A. Fitzgerald, Operational Archives Branch, NHC, Washington, D.C.; Martindale, p. 198; Johan Arthur Johansen, *Krigsseileren*, issue 4, 1990, translated from Norwegian by Nina B. Smith; Frank Tremaine, "Tokyo in Flames After Record Bombing Attack," *Brainerd* (Minn.) *Daily Dispatch*, February 16, 1945; "Navy Planes Rip Tokyo," *Nebraska State Journal* (Lincoln), February 16, 1945; "Devastating War to Tokyo," *Nebraska State Journal* (Lincoln), February 16, 1945.

274 American Hellcat pursues Japanese fighter: John A. Fitzgerald, POW diary, Papers of John A. Fitzgerald, Operational Archives Branch, NHC, Washington, D.C.; Louis Zamperini, telephone interview.

274 February 24 air raid: "1,600 Planes Bomb Jap Capital as All-Out Drive Launched on Iwo," *Sunday Times-Signal* (Zanesville, Ohio), February 25, 1945; Kerr, *Flames*, pp. 138–44.

275 Transfer of POWs: Louis Zamperini, telephone interview; John A. Fitzgerald, POW diary, Papers of John A. Fitzgerald, Operational Archives Branch, NHC, Washington, D.C.

275 Journey through Tokyo: Louis Zamperini, telephone interview.

275 Shadow factories: Martindale, p. 214; Kerr, *Flames*, p. 153.

275 Arrival at Naoetsu: John A. Fitzgerald, POW diary, Papers of John A. Fitzgerald, Operational Archives Branch, NHC, Washington, D.C.; Wade, pp. 146–47.

275 "It was as if a giant frosted cake": Wade, p. 144.

276 Louie collapses: Louis Zamperini, telephone interview.

Chapter 28: Enslaved

277 Bird beaming: Frank Tinker, telephone interview, February 20, 2005.

277 Description of Naoetsu: Wade, pp. 148–49, 152–53; Frank Tinker, telephone interview, February 20, 2005; Alan B. Lyon, *Japanese War Crimes: Trials of the Naoetsu Camp Guards* (Loftus, Australia: Australian Military History Publications, 2000), pp. 25–34; John Cook, "Japan: C Force," unpublished memoir; "List of Death Naoetu [sic] POW Camp, 1942–44," *Taheiyo ni Kaleru Hashi: Horyo Shuyojono Higeikei wo Keoete* (Japan-Australia Society, 1996), translated from Japanese.

278 Zamperini Invitational: "United Nations Olympics Talked—New Golden Era in Track Seen When Peace Comes," *Abilene* (Tex.) *Reporter-News*, March 5, 1945.

279 Glickman crying: CBS Television, "48 Hours: Race to Freedom," 1998.

279 Louie sick: "42nd Bombardment Squadron: Addendum to Squadron History," September 11, 1945, AFHRA, Maxwell AFB, Ala.; Louis Zamperini, 1946 notes on captive experience.

279 Food, guards smoking: Louis Zamperini, telephone interview; Louis Zamperini, 1946 notes on captive experience; Wade, p. 151; Ken Marvin, telephone interview, January 21, 2005.

279 "a roaring Hitlerian animal": Wade, p. 159.

279 Officers picked by the Bird: Tom Wade, telephone interview, January 2, 2005.

280 "just for drill": Ken Marvin, telephone interview, January 21, 2005.

280 Slave labor: Wade, pp. 151–52; John Cook, "Japan: C Force," unpublished memoir; Tom Wade, telephone interview, January 2, 2005.

280 Men falling into snow crevasses: Wall, p. 303.

280 Melting snow, pig's appearance: Wade, pp. 156, 149.

281 Potato-field work: John A. Fitzgerald, POW diary, Papers of John A. Fitzgerald, Operational Archives Branch, NHC, Washington, D.C.; Louis Zamperini, telephone interview; Wade, p. 157; Affidavit, Louis Zamperini, from files on Mutsuhiro Watanabe (Sgt.), vols. 1–3, 1945–1952, POW 201 File 1945–1947, SCAP, Legal Section, Administrative Division, RAOOH, RG 331, NACP.

281 B-29 seen: Louis Zamperini, telephone interview; Wade, p. 157; Wall, p. 298.

282 Roosevelt's death: Louis Zamperini, telephone interview; Wall, p. 298.

282 Barge duty: Louis Zamperini, telephone interview; John A. Fitzgerald, POW diary, Papers of John A. Fitzgerald, Operational Archives Branch, NHC, Washington, D.C.; Ken Marvin, telephone interview, January 21, 2005; Louis Zamperini, 1946 notes on captive experience; John Cook, "Japan: C Force," unpublished memoir; Wade, pp. 160–63.

283 Bathing options: Ken Marvin, telephone interview, January 21, 2005; John Cook, "Japan: C Force," unpublished memoir.

283 Wade shaves head: Wade, p. 161.

284 Man injured on barge: Louis Zamperini, telephone interview.

284 Salt stealing: John Cook, "Japan: C Force," unpublished memoir.

285 Rice stealing: Louis Zamperini, telephone interview.

285 Marvin teaching Bad Eye: Ken Marvin, telephone interview, January 21, 2005.

286 Leg injured: Louis Zamperini, telephone interview; Louis Zamperini, POW diary.

286 Louie's fever spikes: Louis Zamperini, telephone interview.

286 Louie tailors clothes: Ibid.

286 Pig duty: Ibid.; Wade, p. 149; Louis Zamperini, 1946 notes on captive experience.

Chapter 29: Two Hundred and Twenty Punches

287 May 5, 1945, B-29 raid: Wall, p. 299; John Cook, email interview, October 30, 2004.

288 Four hundred POWs arrive: John A. Fitzgerald, POW diary, Papers of John A. Fitzgerald, Operational Archives Branch, NHC, Washington, D.C.

288 "You must be sober!": Ken Marvin, telephone interview, January 21, 2005.

288 The Bird at Mitsushima: Weinstein, pp. 287–94; Mutsuhiro Watanabe (Sgt.), vols. 1–3, 1945–1952, POW 201 File 1945–1947, SCAP, Legal Section, Administrative Division, RAOOH, RG 331, NACP.

288 Murder plots at Mitsushima: Weinstein, pp. 287–94.

289 "whimpering," "almost hysterically": Ibid.

289 Beating after theft of fish: Mutsuhiro Watanabe (Sgt.), vol. 1, 1945–1952, POW 201 File 1945–1947, SCAP, Legal Section, Administrative Division, RAOOH, RG 331, NACP; Louis Zamperini, telephone interview; Frank Tinker, telephone interview, February 20, 2005; Wade, pp. 163–64; Louis Zamperini, 1946 notes on captive experience, 1946; Robert Trumbull, "Zamperini, Olympic Miler, Is Safe After Epic Ordeal," *NYT,* September 9, 1945.

290 Some 220 punches: Wade, p. 163.

290 "the Lone Ranger": Wall, p. 300.

290 "all lit up": Ibid.

291 Man dies after work: Louis Zamperini, telephone interview.

291 The Bird breaks man's jaw: Affidavit, Arthur Klein, from files on Mutsuhiro Watanabe (Sgt.), vol. 1, 1945–1952, POW 201 File 1945–1947, SCAP, Legal Section, Administrative Division, RAOOH, RG 331, NACP.

291 POWs ask for meat, dog killed: Louis Zamperini, telephone interview.

291 Rations to be cut in winter: Wade, p. 165.

291 "hanging on from day to day": Wall, p. 300.

291 "Frisco dive in '45": Knox, p. 417.

291 beriberi in civilians: Wade, p. 158.

291 men stop stealing: Ken Marvin, telephone interview, January 21, 2005.

292 Women with sharpened sticks, children with wooden guns: Milton McMullen, telephone interview, February 16, 2005.

292 Batu Lintang: Ooi Keat Gin, ed., *Japanese Empire in the Tropics: Selected Documents and Reports of the Japanese Period in Sarawak, Northwest Borneo, 1941–1945* (Athens: Ohio University Center for International Studies, 1998), vol. 2, pp. 612, 648.

292 Written death orders in camp offices: Ibid., p. 648.

292 Omori POWs told of death plan: Martindale, p. 223; Robert Martindale, telephone interview, January 2, 2005; Affidavit, Arthur Laurence Maher, from files on Mutsuhiro Watanabe (Sgt.), vol. 1, 1945–1952, POW 201 File 1945–1947, SCAP, Legal Section, Administrative Division, RAOOH, RG 331, NACP.

292 Preparations for killing: Ken Marvin, telephone interview, January 31, 2005; Wade, p. 167; Daws, pp. 324–25; Tom Wade, telephone interview, January 2, 2005.

293 Rokuroshi: George Steiger, "Captain George Steiger: A POW Diary," http://www.fsteiger.com/gsteipow.html (accessed October 2, 2009); K. C. Emerson, *Guest of the Emperor* (Sanibel Island: 1977), pp. 77–79; Donald T. Giles, Jr., ed., *Captive of the Rising Sun: The POW Memoirs of Rear Admiral Donald T. Giles* (Annapolis: Naval Institute Press, 1994), pp. 146–54.

293 *This is the place:* Giles, p. 154.

293 Naoetsu POWs to be taken into the mountains: Wade, p. 166; Wall, p. 300.

293 Civilian gives death date: John Cook, "Japan: C Force," unpublished memoir.

Chapter 30: The Boiling City

294 B-29s coming over every night: Wall, p. 300.

294 The Bird tormenting men after raids: Louis Zamperini, telephone interview; Louis Zamperini, 1946 notes on captive experience.

294 Face slapping: Louis Zamperini, telephone interview; Louis Zamperini, 1946 notes on captive experience.

294 Louie clubbed on ankle: Louis Zamperini, letter to Edwin Wilber, May 1946.

294 Port closed, shipping hit: Wall, p. 300; "Jap Shipping, Planes Hard Hit in July," *Walla Walla Union-Bulletin*, August 1, 1945.

295 Louie begs the Bird for work: Louis Zamperini, telephone interview.

295 "Goat die, you die": Ibid.

295 Marvin steals rope: Ken Marvin, telephone interview, January 31, 2005.

295 Goat dies: Tom Wade, telephone interview, January 2, 2005; Louis Zamperini, telephone interview; Louis Zamperini, 1946 notes on captive experience.

295 The Bird forces Louie to hold beam: Louis Zamperini, telephone interview; Frank Tinker, telephone interview, February 20, 2005; Wade, p. 166; Tom Wade, telephone interview, January 2, 2005; Louis Zamperini, 1946 notes on captive experience; Affidavit, Louis Zamperini, from files on Mutsuhiro Watanabe (Sgt.), vols. 1–3, 1945–1952, POW 201 File 1945–1947, SCAP, Legal Section, Administrative Division, RAOOH, RG 331, NACP.

296 Thirty-seven minutes: Wade, p. 166.

296 B-29 flyover on August 1: "Record Raid Hits Four Jap Cities," *Walla Walla Union-Bulletin*, August 1, 1945.

296 Biggest World War I raid by tonnage: Kerr, *Flames*, pp. 269–70.

296 Nagaoka civilians think napalm is rain: "Nagaoka Air Raid, August 1, 1945," http://www.echigonagaoka.com/index.html (accessed October 5, 2009).

296 The Bird beats men on August 1: Louis Zamperini, telephone interview.

297 Skyline glowing: Wall, p. 300.

297 Leaflets, Japanese government forbids people from keeping, sharing leaflets: Josette H. Williams, "The Information War in the Pacific, 1945: Paths to Peace," Central Intelligence Agency Center for the Study of Intelligence, May 8, 2007, https://www.cia.gov/library/center-for-the-study-of-intelligence/csi-publications/csi-studies/studies/vol46no3/article07.html (accessed April 29, 2010).

297 Louie sicker: Louis Zamperini, POW diary; Louis Zamperini, letter to Edwin Wilber, May 1946.

297 Boot licking: Louis Zamperini, telephone interview; Affidavit, Louis Zamperini, from files of Mutsuhiro Watanabe (Sgt.), vols. 1–3, 1945–1952, POW 201 File 1945–1947, SCAP, Legal Section, Administrative Division, RAOOH, RG 331, NACP; Louis Zamperini, POW diary; "42nd Bombardment Squadron: Addendum to Squadron History," September 11, 1945, AFHRA, Maxwell AFB, Ala.

297 Push-ups over latrine: Louis Zamperini, telephone interview; Robert Trumbull, "Zamperini, Olympic Miler, Is Safe After Epic Ordeal," *NYT*, September 9, 1945.

297 Bird threatens to drown Louie: Louis Zamperini, telephone interview; Robert Trumbull, "Zamperini, Olympic Miler, Is Safe After Epic Ordeal," *NYT*, September 9, 1945.

298 Murder plot: Louis Zamperini, telephone interview; Louis Zamperini, interview by George Hodak, Hollywood, Calif., June 1988, AAFLA.

298 The Bird sees man sneering: Mutsuhiro Watanabe, "I Do Not Want to Be Punished by America," *Bingei Shunjyu*, April 1956, translated from Japanese.

299 Hiroshima: Paul Tibbets, interview by Studs Terkel, 2002, http://dalesdesigns.net/interview.htm (accessed September 14, 2007); Matthew Davis, "The Men Who Bombed Hiroshima," BBC News, August 4, 2007; "Paul Tibbets," AcePilots.com, www.acepilots.com/asaaf_tibbets.html (accessed September 13, 2007).

300 Ferron Cummins feels effect of bomb: Knox, p. 435.

Chapter 31: The Naked Stampede

301 Civilians' hands in fists: Frank Tinker, telephone interview, February 20, 2005.

301 Guard says Hiroshima hit by cholera: Louis Zamperini, telephone interview.

301 Civilian says one bomb destroyed city: Frank Tinker, telephone interview, February 20, 2005.

301 "electronic bomb": Tom Wade, telephone interview, January 2, 2005.

301 Omori commander speaks to POWs: Milton McMullen, telephone interview, February 16, 2005.

302 Men discuss self-defense: Tom Wade, telephone interview, January 2, 2005.

303 The Bird in mountains: Wade, p. 166; John Cook, email interview, October 30, 2004.

303 Louie's illness, weight loss: Louis Zamperini, letter to Edwin Wilber, May 1946; Louis Zamperini, POW diary; Louis Zamperini, telephone interview.

303 Louie struck by Ogawa: Louis Zamperini, letter to Edwin Wilber, May 1946; Louis Zamperini, telephone interview.

303 Japanese walk out: Ken Marvin, telephone interview, January 31, 2005.

303 Japanese at radio: Frank Tinker, telephone interview, February 20, 2005.

303 Marvin's talk with Bad Eye: Ken Marvin, telephone interview, January 31, 2005.

304 Rumors: Ken Marvin, telephone interview, January 31, 2005; John Fitzgerald, POW diary, Papers of John A. Fitzgerald, Operational Archives Branch, NHC, Washington, D.C.; Wall, pp. 300, 304; "Letters Recall End of Captivity," *Idaho Press-Tribune*, undated article from *Idaho Press-Tribune* archives; John Cook, email interview, October 30, 2004.

304 Naoetsu to be bombed: Louis Zamperini, letter to Edwin Wilber, May 1946.

304 Marvin's thoughts: Ken Marvin, telephone interview, January 31, 2005.

304 Work crews dismissed: Wall, p. 304.

304 Louie vomiting, gets letters: Louis Zamperini, POW diary.

304 Town illuminated, POWs take shades down: Wall, p. 304.

304 "Look like skeleton": Louis Zamperini, POW diary.

305 The Bird reappears: Louis Zamperini, telephone interview.

305 Rokuroshi: Emerson, pp. 80–84; Giles, pp. 154–57; Robert S. La Forte, Ronald E. Marcello, and Richard L. Himmel, eds., *With Only the Will to Live: Accounts of Americans in Japanese Prison Camps, 1941–1945* (Wilmington, Del.: SR Books, 1994), pp. 260–61; George Steiger, "Captain George Steiger: A POW Diary," http://www.fsteiger.com/gsteipow.html (accessed October 2, 2009).

305 Men told war over: Louis Zamperini, telephone interview; John Fitzgerald, POW diary, Papers of John A. Fitzgerald, Operational Archives Branch, NHC, Washington, D.C.; John Cook, email interview, October 30, 2004; Frank Tinker, telephone interview, February 20, 2005.

305 "The war has come": John Cook, email interview, October 30, 2004.

306 Commander asks POWs to fight "Red Menace": Frank Tinker, telephone interview, February 20, 2005; John Cook, email interview, October 30, 2004; John Cook, "Japan: C Force," unpublished memoir. One published account of the speech gives a different version of events, stating that according to Cook, it was Fitzgerald who asked that the POWs of other nations join America in fighting the Soviets. But in Cook's memoir, as well as his interview with this author, he stated that it was the Japanese commander, not Fitzgerald, who wanted POWs to join Japan in the fight against the Soviets. "The Camp Commander, through the Interpreter," Cook wrote, "informed the POWs that the War with Japan was over and he appealed to them to join with Japan to fight the Red Menace. (Russia.)" This account makes far more sense, as America was not fighting the Soviet Union, then

its ally, but Japan was, having seen its Kuril Islands seized by the Soviets two days before. According to POW Johan Arthur Johansen, the commander at Omori also asked the POWs to join Japan in fighting the Russians.

306 Flyover, reaction: Frank Tinker, telephone interview, February 20, 2005; Louis Zamperini, telephone interview; John Cook, email interview, October 30, 2004; Robert Rasmussen, "A Momentous Message of Hope," *National Aviation Museum Foundation Magazine,* vol. 8, no. 1, Spring 1987; Louis Zamperini, interview by George Hodak, Hollywood, Calif., June 1988, AAFLA; Ken Marvin, telephone interview, January 31, 2005.

307 Clift: Robert Rasmussen, "A Momentous Message of Hope," *National Aviation Museum Foundation Magazine,* vol. 8, no. 1, Spring 1987.

307 OUR TBFS HAVEN'T BEEN ABLE: Ibid.

307 Chocolate, cigarettes: Louis Zamperini, telephone interview; Ken Marvin, telephone interview, January 31, 2005; Wade, p. 169.

307 Pants drop from plane: Louis Zamperini, telephone interview; Louis Zamperini, interview by George Hodak, Hollywood, Calif., June 1988, AAFLA.

308 The Bird leaves: Frank Tinker, telephone interview, February 20, 2005.

Chapter 32: Cascades of Pink Peaches

309 End of war at Rokuroshi: Emerson, pp. 80–84; Giles, pp. 154–57; La Forte, pp. 260–61; George Steiger, "Captain George Steiger: A POW Diary," http://www.fsteiger.com/gsteipow.html (accessed October 2, 2009).

311 Little food, no tobacco: John Fitzgerald, POW diary, Papers of John A. Fitzgerald, Operational Archives Branch, NHC, Washington, D.C.; Wall, p. 302.

311 Fitzgerald demands food: John Fitzgerald, POW diary, Papers of John A. Fitzgerald, Operational Archives Branch, NHC, Washington, D.C.

311 Cow, pigs brought: Ken Marvin, telephone interview, January 31, 2005.

311 Fitzgerald's dispatch, fight with commander: John Fitzgerald, POW diary, Papers of John A. Fitzgerald, Operational Archives Branch, NHC, Washington, D.C.

311 Fighters fly over: Ibid.; Wade, p. 169; Wall, p. 302; "Letters Recall End of Captivity," *Idaho Press-Tribune,* undated article from *Idaho Press-Tribune* archives.

311 "Wonderful?": "Letters Recall End of Captivity," *Idaho Press-Tribune,* undated article from *Idaho Press-Tribune* archives.

311 Commander gives in: John Fitzgerald, POW diary, Papers of John A. Fitzgerald, Operational Archives Branch, NHC, Washington, D.C.

311 Supplies drop, men gorge themselves: John Cook, email interview, October 30, 2004; John Fitzgerald, POW diary, Papers of John A. Fitzgerald, Operational Archives Branch, NHC, Washington, D.C.; Wade, p. 170; Wall, pp. 302, 304; Robert Rasmussen, "A Momentous Message of Hope," *National Aviation Museum Foundation Magazine,* vol. 8, no. 1, Spring 1987; "Letters Recall End of Captivity," *Idaho Press-Tribune,* undated article from *Press-Tribune* archives; Frank Tinker, telephone interview, February 20, 2005.

312 BOMBED HERE IN MAY 45: Wall, p. 302.

313 Louie sleeps in parachute: Louis Zamperini, interview by George Hodak, Hollywood, Calif., June 1988, AAFLA.

313 "'Tis about 6 p.m., and I'm lying here": "Letters Recall End of Captivity," *Idaho Press-Tribune,* undated article from *Press-Tribune* archives.

313 Kinney's flyover: Byron Kinney, telephone interview, April 23, 2007; Louis Zamperini, telephone interview; Byron Kinney, *A Mission of Mercy Touches Two Lives* (Chicago: United Letter Service, 1995).

314 Harris taken to surrender ceremony: Whitcomb, p. 285.

314 Some 132,000 Allied POWs: Tanaka, p. 70; Brian MacArthur, *Surviving the Sword: Prisoners of the Japanese in the Far East, 1942–45* (New York: Random House, 2005), p. xxvi.

314 Nearly 36,000 Allied POWs die: Tanaka, p. 70.

315 More than 37 percent versus 1 percent: Charles A. Stenger, PhD, telephone interview with author, October 17, 2009; Charles A. Stenger, PhD, *American Prisoners of War in World War I, World War II, Korea, and Vietnam: Statistical Data,* Veterans Administration Central Office, June 30, 1979, p. 20.

315 More than 215,000 other POWs: Tanaka, p. 2.

315 Death marches: Kerr, *Surrender,* p. 60.

315 Burma-Siam Railway: Children of Far East Prisoners of War, "SE Asia Under Japanese Occupation," http://www.cofepow.org.uk/pages/asia_thailand1.html (accessed March 18, 2010).

315 Medical experiments: Tanaka, pp. 135–65; Gary K. Reynolds, *U.S. Prisoners of War and Civilian American Citizens Captured and Interned by Japan in World War II: The Issue of Compensation by Japan,* Congressional Research Service, December 17, 2002, pp. 17–19.

315 Cannibalism: James, p. 259; Tanaka, pp. 111–34; "Claim Japs Practiced Cannibalism," *Hammond Times,* September 16, 1945; "Jap Soldiers Eat Flesh of U.S. Prisoners, Australia Discloses," *Abilene Reporter-News,* September 10, 1945.

315 Sandakan: Tanaka, pp. 11–43.

315 Tinian massacre: Eric Lash, "Historic Island of Tinian," *Environmental Services,* October 2008, vol. 1, 2nd edition; Major General Donald Cook, "20th Air Force Today," *20th Air Force Association Newsletter,* Fall 1998.

315 Ballale: Peter Stone, *Hostages to Freedom* (Yarram, Australia: Oceans Enterprises, 2006).

315 Wake: Major Mark E. Hubbs, "Massacre on Wake Island," Yorktown Sailor, http://www.yorktownsailor.com/yorktown/massacre.html (accessed October 18, 2009); Daws, p. 279.

315 Tarawa: Daws, p. 278.

315 Palawan: Sides, pp. 7–17; Kerr, *Surrender,* pp. 212–15; V. Dennis Wrynn, "American Prisoners of War: Massacre at Palawan," *World War II,* November 1997.

315 POWs giving supplies to civilians, guards: Kerr, *Surrender,* p. 273.

316 Kono hides in office: Wade, p. 169.

316 Kono's flight, capture, trial: Hiroaki Kono records from the NACP: Hiroaki Kono et al., 1946–1947, File Unit from RG 331: RAOOH, WWII, 1907–1966, SCAP, Legal Section, Manila Branch (1945–11/1949) Series: Orders and Summaries, compiled 1946–1947; Narumi Oota et al., 1945–1949, File Unit from RG 331: RAOOH, WWII, 1907–1966, SCAP, Legal Section, Prosecution Division (1945–1949) Series: USA Versus Japanese War Criminals Case File, compiled 1945–1949; Hiroaki Kono, 1948–1953, File Unit from RG 84: Records of the Foreign Service Posts of the Department of State, 1788–ca. 1991, Department of State. U.S. Embassy, Japan.

(04/28/1952–) (Most Recent) SCAP, Legal Section (10/02/1945–04/28/1952?) (Predecessor) Series: Japanese War Crimes Case Files, compiled 1946–1961.

316 Guard thrown from galley: Ken Marvin, telephone interview, January 31, 2005.

316 NO MORE—THANKS: Robert Rasmussen, "A Momentous Message of Hope," *National Aviation Museum Foundation Magazine*, vol. 8, no. 1, Spring 1987.

316 one thousand planes, 4,500 tons of supplies: Daws, p. 340.

316 Cocoa hits office: Martindale, p. 233; Robert Martindale, telephone interview, January 2, 2005.

317 Louie washes shirt: Louis Zamperini, telephone interview.

317 Industrial machines in private houses: Ken Marvin, telephone interview, January 31, 2005.

317 Tinker buys record: Louis Zamperini, telephone interview.

317 fifteen hundred Red Cross boxes in storehouse: Ken Marvin, telephone interview, January 31, 2005.

317 Men find brothel: Wade, p. 170.

317 Marvin on bicycle and in bath: Ken Marvin, telephone interview, January 31, 2005.

317 Occupying forces don't arrive: John Fitzgerald, POW diary, Papers of John A. Fitzgerald, Operational Archives Branch, NHC, Washington, D.C.

318 Fitzgerald hits official: Ken Marvin, telephone interview, January 31, 2005.

318 POWs walk to train: Wall, p. 304; Wade, p. 170; Louis Zamperini, telephone interview.

318 Fitzgerald stays: John Fitzgerald, POW diary, Papers of John A. Fitzgerald, Operational Archives Branch, NHC, Washington, D.C.

318 Japanese saluting: Wall, p. 304.

Chapter 33: Mother's Day

319 POWs on train: Ken Marvin, telephone interview, January 21, 2005; Wade, p. 171; Knox, p. 452; Louis Zamperini, telephone interview.

320 "First there were trees": Knox, p. 451.

320 "Welcome back, boys": Wade, p. 171.

320 "Before me in immaculate khaki uniform": Ibid.

320 Women like goddesses: Ken Marvin, telephone interview, January 21, 2005.

320 Trumbull encounters Louie: Louis Zamperini, telephone interview; "Zamperini Gives Sidelights of His Dramatic Trip Back," October 1, 1945, NPN, from papers of Louis Zamperini; Louis Zamperini, interview by George Hodak, Hollywood, Calif., June 1988, AAFLA.

320 "Zamperini's dead": Louis Zamperini, telephone interview.

321 "If I knew": Robert Trumbull, "Zamperini, Olympic Miler, Is Safe After Epic Ordeal," *NYT*, September 9, 1945.

321 Hoarding K rations: Louis Zamperini, telephone interview; Louis Zamperini, interview by George Hodak, Hollywood, Calif., June 1988, AAFLA.

321 Rosynek watches men deplane: Frank Rosynek, email interview, June 21, 2005.

321 POW told his wife married his uncle: "Sends Love Message to Soldier Husband," *Council Bluffs Nonpareil*, September 11, 1945.

321 Louie interviewed: Frank Rosynek, written interview, December 8, 2007.

322 "Well, I'll be damned": Jack Krey, telephone interview, August 18, 2005.

322 11th Bomb Group, 42nd squadron men lost: Cleveland, pp. 484–85.

322 Only four of sixteen men from barracks alive: Jesse Stay, "Twenty-nine Months in the Pacific," unpublished memoir.

322 four hundred athletes killed: "400 Stars Give Lives in Service," *Oakland Tribune,* December 30, 1944; Walt Dobbins, "I May Be Wrong," *Lincoln* (Neb.) *Journal,* January 6, 1944.

322 Louie not allowed food, clothes: Louis Zamperini, telephone interview.

322 Louie assessed by physicians: "Lou Zamperini Has Won Final Race on Track," *Olean* (N.Y.) *Times-Herald,* September 13, 1945.

323 "It's finished": "Zamperini Drifted 1,200 Miles on Raft," *Stars and Stripes,* September 14, 1945.

323 "Darling, we will": Sylvia Zamperini, letter to Louis Zamperini, August 31, 1945.

324 Pete learns Louie free: "Lou Zamperini's Release Thrills Brother at NTC," *Hoist* (U.S. Naval Training Center, San Diego), September 14, 1945.

324 Preparing for homecoming, family quotations: "Zamperini's Mother Sheds Tears of Joy," undated article from papers of Peter Zamperini, NPN.

324 Freeing Rokuroshi: George Steiger, "Captain George Steiger: A POW Diary," http://www.fsteiger.com/gsteipow.html (accessed October 2, 2009); Emerson, pp. 86–87; Giles, pp. 155–65; Kerr, *Surrender,* pp. 288–89.

324 History of American flag: Giles, pp. 156–57.

325 Kelsey Phillips learns Allen is free: "Lt. Allen Phillips Back in Care of U.S. Army, Mother Informed," *Terre Haute Star,* September, 1945.

325 "That day": Ibid.

325 Louie remains in Okinawa: Louis Zamperini, telephone interview; Louis Zamperini, letter to Edwin Wilber, May 1946.

325 Hospital parties: Louis Zamperini, telephone interview.

325 Louie startling USC recruiter: Ibid.

326 Typhoon: Ibid.

326 Louie flies in B-24: Ibid.; Louis Zamperini, letter to Edwin Wilber, May 1946.

326 Overloaded B-24 crashes: Martindale, p. 243.

326 "This is Kwajalein": Louis Zamperini, telephone interview.

326 One tree left on island: Ibid.

327 Hospitalization mandatory: Bernard M. Cohen and Maurice Z. Cooper, *A Follow-up Study of World War II Prisoners of War* (Washington, D.C.: Government Printing Office, 1955), p. 40.

327 Garrett and Louie stay together: Ibid.

327 Louie loses beloved shirt: Ibid.

327 Louie and Garrett wrestle on beach: Ibid.

327 "I just thought I was empty": Ibid.

327 Wade goes home: Wade, p. 179; Tom Wade, letter to Louis Zamperini, August 20, 1946.

327 Phil's homecoming: Kelsey Phillips, "A Life Story," unpublished memoir; telegram and photographs from Phillips scrapbook.

329 Pete and Louie meet: Peter Zamperini, telephone interview, October 19, 2004; Louis Zamperini, telephone interview.

329 Louie flown home: Louis Zamperini, letter to Edwin Wilber, May 1946; "Lou

Zamperini Back in L.A.," undated article from papers of Peter Zamperini, NPN; Peter Zamperini, telephone interview, October 19, 2004.

329 *"Cara mamma mia":* "Lou Zamperini Back in L.A.," undated article from papers of Peter Zamperini, NPN.

PART V

Chapter 34: The Shimmering Girl

333 "This, this little home": "Lou Zamperini Back in L.A.," undated article from papers of Peter Zamperini, NPN.

333 Homecoming: Peter Zamperini, telephone interview, October 19, 2004; Louis Zamperini, telephone interview; Sylvia Flammer, telephone interviews, October 25, 27, 2004.

334 Louie hears record: Sylvia Flammer, telephone interviews, October 25, 27, 2004.

334 Nightmare about the Bird: Louis Zamperini, telephone interview.

334 Wade named Watanabe: Wade, p. 176.

334 MacArthur arrest list: "MacArthur's Round Up of Criminals," *Argus* (Melbourne), September 25, 1945; "Tojo Shoots Self to Avoid Arrest; MacArthur Orders 39 Other Criminals Arrested," *Port Arthur News,* September 11, 1945.

335 Tojo suicide attempt: "Think Tojo Had Planned Suicide," *Council Bluffs* (Iowa) *Nonpareil,* September 11, 1945; "Blood of Men He Sought to Destroy May Save Life of Man Ordering Pearl Harbor Attack," *Council Bluffs* (Iowa) *Nonpareil,* September 11, 1945; Robert Martindale, telephone interview, January 2, 2005.

335 Watanabe flees: Mutsuhiro Watanabe, "I Do Not Want to Be Punished by America," *Bingei Shunjyu,* April 1956, translated from Japanese.

335 Watanabe hears name listed with Tojo, resolves to disappear: Ibid.

335 Manhunt: Mutsuhiro Watanabe (Sgt.), vols. 1–3, 1945–1952, POW 201 File 1945–1947, SCAP, Legal Section, Administrative Division, RAOOH, RG 331, NACP.

336 Fake letter: Mutsuhiro Watanabe, "I Do Not Want to Be Punished by America," *Bingei Shunjyu,* April 1956, translated from Japanese.

337 Watanabe said he'd rather die than be captured: Mutsuhiro Watanabe (Sgt.), vols. 1–3, 1945–1952, POW 201 File 1945–1947, SCAP, Legal Section, Administrative Division, RAOOH, RG 331, NACP.

337 Wave of suicides: Philip R. Piccigallo, *The Japanese on Trial: Allied War Crimes Operations in the East, 1945–1951* (Austin: University of Texas Press, 1979), p. 45.

337 Affidavits: Mutsuhiro Watanabe (Sgt.), vols. 1–3, 1945–1952, POW 201 File 1945–1947, SCAP, Legal Section, Administrative Division, RAOOH, RG 331, NACP.

337 Two thousand letters: Louis Zamperini, letter to Cynthia Applewhite, April 5, 1946.

337 Ringing phone, ninety-five speeches: Louis Zamperini, letter to Edwin Wilber, May 1946.

338 "It was like he got hit": Payton Jordan, telephone interviews, August 13, 16, 2004.

338 Louie drives to forest: Louis Zamperini, telephone interview.

338 *Los Angeles Times* dinner, drinking: Ibid.

339 Zamperini Invitational Mile: "Hero Takes Mile Without Running," *Kingsport* (Tenn.) *News,* March 4, 1946.

339 Louie meets Cynthia: Louis Zamperini, telephone interview; Louis Zamperini, letters to Cynthia Applewhite, April 15 and May 9, 1946; Ric Applewhite, telephone interview, March 12, 2008; Sylvia Flammer, telephone interviews, October 25, 27, 2004.

339 "I want to see you again": Ric Applewhite, telephone interview, March 12, 2008.

339 Cynthia dating Macs, first date: Louis Zamperini, telephone interview.

340 Cynthia's history: Ric Applewhite, telephone interview, March 12, 2008.

340 Drinking gin at sixteen: Louis Zamperini, letter to Cynthia Applewhite, May 8, 1946.

341 Louie throws toilet paper down hotel wall: Louis Zamperini, telephone interview.

341 Louie proposes: Louis Zamperini, letter to Cynthia Applewhite, May 9, 1946.

341 Engagement concerns Applewhites: Louis Zamperini, letter to Cynthia Applewhite, April 13, 1946; Louis Zamperini, telephone interview.

341 Cynthia ignorant of POW experiences: Louis Zamperini, telephone interview.

341 Easy on rice, barley: Louis Zamperini, letter to Cynthia Applewhite, May 2, 1946.

341 Louie gets drunk on date: Louis Zamperini, telephone interview.

341 Louie warns Cynthia: Louis Zamperini, letter to Cynthia Applewhite, April 23, 1946.

341 "We have got to set": Louis Zamperini, letter to Cynthia Applewhite, April 15, 1946.

342 "If you love me enough": Louis Zamperini, letter to Cynthia Applewhite, April 23, 1946.

342 Louie prepares for wedding: Louis Zamperini, letters to Cynthia Applewhite, April 5, 9, 27 and May 8, 1946.

342 Cynthia wants a home: Louis Zamperini, letter to Cynthia Applewhite, April 23, 1946.

342 Sleeping on floors: Louis Zamperini, letter to Cynthia Applewhite, May 10, 1946.

342 Concerns about Applewhites: Louis Zamperini, telephone interview; Ric Applewhite, telephone interview, March 12, 2008; Louis Zamperini, letter to Eric Applewhite, April 1946; Eric Applewhite, letter to Louis Zamperini, April 16, 1946.

343 Louie trains: Louis Zamperini, letter to Cynthia Applewhite, April 13, 1946; Louis Zamperini, letter to Edwin Wilber, May 1946.

343 Cynthia's deal with parents: Louis Zamperini, letter to Cynthia Applewhite, April 25, 1946; Ric Applewhite, telephone interview, March 12, 2008.

343 Ric's fears: Ric Applewhite, telephone interview, March 12, 2008.

343 Louie, Cynthia argue: Louis Zamperini, telephone interview.

343 Cynthia calls home, Louie drinks: Ibid.

Chapter 35: Coming Undone

346 Garrett upset over rice: Louis Zamperini, telephone interview.

346 Toll of captivity: Norman S. White, MD, letter to the editor, *Hospital and Community Psychiatry,* November 1983; Bernard M. Cohen and Maurice Z. Cooper, *A Follow-up Study of World War II Prisoners of War* (Washington, D.C.: Govern-

ment Printing Office, 1955); D. Robson et al., "Consequences of Captivity: Health Effects of Far East Imprisonment in World War II," *JM: An International Journal of Medicine,* vol. 102, no. 2, 2009, pp. 87–96; Robert Ursano, MD, and James Rundell, MD, "The Prisoner of War," *War Psychiatry* (Washington, D.C.: Office of the Surgeon General, 1995), pp. 431–56.

347 Nightmares, sleeping on floors, ducking, hallucinations: Knox, pp. 461, 463, 478–79.

347 McMullen speaking Japanese: Milton McMullen, telephone interview, February 16, 2005.

347 Weinstein's urges to scavenge in garbage cans: Weinstein, p. 316.

347 Weinstein housing complex: "Georgia: No Shenanigans," *Time,* January 2, 1950.

347 Halloran's experience: Raymond Halloran, email interview, March 3, 2008.

348 Former POW spitting at Asians: Burke, p. 184.

348 Former POWs try to attack hospital staffer: Knox, p. 465.

348 McMullen after Japan: Milton McMullen, telephone interview, February 16, 2005.

349 "a seething, purifying": Jean Améry, *At the Mind's Limits: Contemplations by a Survivor of Auschwitz and Its Realities* (Bloomington: Indiana University Press, 1998), p. 40.

349 "You must look": Louis Zamperini, letter to Cynthia Applewhite, May 4, 1946.

350 Louie's torment, resumption of running: Louis Zamperini, telephone interviews.

351 Louie injured: Louis Zamperini, telephone interview; Louis Zamperini, letter to Edwin Wilber, May 1946; John P. Stripling, "Striptees," *Torrance Herald,* November 28, 1946.

351 Louie's nightmares, drinking, decline, resolution to kill the Bird: Louis Zamperini, telephone interviews.

Chapter 36: The Body on the Mountain

354 Manhunt: Mutsuhiro Watanabe (Sgt.), vols. 1–3, 1945–1952, POW 201 File 1945–1947, SCAP, Legal Section, Administrative Division, RAOOH, RG 331, NACP.

354 Officer's visit: Mutsuhiro Watanabe, "I Do Not Want to Be Punished by America," *Bingei Shunjyu,* April 1956, translated from Japanese.

355 Watanabe's flight and quotes in this section: Ibid.

356 Conviction rates: John W. Dower, *Embracing Defeat: Japan in the Wake of World War II* (New York: Norton, 1999), p. 447.

356 Ofuna convictions: "Jap Officers to Be Hanged for POW Brutality," *San Mateo* (Calif.) *Times,* October 13, 1948; William R. Gill and Davis P. Newton, "A Compilation of Biographical Source Documents Concerning Major William Herald Walker, U.S. Army Air Force (1919–1945), a Prisoner of War in Japan During World War II," 1999; "8th Army Commission Court Gives Sentence to POW Torturers," *Pacific Stars and Stripes,* February 29, 1948.

356 Naoetsu convictions: Lyon, pp. 49–51.

356 Sasaki's capture, trial, imprisonment: Kunichi Sasaki and James Kunichi Sasaki records from RG 331, RAOOH, WWII, 1907–1966, SCAP, Legal Section, Administration Division and Prosecution Division, NACP: Kunichi Sasaki, Isamu Sato,

Kazuo Akane, 1945–1948, Investigation and Interrogation Reports; Nakakichi Asoma et al., trial, exhibits, appeal, and clemency files; Nakakichi Asoma et al., 1945–1952, POW 201 File, 1945–1952, Charges and Specifications, 1945–1948.

357 Kano: Martindale, pp. 230, 240; Gamble, p. 339; Yukichi Kano, "Statement of Yukichi Kano, Tokio P.O.W. Camp H.Q. (Omori)," undated, from papers of Robert Martindale; Yukichi Kano, SCAP, Legal Section, Administration Division (10/02/1945–04/28/1952), File Unit from RG 331: RAOOH, WWII 1907–1966, Series POW 201 File, 1945–1952, NACP.

357 Kato accused of kicking a man nearly to death: Martindale, p. 141.

357 "Cross my heart": Yukichi Kano, "Statement of Yukichi Kano, Tokio P.O.W. Camp H.Q. (Omori)," undated, from papers of Robert Martindale.

358 "I thought I": Yukichi Kano, letter to Robert Martindale, December 23, 1955.

358 Watanabe in hiding: Mutsuhiro Watanabe, "I Do Not Want to Be Punished by America," *Bingei Shunjyu,* April 1956, translated from Japanese.

358 Intensified manhunt: Mutsuhiro Watanabe (Sgt.), vols. 1–3, 1945–1952, POW 201 File 1945–1947, SCAP, Legal Section, Administrative Division, RAOOH, RG 331, NACP.

359 Watanabe goes to Tokyo: Mutsuhiro Watanabe, "I Do Not Want to Be Punished by America," *Bingei Shunjyu,* April 1956, translated from Japanese.

360 "You have plenty of room": Ibid.

360 Watanabe approached for arranged marriage: Ibid.

360 "if she liked books": Ibid.

360 "a burden which would make her unhappy": Ibid.

360 Watanabe becomes cowherd: Ibid.

361 Bodies found on Mitsumine: "From Chief of Hyogo Prefectural Police Force," November 21, 1950, report, from papers of Frank Tinker; Mutsuhiro Watanabe (Sgt.), vols. 1–3, 1945–1952, POW 201 File 1945–1947, SCAP, Legal Section, Administrative Division, RAOOH, RG 331, NACP.

361 Shizuka taken to body: Mutsuhiro Watanabe, "I Do Not Want to Be Punished by America," *Bingei Shunjyu,* April 1956, translated from Japanese.

361 Watanabe's death announced: Ibid.

Chapter 37: Twisted Ropes

362 Louie plans to go back to Japan: Louis Zamperini, telephone interview.

363 Louie's decline, troubled marriage: Ric Applewhite, telephone interview, March 12, 2008; Louis Zamperini, telephone interview; Payton Jordan, telephone interviews, August 13, 16, 2004; Peter Zamperini, telephone interview, October 22, 2004; Sylvia Flammer, telephone interviews, October 25, 27, 2004.

367 "nails every one of us": Améry, p. 68.

367 Shizuka sees dead son: Mutsuhiro Watanabe, "I Do Not Want to Be Punished by America," *Bingei Shunjyu,* April 1956, translated from Japanese.

Chapter 38: A Beckoning Whistle

368 Relatives think dead man is Mutsuhiro: Mutsuhiro Watanabe, "I Do Not Want to Be Punished by America," *Bingei Shunjyu,* April 1956, translated from Japanese.

368 Shizuka believes Mutsuhiro is alive, Mutsuhiro promises to return: Ibid.

368 Authorities question identity of body, tail family: "From Chief of Hyogo Prefectural Police Force," November 21, 1950, report, from papers of Frank Tinker; Mutsuhiro Watanabe, "I Do Not Want to Be Punished by America," *Bingei Shunjyu,* April 1956, translated from Japanese.

369 Meeting at restaurant: Mutsuhiro Watanabe, "I Do Not Want to Be Punished by America," *Bingei Shunjyu,* April 1956, translated from Japanese.

369 Shizuka refers to deaths at Mitsumine: "From Chief of Hyogo Prefectural Police Force," November 21, 1950, report, from papers of Frank Tinker.

369 Rumors: Martindale, p. 248; Frank Tinker, telephone interview, February 20, 2005; Johan Arthur Johansen, *Krigsseileren,* issue 1, 1991, translated from Norwegian by Nina B. Smith.

369 *if I am alive:* Mutsuhiro Watanabe, "I Do Not Want to Be Punished by America," *Bingei Shunjyu,* April 1956, translated from Japanese.

370 Billy Graham history: Cliff Barrows, Graham musical director, telephone interview, February 22, 2007; Billy Graham, *Just as I Am: The Autobiography of Billy Graham* (HarperSanFrancisco and Zondervan, 1997), pp. 92–158.

370 Los Angeles campaign: Graham, pp. 143–158; "Billy Graham Acclaimed: Crusade Continues as Over 300,000 Attend," *Van Nuys* (Calif.) *News,* November 17, 1949; "Old Fashioned Revival Hits Los Angeles," *Gettysburg* (Pa.) *Times,* November 2, 1949.

370 Movie contract: Virginia MacPherson, "Preacher Laughs Off Film Offers to Make Him Star," *San Mateo* (Calif.) *Times,* November 12, 1949.

371 Louie and Cynthia meet neighbor: Louis Zamperini, telephone interview.

371 Cynthia goes to Graham: Ibid.; Cliff Barrows, Graham musical director, telephone interview, February 22, 2007.

371 Dinner at Sylvia's: Sylvia Flammer, telephone interviews, October 25, 27, 2004.

371 Cynthia talks Louie into seeing Graham: Louis Zamperini, telephone interview.

371 Graham exhausted, doesn't recognize daughter: Graham, pp. 156–57.

372 Train whistle: Billy Graham, "The Only Sermon Jesus Ever Wrote," Los Angeles, October 22, 1949, audio recording, BGEA.

372 Louie's impression of Graham: Louis Zamperini, telephone interview.

372 Graham's sermon, Louie's reaction: Billy Graham, "The Only Sermon Jesus Ever Wrote," Los Angeles, October 22, 1949, BGEA; Louis Zamperini, telephone interviews.

374 Cynthia gets Louie to return to Graham: Louis Zamperini, telephone interview.

374 Graham's second sermon, Louie's reaction: Ibid.; Billy Graham, "Why God Allows Communism to Flourish and Why God Allows Christians to Suffer," Los Angeles, October 23, 1949, BGEA.

375 Louie's last flashback: Louis Zamperini, telephone interviews.

376 Louie and Cynthia return home: Ibid.

376 Louie at park, new view of his life: Ibid.

Chapter 39: Daybreak

377 Louie goes to Sugamo: Louis Zamperini, telephone interview; Louis Zamperini, interview by George Hodak, Hollywood, Calif., June 1988, AAFLA.

379 Shizuka goes to see son: "From Chief of Hyogo Prefectural Police Force," November 21, 1950, police report.

379 "Mutsuhiro," Shizuka had said: Ibid.

379 Shizuka's shrine: Frank Tinker, telephone interview, February 20, 2005.

379 Louie at Sugamo: Louis Zamperini, telephone interview.

Epilogue

381 Victory Boys Camp: Louis Zamperini, telephone interview; Louis Zamperini, interview by George Hodak, Hollywood, Calif., June 1988, AAFLA.

382 Louie's postwar life: John Hall, "Lou and Pete," *Los Angeles Times,* June 2, 1977; Louis Zamperini, interview by George Hodak, Hollywood, Calif., June 1988, AAFLA; Morris Schulatsky, "Olympic Miler at 19, Skateboards at 70," undated article from papers of Peter Zamperini, NPN; Louis Zamperini, telephone interview; Cynthia Zamperini Garris, telephone interview, December 13, 2008.

384 "When I get old": National Geographic Channel, "Riddles of the Dead: Execution Island," October 13, 2002.

384 "When God wants": Peter Zamperini, telephone interview, December 12, 2006.

384 Not angry for forty years: Louis Zamperini, telephone interview.

384 Falls down stairs, stays in hospital: Ibid.; Cynthia Zamperini Garris, telephone interview, December 13, 2008.

384 "I never knew anyone": Peter Zamperini, telephone interview, October 17, 2004.

385 Phil's postwar years: Karen Loomis, telephone interview, November 17, 2004; Monroe and Phoebe Bormann, telephone interview, June 7, 2005.

385 Phil's irritation: Karen Loomis, telephone interview, November 17, 2004.

386 *This Is Your Life:* Louis Zamperini, interview by George Hodak, Hollywood, Calif., June 1988, AAFLA.

386 "Dad must have": Karen Loomis, telephone interview, November 17, 2004.

386 "a little grin underneath": Ibid.

386 Life, death of Harris: Katey Meares, email interviews, March 14, 17, 18, 27, 2008; Whitcomb, pp. 286–87; Edwin H. Simmons, *Frozen Chosin: U.S. Marines at the Changjin Reservoir* (Darby, Pa.: Diane Publishing), p. 94; "Jamestown Man Gets Navy Cross," *Newport Daily News,* December 6, 1951; "Marine Officer Missing in Korea," *Newport Mercury and Weekly News,* December 29, 1950.

388 Pete's life, death, Cynthia's death: Peter Zamperini, telephone interviews, October 15, 17, 19, 22, 2004; Louis Zamperini, telephone interview.

390 Louie learns the Bird is alive: Louis Zamperini, telephone interview.

390 Watanabe's return: Mutsuhiro Watanabe, "I Do Not Want to Be Punished by America," *Bingei Shunjyu,* April 1956, translated from Japanese.

390 Pressure to resolve war-crimes issue: Piccigallo, p. 47; Daws, p. 373; Awaya Kentaro, "The Tokyo Tribunal, War Responsibility and the Japanese People," *Shukan Kinboyi,* December 23, 2005, translated by Timothy Amos; Ernie Hill, "Japan's Revival," *Oakland Tribune,* March 17, 1953.

390 "Christmas amnesty": "Amnesty for 17 Top Jap War Suspects," *Lowell* (Mass.) *Sun,* December 24, 1948; Dower, p. 454.

391 Kishi: Michael Schaller, "America's Favorite War Criminal: Kishi Nobusuke and the Transformation of U.S.-Japan Relations," *This Is Yomiuri,* August 1995.

391 Many defendants believed to be guilty: "Amnesty for 17 Top Jap War Suspects," *Lowell* (Mass.) *Sun,* December 24, 1948.

391 Last man tried: Tom Lambert, "Last Trial Held on War Crimes by U.S. Tribunal,"

Stars and Stripes, October 20, 1949; "All Known Japanese War Criminals Brought to Trial," *Independent* (Long Beach, Calif.), October 20, 1949.

391 Sentences reduced: "War Criminal Is Due Parole," *Lubbock Evening Journal,* March 7, 1950.

391 Treaty of Peace and reparations: Gary Reynolds, *U.S. Prisoners of War and Civilian American Citizens Captured and Interned by Japan in World War II: The Issue of Compensation by Japan,* Congressional Research Service, December 17, 2002, pp. 3–9, 9–10.

391 Order for apprehension revoked: Mutsuhiro Watanabe, "I Do Not Want to Be Punished by America," *Bingei Shunjyu,* April 1956, translated from Japanese.

392 War criminals paroled, amnesty declared: Daws, p. 373; "U.S. Pardons Last 83 Japan War Criminals," *Stars and Stripes,* December 31, 1958.

392 Watanabe blames war, not self: Mutsuhiro Watanabe, "I Do Not Want to Be Punished by America," *Bingei Shunjyu,* April 1956, translated from Japanese.

392 "I was just in a great joy": Ibid.

392 Watanabe's postexile life: Lyon, p. 63; Martindale, p. 250.

392 Visited America, rumors that the Bird is alive: Draggan Mihailovich, email interview, August 3, 2007; Martindale, p. 249.

393 *Daily Mail* interviews with the Bird, Wade: Peter Hadfield and Clare Henderson, "Deathcamp Monster Finally Says I'm Sorry," *Daily Mail* (London), August 20, 1995.

394 Naoetsu park movement: Yoshi Kondo, email interview, February 14, 2009; Shoichi Ishizuka, "About Naoetsu POW Camp," *Gaiko Forum,* June 2006.

395 Mihailovich seeks the Bird, interview: Draggan Mihailovich, email interview, August 3, 2007; CBS Television, "48 Hours: Race to Freedom," 1998.

396 Louie writes to the Bird: Louis Zamperini, letter to Mutsuhiro Watanabe, May 19, 1997; Louis Zamperini, telephone interview.

397 The Bird refuses to see Louie: Draggan Mihailovich, email interview, August 3, 2007.

397 Watanabe dies: Yuichi Hatto, written interview, July 16, 2004.

397 Louie runs with torch: Louis Zamperini, telephone interview; Chris Boyd, "Legendary Zamperini Carries the 'Eternal Flame,'" *Palos Verdes Peninsula News,* March 5, 1998; R. J. Kelly, "Olympic Torch Relay Rekindles Ex-POWs Flame of Forgiveness," *Stars and Stripes,* January 30, 1998; "Zamperini: War Survival Was a Matter of Miracles," *Stars and Stripes,* January 26, 1998.

INDEX

Page numbers in *italics* refer to illustrations.